Study Guide

AN INTRODUCTION TO
MICROECONOMICS

■ ■ ■

■ ■

ALSO AVAILABLE FROM McGRAW-HILL RYERSON:

ECONOMICS
Third Canadian Edition
by Blomqvist/Wonnacott/Wonnacott
ISBN: 0-07-549915-0

AN INTRODUCTION TO MACROECONOMICS
Third Canadian Edition
by Blomqvist/Wonnacott/Wonnacott
ISBN: 0-07-549160-5

AN INTRODUCTION TO MICROECONOMICS
Third Canadian Edition
by Blomqvist/Wonnacott/Wonnacott
ISBN: 0-07-549916-9

STUDY GUIDE to accompany
AN INTRODUCTION TO MACROECONOMICS
Third Canadian Edition
by Blomqvist/Wonnacott/Wonnacott
ISBN: 0-07-551007-3

INSTRUCTOR'S MANUAL to accompany **ECONOMICS**
Third Canadian Edition
by Blomqvist/Wonnacott/Wonnacott/Sephton
ISBN: 0-07-549918-5

TEST BANK to accompany **ECONOMICS**
Third Canadian Edition
by Blomqvist/Wonnacott/Wonnacott/Sephton
ISBN: 0-07-551028-6

■ ■ ■

Study Guide

AN INTRODUCTION TO
MICROECONOMICS

THIRD CANADIAN EDITION

■ ■

ÅKE BLOMQVIST
University of Western Ontario

PAUL WONNACOTT
University of Maryland

RONALD WONNACOTT
University of Western Ontario

McGRAW-HILL RYERSON LIMITED

Toronto   Montreal   New York   Auckland   Bogotá
Caracas   Hamburg   Lisbon   London   Madrid   Mexico
Milan   New Delhi   Paris   San Juan   São Paulo   Singapore
Sydney   Tokyo

■ ■ ■

■ ■

STUDY GUIDE
AN INTRODUCTION TO MICROECONOMICS
Third Canadian Edition

Copyright © McGraw-Hill Ryerson Limited, 1990,
1987, 1983. Copyright © 1990 John Wiley and Sons,
Inc. Copyright © McGraw-Hill, Inc. 1986, 1982,
1979. All rights reserved. No part of this publication
may be reproduced, stored in a retrieval system, or
transmitted, in any form or by any means, electronic,
mechanical, photocopying, recording, or otherwise,
without prior written permission of McGraw-Hill
Ryerson Limited.

ISBN: 0-07-549919-3

2 3 4 5 6 7 8 9 0 MP 9 8 7 6 5 4 3 2 1 0

Typesetting by Jay Tee Graphics Ltd.
Printed and bound in Canada

Care has been taken to trace ownership of copyright
material in this text. The publishers will gladly take
any information that will enable them to rectify any
reference or credit in subsequent editions.

Canadian Cataloguing in Publication Data

Main entry under title:

Study guide to accompany An introduction to
   microeconomics, third Canadian edition

Supplement to: Blomqvist, Åke G., date—
An introduction to microeconomics. 3rd Canadian ed.
ISBN 0-07-549919-3

1. Microeconomics. I. Blomqvist, Åke G., date—
II. Blomqvist, Åke G., date—   . An introduction
to microeconomics. 3rd Canadian ed.

HB172.B672 1990   338.5   C90-094053-0

■ ■ ■

Contents

■ ■

■ ■ ■

Preface

■■■■■■■■■■■■■■■■■■■■■■■■■■■■■■■■■■■■■

This study guide is intended to help the student who is taking an introductory economics course using the third Canadian edition of *An Introduction to Microeconomics* by Blomqvist, Wonnacott, and Wonnacott. It makes no attempt to be self-contained: it can be used as a supplement to, not as a substitute for, the textbook.

Each chapter is designed for you to read and work through after reading the corresponding chapter in the textbook. Each study-guide chapter contains nine sections:

1. *Major purpose.* This section sets out very briefly the basic ideas that will be developed in the chapter.

2. *Learning objectives.* This section consists of a list of tasks that you should be able to accomplish after you have studied the chapter in the textbook and in the study guide. The purpose of this section is twofold. First, it should help to give you direction and purpose while studying the rest of the chapter. Second, it should serve as a checklist to test your comprehension after reading the chapter.

3. *Highlights of the chapter.* This section contains a summary of the important points of the chapter. Its purpose is mainly to reinforce the textbook by going over these main points from a somewhat different perspective and adding illustrative examples. To a student learning a subject for the first time, everything is likely to appear equally important. This section should help sort out the more important from the less by focusing more narrowly than the text and by drawing attention to the particularly important material.

4. *Important terms: Match the columns.* This section sets out the important concepts along with the definition of each. Your task is to match each term with its definition. One of the best ways of doing this is to write out your own definition first; this provides the most effective form of review.

5. *True-false questions.*

6. *Multiple-choice questions.*

7. *Exercises.*

These three sections are meant to help you learn by doing. Besides providing reinforcement through repetition, many of the questions and exercises are designed to guide you toward discovering ideas that will not be explicitly introduced until later in the textbook. Spend a few minutes going over the true-false and multiple-choice questions as a self-test, even if you believe you understand the textbook chapter well enough to proceed without using the study guide in any other way. Answers to questions in these sections are provided at the end of each chapter.

8. *Essay questions.* This section is designed to help you apply important concepts that have been developed in the text, as well as to stimulate your imagination. No answers have been provided for this section. Thus the questions may be used as material for classroom discussion.

9. *Crossword puzzles.* These appear intermittently throughout the study guide. Our hope is that you will find them entertaining, whether or not you are a crossword puzzle enthusiast. Each puzzle, of course, draws heavily on the terms introduced in the related chapter.

This third edition of the study guide, now in Macro and Micro volumes, has a number of new or extensively revised chapters, corresponding to the changes in the textbook. We have also rewritten the old chapters in several places, with a view to improving the clarity of exposition. Many of the old true-false and multiple-choice questions have been replaced or reworked. The inclusion of suggested answers to some of the review problems that appear in the textbook is another new feature of this edition. They were added in response to the suggestion by a number of our students that ready access to "model answers" would enhance the value of the problems as aids in learning.

Åke Blomqvist
Paul Wonnacott
Ron Wonnacott
London, Ontario, and
College Park, Maryland

Note to Students and Instructors

Economics, Third Canadian Edition, by Blomqvist, Wonnacott, and Wonnacott, exists in three forms: the combined volume (chapters 1–40), the macroeconomics volume (chapters 1–20), and the microeconomics volume (chapters 1–5 and 21–40).

This study guide is designed for the convenience of students who begin their study of economics with microeconomics. It follows the content of the microeconomics volume of *Economics*, Third Canadian Edition, beginning with chapters 1–5 and following with chapters 21–40.

A study guide to accompany the macroeconomics volume and the macroeconomics chapters of *Economics*, Third Canadian Edition, is available as well.

Part One

Basic Economic Concepts

Chapter 1

■ ■

Economic Problems and Economic Goals

MAJOR PURPOSE

The major purpose of this chapter is to provide a broad overview of *economic developments* and *economic objectives* as a background for the more detailed topics of the following chapters. Five major economic objectives are discussed: *high employment*, a *stable average level of prices, efficiency, equity*, and *growth*. You should gain some understanding of the problems which have arisen in the Canadian economy, and why it is not always easy to solve these problems. In particular, it may be difficult to deal with problems when the government has a number of goals, some of which are *in conflict*. That is, solving one problem may make others more difficult to solve. For example, inflation generally gets worse as the unemployment rate falls.

LEARNING OBJECTIVES

After you have studied this chapter in the textbook and study guide, you should be able to
- List five major economic goals
- Describe, in broad terms, what has happened to Canadian unemployment, inflation, growth, and the distribution of income in recent decades
- Distinguish the views of Adam Smith and J.M. Keynes with respect to the proper role of the government
- Define terms such as inflation, deflation, recession, and efficiency
- Distinguish between *allocative efficiency* and *technological efficiency*
- Describe briefly how changes in relative prices may contribute to allocative efficiency
- Explain why it is harder to identify the problems created by inflation than those created by unemployment
- Explain the distinction between equity and equality
- Explain how some goals may be *complementary*, while others are *in conflict*

If you have studied the appendix to Chapter 1 in the textbook, you should also be able to
- Describe some of the ways in which people may be misled by graphs
- Explain the advantage of using a ratio (or logarithmic) scale
- Explain the difference between a nominal and a real measure

HIGHLIGHTS OF THE CHAPTER

Economics is one of the social sciences—it involves the systematic study of human behaviour. The aspects of behaviour which interest economists is how people earn a living and the problems which may make it difficult for them to do so. In the words of Alfred Marshall, economics is the study of people "in the ordinary business of life."

The objective of *economic theory* is to discover and explain the basic principles and laws that govern economic life. Economic theory helps us to understand questions such as: Why are some prices higher than others? Why does the average level of prices rise? Why are some people richer than others? What causes large-scale unemployment?

Economic policy addresses such questions as: How can the government reduce inflation? How can it reduce the unemployment rate? What steps can individuals take to increase their incomes or reduce the risks of unemployment? How does a business increase its profits?

Economic theory and economic policy go hand-in-hand. Just as a physician needs to know how the human body works in order to heal patients, so the economic policy maker needs to understand economic theory in order to prescribe economic policies that will be successful. Scientific studies of how things work are often inspired by a policy motive—to do something about problems. Thus, scientists strive to unlock the mysteries of the human cell in order to find out why cancer occurs and, ultimately, to be able to cure cancer. Similarly, studies of how the economy works are often motivated by the desire to solve economic problems such as recession and large-scale unemployment.

Perhaps the most hotly contested issue in all of economics is the question of how much the government should intervene in the economy. Many of those in government are motivated by the desire to promote the public welfare. But well-meaning policy makers do not always adopt policies that work in practice. Furthermore, the government may be used to benefit individuals or groups at the expense of the public as a whole.

In the late 1700s, Adam Smith attacked many governmental interventions in the economy as being contrary to the public interest. Even though tariffs benefitted the protected sectors of the economy, they inflicted higher costs on consumers and acted as a drag on efficiency. Smith conceived of the private economy as a self-regulating mechanism. By pursuing their own interests, individuals would unwittingly contribute to the common good. There was no need for extensive government interference to ensure that things would come out all right.

A century and a half later, J.M. Keynes was skeptical of Smith's message of laissez-faire. Things were not coming out all right. The economy was in a deep depression, with many people out of work. It was the responsibility of the government, said Keynes, to do something about this tragic situation. He recommended government spending on roads and other public works as a way to provide jobs.

Full employment is one of the major economic objectives. Four others are also described in this chapter: a *stable average level of prices, efficiency,* an *equitable distribution of income*, and economic *growth.* Other goals might be added to this list, for example, economic freedom, economic security, protection of the environment, and a reduction in Canada's dependence on foreign influences.

The first two goals—full employment and stable prices—come under the heading of maintaining a stable *equilibrium* in the economy. There has been, in fact, considerable instability in the Canadian economy. The most notable disturbance occurred during the Great Depression of the 1930s, when output and employment dropped sharply and remained at very low levels for a full decade. During World War II, there was an effort to produce as many munitions as possible. Unemployment ceased to be a significant problem, but prices began to rise substantially. Since the end of World War II in 1945, we have avoided severe disturbances comparable to those from 1929 to 1945. However, there have been periodic recessions, with rising unemployment; the most severe one occurred as late as 1982. Inflation was severe during the late 1940s and the 1970s. During the decade of the 1970s, the average level of prices doubled.

Of the major economic problems, unemployment is perhaps the most obvious. When employment declines, we have less output to enjoy. We not only forgo the output which might have been produced, but we also must face the demoralization that comes with unemployment.

The problems with inflation are less obvious. When people buy goods, they obviously dislike higher and higher prices. But there are two sides to every transaction—the buyer's side, and the seller's. With widespread inflation, not only do the prices of what we buy increase, but wage rates also go up as do the prices of what we sell. It is not clear whether individuals are net gainers or net losers.

However, there are certain segments of the population that do lose. Those who have pensions set in money terms lose: As prices rise, their pensions buy less. (However, some pensions, including the Old Age Security and Canada Pension Plan benefits paid by the government, are increased to compensate for inflation.) Those who own government bonds or other interest-bearing securities lose. Through the years, they receive payments whose value becomes smaller and smaller as prices rise. On the other hand, people who have borrowed can benefit: They repay their loans in money whose value has declined.

Inflation generates a feeling that the economic system is unfair. There are arbitrary redistributions of income and wealth, such as the gains to debtors and losses to bond owners. Inflation can also make it more difficult to make wise and well-informed decisions. *Prices* provide an important source of information to the business executive and consumer. During periods of rapid inflation, when all prices are rising at a brisk pace, the message carried by prices may be obscured. It becomes more difficult to make good decisions.

If inflation accelerates to very high rates—such as 1,000% per year—it becomes known as *hyperinflation.* Money is losing its value so rapidly that people may refuse to accept it. Because money is practically useless, sellers may feel compelled to barter their products for other goods. Such barter transactions are very cumbersome and time-consuming.

Most inflations do not accelerate into hyperinflation. Hyperinflation is relatively rare, except during wartime or early postwar periods in countries that have been defeated in wars. There are, however, a few cases where countries have had very rapid rates of inflation even though they have not been defeated in a war—for example, during some periods in Brazil.

There are two important types of efficiency. *Technological efficiency* means getting the most output from a given set of inputs (labour, machinery, raw materials). *Allocative efficiency* occurs when the economy is producing the best combination of outputs, using the lowest-cost combination of inputs. Allocative efficiency means producing the goods and services that the Canadian consuming public wants most, or that can be sold in foreign countries in exchange for goods and services that are difficult to produce here. It is possible for an economic system to produce "white elephants" in a technologically efficient manner. But this system would not be producing what people want; it would not be allocatively efficient. Similarly, if everyone were a lawyer and no one a doctor, there would be allocative inefficiency—even if everyone were a superb lawyer.

Equity means *fairness,* and that raises the question of what fairness means. There can be obvious disagreements. Those with low incomes are likely to argue that a more equal distribution of income would be fairer. Those with higher incomes often argue that their high incomes are the result of hard work; it is fair for them to be paid more because they have worked harder.

Most people agree that the government should take steps to help those who are poverty-stricken, for example, by taxing the rich to provide services for the needy. The question arises, however, as to how far this process should be taken. Clearly, if the government confiscated all incomes above the average, and gave the revenues to low-income people, then it would severely interfere with the incentive to work hard. (This would also greatly increase the incentive to cheat on taxes!) Even less drastic steps to redistribute income can decrease incentives, and thus decrease the size of the national "pie." The size of the pie depends in part on how it is cut up.

Economic growth is often advocated for its own sake. In a growing economy, we enjoy more goods and services. Furthermore, growth may make it easier to meet other goals, such as reducing poverty. However, we should not simply assume that the more growth, the better. Growth comes at a cost. Most obviously, if we produce more machinery and equipment to help us grow, then we will give up the current consumer goods that might have been produced instead of the machinery and equipment. And, in recent years, we have become increasingly aware of the potentially devastating consequences of the pollution that industrial growth may cause, unless it is properly controlled.

Some goals—such as a high level of employment and an elimination of poverty—are *complementary.* Progress on the one contributes to progress on the other. If jobs are provided for people, they are less likely to be poor.

Other goals are *in conflict.* If people buy more goods and services, they will help to increase the number of jobs. But they will also make it easier for sellers to raise their prices. Thus, if the government takes steps to encourage spending, it may help ease one problem (unemployment) while making another worse (inflation). In such circumstances, good policies may be particularly difficult to develop.

IMPORTANT TERMS: MATCH THE COLUMNS

Match each term in the first column with the corresponding explanation in the second column.

_N_	**1.** Laissez-faire	**a.**	Put forward the idea of the "hidden hand"
_C_	**2.** Great Depression	**b.**	Pursuing one helps in attainment of other
_L_	**3.** Labour force	**c.**	When large-scale unemployment existed
_J_	**4.** Population	**d.**	A change in relative prices
_H_	**5.** Recession	**e.**	A tax on an import
_E_	**6.** Duty	**f.**	Pursuing one makes other more difficult to attain

_____ K **7.** J.M. Keynes
_____ A **8.** Adam Smith
_____ M **9.** Inflation
_____ G **10.** Deflation
_____ O **11.** Allocative efficiency
_____ I **12.** Technical efficiency
_____ B **13.** Complementary goals
_____ F **14.** Conflicting goals
_____ D **15.** This can help promote allocative efficiency

g. A decrease in the average level of prices
h. A broad decline in production, involving many sectors of the economy
i. Avoiding sloppy management and wasted motion
j. Total number of people in a country
k. Put forward the idea that government should spend for public works when necessary to get economy out of depression, and restore full employment
l. Sum of those employed and those unemployed
m. An increase in the average level of prices
n. Leave the economy alone
o. Producing the best combination of outputs, using the lowest-cost combination of inputs

TRUE-FALSE

T (F) **1.** Adam Smith argued that the government should build public works whenever needed to reduce the rate of inflation.

T (F) **2.** By definition, a depression occurs whenever the output of the nation falls.

(T) F **3.** During the Great Depression of the 1930s, the unemployment rate rose above 15% of the labour force.

(T) F **4.** Between 1965 and 1986, output per person in the 30 poorest countries in the world grew at an average annual rate of less than 1.25%, much slower than in most advanced countries.

until 1982 (T) (F) **5.** Since 1970, recessions have been much less severe than those of the 1950s and 1960s.

(T) F **6.** A recession is a decline in total output, employment, and income, and is marked by a widespread contraction in *many* industries.

T (F) **7.** Changes in the average level of inflation make an important contribution, since they are the key to improvements in allocative efficiency.

T (F) **8.** Throughout the 1980s, the percentage of the population living in poverty declined slowly but consistently.

T (F) **9.** Over the past three decades, there has been a consistent trend in Canada: the rich have gotten richer, and the poor have gotten poorer.

(T) (F) **10.** Inflation is caused by a decline in purchases by consumers.

MULTIPLE CHOICE

1. Since 1900, output per capita in Canada
   a. has approximately doubled, while the length of the work week has declined
   b. has grown more than fivefold, while the length of the work week has declined
   c. has approximately doubled, while the length of the work week has remained stable
   d. has grown more than fivefold, while the length of the work week has remained stable
   e. has remained stable, while the length of the work week has declined sharply; all the gains have come in the form of more leisure

2. Between 1960 and 1986/87, which of the following countries grew most rapidly?
   a. France
   b. Canada
   c. Japan
   d. United States
   e. West Germany

3. By the phrase, "invisible hand," Adam Smith was expressing the idea that
   a. there are no economic conflicts among nations
   b. there would be no economic conflicts among nations if countries would eliminate tariffs
   c. there are no conflicts between what is good for an individual and what is good for society as a whole
   d. by pursuing their own individual interests, people frequently promote the interests of society

e. business executives have a natural interest in keeping prices down and preventing inflation

4. Suppose that the American government is considering increasing the tariffs on steel imported from Canada. Which organizations in the United States are *most likely* to *oppose* such an increase?

    a. steelworkers' union and auto workers' union
    b. General Motors and Caterpillar
    c. steelworkers' union and the U.S. Treasury
    d. U.S. Steel and the U.S. Treasury
    e. U.S. Steel and General Motors

5. In his *General Theory*, Keynes' principal concern was with the goal of

    a. stable prices
    b. low unemployment
    c. allocative efficiency
    d. technological efficiency
    e. an equitable distribution of income

6. Unemployment is likely to be highest during

    a. war
    b. peacetime prosperity
    c. rapid growth
    d. recession
    e. depression

7. Between 1929 and 1933 (the early part of the Great Depression) total output in Canada

    a. declined about 30%
    b. declined about 20%
    c. declined about 10%
    d. declined about 5%
    e. remained approximately stable; the Depression represented an interruption of growth, not an actual decline in output

8. Which of the following is counted as being unemployed?

    a. someone who has just retired at age 65
    b. a full-time student not looking for a job
    c. someone who has recently graduated from college and is looking for his or her first full-time job
    d. convicts in prisons
    e. all of the above

9. A moderate rate of inflation (of, say, 4% per annum)

    a. creates no problems in the economy
    b. hurts people living on fixed money incomes
    c. hurts people who have borrowed money
    d. occurs whenever money wages rise more rapidly than prices
    e. is likely to be caused by war

10. The key role in promoting allocative efficiency is played by changes in

    a. the average level of prices
    b. the rate of inflation
    c. the rate of growth
    d. relative prices
    e. the distribution of income

11. Economists distinguish changes in the *average* level of prices and changes in *relative* prices. Changes in the average level of prices are generally considered

    a. undesirable, while changes in relative prices can perform a useful function in promoting efficiency
    b. undesirable, but changes in relative prices are even more undesirable, since they hurt some people while helping others
    c. undesirable, but changes in relative prices are neither good nor bad; they just happen
    d. desirable, but the government should attempt to prevent changes in relative prices
    e. desirable, but changes in relative prices are even more desirable, and the government should take steps to increase changes in relative prices

12. Suppose that every factory worker were in the job best suited for him or her, working as productively as possible, but producing cars that nobody wanted to buy. This would be an example of

    a. technical inefficiency and allocative inefficiency
    b. technical efficiency and allocative inefficiency
    c. technical inefficiency and allocative efficiency
    d. technical efficiency and allocative efficiency
    e. technical efficiency and allocative efficiency, but slow growth

13. During the past two decades, the prices of computers have fallen, while the price of oil has risen. As a result, manufacturers and other businesses have used more computers, and have conserved on energy. This switch toward more computers and less energy consumption is an illustration of

    a. allocative efficiency
    b. technological efficiency
    c. the effects of inflation
    d. a less equal distribution of income
    e. a more equal distribution of income

14. Which is the best example of *technological* inefficiency?

    a. producing too many cars, and not enough housing
    b. slow growth
    c. inflation
    d. inequality of incomes
    e. sloppy management

15. *Equity* in the distribution of income means

    a. equality
    b. fairness
    c. more for everyone as a result of growth
    d. more for those who can't work
    e. more for those who work hard

16. Suppose that the incomes of all families are perfectly equal. Then what share of total income will the poorest 10% of the families get?
    a. 5%
    b. 10%
    c. approximately 15%
    d. 20%
    e. 25%

17. Which of the following pairs is the clearest example of conflicting goals?
    a. less unemployment and less inflation
    b. less unemployment and less poverty
    c. less unemployment and more growth
    d. less unemployment and more efficiency
    e. more efficiency and less poverty

18. If, during the coming six months, there is a boom in the purchases of machinery by businesses, then we would be most likely to observe
    a. an increase in the rate of inflation and a decline in the rate of unemployment
    b. a decrease in the rate of inflation and a decline in the rate of unemployment
    c. an increase in the rate of inflation and an increase in the rate of unemployment
    d. a decrease in the rate of inflation and an increase in the rate of unemployment
    e. a decrease in inflation, growth, and unemployment

19. Economists study
    a. inflation
    b. unemployment
    c. efficiency
    d. poverty
    e. all of the above

(Appendix)

20. A reason for using a logarithmic or ratio scale on the vertical axis of a chart is that this
    a. makes it easier to start measuring from zero
    b. allows readers to quickly see when the rate of increase was most rapid
    c. avoids the necessity of choosing an arbitrary beginning year
    d. shows when profits were at a maximum
    e. shows when profits were at a minimum

EXERCISE

In the following passage, choose the correct word or phrase from those given in the brackets.

Economic history is a story of both progress and problems. Some evidence of progress shows up in Figure 1.1 in the textbook. Here we see that output per person has increased by a little more than (150%, 200%, 300%) since 1926, and about (25%, 100%, 200%) since 1960. If we were to look at total output of the economy—rather than at output *per person*—we would find that total output has increased by (an even greater percentage than output per person, a somewhat smaller percentage).

The right-hand panel of Figure 1.1 shows another source of gain. Not only have we produced more, but we have done so with a shorter work week. The decline in the work week was approximately (20%, 40%, 60%) between 1926 and the mid-1980s. Notice also the very sharp drop between 1926 and 1935. This decrease was the result of (a much more rapidly improving economy which allowed more leisure, the Depression which reduced the demand for output, a loss of the work ethic).

Successes and problems also show up in Figure 1.3 in the textbook. The (upward trend in output, downward trend in unemployment, both) since 1950 show(s) how things have improved. However, from time to time there have been problems such as in 1981/82 when (the unemployment rate increased, output declined, both). This was only one of several instances since 1950 when the Canadian economy suffered from the problem of (recession, depression, inflation, poverty).

Figure 1.4 shows the average level of prices. A rise in this curve is an indication of inflation. The more rapid is inflation, the steeper is the curve. We see that inflation was particularly rapid between (1950 and 1960, 1960 and 1970, 1970 and 1980).

Finally, Figure 1.5 shows the percentage of the population living in poverty; a decline in the percentage is a sign of success. Observe that, at the beginning of the period shown, the incidence of poverty declined, from about (15%, 22%, 35%) in the mid-1960s to about (8%, 11%, 14%) in the mid-1980s.

ANSWERS

Important Terms: 1n, 2c, 3l, 4j, 5h, 6e, 7k, 8a, 9m, 10g, 11o, 12i, 13b, 14f, 15d
True-False: 1F, 2F, 3T, 4T, 5F, 6T, 7F, 8F, 9F, 10F
Multiple Choice: 1b, 2c, 3d, 4b, 5b, 6e, 7a, 8c, 9b, 10d, 11a, 12b, 13a, 14e, 15b, 16b, 17a, 18a, 19e, 20b
Exercise: 300%, 100%, an even greater percentage than output per person, 40%, the Depression which reduced the demand for output, upward trend in output, both, recession, 1970 and 1980, 35%, 11%.

ANSWERS TO SELECTED REVIEW QUESTIONS FROM THE TEXT

1-1. In the first instance, the butcher gets money in exchange for the meat. In turn, this money can be used to buy the things the butcher wants—clothing, housing, etc. The butcher and the baker find that, by specializing in the preparation of food, they can obtain more clothing and housing than they could make themselves in an equivalent time.

1-2. Unemployment is the major problem of a depression. After a collapse, as many as 10% or 25% of the labour force may be unable to find jobs. Furthermore, joblessness tends to be of much longer duration during a depression than in more normal times. Unemployment is particularly severe for young people. During hard times, those who have jobs try to keep them. It is the new entrants into the labour force who are hit particularly hard when job openings dry up.

1-4. As people buy more clothes, cars, etc., more jobs become available in textiles, clothing, automobiles, rubber, steel, etc. As people are more eager to buy, producers find it easier to raise prices. Thus, the increase in purchases that helps to ease unemployment will make inflation worse; high employment and price stability are conflicting goals.

1-5.(a) Presumably, the main reason that the length of the work week has declined is that as real incomes have increased, people have felt that they could afford more leisure. In Sweden, tax rates are very high. This means that the "price of leisure" (that is, the after-tax income you forgo by not working) is relatively low, which may explain why Swedes choose more leisure. The difference between Canada and the United States also may be explained by higher taxes here.

(b) No; if people value leisure, they may be happy to give up some growth in income in order to have more leisure.

APPENDIX

This appendix provides additional information and practice for those who have already studied the appendix to Chapter 1 in the textbook.

Graphs

During rainy spells, sales of lawn furniture decline. A simple version of the relationship between weather and the sales of lawn furniture is illustrated in Figure 1.1 below.

The two measures used in this graph—sales of furniture and rainfall—are examples of **variables**. A variable is something that can change, or vary, from time to time or from place to place. For example, the amount of rain in April is generally different from the amount in July.

The statement that the sales of lawn furniture decline during rainy weather means that there is a relationship between the two variables in Figure 1.1. In particular, it means that when rainfall increases, sales decline. This idea can be illustrated in the figure.

The two *axes*, marked with numbers, meet at the **origin** 0. The vertical axis shows the quantity of lawn furniture sold. The horizontal axis shows the amount of rainfall. The relationship between the two variables is depicted by the line marked with the letters *A* through *F*. For example, point *A* shows that when the rainfall is 1 cm per month (measured along the horizontal axis), there are $6,000 worth of sales of lawn furniture (measured up the vertical axis). Likewise, at point *B*, 2 cm of rainfall result in sales of $5,000. In this way, each time you read a point on the line you get one bit of information. These "bits" are shown in Table 1.1.

Table 1.1.

Point	A	B	C	D	E	F
Rainfall	1	2	3	4	5	6
Sales	6	5	4	3	2	1

Thus, the rule for reading the graph is as follows. If you want to find out how much furniture will be sold

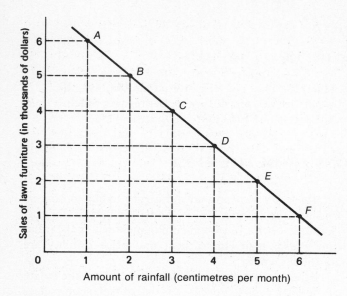

Figure 1.1

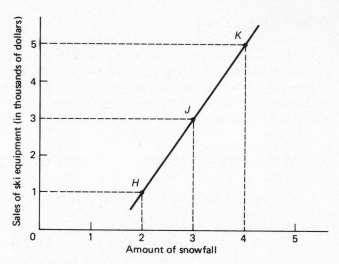

Figure 1.2

when there is some particular amount of rain (say, 3 cm), go along the horizontal axis to 3 units. Then go directly up to the line. This shows sales of $4,000 worth of furniture when the rainfall is 3 cm. Question 1 at the end of this appendix provides an exercise in reading graphs.

Slope

Figure 1.1 shows not only that rainfall and sales are related. It shows the *direction* of that relationship.

Specifically, when rainfall *increases*, sales *decrease*. In other words, sales are **negatively** or **inversely** related to rainfall. This negative relationship means that the line in Figure 1.1 slopes downward to the right. As you move to the right (as rainfall increases), the height of the line decreases (sales decrease). For example, by comparing points *A* and *B*, we see that when rainfall increases from 1 to 2 cm, sales decrease from $6,000 to $5,000.

A **positive** or **direct** relationship is illustrated in Figure 1.2; both variables change in the same direction. When snowfall increases, sales of skis increase, too. This means that as we move to the right (more snow), the line slopes upward (more sales of skis).

A graph such as Figure 1.2 shows not only the *direction* of the relationship between the two variables, it also shows the *strength*. For example, it shows that when snow increases by 1 cm (from 2 to 3 cm), 2000 more skis are sold. The *strength* of the relationship is shown by the **slope** of the line. The slope of the line is defined as the amount by which the height of the line changes when you go one more unit to the right on the horizontal axis. In Figure 1.2, the slope is 2; a 1 unit increase in snow causes a 2 unit increase in the sales of skis. Alternatively, the

slope of a line between two points (such as *H* and *K* in Figure 1.2) is defined as the *rise* (that is, the vertical change of 4 units) *divided by the run* (the horizontal change of 2 units). Again, we see that the slope of the line is 2 (that is, 4 divided by 2).

Observe that ski sales respond much more strongly to snow in Figure 1.2 than in Figure 1.3. In Figure 1.3, the much weaker response is illustrated by the relatively flat curve; when snowfall increases by 1 unit, ski sales increase only a half unit; the slope is only 1/2.

Back in Figure 1.1, an increase in one variable (rain) caused a decrease in the other variable (sales of lawn furniture). The line slopes downward; that is, the slope is negative. (For example, between points *A* and *C*, the rise is − 2 while the run is 2; thus the slope is − 1.) A negative slope means, therefore, that the two variables are negatively or inversely related.

In summary, the slope of the line shows two ideas—the direction and strength of the relationship between two variables. The *direction* of the relationship depends on whether the line slopes up or down—that is, whether the slope is positive or negative. The *strength* of the relationship depends on the steepness of the line. Questions 3 and 4 at the end of this appendix deal with the concept of slope.

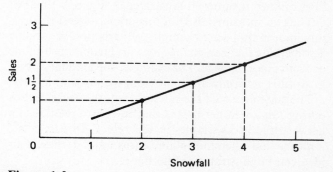

Figure 1.3

Linear Equations

Sometimes the relationship between two variables is shown not by a graph, but by an equation. For example, suppose that you are told that my expenditures on consumer goods (C) each month depends on my income (Y) according to the equation:

$$C = \$400 + 0.50Y$$

(Economists almost always use the letter Y for income. I is used to denote investment.)

In simple English, this equation says that I spend $400 plus half of my income that month. As my income varies from month to month, the equation tells you how my expenditures will vary. Whatever my income (Y) is, you can figure out how much I am likely to spend for consumer goods (C).

For example, choose some convenient value for my income, such as $1,000. Then substitute this into the equation to get $C = 400 + 0.5 \times 1,000 = 400 + 500 = 900$. This tells us that when my income is $1,000, my expenditures on consumer goods is $900. Now choose any other convenient value, such as $1,100. Substituting this value into the equation shows us that when my income is $1,100, my expenditures on consumer goods is $400 + 0.5 \times 1,100$ or $950. Each time you choose a value for Y and make this substitution, you get one bit of information. These two bits are shown in Table 1.2. As an exercise, fill in the rest of the table.

Table 1.2

Y	100	200	300	400	500	600	700	800	900	1,000	1,100
C										900	950

Figure 1.4 shows this relationship in a graph. The slope of the line is 0.5. This is because every time my income increases by $100 (shown as a move of one unit along the horizontal axis), I spend another $50 (shown as a rise of 0.5 of a unit). In contrast, the equation $C = 400 + 0.75Y$ represents the behaviour of individuals who spend $400 plus three-quarters of their income. In this case, the slope of the line would be 0.75, because every increase of $100 in income would cause an increase of $75 in consumption.

In general, any equation of the sort $C = a + bY$ represents a line with a slope equal to b. Such an equation is a **linear** equation. For example, the linear equation illustrated in Figure 1.4 has $a = 400$ and $b = 0.5$.

The number b (in this example, 0.5) is known as the **coefficient** of the variable Y. It indicates the slope of the line. The number a (400) shows how high the line is where it meets the vertical axis (point A). Thus, a is often called the **vertical intercept** of this equation. For example, the vertical intercept in Figure 1.4 is 400; this corresponds to the equation where $a = 400$.

At this time, you should do questions 5 and 6, which deal with linear equations.

Curves

So far we have drawn only straight lines. A straight line is easy to use because it has a *constant* slope. For example, in Figure 1.1, the slope of the line is the same between A and B as it is between any other two points on the line.

However, sometimes a relationship is described better by a curve, like the one in Figure 1.5 which illustrates how a student's final grade depends on how many hours he or she spends studying during the average week. A curve does not have a constant slope; as you move to the right on this curve, it gets flatter. For example, the first hour of studying causes an increase in the grade by 30 points—from 20 to 50. However, the second hour makes it rise by only 20 more (to 70), and the third hour causes an increase of only 5 more points. Each move to the right

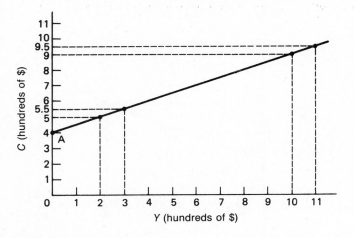

Figure 1.4

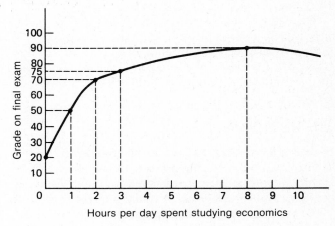

Figure 1.5

of 1 hour per week causes a smaller increase in the grade. In this example, it would obviously be impossible for the relationship to continue in a straight line in the way it began. The first hour caused an increase of 30 points. Four hours obviously couldn't cause an increase of 120 points, for the simple reason that the exam has a maximum grade of 100 points.

In this curve, as before, the slope is still identified as the amount by which the height of the curve changes as you go one more unit to the right along the horizontal axis. But, in this case, the slope changes as you go to the right. For the first hour, it is 30; for the second, 20; then 5; and so on.

The decreasing slope in Figure 1.5 indicates that as the student spends more and more time studying, each additional hour may raise the grade, *but not by as much as the previous hour*. The first hour raises the grade by 30 points, the next by only 20. This is an example of diminishing returns; the payoff (in terms of a higher grade) diminishes as a person studies more and more.

Notice that, according to Figure 1.5, the curve reaches its maximum. No matter how much time the student spends studying, he or she can't get more than 90. Indeed, after 8 hours, the student gets tired and stale. Any more time with the books will be counterproductive. The slope of the curve becomes negative; each additional hour results in a lower grade.

Other Graphs

Sometimes, in presenting a general argument, we don't bother to put numbers on the axes. For example, the linear relationship in Figure 1.6 shows no numbers (except for the 0 at the origin). Without numbers, we can't tell exactly how strong the relationship is between the variables X and Y. But the graph still provides important information—that the relationship is linear, with a constant direction and slope. In this diagram, we can put in letters as points of reference. Point E represents $0A$ units of X, and its height is measured as $0C$ units of Y.

When describing the movement from E to F along the line, it helps to look at triangle EFG. The change in X is the difference between distance $0B$ and $0A$, that is, distance AB. Likewise, the change in Y can be read from the vertical axis as CD, or from the triangle as distance GF.

The Ratio Scale

In the standard diagram (such as Figure 1.2) each vertical increase of one notch represents the same increase—in this example, an increase of 1000 skis. Equal distances along an axis represent equal changes in the variable.

But there is an important exception to this rule. Look at Figure 1.7. In this graph, going up one notch on the vertical axis doesn't always mean the same change in the

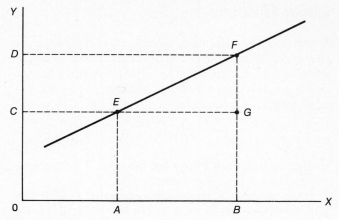

Figure 1.6

price level. The first notch takes you from 25 to 50—a change of 25. But, when you move up to the second notch, the price level goes from 50 to 100—a change this time of 50. The vertical axis measures the price level, not on the usual scale, but on the **ratio scale**, or **logarithmic scale**.

As you move up a ratio scale, equal distances represent equal *percentage* changes. Going up from 25 to the first notch, the price level goes up by 100% to 50. Going to the second notch, it again goes up by 100%—this time to 100. In this case, every notch higher represents a price level that is 100% higher.

In economics, a ratio scale is used most frequently along the vertical axis, with time shown on the horizontal axis (as in Figure 1.7). Such a diagram is used when we're interested in the percentage rate of growth of something—for example, the percentage rate of growth of population or the percentage increase in prices. When such a curve becomes steeper, the percentage rate of increase in population or prices is becoming greater. We can identify the period when the rate of growth was the most rapid. It is the period when the curve is the steepest.

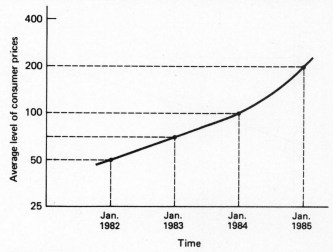

Figure 1.7

QUESTIONS

1. Point *A* in Figure 1.8 has a height of ___8___ and lies distance ___2___ to the right of the origin. Thus, it indicates that when there is a light rainfall of ~~ten~~ 2 centimetres during rush hour, ___8___ thousand workers will arrive to work on time. If rain is heavier, at 6 cm, only ___6___ thousand workers will be on time. With a very heavy rain of 10 cm, ___4___ thousand workers will be on time.

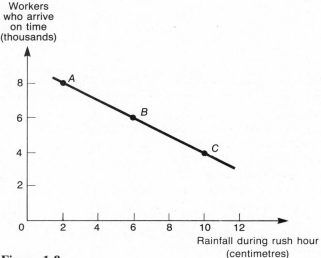

Figure 1.8

2. From Figure 1.2 fill in Table 1.3.

Table 1.3

Amount of snow	2	3	4
Sales of skis	1	3	5

3. There are six different lines in Figure 1.9. In Table 1.4, fill in the slope of each line.

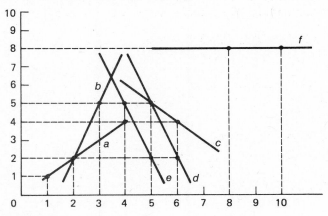

Figure 1.9

Table 1.4

Line	a	b	c	d	e	f
Slope	1	3	-1	-3	-3	0

4. Which of the lines in Figure 1.10 show a positive relationship between variables *X* and *Y*? a, b, e, f. When *X* increases by 1 unit, which of these lines shows the greatest increase in *Y*? ___e___. When *X* increases by 1 unit, which of these lines shows the greatest decrease in Y? ___c___.

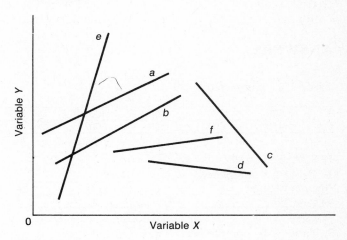

Figure 1.10

5. Consider two variables, *X* and *Y*, that are related according to the linear equation $Y = 8 - 2X$. From this equation, fill in Table 1.5.

Table 1.5

X	0	1	2	3	4
Y	8	6	4	2	0

Draw the line representing this equation in Figure 1.11. The slope of this line is ___-2___. The vertical intercept is ___8___.

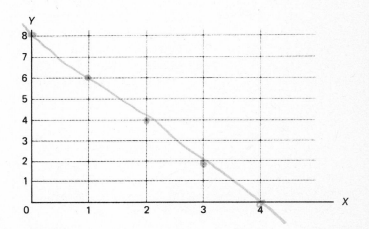

Figure 1.11

6. The following linear equations show how one variable, *Y*, depends on another variable, *X*.

(a) $Y = 90 + 10X$ *Pos*
(b) $Y = 50 + 15X$ *Pos*
(c) $Y = 80 - 5X$
(d) $Y = 3X$ *Pos*
(e) $Y = -10 + 5X$ *Pos*
(f) $Y = 50$

Line __*A*__ has the largest vertical intercept and line __*B*__ has the largest slope. When *X* increases by 1 unit, which line shows the largest increase in *Y*? __*B*__. When *X* = 0, the highest line is __*A*__.
Which equations show a positive relationship between *X* and *Y*? __*ABDE*__. Which a negative relationship? __*C*__. What is the slope of (**f**)? __0__. Which line has a vertical intercept of zero? __*D*__. Which line passes through the origin? __*D*__.

ANSWERS

Table 1.2 completed:

Y	100	200	300	400	500	600	700	800	900	1000	1100
C	450	500	550	600	650	700	750	800	850	900	950

1. 8, 2, 2, 8, 6, 4
2. Table 1.3 completed:

Amount of snow	2	3	4
Sales of skis	1	3	5

3. Table 1.4 completed:

Line	a	b	c	d	e	f
Slope	1	3	−1	−3	−3	0

4. (*a, b, e, f*), *e, c*
5. Table 1.5 completed:

X	0	1	2	3	4
Y	8	6	4	2	0

−2, 8
6. *a, b, b, a,* (*a, b, d, e*), *c,* 0, *d, d*

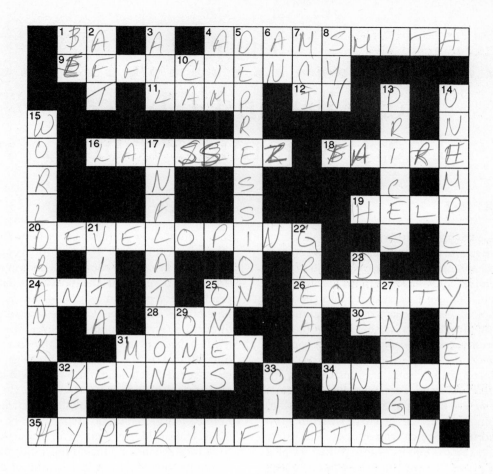

Across

1. university degree
4. His *Wealth of Nations* was an early classic (2 names).
9. getting the most from productive efforts
11. shedder of light
12. preposition
16, 18. keeping government involvement in economy to a minimum
19. assist (verb)
20. the _____ nations, also known as the Third World
24. industrious insect
25. above
26. fairness
28. charged particle
30. _____ garde! (French)
31. During hyperinflation, this becomes practically worthless.
32. advocated goverment spending to restore full employment
34. represents workers
35. Losing countries in war may suffer this.

Down

1. exist
2. toward the stern of a boat
3. be ill
4. purpose, or line up in your sights
5. the economic disease of the 1930s
6. indefinite article
7. 1101 in Roman numerals
8. artificial (abbrev.)
10. a professional business degree
13. important source of information to buyers and sellers
14. a major economic problem
15. international institution lending to developing nations (2 words)
17. rise in the average level of prices
21. document needed when looking for a job
22. large, powerful
23. owing
25. individuals
27. a deep violet-blue colour
29. number
31. first person possessive
32. under lock and _____
33. Its price skyrocketed in the 1970s.

Chapter 2

■ ■

Scarcity and Choice:
The Economic Problem

MAJOR PURPOSE

The major purpose of this chapter is to introduce the concept of *scarcity*. Because of limited resources, we cannot have all the goods and services that we want. Therefore, we must *make choices*, picking some items and forgoing others. This idea—that we face scarcity and therefore have to make choices—is at the centre of economics. A standard definition of economics is "the study of the allocation of scarce resources to satisfy alternative, competing human wants."

The ideas of scarcity and choice are illustrated by the *production possibilities curve*. This illustrates the idea of scarcity because we are limited to a point on (or within) the curve; we cannot go outside the curve with our present resources and technological capabilities. The curve also illustrates the need to *make choices*. When we pick one point on the production possibilities curve, we pass over all the other points and forgo the goods which we might have had if we had picked some other point.

This chapter applies the production possibilities curve to illustrate the choice between consumer goods now and consumer goods in the future. We can forgo some consumer goods now and use the resources to produce capital equipment instead. The additional capital will help us to produce even more consumer goods in the future. Mention is also made of the possibility that a country's productive capacity may grow—that is, its production possibilities curve may shift up and out—because it is importing *foreign* capital. However, when this happens, it must be kept in mind that the future *consumption* opportunities of the country's citizens will not be as great, because the foreign capital owners will be paid a return on the capital they have invested in the country.

Finally, this chapter provides an introduction to *economic theory*. Economic theory *must* be a *simplification* of the real world. If we strove for a complete theory which took into account all the complexities of our world, we would get bogged down in a swamp of detail. When we simplify, we should keep in mind a central question: Does our theory include the most important relationships in the economy, or *have we left out something of critical importance*?

LEARNING OBJECTIVES

After you have studied this chapter in the textbook and study guide, you should be able to
- Understand why the combination of limited resources and unlimited wants requires us to make choices
- Define the three major factors of production
- Explain the difference between real capital and financial capital, and explain why economists focus on real rather than financial capital when studying the productive capacity of the economy
- Explain the functions of the entrepreneur
- Explain the concept of opportunity cost and how it is related to the production possibilities curve (PPC)
- Explain why the PPC slopes downward to the right
- Explain why the PPC usually bows outward from the origin
- Explain a circumstance in which the PPC might be a straight line, instead of bowing outward
- Explain why production occurs *within* the PPC if there is large-scale unemployment

• Explain the difference between a high-growth and a low-growth policy, using a PPC with capital goods on one axis and consumer goods on the other (Figure 2-5 in the textbook)
• Explain the effects of an increase in the capital stock in Canada through a capital inflow from foreign countries
• Explain why it is impossible to develop a theory without making simplifying assumptions

HIGHLIGHTS OF THE CHAPTER

Scarcity is one of the most important concepts in economics. Scarcity requires us to *make choices*; we cannot have everything we want. Why? The answer is that our resources are limited, while our wants are not.

When we make choices, we pick some goods and services and forgo others. If we pick a college education, for example, we may have to put off buying a car for several years. The opportunity cost of our education is the car and other goods and services that we forgo to pay tuition and room and board. Similarly, for the society as a whole, opportunity cost is an important concept. For example, when we decide to produce more weapons, we forgo the consumer goods and services we might have produced instead. Individuals, corporations, and governments are constantly making choices among the options open to them.

The ideas of scarcity, of the need to make choices, and of opportunity cost are summarized by the production possibilities curve (PPC). The PPC shows the options from which a choice is made. The fact that we are limited by the PPC, and cannot pick a point outside it with our present resources and technology, illustrates the idea of scarcity. The slope of the PPC shows how much of one good we must forgo when we choose more of another. In other words, the slope shows the *opportunity cost* of choosing more of a specific good.

The PPC has two important properties. First, it slopes downward to the right. This means that if we decide to produce more of one good, we give up some of the other. The idea that there is an opportunity cost when we produce more of one good is illustrated by the downward slope of the PPC curve.

The second feature of the typical PPC curve is that it is bowed out—that is, it is *concave* to the origin. This is so because resources are *specialized*. If we decide to produce more and more wheat, we will use land which is less and less suited to the production of wheat, even though it was very good for producing wool. For each additional unit of wheat, we will have to give up more wool. Thus, the outward bend in the PPC illustrates the idea of *increasing opportunity cost*.

Under certain circumstances, however, the PPC need not bow outward. It is possible that two goods might require the same set of resources in their production. For example, radios and telephones might take the same combination of resources in their production—the same combination of copper, plastic, silicon, labour, etc.—in which case, the PPC would be a straight line. In this particular case, the *opportunity cost of radios would be constant* in terms of the telephones forgone. (The opportunity cost of both radios and telephones might nevertheless still increase, in terms of the food or clothing forgone. In other words, the PPC would be a straight line if we put radios and telephones on the two axes, but would bow out if we put radios on one axis and food on the other.)

It is worth emphasizing that a downward slope and an outward bow are two *different* features. A PPC can slope downward without bowing outward—as in the example of radios and telephones. A downward slope means that the opportunity cost is *positive*. An outward bow means that the opportunity cost *increases* as more of a good is produced.

One of the important choices facing the society is the choice between consumer goods and capital goods. If we produce only a little capital, we will be able to enjoy a large quantity of consumer goods now. But, with little investment, we will have slow growth. In other words, there is a *trade-off between a high current level of consumption and high growth*. This trade-off or choice is illustrated when we draw a PPC curve with consumer goods on one axis and capital goods on the other. For example, Figure 2.5 in the textbook illustrates the difference between a high-growth and a low-growth strategy. A high-growth strategy requires that a sizeable fraction of our resources be committed to investment in plant and equipment (capital goods). But this makes possible a rapid growth—that is, a rapid outward movement of the PPC.

When a nation is receiving a capital inflow from foreign countries, its stock of capital goods may expand rapidly even if the nation's citizens use most of their resources for present consumption. But there is an offsetting disadvantage: Part of the increased future production that is made possible by the nation's larger capital stock will have to be paid to the foreign investors or lenders who initially supplied the capital inflow, as a return on their investment.

This chapter provides a brief introduction to economic theory. When we develop economic theories, we must simplify. The world is much too complex to describe in all its detail. The objective of theory is to strip away the non-essential complications in order to see the important relationships within the economy. Theory should not be dismissed because it fails to account for everything, just as a road map should not be discarded as useless just because it doesn't show everything. But, because of simplifications, theory must be used carefully. Just as last week's weather map is useless for planning a trip in a car, so the theory which helps to explain one aspect of the economy may be inappropriate or useless for explaining others.

Finally, this chapter explains the distinction between *positive* and *normative* economics. Positive or descriptive economics is aimed at explaining what has been happening and why. Normative economics deals with policies; it deals with the way things *ought* to be.

IMPORTANT TERMS: MATCH THE COLUMNS

Match each term in the first column with the corresponding phrase in the second column.

1. Economic resources
2. Capital inflow
3. Financial capital
4. Real capital
5. Increase in real capital
6. Entrepreneur
7. PPC
8. Opportunity cost
9. Increasing opportunity cost
10. Constant opportunity cost
11. Cause of outward bow of PPC

a. Outward bow of PPC
b. Choices open to society
c. Specialized resources
d. Foreign-financed investment
e. Stocks and bonds
f. Straight-line PPC
g. Organizer of production
h. Basic inputs used in the production of goods and services
i. Investment
j. Alternative forgone
k. Machinery, equipment, and buildings

TRUE-FALSE

T F 1. Resources are said to be scarce because they are incapable of producing all the goods and services that people want; therefore, choices must be made.

T F 2. Wants were "unlimited" during the early days of the study of economics in the eighteenth and nineteenth centuries. But they are no longer unlimited in the affluent countries of North America and Western Europe.

T F 3. Suppose that a production possibilities curve meets the axes at 5 units of clothing and at 20 units of food. This illustrates that the society can have a total of 5 units of clothing plus 20 units of food, but no more.

T F 4. The production possibilities curve bends outward because resources are not uniform in quality; some are better at producing one good than the other.

T F 5. Just as it is possible to select a combination of goods inside the PPC, so it is possible to choose a combination of goods that lies outside the PPC.

T F 6. An increase in the quantity of labour causes the production possibilities curve to move outward from the origin.

T F 7. Suppose that two countries, A and B, were identical in 1979. Suppose that, between 1979 and 1989, the economy of A grew at 4% per annum, while B grew at 3% per annum. Then, from that fact, we may conclude that economy A was allocatively more efficient than B during the 1979-1989 period.

T F 8. Positive economics is the study of how policy makers can achieve desirable (that is, "positive") social goals.

T F 9. Less developed countries have a special problem. If they want to grow through creating more capital, they have to forgo some consumer goods or import capital. In the affluent countries in North America and Western Europe, no such choice is necessary.

T F 10. An inflow of American capital into Canada would help shift Canada's PPC outward from the origin.

T F 11. In most less developed countries, an increase in the population and in the quantity of labour will make it more difficult to raise income per person. In such a country, such a population increase will generally cause an inward movement of its PPC.

MULTIPLE CHOICE

1. Economists often speak of wants being "unlimited" because
   a. the cost of living has increased; it costs more to meet our basic needs now than it did twenty years ago
   b. more people live in the cities now than in an earlier age, and it is more expensive to live in cities than on the farm
   c. even though our incomes have risen, we still want "more"; we do not believe all our wants are satisfied
   d. resources such as oil have become scarcer because we have been using them up
   e. as people's incomes have risen, they have decided to take more leisure, and work fewer hours

2. By real capital, economists mean
   a. real estate, particularly land
   b. plant and equipment
   c. the real value of bonds, adjusted for inflation
   d. the real value of common stock, adjusted for inflation
   e. both c. and d.

3. The production possibilities curve has one major purpose: to illustrate the need to
   a. stop inflation
   b. cut taxes
   c. cut government spending
   d. make choices
   e. stop pollution

4. The textbook has a picture of a production possibilities curve (PPC), joining six points.
   a. all six points are equally desirable, since they all represent full employment
   b. all six points are equally desirable, since they all are consistent with zero inflation
   c. all six points are equally desirable, since they all provide for some growth
   d. all six points are possible, but the PPC curve doesn't give enough information to tell which point is best
   e. only one of the six points is presently achievable; the others can be achieved only if the economy grows

5. An outward bow in the production possibilities curve illustrates what concept?
   a. scarcity
   b. unlimited wants
   c. increasing opportunity cost
   d. unemployment
   e. inflation

6. The opportunity cost of a good is measured by
   a. the slope of the PPC
   b. how far the PPC is from the origin
   c. the slope of a line from the origin out to the PPC
   d. how far the economy is operating within the PPC
   e. how fast the PPC is shifting outward

7. Suppose the production possibilities curve is a straight line if goods X and Y are put on the axis. Then we know that
   a. X and Y are really the same good
   b. the problem of scarcity has been solved
   c. we can have all the X and Y we want without incurring an opportunity cost, even though the general problem of scarcity has not been solved
   d. the opportunity cost of X is zero, in terms of Y forgone
   e. the opportunity cost of X is constant, in terms of Y forgone

8. We speak of a production possibilities curve as a "frontier" because
   a. we can produce within it or on it, but not beyond it, with presently available resources and technology
   b. it reflects the concept of scarcity, and goods were particularly scarce for settlers on the western frontier in the nineteenth century
   c. it is no longer relevant, now that the frontier has been tamed and we have an affluent society
   d. unemployment problems provide the frontier for economic research
   e. differences among resources provide the frontier for economic research

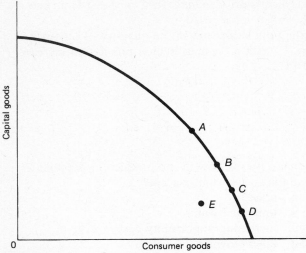

Figure 2.1

Table 2.1 Production Possibilities

	Options					
Products	A	B	C	D	E	F
Capital goods	0	1	2	3	4	5
Consumer goods	25	24	21	16	9	0

9. Suppose that the society has only one objective, to maximize growth. Then, the best choice among the five points shown on Figure 2.1 is

  a. A
  b. B
  c. C
  d. D
  e. E

10. In Figure 2.1, a growth of the economy can be illustrated by

  a. a move from point A to B
  b. a move from point B to A
  c. a move from point A to E
  d. a move from point D to E
  e. an outward shift of the production possibilities curve

11. In Figure 2.1, suppose that the economy is originally at point E. Then there will be

  a. rapid growth
  b. no capital formation
  c. more capital formation than at points A, B, or C
  d. a high rate of unemployment
  e. rapid inflation

12. The production possibilities curve generally bends outward because

  a. sensible people want to divide their purchases; they want to choose some food and some clothing
  b. there are economies of large-scale production
  c. most people have a comparative advantage in the production of at least one good
  d. there is much less unemployment now than during the Great Depression of the 1930s
  e. resources are not uniform in quality; some are better for producing one good than the other

13. In Table 2.1, the opportunity cost of the second unit of capital goods is how many units of consumer goods?

  a. 1
  b. 3
  c. 5
  d. 7
  e. 9

14. Given the options in Table 2.1, a total output of 5 units of capital goods and 25 units of consumer goods

  a. is unattainable at present
  b. represents a situation of large-scale unemployment
  c. can be achieved only if the economy achieves technological efficiency
  d. can be achieved only if the economy achieves allocative efficiency
  e. can be achieved only if the economy achieves both allocative and technological efficiency

15. Given the options in Table 2.1, a total output of 2 units of capital goods and 10 units of consumer goods

  a. is unattainable at present
  b. represents a situation of large-scale unemployment
  c. can be achieved only if the economy achieves technological efficiency
  d. can be achieved only if the economy achieves allocative efficiency
  e. can be achieved only if the economy achieves both allocative and technological efficiency

16. The choice of option C rather than B

  a. represents a mistake, since only 23 total units are produced (that is, 2 + 21) rather than 25 (that is, 1 + 24)
  b. represents a mistake, since consumers have fewer goods
  c. means that there will be more unemployment
  d. represents a choice of more growth
  e. represents a choice of less growth

17. The production possibilities curve shifts outward, away from the origin

  a. if the number of workers increases
  b. if the skill of workers increases
  c. if there is more capital
  d. if technology improves
  e. if any of the above happens

18. Oil now being pumped in a pipeline is an example of
   a. the land resource, because oil comes out of the ground
   b. real capital, because it has been produced in the past and will be used in the production of other goods
   c. financial capital, because it is valuable and is worth money
   d. financial capital, because it can be used as collateral for bank loans
   e. financial capital, because it was costly to pump out of the ground

19. Which of the following is an example of a capital inflow into Canada?
   a. a Canadian student spends $10,000 to study business administration at a U.S. university
   b. a Japanese construction firm buys $100,000 worth of timber from British Columbia
   c. a Finnish firm builds a plant in Quebec to produce cross-country skis
   d. an American couple spends $100 for a room and meals in Niagara Falls, Ontario
   e. a Canadian tourist brings back $100 worth of Mexican currency after a vacation in Acapulco

EXERCISES

1. Consider the following production possibilities table:

Table 2.2

	Options:							
	A	B	C	D	E	F	G	H
Consumer goods	0	1	2	3	4	5	6	7
Capital goods	23	22	20	17	13	9	5	0
Opportunity cost of consumer goods		1	2	3	4	4	4	5

   a. Complete the third line, showing the opportunity cost of each additional unit of consumer goods.
   b. Draw the PPC on Figure 2.2.

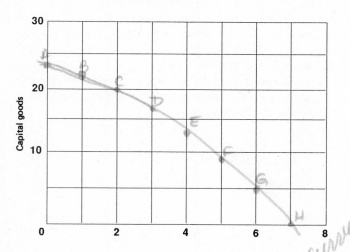

Figure 2.2

   c. What is unusual about this curve?
   d. In the range between points A and D, the PPC (bows outward, bows inward, is a straight line). This shows that opportunity cost is (increasing, decreasing, constant) in this range. However, between points D and G, the curve (bows outward, bows inward, is a straight

line). This shows that opportunity cost is (increasing, decreasing, constant) in this range.
   2. Consider a hypothetical economy with a labour force of 10 000 workers, each of whom can be put to work building either houses or roads. Each worker is available for 2000 hours per year. Thus, there are 20 million labour hours available during the year to produce houses and roads. Table 2.3 shows how many labour hours it takes to build various quantities of houses. For example, in order to build 18 000 houses, 15 million labour hours are needed. Likewise, Table 2.4 indicates how many labour hours are needed to build various amounts of roadway. In Figure 2.3, only one point, A, on the PPC has been plotted. It shows that if no houses are built, the 20 million labour hours can be used to produce 1000 kilometres of road. Using the data in Tables 2.3 and 2.4, plot four other points, and draw a PPC to connect them.

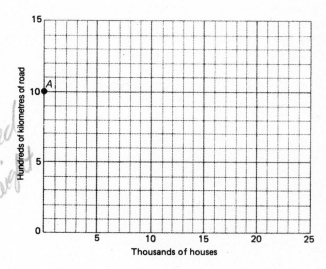

Figure 2.3

Table 2.3

Millions of labour hours	Thousands of houses
20	20
15	18
10	14
5	8
0	0

Table 2.4

Millions of labour hours	Hundreds of kilometres of road
20	10
15	9
10	7
5	4
0	0

ANSWERS

Important Terms: **1**h, **2**d, **3**e, **4**k, **5**i, **6**g, **7**b, **8**j, **9**a, **10**f, **11**c
True-False: **1**T, **2**F, **3**F, **4**T, **5**F, **6**T, **7**F, **8**F, **9**F, **10**T, **11**F
Multiple Choice: **1**c, **2**b, **3**d, **4**d, **5**c, **6**a, **7**e, **8**a, **9**a, **10**e, **11**d, **12**e, **13**b, **14**a, **15**b, **16**d, **17**e, **18**b, **19**c
Exercises: **1a.** 3, 4, 4, 4, 5. **1c.** over part of its range, it is a straight line (between D and G). **1d.** bows outward, increasing, is a straight line, constant. **2.** Four other points are:

	B	C	D	E
Hundreds of kilometres	9	7	4	0
Thousands of houses	8	14	18	20

ANSWERS TO SELECTED REVIEW QUESTIONS FROM THE TEXT

2-1. The first definition covers the problem of unemployment, but the second does not. (If there is large-scale unemployment, production is not limited by the scarcity of productive factors.) The importance of the unemployment problem is one of the reasons Chapter 1 uses the broader definition of economics.

2-2. It may be true that Pocklington's material wants have been completely satisfied, but the vast majority of people consume less than they would if they had an unlimited budget. For society as a whole, scarce resources constrain behaviour even though some individuals may have great personal wealth. Although the wealth of very rich families is great, it is not capable of solving the economic problems of society as a whole.

2-3. No clearly correct answer; the best rate of growth is an interesting policy issue. In addressing this question, it is important to recognize that growth comes at a cost. When we direct more of our resources toward capital formation, we have less for current consumption (Figure 2-5 in text). Unless there are unemployed resources which can be directed toward capital formation, higher growth represents a choice between consumption today and consumption in the furture.

2-4. Question 2-3 falls within the category of normative economics. It addresses the question of the best rate of growth of the economy.

Chapter 3

∎ ∎

Specialization, Exchange, and Money

MAJOR PURPOSE

In this chapter, we study specialization, exchange, and money. People specialize and engage in exchange because there are *gains* from doing so. By specializing, people can achieve higher standards of living. There are *two major sources* of gain from specialization: (1) *comparative advantage,* and (2) *economies of scale.* These two phenomena are the forces that motivate specialization and exchange; that is, they are the *twin engines that drive commerce.*

Money, on the other hand, *is the oil* which makes the machinery of commerce run smoothly, with a minimum of friction. Without money, people would engage in cumbersome barter. But, if some money helps to make the system work smoothly, we should not conclude that more money would make it work even better. Just as too much oil can gum up an engine, so too much money can cause difficulty. Specifically, it causes inflation. The Bank of Canada (Canada's central bank), acts as the chief mechanic. Its task is to create the right amount of "oil" (money)—neither too much, nor too little. The operations of the Bank of Canada will be considered in detail in Chapter 12.

LEARNING OBJECTIVES

After you have studied this chapter in the textbook and study guide, you should be able to
- Explain why specialization and exchange go hand in hand
- Explain why barter is inferior to exchange with money
- Explain why people may nevertheless revert to barter in some circumstances
- Give an example of Gresham's law
- Explain the two major reasons that there can be gains from specialization and exchange
- Explain the difference between absolute advantage and comparative advantage
- Explain why a country may have an absolute advantage in a product without having a comparative advantage in that product
- Explain why a country cannot have a comparative advantage (or a comparative disadvantage) in every product
- Explain why economies of scale may lead to substantial gains from freer international trade, especially for small countries

HIGHLIGHTS OF THE CHAPTER

One reason for economic progress has been an increase in *specialization*. Individuals, cities, and countries are now more specialized than they were a hundred years ago. When production is specialized, people engage in exchange, selling the products they produce to buy the wide variety of goods and services that they want to consume. We live in a highly interdependent economy, in which each of us depends on the specialized production of others.

Specialization and exchange would be very cumbersome without money. It is easy to imagine the difficulties that would arise if we tried to do without money and engaged in barter exchange instead. Barter requires a *coincidence of wants*—people engaging in exchange must each be able to provide a good or service that the other wants. Furthermore, for barter to work, there must be some rough equivalence in the value of the two goods or services to be exchanged. To buy toothpaste, a farmer would scarcely offer a cow in exchange. However, with money, such problems of indivisibility do not arise. The farmer may sell the cow for $1,000 and spend just a bit of the money to buy toothpaste, using the rest for a wide variety of other purchases. Money provides people with *general purchasing power*; money can be used to buy any of the wide variety of goods and services on the market. Those wishing to make exchanges no longer have to search for unlikely coincidences (such as the ill-clad farmer looking for someone who not only has clothes to exchange, but who also wants to get beef in return).

Because it is so useful for those who wish to engage in exchange, money is used even in rudimentary societies with little or no government. The prisoner-of-war camp provides an example of such a simple society. However, governments have gotten deeply involved in the monetary system. Every country uses paper money printed by a central bank.

One reason for the government to be involved in the monetary system is that the government can provide a *uniform* currency. In Canada, for example, every $5 Bank of Canada note (five-dollar bill) is always worth exactly the same as every other five-dollar bill, or as five "loonies" (one-dollar coins). This uniformity of the money stock is very convenient. When selling something for $5, we have to find out only if the buyer has a $5 bill or the equivalent in other standard coins and bills. Except for the rare cases where counterfeiting is suspected, we do not need to ask the much more complicated question of whether the buyer's bills or coins are inferior to someone else's bills or coins.

(Canada has not always had a uniform currency. In the nineteenth century, privately owned banks issued currency. The value of this currency depended on the soundness of the bank that issued it. Thus, sellers did have to worry about the value of the notes or dollar bills they accepted. Similar problems have arisen throughout history. For example, when gold coins were in use, their value could depend on the amount of gold they contained. Before the development of modern methods of producing coins with hard edges, such coins were sometimes clipped. That is, people chipped off bits before spending them. As a result, not every coin was worth the same as every other coin of the same denomination. People had to examine the physical condition of the coins they were accepting.)

In addition to providing a uniform currency, the Bank of Canada has the responsibility of providing an appropriate *quantity* of money. If too many bills or coins are issued, there will be "too much money chasing too few goods." Inflation will result; the currency will decline in value. On the other hand, if the quantity of money is allowed to decline sharply, spending will decline. Sellers will have a very difficult time finding buyers. Sales will fall, unemployment will rise, and prices will be under downward pressure. The authorities do not always perform their monetary duties well. In some countries—for example, Brazil—prices are galloping ahead by more than 100% per year. This reduces the convenience of money. If prices are rising rapidly, sellers feel under pressure to spend their money as soon as possible, before its value declines significantly.

With the proper quantity of money, the monetary system can work very smoothly, making transactions very convenient. But this is all that money does—it makes exchange convenient. It is not the reason that exchange is desirable in the first place.

There are two reasons that specialization and exchange can yield benefits. The first is *comparative advantage*. The notion of comparative advantage is illustrated in the textbook by the example of the gardener and the lawyer. The lawyer has an absolute advantage in both the law and gardening; she can do both quicker than the gardener. It follows that the gardener has an absolute disadvantage in both the law and gardening—he is slower at both. However, the gardener has a comparative advantage in gardening, while the lawyer has a comparative advantage in the law. Comparative advantage provides the basis for mutually beneficial trade. Both the gardener and the lawyer can gain from specialization and exchange. (Details are provided in Box 3-2 in the text.)

Two points should be emphasized. (1) Absolute advantage is not necessary for gain; the gardener can gain by specializing in gardening, even though he is not the best gardener. (2) A person (or a nation) cannot have a comparative disadvantage in everything. In the simple case of two people and two activities (law and gardening), if one person has a comparative advantage in one activity, the other person must have the comparative advantage in the other activity.

Economies of scale provide the second major reason that there are gains from specialization and exchange. Economies of scale exist if an increase of x% in all inputs (labour, machinery, land, steel, etc.) leads to an increase of more than x% in output. Economies of scale are the major reason that big firms have an advantage in many industries, such as automobiles and mainframe computers. Economies of scale are the major reason that costs per unit of output often decline as more is produced. For example, a car company can produce 100 000 cars at a much lower cost per car than if it produces 1000 cars. Clearly, if a person tried to put together a car in the back yard or in a small shop, it would be very expensive. There are gains when car production is left to the specialists.

Comparative advantage and economies of scale also help explain international trade and specialization among *countries* in producing different goods. For example, land in Florida is not used to produce trees for wood-pulp even though Florida land can produce more wood-pulp per hectare per year than land in Northern Alberta. Instead, Florida produces oranges while wood-pulp is produced in Northern Alberta, even though Alberta (like the gardener in Box 3-2) has an absolute disadvantage in *both* wood-pulp and oranges.

Similarly, the desire to gain economies of scale was part of the explanation for Canada entering into an agreement with the United States to allow free trade in cars and car parts (the Auto Pact) in the 1960s. With this agreement, Canadian auto plants could gain scale economies by specializing and producing a narrow range of models for the whole North American market, rather than producing a wide range of models, each on a small scale, for the Canadian market alone. And the hope for greater efficiency through increased scale economies was an important reason for Canada's decision to enter into the wide-ranging Free Trade Agreement with the United States that came into effect in 1989.

IMPORTANT TERMS: MATCH THE COLUMNS

Match each term in the first column with the corresponding phrase in the second column.

D	**1.**	Barter
I	**2.**	Required by barter
F	**3.**	General purchasing power
A	**4.**	A function of money
J	**5.**	Inflation
K	**6.**	Cause of inflation
H	**7.**	Absolute advantage
C	**8.**	Comparative advantage
E	**9.**	Economies of scale
G	**10.**	Example of economies of scale
B	**11.**	Gresham's law

~~a.~~	Acting as medium of exchange
b.	Bad money drives out good
c.	Reason the lawyer gains by practising law
~~d.~~	Exchange of one good or service for another
e.	Reason costs per unit fall as more is produced
~~f.~~	Money
g.	Adam Smith's pin factory
h.	Good can be produced with fewest resources
i.	Coincidence of wants
~~j.~~	Fall in value of money
~~k.~~	Too much money chasing too few goods

TRUE-FALSE

(T) F **1.** One reason that barter is inconvenient is that many commodities cannot easily be divided into smaller parts.

T (F) **2.** Monetary systems develop only when there is a strong national government, since strong national governments are required to provide money with value.

T (F) **3.** Suppose that, in the prisoner-of-war camp with its "cigarette money," the value of cigarettes rises compared to the value of other items (such as beef, etc.). Such an increase is known as inflation.

(T) F **4.** Comparative advantage is the reason wheat is grown in rural Manitoba and not in downtown Vancouver.

T (F) **5.** If everyone had exactly the same talents and training, and exactly the same quantity of capital, then economies of scale would not exist.

T (F) **6.** In the absence of a government, money is valuable only if it is useful. Therefore, cigarette money would be used exclusively in transactions between smokers in the prisoner-of-war camp.

T   F   7. Economies of scale are the primary reason wood-pulp is produced in Northern Quebec rather than on the Niagara peninsula.

T   F   8. Even if everyone has the same abilities, specialization may be beneficial if there are economies of scale.

T   F   9. International trade is more important for a country such as the United States than for Canada because large-scale U.S. factories have a more urgent need for access to world markets.

T   F   10. If scale economies are important in many industries, then free international trade is likely to mean both cheaper products and a wider choice for consumers.

MULTIPLE CHOICE

1. One of the problems with barter is that it requires a "coincidence of wants." This means that
   a. everybody must want money
   b. everybody must want the same good
   c. at least two people must want the same good
   d. everybody must want my good, before I am able to exchange it
   e. for there to be an exchange between individuals A and B, individual A must want what B has, while B must want what A has

2. When a monetary system first replaces barter, it becomes possible for the first time to distinguish between
   a. a good and a service
   b. the buyer and the seller
   c. private enterpreneurs and the government
   d. owners of capital and workers
   e. all of the above

3. Money is said to represent "general purchasing power" because
   a. it can be used to buy any of the goods and services offered for sale
   b. the government guarantees its value
   c. the government is committed to accept money in payment of taxes
   d. Gresham's law no longer is valid
   e. Gresham's law applies to other goods, but not money

4. When we draw a diagram showing the circular flow of payments between households and businesses, the two major markets we show are
   a. goods and services
   b. capital and labour
   c. capital and land
   d. consumer goods and economic resources
   e. products made by private entrepreneurs, and those provided by the government

5. In the present-day Canadian economy, what would an economist consider to be the "medium of exchange"?

   a. supermarkets
   b. corner drug stores
   c. the Sear's catalogue
   d. real estate brokers
   e. 5-dollar bills

6. When the best-tasting cigarettes started to disappear from circulation in the prisoner-of-war camp, this was an example of
   a. economies of scale
   b. absolute advantage
   c. comparative advantage
   d. inflation
   e. Gresham's law

7. In the prisoner-of-war camp, in which cigarettes acted as money, suppose that the quantity of cigarettes coming into the camp remained constant, while the quantity of all other goods decreased. Then the most probable result would be
   a. a rise in the value of cigarettes, measured in terms of other items
   b. a fall in the prices of other goods, measured in terms of cigarettes
   c. inflation
   d. deflation
   e. bad money driving out good money

8. Suppose that a building supervisor can lay bricks more rapidly and better than a bricklayer. Then, considering only these two individuals, we may conclude that
   a. the bricklayer has an absolute advantage in bricklaying
   b. the supervisor has an absolute advantage in bricklaying
   c. the bricklayer has a comparative advantage in bricklaying
   d. the supervisor has a comparative advantage in bricklaying
   e. we can't tell which of the above is true without knowing how much bricks cost, compared to the wage for bricklayers

9. The theory of comparative advantage was put forward by
   a. Adam Smith
   b. John Maynard Keynes
   c. David Ricardo
   d. David Hume
   e. Karl Marx

10. Suppose that there are only two countries, A and B, and only two goods, food and clothing. If country A has a comparative advantage in the production of food, B is most likely to have a comparative advantage in
   a. food also
   b. clothing
   c. both food and clothing
   d. neither food nor clothing
   e. we don't have enough information to decide

11. Suppose 10 workers with 1 machine can produce 100 TV sets in a month, while 20 workers with 2 machines can produce 250 TV sets in a month. This is an example of
   a. technological efficiency
   b. allocative efficiency
   c. economies of scale

   d. comparative advantage
   e. absolute advantage

12. Suppose that (1) there are economies of scale in the production of each good, and (2) land and labour have specialized capabilities—for example, land and the climate give Brazil a comparative advantage in coffee. Then the gains from specialization will be
   a. larger than if either (1) or (2) had existed alone
   b. small, since (1) and (2) tend to offset each other
   c. negative, since the combination of (1) and (2) creates confusion
   d. about the same as with (1) alone, since (2) doesn't make much difference
   e. about the same as with (2) alone, since (1) doesn't make much difference

13. When tariffs among countries are reduced, this generally leads to gains from
   a. economies of scale
   b. wider use of money rather than barter
   c. comparative advantage
   d. a. and b.
   e. a. and c.

EXERCISES

1. This exercise illustrates the idea of comparative advantage. Assume the following. A doctor working on home repairs can fix a leaky faucet in 10 minutes. A plumber takes 15 minutes. Then the (doctor, plumber) has an absolute advantage in plumbing. The doctor's time is worth $80 per hour in the practice of medicine. The plumber is paid $20 per hour.

Suppose the doctor's house has six leaky faucets. If he fixes them himself, it will take _____ minutes. Thus, to fix the faucets, the doctor will use $ _____ worth of his time. If the plumber is hired to fix the faucets, he will take _____ minutes, which is (longer, shorter) than the doctor would take. The cost in this case is $ _____, which is (more, less) by $ _____ than if the doctor fixed the faucets himself. The (doctor, plumber) has a comparative advantage in plumbing.

2. Table 3.1 shows how many cars can be produced in a country with various amounts of inputs. Each unit of input represents a specific quantity of labour and capital. Table 3.2 provides similar information for TV sets. Table 3.1, by itself, illustrates the idea of (comparative advantage, absolute advantage, economies of scale, none of these). Table 3.2, by itself, illustrates the idea of (comparative advantage, absolute advantage, economies of scale, none of these).

Suppose that the economy has 5 units of inputs to be devoted to cars and TV sets. Plot the PPC for these 5 units of input in Figure 3.1. How is the shape of the PPC different from the PPCs in Chapter 2? _____. The opportunity cost of producing cars (increases, decreases, remains constant) as more are produced.

Table 3.1 Production of Cars

Number of cars (millions)	Units of input
1	1
3	2
6	3
12	4
20	5

Table 3.2 Production of TV Sets

Number of TV sets (millions)	Units of input
20	1
40	2
60	3
80	4
100	5

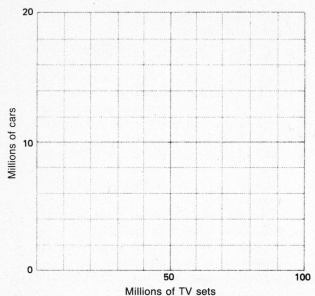

Figure 3.1

ESSAY QUESTIONS

1. The textbook explains why comparative advantage can mean that there are benefits from specialization and exchange. But it does not explain *why* specific people or nations might have a comparative advantage. How would you explain Saskatchewan's comparative advantage over New Brunswick in producing wheat? Why does Quebec have a comparative advantage over most American states in the production of wood-pulp and newsprint? Why does Taiwan have a comparative advantage in the production of transistor radios and TV sets?

2. Why do you think that most economists are usually in favour of reducing tariffs and other barriers to international trade? In the intense debate that preceded the signing of the 1989 Canada/United States Free Trade Agreement, many Canadians (including some economists) nevertheless opposed the removal of barriers to Canada-United States trade. What, do you think, were their reasons?

3. There are disadvantages associated with specialization as well as advantages. What are they?

ANSWERS

Important Terms: **1**d, **2**i, **3**f, **4**a, **5**j, **6**k, **7**h, **8**c, **9**e, **10**g, **11**b
True-False: **1**T, **2**F, **3**F, **4**T, **5**F, **6**F, **7**F, **8**T, **9**F, **10**T
Multiple Choice: **1**e, **2**b, **3**a, **4**d, **5**e, **6**e, **7**c, **8**b, **9**c, **10**b, **11**c, **12**a, **13**e
Exercises: **1.** doctor, 60, $80, 90, longer, $30, less, $50, plumber. **2.** economies of scale, none of these, it bows inward, decreases

ANSWERS TO SELECTED REVIEW QUESTIONS FROM THE TEXT

3-1. The simple answer to (a) and (b) is that we export those goods in whose production we have a comparative advantage, and import those goods for which our trading partners have a comparative advantage (that is, for which we have a comparative *dis*advantage).

In the case of an industry like cars (item (c)), economies of scale provide a reason for exporting some models and importing others, as discussed in the text.

3-3. One reason for greater specialization is the development of more specialized machinery. The advantage is more output. One possible disadvantage is the boredom that can come from producing only one narrow product.

3-4. Measuring "number of wills per week" on the vertical axis and "flowers planted per week" on the horizontal axis, the lawyer's PPC will be a straight line from 40 wills on the vertical axis to 800 flowers on the horizontal axis. It is different because it is a straight line.

Chapter 4

■ ■

Demand and Supply: The Market Mechanism

MAJOR PURPOSE

This chapter is one of the most important in the book. It introduces the concepts of *demand* and *supply*, which help us to understand what is happening in the market for a specific product. The demand curve illustrates how buyers respond to various possible prices: At lower prices, they buy more. On the other hand, sellers react negatively to low prices: They offer less for sale. This response of sellers is illustrated by the supply curve.

When drawing a demand or supply curve, we isolate the effect of *price alone* on the behaviour of buyers and sellers. Of course, many other things besides price can affect their behaviour. When we draw a demand or supply curve and look at the effect of price alone, we make the *ceteris paribus* assumption—that all these other things do not change. In cases where they do, in fact, change, we are no longer on a single demand or supply curve; the demand or supply curve *shifts*.

Other important concepts introduced in this chapter are the concepts of *equilibrium, surplus* and *shortage,* and *substitutes* and *complementary goods*.

LEARNING OBJECTIVES

After you have studied this chapter in the textbook and study guide, you should be able to

- Explain why the supply curve slopes upward to the right
- Explain why a price that begins away from equilibrium will move to equilibrium
- List and explain three things that can shift the demand curve and four that can shift the supply curve
- Give one example each of two goods that are (1) substitutes in use, (2) complements in use, (3) substitutes in production, and (4) complements in production. In each case, you should be able to explain why they fit into the category.
- Explain the distinction between product markets and markets for factors of production
- Explain how the factor markets can help answer the question, *For whom*?
- Explain how changes in factor markets can affect what happens in a product market, and vice versa
- Explain the main strengths and main shortcomings of the market mechanism as a way of answering the questions, *What*?, *How*?, and *For whom*?

HIGHLIGHTS OF THE CHAPTER

In every economy, some mechanism is needed to decide three major questions: *What* will be produced? *How* will it be produced? And *for whom* will it be produced? There are two major ways of answering these questions: (1) through the market—that is, through voluntary exchanges between buyers and sellers, and (2) through governmental decision making. (Other ways are sometimes used—for example, in a family or in a monastery. But we are not primarily interested in these alternatives.)

All nations have some reliance on markets and some reliance on governmental decision making. However, there are substantial differences among nations. In Canada and the United States, the market is the most important mechanism, although the government does play a significant role in modifying the outcome of the market. In the U.S.S.R., government plays a much more central role, although there is some reliance on markets.

The central feature of a market is *price*. Different prices for different goods provide *incentives* for producers to make some goods rather than others, and incentives for consumers to purchase cheap goods rather than expensive ones. Prices also provide *signals* and *information* to buyers and sellers. For example, the willingness of buyers to pay a high price acts as a signal to producers, showing that people are eager to obtain the product.

To study how buyers respond to different prices, we use a *demand curve* or *demand schedule*. This curve or schedule shows the quantity of a specific good that buyers would be willing and able to purchase at various different prices. The demand curve slopes downward to the right, illustrating that people are more eager to buy at lower prices. A major reason is that, at a lower price, people have an incentive to *switch* away from other products and buy the product whose price is lower instead.

On the other side of the market, the supply curve shows how much sellers would be willing to offer at various prices. It slopes upward to the right, because sellers will be increasingly eager to sell as the price rises. Again, the willingness to *switch* is an important reason for the slope. If the price of a good is higher, firms have an incentive to drop other products, and make more of this good instead.

What happens in the market depends on both demand and supply. To find the *equilibrium* price and quantity, we put the demand and supply curves together, to find where they intersect. At this price, the quantity offered by sellers is equal to the quantity which buyers want to purchase. There is no unfulfilled demand to pull prices up, nor any excess offers to pull prices down.

When the price is not at its equilibrium, there are pressures for it to change. If the price is below its equilibrium,

for example, there are eager buyers who are unable to find the good for sale. In other words, there is a *shortage*. Producers notice this and conclude that they can sell at a higher price. The price rises to its equilibrium level. On the other hand, if the price is initially above its equilibrium, there is a *surplus*. Eager sellers are unable to find buyers. They are willing to sell at a lower price. The price falls to its equilibrium.

When we draw a demand or supply curve, we are looking at the way in which buyers and sellers respond to price, and to price *alone*. In practice, of course, buyers and sellers are influenced by many other things than the price of the good—for example, buyers generally purchase more when their incomes rise, and sellers are less willing to sell when the costs of their inputs rise. But these other things are held constant when a single demand or supply curve is drawn. This is the important assumption of *ceteris paribus*, that other things do not change. If they do change, the demand or supply curve shifts. For example, an increase in income generally causes a rightward shift in the whole demand curve. However, in the case of inferior goods, the demand curve shifts left; when people can afford better alternatives, they choose them instead.

If the demand curve shifts to the right while the supply curve remains stable, then both price and quantity will increase. On the other hand, if the supply curve shifts to the right while the demand curve remains stable, then quantity will increase but price will fall. In brief, *a change in demand makes price and quantity change in the same direction, whereas a change in supply makes price and quantity move in opposite directions*. In practice, of course, many things can happen at once; often the demand and supply curves both shift. In this case, it becomes more difficult to predict what will happen.

Supply and demand theory is often used to study the market for a single good. However, there are strong connections among markets. When a price changes in one market, it can change conditions in other markets. For example, an increase in the price of gasoline in the 1970s caused a decline in the demand for large cars. This is an example of *complementary goods*—large cars and gasoline are used *together*. When the price of gasoline increases, the demand for large cars shifts left.

Whereas gasoline and cars are complements, some other products—such as bus tickets and train tickets—are *substitutes*. A person wanting to travel to the next city can go either by train or by bus. The higher is the train fare, the more people will use busses instead. Thus, a higher price of train tickets causes the demand for bus tickets to shift to the right.

Goods may also be substitutes or complements in

production. Substitutes in production are goods which use the same inputs; the inputs can be used to produce either the one good or the other. For example, land can be used to produce either wheat or corn. If there is a crop failure abroad and an increase in North American exports of wheat, the price of wheat will be bid up. Farmers will be encouraged to switch out of the production of corn and produce additional wheat instead. The supply curve for corn will shift to the left.

On the other hand, complements are produced together. For example, wheat and straw are produced together. If the price of wheat is bid up, more wheat will be produced. In the process, more straw will be produced as a by-product. The supply curve of straw will shift to the right.

The question of *what* will be produced is decided primarily in the product market. To throw light on the other two questions—*how?* and *for whom?*—we look first at the markets for inputs. For example, the market for labour helps to answer these two questions. If the demand for labour is high compared to its supply, then wage rates will be high. Thus, wage rates are much higher in Canada than in India because there are fewer workers for each unit of land and capital in Canada. As a result of the high wage, producers in Canada have an incentive to use only a little labour, and substitute capital instead. In an Indian factory, in contrast, many more things are done by hand because of the low wage rate. The wage rate not only helps to determine how things are produced, but it also helps to determine who gets the product. Because wage rates are high in Canada, a typical worker here can buy and consume many more products than the Indian worker.

Observe that high wage rates affect what the worker can buy; with high wages, workers are more likely to buy TV sets and homes. This means that wages—determined in the factor markets in the lower box in Figure 4-8 in the textbook—have an impact on the demand for TV sets, homes, and other products in the upper box. Thus, there are important connections among markets.

Finally, this chapter summarizes the strengths and weaknesses of the market as a mechanism for answering the three central questions—*What?, How?,* and *For whom?* The strong points of the market are that (1) it encourages producers to make what consumers want, (2) it provides people with an incentive to acquire useful skills, (3) it encourages consumers to conserve scarce goods, (4) it encourages producers to conserve scarce resources, (5) it provides a high degree of economic freedom, and (6) it provides buyers and sellers with information on market conditions, including local conditions.

The market mechanism is also subject to major criticisms: (1) some people may be left in desperate poverty, (2) markets don't work in the case of public goods such as defence and the police, (3) monopolies and oligopolies may have the power to keep production down and keep prices up, (4) the market does not provide a strong incentive for producers to limit pollution and other negative side effects, (5) a market economy may be unstable (although government policies will not necessarily increase stability), and (6) producers may simply be satisfying a want that they have created in the first place through advertising.

To evaluate the market, it is important to compare it with the alternatives that exist in fact, not with some ideal, unattainable system. The textbook outlines a few of the problems which can arise when the government sets prices—in particular, the problem of black markets and shortages. A number of countries that have interfered very heavily in economic activity—such as the Soviet Union—have run into severe problems, including shortages.

IMPORTANT TERMS: MATCH THE COLUMNS

Match each term in the first column with the corresponding phrase in the second column.

D	1. Capitalism	a. All the producers of a single good
H	2. Monopoly	b. If price of A rises, demand for B increases
L	3. Oligopoly	c. Surplus
I	4. Perfect competition	d. Free enterprise
A	5. Industry	e. Demand for this declines as income rises
K	6. Firm	f. Nothing else changes
C	7. Excess supply	g. Goods used together
J	8. Excess demand	h. Market with only one seller
E	9. Inferior good	i. Where every buyer and seller is a price taker
G	10. Complementary goods	j. Shortage
B	11. Substitutes	k. A single business organization, such as Canadian General Electric
F	12. Ceteris paribus	l. Market dominated by a few sellers

TRUE-FALSE

T (F) ✓ 1. Perfect competition exists only when the government fixes the price, so that no single buyer or seller is able to influence the price of the good.

(T) F ✓ 2. Perfect competition will not exist in a market if there is only one seller, or if there is only one buyer.

T (F) ✓ 3. In a perfectly competitive industry, every buyer and seller takes the quantity as given, and is left with only a pricing decision.

(T) F ✓ 4. Even if there are many buyers, imperfect competition can exist in a market.

(T) F ✓ 5. Even if there are many sellers, imperfect competition can exist in a market.

T (F) ✓ 6. In a capitalist economy, most of the capital equipment is owned by the government.

(T) F ✓ 7. A surplus drives the price down; a shortage drives the price up.

(T) F ✓ 8. If the price of wheat increases, the supply curve of straw will probably shift to the right.

(T) F ✓ 9. The demand curve for Pepsi-Cola will probably shift to the right if the price of Coke rises.

T (F) ✓ 10. If the price of paper increases, the supply curve of books will probably shift to the right.

(T) F ✓ 11. If demand increases while supply decreases, the price will increase.

(T) F ✓ 12. If the demand curve shifts to the right, the result will be an increase in the quantity sold and an increase in the market price.

depends how both (T) (F) 13. If both the demand and supply curves for a product shift to the right, we can expect the quantity sold to increase, but we cannot be sure whether the price will rise or fall.

T (F) 14. One essential characteristic of a free enterprise economy is that the government make it easier to enter businesses freely by subsidizing new businesses.

T (F) 15. Factor markets are different from the markets for most goods, in that goods markets are generally perfectly competitive, while the markets for factors are usually monopolized.

MULTIPLE CHOICE

1. Economists sometimes speak of a "free" market. By "free," they mean
   a. prices are low
   b. people do not have to pay admission to the marketplace
   (c.) transactions take place with little or no government interference
   d. the government is not a buyer or seller in the market
   e. there is perfect competition in that market

2. The Canadian government uses four major ways to influence what will be produced, how, and for whom. It uses every one of the following except one. Which one does not belong on this list?
   a. spending
   b. taxes
   c. regulation
   (d.) comprehensive central planning
   e. public enterprises

3. What is the most important characteristic of perfect competition?
   a. each seller has at least one powerful competitor to worry about
   b. there is at least one powerful, efficient producer who acts to keep prices down

c. every buyer can go to at least three or four sellers to see who has the lowest price
   (d.) every buyer and seller is a price taker; none has any power to set price
   e. there must be many buyers, and at least three or four sellers

4. A market with one seller and a few buyers is an example of
   (a.) monopoly
   b. oligopoly
   c. perfect competition
   d. technological inefficiency
   e. a black market

5. It is most accurate to speak of Abitibi Paper Ltd. as
   a. a plant
   (b.) a firm
   c. an industry
   d. a monopoly
   e. a perfect competitor

6. A surplus of turnips exists when
   a. turnip production is lower than last year
   b. turnip production is higher than last year
   c. turnip production exceeds the production of all other vegetables combined

d. the quantity of turnips demanded exceeds the quantity supplied

e. the quantity of turnips supplied exceeds the quantity demanded

7. Suppose that a surplus exists in a market. Then we may conclude that
   a. the price is below the equilibrium
   b. the price is above the equilibrium
   c. the government has imposed a price ceiling
   d. the quantity demanded has decreased
   e. the quantity supplied has increased

8. When we draw the demand curve for a product, we assume that
   a. there are many sellers
   b. there are only a few sellers
   c. all "supply shifters" are held constant
   d. all "demand shifters" are held constant
   e. both **c.** and **d.**

9. When incomes increase, the demand curve for an individual good
   a. usually shifts down
   b. always shifts down
   c. usually shifts to the right
   d. always shifts to the right
   e. doesn't move, since only price affects demand

10. Suppose that we know that an increase in the price of good A will cause a rightward shift in the demand curve for good B. Then we may conclude that
   a. producers of A and B use the same set of inputs
   b. consumers of A and B have the same levels of income
   c. consumers of A and B have different incomes
   d. A and B are complementary goods
   e. A and B are substitutes

11. Tennis rackets and tennis balls are
   a. substitutes
   b. complementary goods
   c. inferior goods
   d. independent goods
   e. monopolistic goods

12. Apples and textbooks are
   a. substitutes
   b. complementary goods
   c. inferior goods
   d. independent goods
   e. monopolistic goods

13. Which illustrate best the idea of substitutes in production?
   a. copper and aluminum
   b. wheat and barley
   c. wheat and bananas
   d. beef and leather
   e. cream and sugar

14. Peanuts and tobacco can be grown on similar land. Therefore, they are
   a. substitutes in production
   b. joint products
   c. inferior goods
   d. normal goods
   e. an oligopoly

15. Suppose that the demand for beef increases. This is most likely to cause
   a. a rightward shift in the supply curve for beef
   b. a leftward shift in the supply curve for beef
   c. a fall in the price of beef
   d. a fall in the price of leather
   e. an upward shift in the demand for leather

16. In a typical market
   a. an increase in demand, with no change in supply, will result in a fall in price
   b. an increase in demand, with no change in supply, will result in a decrease in quantity
   c. an increase in demand, with no change in supply, will result in an increase in both price and quantity
   d. an increase in supply, with no change in demand, will result in a decrease in quantity
   e. an increase in supply, with no change in demand, will result in an increase in price

17. Suppose that, between year 1 and year 2, the demand curve and the supply curve for wheat both shift to the right. From this information, we may conclude that, in year 2,
   a. the quantity of wheat sold will be larger, while the price will be higher
   b. the quantity of wheat sold will be larger, while the price will be lower
   c. the quantity of wheat sold will be larger, while we do not have enough information to tell if the price will be higher or lower
   d. the quantity of wheat sold will be smaller, while we do not have enough information to tell if the price will be higher or lower
   e. we do not have enough information to tell what will happen to either the price or the quantity

18. Incomes are determined primarily in the markets for
   a. goods
   b. services
   c. factors of production
   d. machinery
   e. parts

19. The advantages of the market mechanism (as contrasted to government controls) as a way of deciding What?, How?, and For whom? include
   a. prices provide incentives for producers to make what the public wants

b. prices provide incentives for producers to conserve scarce resources

c. prices provide incentives for consumers to conserve scarce goods

d. high wages in skilled occupations act as an incentive for workers to undertake training

e. all of the above

20. A black market is most likely to exist when

a. the government controls the price of a good

b. the supply of a good is controlled by a monopolist

c. the supply of a good is controlled by two or three producers

d. the government imposes an excise tax on a good

e. the government urges producers to produce more to promote the general welfare of the public

EXERCISES

1. Using the demand schedule in the first two columns of the table below, plot the demand and supply curves in Figure 4.1. Label the axes and mark in appropriate numbers on each axis. Then fill in the last column of the table.

a. The equilibrium quantity is ___400___ .

b. The equilibrium price is ___80¢___ .

c. At the equilibrium price, what is the surplus or shortage shown in the last column? ___∅___ . Does this confirm that this price is an equilibrium? ___yes___ .

d. Now suppose that the government sets a price of 60 cents. At this price, there will be a (surplus, (shortage)) of ___300___ .

2. Figure 4.2 illustrates some of the issues that arise when the government undertakes price supports (for example, in agriculture). **D** shows the demand curve, and S_1 the supply curve. Initially, the equilibrium quantity is ___120___ million bushels, and the price is ___P_2___ . Now suppose that the government passes a rule that says that wheat cannot be sold at a price less than P_3. The result of this law will be a ((surplus), shortage) amounting to ___40___ million bushels.

If all the government does is set a high price, not all wheat farmers will be better off. Those who are better off will be those who ((cut back production), (sell their wheat at the high price)). On the other hand, some will be worse off, specifically those who ((are unable to sell their wheat at the high price), sell their wheat at a low price). To ensure that wheat farmers are better off, the government can ((buy the surplus wheat), reduce the price to P_1).

Now, suppose that the government undertakes irrigation projects to help agriculture in dry areas. This will cause an increase in supply from S_1 to S_2, and the ((surplus), shortage) of wheat will ((increase), decrease) to ___80___ million bushels. The government will find the costs of its price support program ((increasing), decreasing). If it now eliminates the price support, the free market price will settle at ___P_1___ .

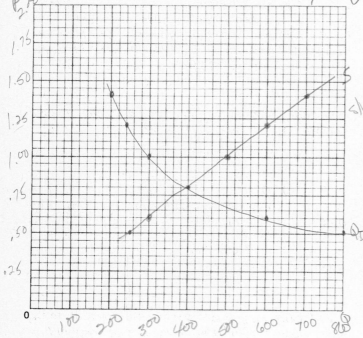

Figure 4.1

Price of Hamburgers	Quantity Demanded (thousands per week)	Quantity Supplied (thousands per week)	Surplus (+) or Shortage (−)
$1.40	200	700	+500
$1.20	240	600	+360
$1.00	300	500	+200
$0.80	400	400	0
$0.60	600	300	−300
$0.50	800	250	−550

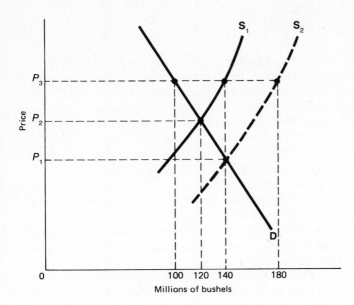

Figure 4.2

3. Suppose that supply is given by the equation:

$$Q = -30 + 4P$$

This supply is plotted in Figure 4.3 in the following way. First, choose some convenient value for P, such as 10. Put this value into the equation to get $Q = -30 + 40 = 10$. This means that when $P = 10$, $Q = 10$, so that point A is on the supply "curve." Then, choose another value of P, say, 15. Substituting this into the equation, we find that the corresponding $Q =$ ___30___. This is plotted as point B. The supply relationship is a straight line; there are no squared terms or other reasons for supply to bend. Thus, with the two points A and B, we can draw the straight-line supply $\mathbf{S_1}$.

a. Suppose that demand is also a straight line:

$$Q = 20 - P$$

Then, if $P = 15$, $Q =$ ___5___, and if $P = 5$, $Q =$ ___15___. Plot demand in Figure 4.3 and label it $\mathbf{D_1}$. On this figure, we see that the equilibrium price is ___$10___ and the equilibrium quantity ___10___. Confirm these figures by solving the two equations algebraically, to find P and Q.

$$Q = -30 + 4P$$
$$Q = 20 - P$$
$$-30 + 4P = 20 - P$$
$$5P = 50 \quad P = 10$$

b. Suppose now that income increases and demand consequently increases, with 15 more units being demanded at each price. Thus, the new demand is

$$Q = 35 - P$$

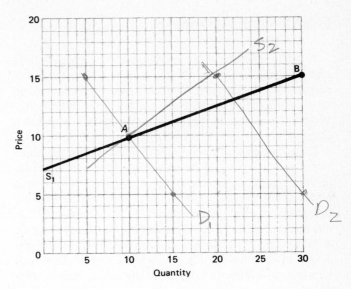

Figure 4.3

To plot this new demand, we find two points. For example, if $P = 15$, $Q =$ ___20___, and if $P = 5$, $Q =$ ___30___. Plot the new equilibrium demand, labelling it $\mathbf{D_2}$. At the new equilibrium, $P =$ ___13___ and $Q =$ ___22___. Again, confirm these numbers by solving the demand and supply equations. The price has (increased, decreased), and the quantity has (increased, decreased) as a result of this increase in demand.

$$-30 + 4P = 35 - P$$
$$5P = 65$$
$$P = 13$$

c. Now, suppose we are back with the original demand, $\mathbf{D_1}$, but that supply is now:

$$Q = -10 + 2P$$

If $P = 10$, $Q =$ ___10___, and if $P = 15$, $Q =$ ___20___. Plot this new supply and label it $\mathbf{S_2}$. With supply $\mathbf{S_2}$ and demand $\mathbf{D_1}$, the equilibrium price is ___10___, while quantity is ___10___. Again, confirm these numbers by solving the demand and supply equations.

$$-10 + 2P = 20 - P$$
$$3P = 30$$
$$P = 10$$

d. Finally, suppose that demand shifts from $\mathbf{D_1}$ to $\mathbf{D_2}$, while supply remains at $\mathbf{S_2}$. At the new equilibrium $P =$ ___15___ and $Q =$ ___20___. When the demand curve shifted this time, why is it that the price rose more, and the quantity less, than in part **b**?

Because of the slope of the Supply curve

Answer: ___S_2 steeper than S_1___.

ESSAY QUESTIONS

1. A demand or supply curve applies to a specific time and a specific location. For example, the market for maple syrup in London, Ontario, is not the same thing as the market for maple syrup in Winnipeg, Manitoba. Would you expect the price of maple syrup in these two cities to be similar? Precisely the same? Explain.

2. Suppose that, as a result of an increase in the number of pancake eaters in Winnipeg, there were an increase in the demand for maple syrup in that city. If you were an all-powerful social planner, you would probably want to persuade people in London to give up some of their maple syrup in order to provide for the higher demand in Winnipeg. What sort of rationing scheme might you devise to accomplish this goal? How would you know how much to allocate to each family? How large a staff do you think you would need?

Suppose, alternatively, that you allowed market forces to work freely. What would happen to the price of maple syrup in London, Ontario? What would happen to the quantity? How would the changing conditions in Lon-don affect the supply curve for maple syrup in Winnipeg? What would happen to the price of maple syrup in Winnipeg? To the quantity? Draw demand and supply curves for London and Winnipeg to illustrate what is happening. Would your intentions as a social planner be carried out by the market instead? Which policy—rationing or the market—works more efficiently? Are there any disadvantages to the more efficient system?

3. The prices printed on a restaurant menu apply whether the restaurant is crowded or half empty on any particular evening. If you ran a restaurant,

a. would you charge higher prices on Friday and Saturday evenings, when the restaurant is crowded, than on other evenings?

b. would you charge higher prices during the evening than for an identical meal at lunch? Why or why not? (Or, under what circumstances might you?)

c. Does McDonald's behave in the way you have suggested? How do you explain that?

ANSWERS

Important Terms: **1**d, **2**h, **3**l, **4**i, **5**a, **6**k, **7**c, **8**j, **9**e, **10**g, **11**b, **12**f
True-False: **1**F, **2**T, **3**F, **4**T, **5**T, **6**F, **7**T, **8**T, **9**T, **10**F, **11**T, **12**T, **13**T, **14**F, **15**F
Multiple Choice: **1**c, **2**d, **3**d, **4**a, **5**b, **6**e, **7**b, **8**d, **9**c, **10**e, **11**b, **12**d, **13**b, **14**a, **15**d, **16**c, **17**c, **18**c, **19**e, **20**a
Exercises: **1a.** 400, **b.** \$0.80, **c.** zero, yes, **d.** shortage, 300
2. 120, P_2, surplus, 40, sell their wheat at the high price, are unable to sell their wheat at the high price, buy the surplus wheat, surplus, increase, 80, increasing, P_1
3. 30, **a.** 5, 15, 10, 10, **b.** 20, 30, 13, 22, increased, increased, **c.** 10, 20, 10, 10, **d.** 15, 20, because S_2 is steeper than S_1.

ANSWERS TO SELECTED REVIEW QUESTIONS FROM THE TEXT

4-1. When there is a freeze on the coffee plantations, the supply of coffee shifts to the left, causing the price to rise. Because tea and coffee are substitutes, the rise in the price of coffee causes a rightward shift in the demand for tea. This causes an increase in the price of tea. The effects are the same as those shown in Figure 4-7.

4-2. Some other relevant questions in deciding careers are these: Is a job interesting? Does it provide satisfaction? Are the surroundings pleasant? Does the job offer prestige? Do you get to meet interesting people? Are you likely to get along with your colleagues? Is the job safe?

4-3. (a) The supply will shift to the left. The demand will also shift to the left, to the extent that social pressures mean less drinking.

(b) The demand for and supply of funds will likewise shift left. Profitability may go up or down, depending on whether the demand or supply shifts more.

4-4. The supply will shift left or upward. Suppliers will not be willing to offer the item unless they are compensated for the risk of prison. The demand is likely to shift to the left, too, although we cannot be certain. (The thrill of doing something mildly illegal may appeal to some users.) The quantity will therefore probably fall, and the price will probably rise. The money incomes of sellers will probably increase (although their risk-adjusted returns will probably fall, unless there is a perverse outward shift of the demand curve).

Chapter 5

■ ■

The Economic Role of the Government

MAJOR PURPOSE

The major objective of this chapter is to explain how the government affects the economy. It does so in four ways: spending, taxation, regulation, and the operation of public enterprises.

There are a number of reasons for government intervention in the economy. (1) The government provides *public goods*—that is, goods that cannot be provided by the private sector because everyone can enjoy them, regardless of who pays for them. An example is police protection; we all gain the benefits from an orderly society, whether we pay taxes or not. (2) The government can control or discourage externalities, such as pollution. Free markets don't work very well in the control of polluting industries, since they provide no incentive to keep pollution down. (3) The government provides merit goods—such as education--that it considers particularly important for the society. (4) The government provides programs to help the poor. (5) Another important objective of the government is to promote stability. Badly designed policies may lead to rapid inflations and deep depressions. An important objective—to be considered in Parts 2 to 5, is to avoid such destabilizing actions.

LEARNING OBJECTIVES

After you have studied this chapter in the textbook and study guide, you should be able to
- Describe the four ways in which the government affects the economy
- Describe the major programs of the three levels of government
- Explain the difference between government spending for goods and services, and transfer payments
- Explain the difference between a progressive and a regressive tax, and give an example of each
- Describe the five major reasons for government intervention in the economy
- Explain the role and significance of Crown corporations in the Canadian economy
- Explain the objectives that should be kept in mind when designing a tax system
- Explain the difference between the *benefit principle* and the *ability to pay principle*
- Explain why the Canadian tax system is less progressive than we might guess by looking at the income tax schedule
- Describe the major elements of Canada's federal tax reform that was begun in the late 1980s

HIGHLIGHTS OF THE CHAPTER

The government affects the economy in four major ways: (1) spending, (2) taxation, (3) regulation, and (4) public enterprises.

Spending

In dollar terms, government spending has risen very rapidly in Canada, from about $4 billion per year in 1950 to $267 billion by 1988. However, if we look at the size of the government relative to the economy, we get a much less spectacular picture. For example, government *purchases of goods and services* have increased relatively slowly as a percentage of GDP since the mid-1940s, and the percentage remains well below what it was during World War II. Nevertheless, if transfer payments to individuals are included, government spending has risen substantially as a percentage of GDP in recent decades; in the mid-1980s this percentage surpassed its wartime peak. Thus, most of the increase in the relative size of government reflects the increase in transfer payments such as Old Age Security and Unemployment Insurance benefits, family allowances, and so on.

A large part of government spending at the federal level consists of revenue transfers to *provincial* governments, both as general equalization payments (to provinces with a relatively small tax base), and as conditional transfers for specific programs, such as health care and post-secondary education. Provincial governments, in turn, transfer substantial amounts to local governments.

Taxes

The primary purpose of taxes is to raise the revenue to finance government spending. The personal income tax is the largest revenue raiser, by a large margin, for the federal and provincial governments. Other important sources are the corporate income tax, sales taxes, and local government property taxes. At the federal level, unemployment insurance contributions and mandatory contributions to the Canada/Quebec Pension Plans represent another important revenue source.

On most income—up to a maximum of about $30,000 per year in 1988—a "tax" such as the worker's portion of the unemployment insurance contribution is *proportional*: It is calculated as a fixed percentage of income. However, no contributions are collected on incomes over the maximum, which means that, in this range, the "tax" is *regressive*. That is, it is a smaller percentage of an income of, say, $60,000, than of an income of $30,000. Nevertheless, the impact (*incidence*) of the overall sys-

tem of unemployment insurance, mandatory government pension plans, and other transfer payments, is *progressive* because the net benefits to lower-income people are greater, as a percentage of their incomes, than the benefits to people with higher incomes.

Unlike the "tax" rates for the unemployment insurance contributions, the income tax rates are progressive: The tax rate on high incomes is generally larger than the tax rate on low incomes. However, the overall tax system is less progressive than the tax rates suggest, both because of the existence of regressive components such as unemployment insurance contributions, and because of "loopholes"—that is, special rules in the tax law that allow certain kinds of income to be taxed at a lower rate, or escape tax altogether. The term "loophole" implies that these rules are undesirable, and there is considerable debate over what is desirable and what is not. One item sometimes put on the list of loopholes—the fact that the government does not levy any tax on the implicit return on homeowners' equity—has strong political support and is rarely mentioned in the debate on tax reform.

Other than raising revenues, there are a number of other objectives that should be considered in designing a tax code.

1. One objective is *equity,* or fairness. As we suggested in Chapter 1, there is some controversy over just what is fair. Nevertheless, discussions of fairness usually begin with one of two approaches to taxation:

a. *Ability to pay*. According to this idea, taxes should be imposed according to income or wealth; people with high incomes should pay more because they are better able to do so. The progressive income tax is one application of this principle.

b. *Benefit principle*. According to this idea, taxes should depend on who benefits most from government programs. Those who benefit most should pay the most.

2. *Simplicity* is an important objective in the tax system. Discussions of tax reform in recent years have often centred around the criticism that the income tax has become hopelessly complicated.

3. *Neutrality*. As a starting point, most economists believe that the tax system should be designed to disturb market forces as little as possible. It should not capriciously introduce incentives for people to change their behaviour in order to avoid taxes.

4. *Meeting social objectives*. Nevertheless, in some cases it may be desirable to encourage people to change their behaviour. For example, in order to encourage people to give to charities, the government allows people to deduct their contributions to charities from their taxable income. Taxes may also be used to discourage businesses from polluting the air or water.

In the 1980s, efforts were made to improve the federal tax system in Canada through a number of reforms. While some of the specific measures were controversial, there was widespread support for the basic underlying principles of the reform program: that the tax base should be broadened by reducing the number of loopholes; that income tax rates should be reduced; and that there should be more emphasis on *tax credits* (specific dollar reductions in the amount of tax payable) than on *deductions* from taxable income, as a way of reducing the tax burden on various categories of individuals.

Regulation

More direct means are available for encouraging some behaviour, and discouraging other activities. For example, there are regulations limiting the amount of pollutants that factories are allowed to discharge into the air and water. In the early days of regulation about a hundred years ago, the government took steps to discourage monopolistic behaviour by the industrial cartels—"combines"—that were being organized at the time. Other regulations are aimed at protecting the safety of workers and discouraging discrimination.

Government regulations are generally aimed at reducing major problems. Nevertheless, regulation has been a source of controversy. There are two major problems with regulation: (1) regulatory agencies may require major reporting efforts from business, and sometimes generate expensive red tape of little value; and (2) regulatory agencies sometimes come under the control of the industry they are supposedly regulating. The government may become the means for an industry gaining oligopolistic or monopolistic power.

Public Enterprise

Another important way in which the government influences the economy is through *Crown corporations*, government-owned firms that derive much of their revenue from selling goods or services to the public. In the 1980s, it was estimated that Crown corporations were responsible for as much as 15% of all capital investment in Canada.

Federal and provincial governments establish Crown corporations for a variety of reasons: as an alternative to regulation in the case of a *natural monopoly*; as a way of ensuring the provision of certain services (such as transportation and communications) to communities that would be inadequately served by private firms; to stimulate investment in risky ventures involving new technology. Sometimes Crown corporations are created when the government takes over a financially ailing firm as a way of protecting employment opportunities in particular communities.

A possible problem with Crown corporations has to do with lack of *accountability*. If the political control over the corporation's managers is weak, there may be inadequate control over costs and some corporations may end up running deficits far higher than can be justified by the special objectives they are supposed to serve. One possible way of overcoming this problem is *privatization*—that is, selling Crown corporations to private shareholders. In the 1980s, a number of instances of privatization occurred at both the provincial and federal levels.

Reasons For Government Activity

The government becomes involved in the economy for many reasons. Here are the five most important:

1. Governments often provide goods and services which the private sector would otherwise fail to provide or would provide only with difficulty and at a high cost. Roads are one example. If the roads within a city were run by private entrepreneurs, motorists would have to stop frequently to pay tolls. National defence is unlikely to be organized and paid for privately. There is a problem of *free riders*—people who let others pay because they will reap the benefits even if they don't contribute. If people benefit whether they pay or not, we have an example of a *public good*.

2. The government may intervene when *side effects* prevent people from making socially desirable decisions. For example, vaccinations protect not only the individuals who are vaccinated; they also protect the public from communicable diseases. Smallpox has been eradicated by the combined action of governments and international organizations. Benefits that go to people other than those who are vaccinated (or their doctors) are known as *external benefits*. There also can be *external costs,* such as the cost to people downwind from a polluting factory. Just as the government encourages activities with external benefits—such as vaccinations—so it may discourage those with external costs.

3. The government may provide *merit* goods or services, such as education, that it considers very desirable from a social viewpoint.

4. The government has programs to *help the poor*; for example, subsidized housing and welfare programs.

5. The government may increase or decrease its expenditures in order to *promote economic stability*. For example, during a period of high unemployment, it may undertake public projects in order to provide jobs.

IMPORTANT TERMS: MATCH THE COLUMNS

Match each term in the first column with the corresponding phrase in the second column.

_____	**1.**	Transfer payment
_____	**2.**	Progressive tax
_____	**3.**	Proportional tax
_____	**4.**	Average tax rate
_____	**5.**	Marginal tax rate
_____	**6.**	Deficit
_____	**7.**	Equalization payments
_____	**8.**	Conditional transfers
_____	**9.**	Privatization
_____	**10.**	Externality
_____	**11.**	Public good
_____	**12.**	Neutral tax
_____	**13.**	Tax credit
_____	**14.**	Tax deduction

a. Tax paid divided by income

b. Federal payments to provinces with a low tax base

c. One that takes the same percentage of high and low incomes

d. Sale of government-owned businesses

e. One that takes a higher percentage of high incomes

f. People get the benefit of this, regardless of who pays

g. Expenditure by government, for which government receives no good or service in return

h. Specified reduction in amount of income tax payable

i. Tax which leaves market forces undisturbed

j. Side effect of production or consumption

k. Specified reduction in taxable income

l. Excess of expenditures over revenues

m. Percentage of additional income paid in tax

n. Federal contributions to specific provincial programs

TRUE-FALSE

T F **1.** Payments to the unemployed are a form of transfer payment.

T F **2.** If we include all levels of government (federal, provincial, and local), then government spending on goods and services is more, as a fraction of GDP, than it was even at the height of World War II in 1943/44.

T F **3.** Since 1960, transfer expenditures by the federal government have risen, both as a fraction of total federal government expenditures and as a fraction of GDP.

T F **4.** Public enterprise in Canada is about the same size (in relation to the economy as a whole) as public enterprise in the United States.

T F **5.** A tax is progressive if high-income people pay a larger percentage of their income than low-income people.

T F **6.** Suppose that a province imposes a tax of 5% on all income. Because it "hits the poor as hard as the rich," such a tax is regressive.

T F **7.** Suppose that the government imposes a federal sales tax of 7%. Because high-income people buy more than low-income people, they will pay more sales tax. Therefore, such a tax is progressive.

T F **8.** According to the benefit principle of taxation, government expenditures should be undertaken whenever they benefit the public.

T F **9.** According to the ability to pay principle of taxation, only those who have enough income that they are able to save should be required to pay taxes.

T F **10.** The term "merit good" is used in describing a feature of the British economy. Specifically, a "merit good" is one which the upper class consumes more heavily than the lower classes.

T F **11.** Since poor people are more likely than rich people to live in rented housing, the non-taxation of the implicit return on homeowners' equity makes the Canadian tax system less progressive.

MULTIPLE CHOICE

1. Which of the following is the best example of government expenditure for goods or services?
   a. salaries of judges
   b. Old Age Security benefits paid to the elderly
   c. social assistance payments to poor people
   d. unemployment compensation
   e. the progressive income tax

2. Of the following categories of expenditure for the federal government, which two are the largest: "Debt charges" (interest on the public debt); "Protection of Persons and Property" (national defence, etc.); "Education"; "Social Services" (including transfers to individuals, etc.)?
   a. debt charges and protection of persons and property
   b. protection of persons and property and social services
   c. debt charges and education
   d. debt charges and social services
   e. education and social services

3. The two largest categories of expenditures for provincial and local governments combined are
   a. health care and interest
   b. health care and education
   c. education and social services
   d. health care and social services
   e. interest and social services

4. Over the past three decades, transfer payments by the federal government have been rising as a percentage of GDP. From this we may conclude that
   a. transfer payments have become too large
   b. transfer payments may or may not be too large now, but they were too small in 1960
   c. transfer payments are still too small, since they continue to rise
   d. transfer payments will sooner or later bankrupt the government
   e. we don't have enough information to come to any of the above conclusions

5. In 1988, each person over the age of 65 was allowed to subtract about $550 when computing the amount they had to pay in federal income tax. This illustrates
   a. that the federal income tax is progressive
   b. the benefit principle of taxation
   c. a tax deduction
   d. a transfer payment
   e. a tax credit

6. Of the following, which provides the largest source of revenue for the federal government?
   a. sales taxes
   b. corporate income taxes
   c. personal income taxes
   d. customs duties
   e. excise taxes on cigarettes and alcohol

Table 1   Income Tax Rates (hypothetical)

Income	Tax
$10,000	$1,000
$20,000	$3,000
$30,000	$5,000

7. For a person with an income of $20,000, the *average* tax rate in Table 1 is
   a. 10%
   b. 15%
   c. 20%
   d. 30%
   e. we don't have enough information to tell what the average tax rate is

8. For a person with an income of $20,000, the *marginal* tax rate in Table 1 is
   a. 10%
   b. 15%
   c. 20%
   d. 30%
   e. 50%

9. If a tax takes $1,000 from someone with an income of $10,000, and $2,000 from someone with an income of $50,000, that tax is
   a. neutral
   b. progressive
   c. regressive
   d. proportional
   e. marginal

10. If unemployment insurance contributions are considered as a tax, then it would be characterized as
   a. neutral
   b. marginal
   c. mildly progressive
   d. highly progressive
   e. regressive

11. Last year, the government's debt increased by the amount of last year's
   a. tax revenues − expenditures
   b. interest payments
   c. transfer payments
   d. surplus
   e. deficit

12. During the past decade, the federal government has
   a. run a surplus every year
   b. run a surplus most years, but not every one

   c. had about the same number of surpluses as deficits

   d. run a deficit most years, but not every one

   e. run a deficit every year

13. Prior to 1977, the federal government reimbursed half the total spending of each provincial government for health care and post-secondary education. This was an example of

   a. government provision of public goods

   b. equalization payments

   c. unconditional federal-provincial transfers

   d. the federal government's laissez-faire approach to economic policy

   e. conditional federal-provincial transfers

14. According to the "neutrality" principle of taxation

   a. income taxes should be progressive

   b. taxes should be imposed only on goods about which people are neutral (that is, neither very enthusiastic nor very negative)

   c. taxes should be imposed on tobacco and alcoholic beverages

   d. taxes should be designed to disturb market forces as little as possible

   e. the government should rely on the corporate profits tax, not the personal income tax

15. A public good

   a. creates no positive externalities

   b. creates no negative externalities

   c. cannot be produced by a private corporation

   d. can be enjoyed by all, even those who do not pay for it

   e. must be provided by the federal government if it is to be provided at all

16. Which of the following is the best example of a negative economic externality?

   a. an increase in the international price of oil

   b. an increase in the international price of grain

   c. air pollution created by a steel mill

   d. the rise in the price of steel when the government requires steel mills to reduce pollution

   e. vaccinations

17. Which of the following is designed specifically to be non-neutral?

   a. a proportional income tax

   b. a general sales tax of 5%

   c. a tax on polluting activities

   d. all of the above

   e. none of the above

18. The presence of externalities means that

   a. a tax system that seems to be progressive will, in fact, be regressive

   b. a tax system that seems to be regressive will, in fact, be progressive

   c. the market system will generally not work as well as it would in the absence of externalities

   d. the rich will generally get richer, and the poor poorer

   e. the federal government will find it much more difficult to balance its budget

EXERCISES

1. The table below shows two different taxes—tax A and tax B. For each of these taxes, fill in the column showing the average tax rate at various incomes, and the marginal tax rate. Also note on the last line whether the tax is proportional, regressive, or progressive.

2. Suppose that a family has an income of $35,000 which includes $5000 in benefits from a pension plan.

Suppose the family is allowed to deduct that $5000 when calculating its taxable income. As a result, taxable income falls from $35,000 to $30,000. This would mean a reduction of $ _____ in tax payable under Tax A, and a reduction of $ _____ under Tax B. Thus, the higher is the marginal tax rate, the (greater, less) is the tax saving from a deduction.

Income	TAX A			TAX B		
		Average Rate	Marginal Rate		Average Rate	Marginal Rate
$10,000	$1,500	_____%		$1,500	_____%	
$20,000	3,000	_____%	_____%	3,500	_____%	_____%
$30,000	4,500	_____%	_____%	6,000	_____%	_____%
$40,000	6,000	_____%	_____%	9,000	_____%	_____%

Type of tax: _____ ; _____ .

ESSAY QUESTIONS

1. What would it be like to live in Canada if there were no federal or provincial government regulatory agencies? Describe what would happen if specific agencies, such as Environment Canada, Health and Welfare, the CTC, and the CRTC, were absent. What do you think the effects were when the government revamped, and sharply reduced the role of, the Foreign Investment Review Agency (FIRA) in 1986?

2. In most communities, the following services are provided by the local government:
   a.   Police
   b.   Elementary education
   c.   Street cleaning
   d.   Garbage collection

Could these be provided by private enterprise? Is there any advantage in having them provided by the government? Would there be any advantage in having them provided by the private sector?

3. What externalities are created by individuals who:
   a. drive on a highway
   b. mow the lawn
   c. smoke in a theatre

In each case, do you think that the government should do anything to encourage or discourage the activity? If so, what? and why? If not, why not?

ANSWERS

Important Terms: **1**g, **2**e, **3**c, **4**a, **5**m, **6**l, **7**b, **8**n, **9**d, **10**j, **11**f, **12**i, **13**h, **14**k

True-False: **1**T, **2**F, **3**T, **4**F, **5**T, **6**F, **7**F, **8**F, **9**F, **10**F, **11**T

Multiple Choice: **1**a, **2**d, **3**b, **4**e, **5**e, **6**c, **7**b, **8**c, **9**c, **10**e, **11**e, **12**e, **13**e, **14**d, **15**d, **16**c, **17**c, **18**c

Exercises: **1.** Tax A. Average rates: 15%, 15%, 15%, 15%. Marginal rates: 15%, 15%, 15%. The tax is proportional. Tax B. Average rates: 15%, 17.5%, 20%, 22.5%. Marginal rates: 20%, 25%, 30%. The tax is progressive. **2.** $750, $1,500, greater.

ANSWER TO A SELECTED REVIEW QUESTION FROM THE TEXT

5-3. In the case of defence research, a major reason is the need for secrecy. In the case of agricultural research, it may be necessary for government to do it since individual farmers produce on too small a scale to justify the high cost of doing research just to increase production on their own farms. Moreover, agricultural research often involves technology that cannot be patented or sold under licensing agreements. Thus, a private firm could not cover the cost of its research by selling the rights to its inventions (the way inventors in other sectors sometimes are able to do).

Across

1. It's important to distinguish between these two tax rates (2 words).
8. prefix meaning "two"
9. era
10. preposition
11. desirable characteristic for tax base
13. me (French)
15. what a completely flat tax would do to tax-rate schedule
18. At the end of April, you have to file your tax _____.
20. The United States imposed restrictions on this important Canadian export in 1986.
22. here (French)
23. second person pronoun
24. long time period
26. generally considered an undesirable kind of tax
27. keeps bridges and airplanes floating
30. thus (Latin)
31. When a dog is happy, its tail does this.
33. undertake
35. preposition
37. preposition meaning "belonging to"
39. The federal government had a $30 billion one in the mid-1980s. (2 words)
41. burns you up
42. goes with "either"
43. The federal and provincial governments have this kind of arrangement in health care and post-secondary education.

Down

1. one guide in designing taxes (3 words)
2. where grapes grow
3. what marginal tax rates do as your income increases
4. His theories shook the world.
5. before this time
6. end of the line
7. love (Latin)
12. what the economy was in the 1930s
13. when the crew takes over the ship (plural)
14. tells you who really pays a tax
16. worth
17. ineffectual, or incapable of movement
19. determines what characteristics you inherit from your parents
21. what people do at a bank
25. government payments without quid pro quo
28. the great outdoors
29. can't get it (abbrev.) or it's irrelevant (abbrev.)
32. They were waiting for him in Beckett's absurdist play.
34. happen
36. poem of praise
38. famous upper-class school in Britain
39. prefix meaning "two"
40. sometimes inflated when you don't know your limitations

Part Six

The Foundations of Microeconomics: The Consumer and the Firm

Chapter 21

■ ■

Applications of Demand and Supply: The Concept of Elasticity

MAJOR PURPOSE

In this chapter, we begin the detailed study of microeconomics by picking up the supply and demand curves developed in Chapter 4. In that earlier analysis, we saw how a demand curve describes how buyers increase their purchases of a product if its price falls. For some products, this response by buyers will be very strong; for others it may be weak. To illustrate, visualize two demand curves with different slopes that pass through the same point. The flatter one describes buyers who are sensitive to price; they buy much more when price falls. On the other hand, the steeper demand curve describes buyers who are less responsive to price; the amount they buy changes relatively little as price falls. In this chapter we develop a measure—called the *elasticity of demand*—to describe this responsiveness of buyers to price.

A similar concept—*supply elasticity*—is developed to measure the responsiveness of sellers to price. An important question is then addressed: "Why are demand and supply elastic in some cases, but inelastic in others?" Finally, this chapter includes illustrations of how important elasticity may be in answering policy questions such as: Who bears the burden of a sales tax on a product—the buyers or sellers? How much revenue will the government raise from this tax? and What are the short-run and long-run effects of rent control?

LEARNING OBJECTIVES

After you have studied this chapter in the textbook and the study guide, you should be able to
- Define and calculate elasticity of demand and elasticity of supply
- Describe how a move to a lower point on a demand curve may increase or decrease the total revenue from the sale of a product, depending on the elasticity of demand
- Compare the elasticity of two demand curves that pass through the same point, showing why the flatter one is more elastic, and explain why flatness and elasticity are not the same when curves do *not* pass through the same point
- List four factors that increase the elasticity of demand for a good
- List three factors that increase the elasticity of supply for a good
- Show how a straight-line supply that is elastic will, when extended, intersect the vertical axis, while a supply that is inelastic will intersect the horizontal axis
- Explain how an excise tax will affect buyers and sellers of a good, and why the group that is most sensitive to price (most elastic in its response to a price change) will be able to push the burden of the tax onto the other group
- Understand how the government's ability to raise revenue with an excise tax depends on the elasticities of demand and supply for the good being taxed
- Show the effects of rent control

• Explain how an inelastic demand for their products makes it difficult for some of the world's heavily indebted nations to increase their export earnings and repay their debts
• Define and calculate the income elasticity of demand and the cross elasticity of demand
If you have studied the appendix to Chapter 21, you should be able to
• Describe some of the special problems of agriculture and how they can be related to the concepts of price and income elasticity of demand

HIGHLIGHTS OF THE CHAPTER

In developing demand curves in Chapter 4, it was argued that they slope downward to the right. However, little was said about how steep or flat they may be or, more precisely, about how responsive buyers might be to a change in price. Similarly, in developing supply curves, little was said about how responsive sellers might be. For many problems that can be analysed with supply and demand curves, it is important to have a simple and handy description of this sensitivity of buyers or sellers to price. Elasticity is such a measure.

Elasticity of Demand

This is defined as

$$\frac{\text{elasticity}}{\text{of demand}} = \frac{\%\ \text{change in quantity demanded}}{\%\ \text{change in price}} \quad \textbf{(1)}$$

To illustrate this formula, suppose that, as a result of a shift in the supply of a good to the right, equilibrium moves downward to the right along the demand curve. With the decrease in the per unit price (the denominator above), there is an increase in the amount demanded (the numerator). If these two are equal—that is, if the price and the quantity demanded change at the same rate—then the elasticity of demand in equation (1) above is equal to 1. Moreover, the total payment buyers make to sellers does not change. To see why this is so, suppose that when the price P paid by buyers falls by 20%, the quantity Q that they purchase rises at the same rate. Then the decrease in P is offset by the increase in Q, and there is no change in P times Q, the total payment made by buyers. This is the first conclusion: When the elasticity of demand is 1, there is no change in the total payment by buyers—that is, in the total revenue received by sellers.

Now suppose buyers are more responsive to a price change—as in panel (a) of Figure 21.1 below where the quantity they demand increases by 200% (from 400 to 1,200 units) when the price falls by 25% (from $8 to $6). In this case, demand elasticity exceeds 1 in equation (1)

above, and there is an increase in PQ, the total revenue received by sellers from buyers. In this case, demand is described as "elastic."

In panel (b) of Figure 21.1, buyers are less responsive to a price change: The quantity demanded increases by only 25% when the price falls by 50%. This is the unresponsive, inelastic case; the elasticity ratio in equation (1) above is less than 1, and there is a decrease in the total revenue received by sellers. Before you leave Figure 21.1, it is essential that you are comfortable with the way elasticity and total revenue are related.

In that diagram, slope and elasticity seem to be closely related: The flatter curve in panel (a) is the more elastic. Is this generally true? The answer is yes—but only if the two curves being compared pass through the same point. (In Figure 21.1, the common point is A.)

Once you have mastered these simple and essential ideas of elasticity, return to the text and ensure you understand why, in actual calculations, the midpoint formula should be used.

Elasticity of Supply

This can also be calculated, using a ratio like the one in the equation above. The only difference is the obvious one—quantity demanded is replaced with quantity supplied.

$$\frac{\text{Elasticity}}{\text{of supply}} = \frac{\%\ \text{change in quantity supplied}}{\%\ \text{change in price}} \quad \textbf{(2)}$$

Whereas elasticity of demand has an important "total revenue" interpretation, elasticity of supply does not. The reason is that a move upward and to the right on any supply curve—regardless of its elasticity—will increase total revenue. The one intuitive interpretation of elasticity of supply is this: If a straight-line supply curve passes through the origin, it has an elasticity of supply of 1. If it intersects the vertical axis, it is elastic, and if it intersects the horizontal axis, it is inelastic.

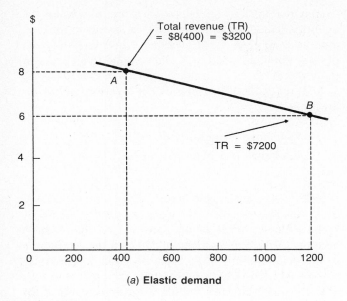

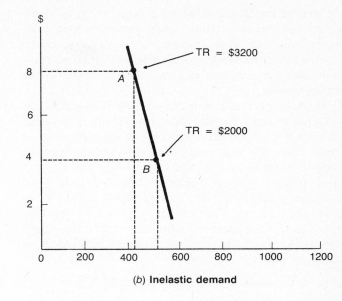

Figure 21.1

What Determines Demand and Supply Elasticity?

Demand elasticity tends to be greater if (a) the product is a luxury rather than a necessity; (2) it is a large item in purchasers' budgets rather than a small one; (3) it is easy for buyers to replace it with substitutes in consumption; (4) we are considering the long-run rather than the short-run demand. The elasticity of supply tends to be greater if (1) the commodity can be inexpensively stored—that is, if it is not perishable and has low storage costs; (2) it is easy for it to be replaced with substitutes in production; (3) we are considering the long-run rather than the short-run supply.

One of the most important of these influences on both supply and demand is time—the short run versus the long run. The reason is simple: If people—whether they are consumers or producers—are given a longer time to adjust to a change in price, they will be able to do more adjusting than if they are given only a short time.

Using Elasticity to Analyse the Burden of a Tax

The first important application of the concept of elasticity is in analysing whether buyers or sellers bear the burden of a commodity tax. The conclusion from this analysis is important because it applies to any marketplace where two groups face each other, with buyers on the one hand and sellers on the other. The "inelastic" group that can't back away from the market but must complete the trans-

action almost without regard to price, will bear more of the burden of a new tax or any other similar disturbance than will the more "elastic" group that is prepared to resist a price change by backing away from the market.

Using Elasticity to Analyse the Amount of Revenue that Will Be Raised by a Sales Tax

A sales tax will raise the price of the good to buyers, and lower the price received by sellers. Thus, typically, both are hurt by the price change. If demand and supply are elastic, both buyers and sellers will be sensitive to this price change and will be willing to reduce their purchases and sales. Therefore, the quantity that will be sold will be substantially reduced. The government's revenue (which is this quantity times the tax) will be disappointing.

If demand and supply are inelastic, then buyers and sellers won't cut back their purchases and sales substantially. The quantity sold will not be reduced very much, and government revenues will not be disappointing.

Rent Control

The key issue here is that the supply of apartments is inelastic in the short run, but more elastic in the long run. When the government keeps rents—the price paid for the use of apartments—below the market equilibrium, the inelastic short-run supply means that there will only be a small reduction in the supply of apartments. But in the long run, the more elastic supply means that there will be an even greater reduction in the supply of rental apartments and thus an even more severe shortage. (New apartments won't be built, and some existing ones may be turned into condominiums—that is, sold to new owners who then occupy them and thus take them out of the rental market.)

When rent controls are removed, there is an initial large increase in rents because short-run supply is inelastic; there is not yet enough time for new apartments to be built. Once new apartments are built—that is, once the supply becomes more elastic in the long run—the new units coming into the market will moderate the price increase and eliminate the shortage. Thus, tenants benefit in the long run. The problem is: How can a government survive the short run when rents take a big jump? One answer is for the government to gradually phase out controls.

Income Elasticity of Demand and Cross Elasticity of Demand

Just as price elasticity of demand measures how much the quantity demanded will respond to a change in price,

the *income* elasticity of demand measures how much the quantity demanded will respond to a change in income, and the *cross* elasticity of demand measures how much the quantity demanded of X will respond to a change in the price of Y.

All three of these measures can be described in the following way:

$$\frac{\%\ \text{change in quantity demanded of X}}{\%\ \text{change in whatever is influencing it}} \quad \textbf{(3)}$$

If the influence on demand in the denominator is the price of X, this ratio becomes the price elasticity of demand. If the influence in the denominator is income, this ratio becomes the income elasticity of demand. If the influence in the denominator is the price of good Y, this ratio becomes the cross elasticity of demand. Note that in each case, the numerator measures how much the demand for X responds to that influence.

IMPORTANT TERMS: MATCH THE COLUMNS

Match each term in the first column with its corresponding explanation in the second column.

C 1. Total revenue
E 2. Elasticity of demand
B 3. Elasticity of supply
A 4. Income elasticity of demand
D 5. Cross elasticity of demand
G 6. Unit elasticity of demand
F 7. Joint products
I 8. Incidence
H 9. Substitutability

a. A measure of how strongly the quantity demanded responds to a change in income. It is defined as the percentage change in quantity demanded divided by the percentage change in income.

b. The percentage change in quantity supplied divided by the percentage change in price, as equilibrium moves from one point to another on a supply curve.

c. The amount of money received by sellers of a product. This also equals the amount of money spent by buyers of the product.

d. A measure of the effect the price of good Y has on the demand for good X. It is defined as the percentage change in the quantity of X divided by the percentage change in the price of Y. This is positive if X and Y are substitutes, and negative if they are complements.

e. The percentage change in quantity demanded divided by the percentage change in price, as equilibrium moves from one point to another on a demand curve.

f. Two products that result from one production process. To illustrate, both beef and hides result from the production of beef.

g. When the percentage change in the quantity demanded is exactly equal to the percentage change in price.
h. Having other goods that can be used instead
i. Burden

TRUE-FALSE

T F ✓ **1.** A move to a new lower price equilibrium on an elastic demand curve means that total revenue falls.

T F ✓ **2.** A straight-line demand curve has the same elasticity at each point on the curve.

T F ✓ **3.** If the elasticity of demand is one, then a 1% change in price will lead to a greater than 1% change in the quantity demanded.

T F ✓ **4.** Elasticity of demand is

$$\frac{\% \text{ change in price}}{\% \text{ change in quantity demanded}}$$

T F ✓ **5.** Elasticity of demand describes how responsive buyers are to a change in price, while elasticity of supply describes how responsive sellers are.

T F ✓ **6.** The elasticity of supply is greater in the short run than in the long run.

T F ✓ **7.** The elasticity of demand tends to be higher for luxuries than for necessities.

T F ✓ **8.** The supply of hides tends to be inelastic because hides and beef are joint products.

T F ✗ **9.** The better the substitutes in production, the more elastic the supply; and the better the substitutes in consumption, the more elastic the demand.

T F ✗ **10.** Over time, demand becomes less elastic, while supply becomes more elastic.

T F ✗ **11.** The past downward trend in farm prices (relative to other prices) has occurred because improvements in farm technology have shifted the supply curve to the right more rapidly than the demand curve has been shifting.

T F ✗ **12.** Because agricultural prices tend to be very stable in the short run, the only price problem in agriculture has been a long-term downward trend.

MULTIPLE CHOICE

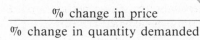

1. When there is a rightward shift in the supply curve, total revenue
  a. must rise
  b. must fall
  c. will rise only if the demand curve is elastic ✓
  d. will rise only if the demand curve is inelastic
  e. will rise only if the supply curve is inelastic

2. If people reduce their consumption of coffee by very little, even when its price skyrockets, we can conclude that
  a. supply is elastic
  b. supply is inelastic
  c. supply has zero elasticity
  d. supply has unit elasticity
  e. demand is inelastic

3. If the elasticity of demand is greater than 1, then a 10% reduction in price will result in
  a. no change in quantity demanded

  b. an increase of less than 10% in the quantity demanded
  c. a decrease of less than 10% in the quantity demanded
  d. a decrease of 10% in the quantity demanded
  e. an increase of more than 10% in the quantity demanded

4. If the elasticity of supply is 3, then a 1% increase in price will
  a. reduce the quantity supplied by 3%
  b. increase the quantity supplied by 3%
  c. increase the quantity supplied by 1%
  d. triple the quantity supplied
  e. increase the quantity supplied by one-third

$$\frac{\% \, \Delta Q_s = 3}{\% \, \Delta P = 1}$$

5. A move to a new, higher-price equilibrium on a supply curve means that total revenue
  a. will not change
  b. may rise or remain unchanged

c. may fall or remain unchanged
d. must fall
e. must rise

6. If the price of X goes from $1.50 per dozen to $2.50 per dozen, and suppliers are willing to increase from 9000 to 11 000 the amount they offer for sale, then the midpoint elasticity of supply is

a. 0.10
b. 0.4
c. 0.8
d. 2.5
e. 4.0

7. If the supply curve for apples shifts to the left
a. the rise in price will be greater in the short run than in the long run
b. the rise in price will be less in the short run than in the long run
c. the rise in price will be the same in the long and short run
d. the fall in price will be the same in the long and short run
e. the price will fall in the short run, and rise in the long run

8. In the long run, the elasticity of demand for foreign travel is high because
a. it is a necessity
b. it is a luxury
c. airliners can easily switch from transporting goods to transporting people
d. travel has no substitutes in consumption
e. travel has no substitutes in production

9. A technological change that shifts the supply curve to the right will cause total revenue to
a. rise if demand is elastic
b. fall if demand is elastic
c. rise if demand is inelastic
d. rise if the elasticity of demand is 1
e. fall if the elasticity of demand is 1

10. If the government places a sales tax on a perfectly competitive good, then the seller will bear the heavier part of the burden if
a. demand is elastic and supply is inelastic
b. demand is inelastic and supply is elastic
c. both demand and supply are inelastic
d. both demand and supply are elastic
e. the elasticity of supply is infinite

11. The burden of a commodity tax is born entirely by buyers
a. in any case
b. if supply has unit elasticity
c. if demand has unit elasticity
d. if demand has infinite elasticity
e. if demand has zero elasticity

12. A bumper crop will lower farm income
a. regardless of demand and supply elasticity
b. if demand is elastic

c. if demand is inelastic
d. if demand and supply have equal elasticity
e. if demand elasticity is infinite

13. If demand for good X is less elastic than the government estimates, then the revenue it will raise from a sales tax on X will be
a. impossible to collect
b. changed, but it is impossible to know in which direction
c. lower than predicted
d. higher than predicted
e. unaffected

14. Annual government revenue from a sales tax on a specific product will be
a. higher in the long run than in the short run
b. lower in the long run than in the short run
c. higher in provinces with a small population
d. higher in provinces with large cities at the border
e. none of the above

15. For most renters, government imposition of rent control
a. provides gains in the short run and the long run
b. imposes losses in the short run and the long run
c. provides gains in the short run but losses in the long run
d. provides losses in the short run but gains in the long run
e. has no effect

16. Relative to other prices, farm prices have been
a. stable in the short run, with a long-term upward trend
b. stable in the short run, with a downward long-term trend
c. unstable in the short run, with neither an upward nor a downward long-term trend
d. unstable in the short run, with a long-term downward trend
e. unstable in the short run, with a long-term upward trend

17. The income elasticity of demand
a. is positive for an inferior good
b. is negative for a normal good
c. is zero for an inferior good
d. is negative for an inferior good
e. a. and b.

18. If, other things equal, the demand for X falls by 20% while the price of Y increases by 10%, then the cross elasticity of demand, E_{XY}, is
a. 0.5
b. −0.5
c. unknown
d. 2
e. −2

19. The income elasticity of demand is the percentage change in

  a. quantity demanded divided by the percentage change in price
  b. income divided by the percentage change in quantity demanded
  c. price divided by the percentage change in quantity demanded
  d. quantity demanded divided by the amount of income
  e. quantity demanded divided by the percentage change in income

20. The cross elasticity of demand is the percentage change in the quantity demanded of X divided by the percentage change in

  a. quantity demanded of Y
  b. quantity supplied of Y
  c. income
  d. the price of X
  e. the price of Y

EXERCISES

1a. If equilibrium is at A in Figure 21.2, total revenue is area _____, which is $ _____. Total revenue at point B is area _____, that is, $ _____. D_1 is (elastic, inelastic, unit elastic) because, as price falls, total revenue (increases, decreases). To be more precise, we can calculate the elasticity of D_1 from the formula:

% change in _____ ÷ % change in _____

= _____ ÷ _____ = _____

1b. D_2 is (more, less) elastic than D_1 because the elasticity of D_2 is:

% change in _____ ÷ % change in _____

= _____ ÷ _____ = _____

2. Draw in a supply curve through point A and mark it S_1. Draw in another supply curve through point B and mark it S_2. Mark the point where S_2 cuts D_2 as F. If supply is initially at S_1, and it shifts to S_2, then the change in price is greater if demand is (D_1, D_2); that is, the change in price resulting from a shift in supply is greater if demand is (more, less) elastic.

3a. In Figure 21.3, supply curve S_1 is (elastic, inelastic, unit elastic) because it _____. If price rises from

P_1 to P_2, then the equilibrium on S_1 moves from point _____ to point _____. On the other hand, for supply curve S_2, this change in price would move equilibrium from point _____ to _____. The quantity response to this change in price is (greater, less) for S_2 than for S_1. S_2 is therefore (more, less) elastic than S_1. It is (true, not true) that if two supply curves pass through the same point—such as A—the flatter one is the more elastic. This conclusion is (the same as, quite different from) the one we arrived at in comparing slopes of demand curves. In general, if any straight line supply curve such as S_2 cuts the quantity axis, it is (elastic, inelastic).

3b. Now consider S_3. As price rises from P_1 to P_2, the quantity response is (greater, less) than for S_1. S_3 is therefore (more, less) elastic than S_1. It is (true, not true) that if two supply curves pass through the same point—such as A—the flatter one is the more elastic. In general, if any straight-line supply curve like S_3 cuts the price axis, it is (elastic, inelastic).

4. Draw in a demand curve through point A and mark it D_1. Draw in another parallel demand curve through point B and mark it D_2. Mark the point where D_2 cuts S_1 as F. If demand is initially at D_1, and it shifts to D_2,

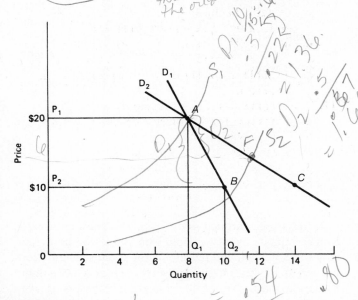

Figure 21.2

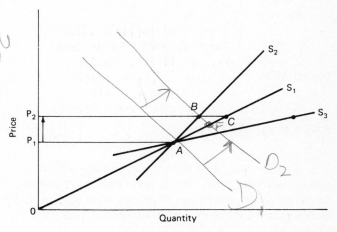

Figure 21.3

then the change in price is greater if supply is (S₁, (S₂)), that is, the change in price resulting from a shift in demand is greater if supply is (more, less) elastic.

5a. The data in Table 21.1 describe hypothetical demand and supply curves for apples. Plot these curves in Figure 21.4 and mark them S and D. Mark the equilibrium as point *A*, where the price of apples is $ ___15___ per bushel, and the equilibrium quantity is ___15___ million bushels. Suppose the government sets a price floor at $19, making it illegal to sell apples at a price below this. Mark the new equilibrium in Figure 21.4 as *B* and draw in an arrow showing the excess (demand, supply). Mark this arrow *BC*.

Table 21.1

Price per bushel	Millions of bushels demanded	Millions of bushels supplied
$ 5	25	5
10	20	10
15	15	15
20	10	20
25	5	25

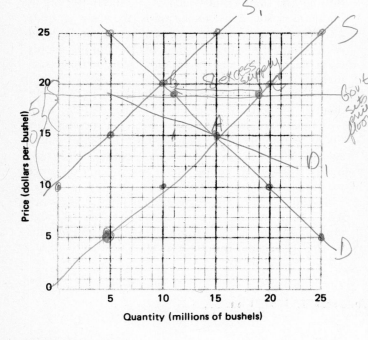

Figure 21.4

5b. In moving from *A* to *B*, the percentage change in price is ___4/17.50 + .22___; the percentage change in quantity demanded is ___4/15 = .30___; and the elasticity of demand is ___1.34___. The percentage change in quantity that sellers would like to supply is approximately ___same___; therefore, the elasticity of supply is ___1___.

6a. Suppose now that the government cancels its price floor, and instead requires the sellers of apples to pay a sales tax of $10 per bushel. When the buyers now pay $15 per bushel, the sellers get to keep only $ ___5___ per bushel after they pay the $10 per bushel tax. Thus, according to Table 21.1, they will supply ___5___ million bushels. Fill in the rest of Table 21.2.

Table 21.2

(1) Price per bushel paid by demanders (including tax)	(2) Amount per bushel received by sellers	(3) Millions of bushels supplied
$10	$ 0	0
15	5	5
20	10	10
25	15	15

6b. Plot the new supply curve in Figure 21.4 and mark it S′. The new equilibrium price (paid by demanders) is $ ___20___, and the new equilibrium quantity is ___10___. Of the $10 per bushel paid in sales tax, sellers are paying $ ___5___, and buyers are paying $ ___5___.

7. Draw a straight-line demand curve D′ passing through point *A* which is more elastic than D. If this new demand curve were to replace the old demand curve, the equilibrium price before the imposition of the tax would be (higher, lower, no different); and the equilibrium quantity before the tax would be (higher, lower, no different). The equilibrium price after the tax would be (higher, lower, no different) than with the old demand curve, and the equilibrium quantity would be (less, more, no different). With the new demand curve, the amount of tax paid by buyers would be (more, less) and the amount paid by suppliers would be (more, less) than with the old demand curve.

ESSAY QUESTIONS

1. Suppose you are a monopolist (a single seller) and you can set your price. If you discover that the demand for your product is inelastic, would you want to raise your price or lower it? Why? How far would you want to change it?

2. It has been argued that stores issue trading stamps to discriminate against people who cannot be bothered collecting, licking, and redeeming the stamps. These people end up paying a higher price for their purchases than those who use the stamps, because only the users receive a "discount" in the form of the items they get with the stamps. Suppose you were the owner of a large chain of stores and you wanted to engage in this kind of price discrimination. (That is, raise the price to nonusers of stamps, and lower it to users.) What would happen to your total revenue if the demand by users of stamps was elastic and the demand by nonusers was inelastic? What would happen to your total revenue if the demand by users was inelastic and the demand by nonusers was elastic?

ANSWERS

Important Terms: 1c, 2e, 3b, 4a, 5d, 6g, 7f, 8i, 9h
True-False: 1F, 2F, 3F, 4F, 5T, 6F, 7T, 8T, 9T, 10F, 11T, 12F
Multiple-Choice: 1c, 2e, 3e, 4b, 5e, 6b, 7a, 8b, 9a, 10a, 11e, 12c, 13d, 14b, 15c, 16d, 17d, 18e, 19e, 20e
Exercises: **1a.** P_1AQ_10, $\$20 \times 8 = \$160$, P_2BQ_20, $\$10 \times 10 = \$100$, inelastic, decreases, quantity, price, 25, 50, 0.5 (or using the more appropriate midpoint formula, $E_d = 0.333$) **1b.** more, quantity, price, 75, 50, 1.5
2. D_1, less **3a.** unit elastic, passes through the origin 0, *A, C, A, B,* less, less, true, the same as, inelastic
3b. greater, more, true, elastic **4.** S_2, less **5a.** $15, 15, supply

Figure 21.4 completed

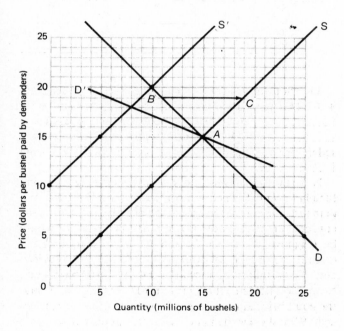

5b. 27%, 27% (slightly different using the midpoint formula), 1, 27%, 1 **6a.** $5, 5

Table 21.2 completed

(1)	(2)	(3)
$10	$ 0	0
15	5	5
20	10	10
25	15	15

6b. $20, 10, $5, $5 **7.** no different, no different, lower, less, less, more

ANSWERS TO SELECTED REVIEW QUESTIONS FROM THE TEXT

21-1. It provides information on the elasticity of demand. To evaluate this, use equation 21-1 in the text.

$$\frac{\% \text{ change in quantity demanded}}{\% \text{ change in price}} = \frac{10\%}{50\%} = 0.2$$

Therefore, demand is inelastic.

If the more precise midpoint formula for elasticity, 21-2, is used, the numbers change a bit, but not the conclusion that demand is inelastic.

21-2. *c, b, a, d, a.*

21-3. We need a measure that is independent of the scale in which P and Q are measured. Elasticity is, but flatness is not. Thus, the quote in part (b) is correct and is the answer to the question in part (a).

21-5. (a) Yes, because with higher prices of imported goods, Brazil would use less foreign currency to pay for imports; thus more money would be available for debt repayment.

(b) If a low U.S. dollar price of exports lowers total dollar earnings, it follows that a *higher* U.S. dollar price would lead to larger dollar earnings, even though the quantity of exports would decrease. Thus, Brazil could try to increase its dollar earnings by *reducing* the quantity of its exports.

21-7. The demand for restaurant meals should be more income elastic than the demand for food (home meals). Since food is a necessity, people must purchase roughly the same amount, whether or not incomes rise or fall. On the other hand, as income rises, people may eat out more often. (They can now afford it.)

Chapter 22

■ ■

Demand and Utility

MAJOR PURPOSE

In the last chapter, we measured elasticity of demand and elasticity of supply and saw how important they are in analysing policy problems. In this chapter, we describe the fundamentals of demand; we examine the foundations of the demand curve. (In Chapters 24 and 25, the fundamentals of supply will be similarly examined.)

Specifically, the four most important objectives in this chapter are (1) to analyse how the consumer, facing a given price, arrives at equilibrium, (2) to examine and measure how much the consumer benefits when the price of a product falls, (3) to describe how a consumer makes a choice among several goods, and (4) to consider the other costs, in addition to price, that are incurred when someone purchases a good or service.

LEARNING OBJECTIVES

After you have studied this chapter in the textbook and the study guide, you should be able to
- Show how the market demand curve is constructed by adding up the individual demand curves
- Define marginal utility and show how it is related to total utility
- Define marginal benefit and explain how it differs from marginal utility
- Describe the principles of diminishing marginal benefit and diminishing marginal utility
- Explain consumer equilibrium which occurs when purchases have been made up to the point where marginal benefit has fallen to price
- Use the demand curve to illustrate consumer surplus and to measure how consumers lose when price rises
- Use Adam Smith's diamonds/water paradox to explain the importance of total benefit as well as marginal benefit
- Explain how a consumer chooses among goods, showing why the consumer is in equilibrium when the marginal utility of a dollar's worth of any good is equal to the marginal utility of a dollar's worth of any other
- Show why purchasers must take into account not only price, but also transactions costs, including search (information) costs
- Explain why search costs include not only out-of-pocket costs, but also time costs, and why time costs are also important in using a product

HIGHLIGHTS OF THE CHAPTER

The first fundamental characteristic of the demand curve that must be recognized is an obvious one: A market demand curve is simply the sum of all the individual demand curves. This is illustrated in Figure 22-1 in the textbook. In turning to the other characteristics of demand, we begin by examining the demand curve of one individual consumer.

The First View of the Consumer: What Does the Demand Curve Tell Us?

Underlying each individual demand curve are the two basic concepts introduced in Chapter 2—scarcity and choice. Thus, the consumer can be viewed as choosing between scarce movies and all other scarce products—that is, between movies and money, since money is the means of acquiring all other goods. The key to describing this choice is to look at the value to the individual of an *additional* unit of a commodity such as movies. We can conceptualize this value by looking at what happens to the individual's *utility* (an index of "satisfaction") as he or she enjoys one more movie. This concept of *marginal utility*—that is, the addition to total utility as one more unit is consumed—has traditionally been used to study consumer behaviour. However, a problem with this concept is that there is no obvious way of actually measuring marginal utility. To get around this problem, we may ask instead how much an additional unit is worth to the individual *in terms of money*. That is, we may ask how much the individual would be *willing to pay* for an additional unit.

Willingness to pay is typically a good indicator of how highly the consumer values each additional unit of a commodity such as movies—that is, willingness to pay measures the *marginal benefit* of movies. The more a consumer buys, the less marginal benefit is derived from another movie. In other words, the further to the right the consumer goes in making more and more purchases in Figure 22-3(a), the shorter these vertical arrows of marginal benefit become. In simplest terms, the more movies you watch, the less interested you become in watching any more. Formally stated, this is the law of diminishing marginal benefit (or its close cousin, the law of diminishing marginal utility), which states that as more and more of any product is acquired, eventually the additional benefit (or utility) provided by one more unit must fall.

Consumer Equilibrium

As the text explains, the curve that describes how an individual's marginal benefit for a good falls as more units are consumed is precisely what we need to describe the equilibrium of the consumer, and his or her demand curve for this good. Because the benefit of, say, the third movie—as shown by the left-hand arrow in Figure 22-3(a) of the textbook—is higher than the market price of $4, the consumer buys that movie. For the same reason, the consumer buys a fourth and fifth movie. Purchases cease at six movies because the marginal benefit has fallen to the level of price. (Beyond that, where marginal benefit has fallen below price—that is, below the marginal cost to the buyer—further purchases are obviously not justified.) This, then, provides an important conclusion: In equilibrium, the consumer purchases up to the point where the marginal benefit of a product equals its price. Thus, we can read the quantity a consumer will demand at any price right off the consumer's marginal benefit curve. This confirms that the demand curve is nothing other than the consumer's marginal benefit curve.

Notice that here we are taking a different approach to the demand curve than we did in previous chapters. Earlier, we viewed the demand curve as telling us, at each given price, how many units (the quantity) the buyer would purchase. As an example, consider Figure 4-1 in the text. At a given price of $4 we horizontally measured the quantity (400) that a buyer would purchase. Now, we are viewing the demand curve as telling us, at each given quantity, how much money the consumer is willing to pay for another movie—as shown by the set of vertical arrows in Figure 22-3(a) of the text.

Consumer Surplus

Figure 22-3(b) in the text shows the concept of consumer surplus. In purchasing the third movie, the consumer enjoys a $3 surplus; the individual is willing to pay $7 for that movie, but it only costs $4. Similarly, there is a $2 surplus on the next movie, and so on. The consumer purchasing six movies acquires a surplus equal to all these arrows above the $4 price line, that is, a surplus equal to the area of the shaded triangle. Thus, consumer surplus is the area of the triangle to the northwest of the point of equilibrium on the demand curve.

Figure 22-4 of the text shows how much the consumer benefits from a price reduction. At the original price of $10 and with equilibrium at E_1, the consumer surplus is area 1. When the price falls to $6 and equilibrium moves to E_2, the consumer surplus is area 1 + 2 + 3, for an increase of 2 + 3—the area enclosed to the left of the demand curve between the old and new price. This is the consumer benefit if the price falls from $10 to $6— or, of course, the consumer loss if the price rises from $6 to $10.

The Second View of the Consumer: The Choice Among Goods

In using the demand curve so far, we have only been studying how a consumer chooses between one product (movies) and money, that is, all other products. In the text, we also show how a rational consumer will choose among movies, apples, shoes, and all other items. So we are no longer concentrating on the purchase just of movies; instead we are examining the purchase of each of the available products. Faced with this variety, what does the consumer do? The answer is: Keep purchasing each item until the marginal utility of the last dollar spent on movies is equal to the marginal utility of the last dollar spent on apples, which, in turn, is equal to the marginal utility of the last dollar spent on shoes, and so on. You can derive this fundamental principle—which appears formally as equation 22-2—by working your way through the example in Table 22-2. Once you have mastered this, you can then always confirm that the principle in equation 22-2 holds by applying the same sort of reasoning that mathematicians frequently use: Assume that this principle does not hold, and then show how the consumer will then change purchases until it does. For example, if the consumer is getting more utility from the

last dollar spent on movies than on shoes, total utility can be increased by switching purchases from shoes to movies until the utility from the last dollar spent on each is equal.

Costs to the Consumer in Addition to Price

The price of a good is not the only cost to a buyer. In addition, the buyer may also face transaction costs. These may include dealer or brokerage fees in making the actual purchase, plus costs of any search (information costs) that must be undertaken. Search costs are the costs incurred in making a purchasing decision. For example, if you are buying a car, search costs will include any out-of-pocket costs of buying magazines that compare cars, plus the "time costs" involved in studying these magazines. There are also time costs in using products once they are purchased. If your new car turns out to be a lemon, you will incur a lot of time costs in taking it back and forth for repair. Thus, if your time is worth a great deal, you are more likely to buy a reliable car that minimizes this time cost. In general, it is important in any purchasing decision to consider not only price, but all of these other costs as well.

IMPORTANT TERMS: MATCH THE COLUMNS

Match each term in the first column with its corresponding phrase in the second column.

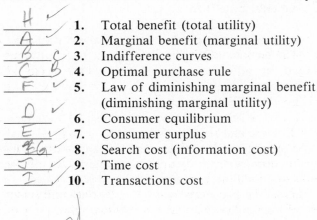

_____ **1.** Total benefit (total utility)
_____ **2.** Marginal benefit (marginal utility)
_____ **3.** Indifference curves
_____ **4.** Optimal purchase rule
_____ **5.** Law of diminishing marginal benefit (diminishing marginal utility)
_____ **6.** Consumer equilibrium
_____ **7.** Consumer surplus
_____ **8.** Search cost (information cost)
_____ **9.** Time cost
_____ **10.** Transactions cost

a. The additional satisfaction derived from one more unit of a product.

b. Utility is maximized when the utility from the last dollar spent on each good is equal.

c. Another way of explaining how a consumer chooses among many goods.

d. A situation in which the marginal benefit of each good just equals its cost.

e. The difference between the amount that a consumer would be willing to pay for a good and the amount that actually is paid for it.

f. As more and more of a good is consumed, a point is eventually reached where marginal benefit (or utility) begins to decline.

g. The time and money spent in collecting the information necessary to make an informed purchase.

h. The total satisfaction derived from a product.

i. All costs (except price) associated with buying or selling anything, including search costs and other costs such as fees or commissions.

j. The time spent shopping for a good and using it.

TRUE-FALSE

T F 1. If marginal benefit has fallen below the price of a good, the consumer has bought too much.

T F 2. If a consumer's purchase of a good is less than the equilibrium amount, marginal benefit will still be greater than the price of the good.

T F 3. The reason a demand curve slopes downward to the right is that ultimately each consumer's marginal benefit falls as the individual consumes more.

T F 4. Because diamonds sell for a higher price than water, they must provide more total benefit to society.

T F 5. When the price of a good falls, the consumer surplus that an individual receives from that good will rise.

T F 6. If the price of a good falls, then both marginal and total benefit will increase as the consumer reaches the new equilibrium.

T F 7. A consumer who gets twice as much marginal utility from a pound of beef as a loaf of bread will be in equilibrium if the price of a loaf of bread is twice as high as the price of a pound of beef.

T F 8. Time costs are incurred in using, but not in purchasing, products.

T F 9. If a consumer is purchasing only 2 goods, and continues to do so until the ratio of the marginal utilities of these 2 goods is equal to their price ratio, then that consumer is in equilibrium.

T F 10. Time-saving devices are more prevalent in low-wage countries than in high-wage countries.

MULTIPLE CHOICE

1. The market demand for a good is the
   a. vertical sum of the individual demands
   b. average of the individual demands
   c. horizontal sum of the individual demands
   d. vertical product of the individual demands
   e. horizontal product of the individual demands

2. The market demand curve has
   a. less slope than the individual demand curves
   b. more slope than the individual demand curves
   c. more slope or less; you can't tell in general
   d. the same slope as the individual demand curves
   e. more slope, if the individual demand curves are elastic

3. The height of a demand curve is
   a. the price consumers would be willing to pay plus consumer surplus
   b. the price consumers would be willing to pay minus consumer surplus
   c. the price consumers would be willing to pay minus the price they actually paid
   d. the price consumers would be willing to pay plus the price they actually paid
   e. the price consumers would be willing to pay

4. Marginal benefit can be viewed as
   a. the height of the demand curve plus the price consumers actually pay
   b. the height of the demand curve minus the price consumers actually pay
   c. the price consumers would be willing to pay plus the price they actually pay
   d. the price consumers would be willing to pay minus the height of the demand curve
   e. the height of the demand curve

5. A consumer will continue to purchase a good until its
   a. marginal benefit falls to zero
   b. marginal benefit falls to the level of its price
   c. total benefit falls to the level of its price
   d. total benefit falls to zero
   e. total benefit rises to the level of its price

6. The amount of a good that a consumer purchases should depend on its
   a. marginal benefit only
   b. search cost only
   c. price only
   d. price and search cost only
   e. marginal benefit, search cost, and price

7. A consumer with diminishing marginal benefit for a good will be willing to pay
   a. more and more for each additional unit
   b. less and less for each additional unit
   c. the same amount for each additional unit
   d. nothing for this good
   e. less than nothing for this good; the individual will have to be subsidized to take it

8. According to the law of diminishing marginal utility
   a. the utility from another unit can never rise
   b. marginal utility must always be negative

c. marginal utility must always be positive

d. marginal utility must rise at first, but eventually it may fall

e. marginal utility may rise at first, but eventually it must fall

9. If water and champagne, both measured in litres, had the same upward-sloping supply curve

 a. they would certainly sell for the same price

 b. the would be likely to sell for the same price

 c. champagne would be more expensive

 d. water would be more expensive

 e. no prediction could be made about their prices

10. If we know only the selling price of a perfectly competitive good, then we know

 a. the total benefit it provides

 b. the total cost of producing it

 c. its total cost and total benefit

 d. the marginal benefit it provides

 e. none of the above

11. If price increases, there is

 a. a gain to the consumer equal to the area to the left of the demand curve between the old and new price

 b. a loss to the consumer equal to the area to the left of the demand curve between the old and new price

 c. a loss to the consumer equal to the area to the left of the supply curve between the old and new price

 d. a gain to the consumer equal to the area to the left of the supply curve between the old and new price

 e. no effect on the consumer

12. Consumer surplus is a "triangle" with two sides being

 a. the vertical axis and the horizontal axis

 b. the horizontal axis and the price line

 c. the horizontal axis and the demand curve

 d. the vertical axis and the price line

 e. none of the above

13. In which case do consumers enjoy the least consumer surplus? (Assume in each case that they face the same price and purchase the same quantity.)

 a. demand elasticity is 1

 b. demand is highly inelastic

 c. demand is highly elastic

 d. supply elasticity is 1

 e. supply is highly elastic

14. If the price of good A increases, then, as the consumer reaches his or her new equilibrium

 a. marginal benefit will decrease, and total benefit will increase

 b. marginal benefit will increase and total benefit will decrease

 c. marginal benefit will decrease, but by less than total benefit decreases

 d. marginal benefit will decrease by more than total benefit decreases

 e. marginal and total benefit will both increase

15. The more willing the public is to bear search costs

 a. the more variation there will be in prices quoted by sellers

 b. the less variation there will be in prices quoted by sellers

 c. the higher will be the price quoted by sellers

 d. the greater the overcharging by wholesalers and retailers

 e. the greater the overcharging by retailers, but not wholesalers

16. Time costs are

 a. greater in a high-income (than a low-income) country, and this is one reason that less reliable cars are purchased there

 b. greater in a high-income country, and this is one reason that more expensive and reliable cars are purchased there

 c. less in a high-income country, and this is one reason that more expensive and reliable cars are purchased there

 d. less in a high-income country, and this is one reason that less expensive and reliable cars are purchased there

 e. less in a high-income country, but this doesn't affect the cars that are purchased there

17. A consumer buying two goods will be in equilibrium if

 a. the ratio of the marginal utilities of these goods is greater than their price ratio

 b. the ratio of the marginal utilities of these goods is less than their price ratio

 c. the ratio of the marginal utilities of these goods is equal to 1

 d. the ratio of the marginal utilities of these goods is equal to their price ratio

 e. some other condition is met; any condition involving marginal utilities is irrelevant

18. If the price of apples rises, the consumer will buy

 a. fewer apples, thus increasing his marginal utility from apples

 b. fewer apples, thus reducing his marginal utility from apples

 c. more cherries, thus reducing his marginal utility from cherries

 d. more cherries, thus increasing his marginal utility from cherries

 e. a. and c.

19. If the marginal utility of a pound of beef is twice as great as the marginal utility of a loaf of bread, then the consumer will be in equilibrium if
  a. the price of a pound of beef is twice the price of a loaf of bread
  b. the price of a pound of beef is four times the price of a loaf of bread
  c. the price of a pound of beef is half the price of a loaf of bread
  d. their prices are the same
  e. their prices are related in some other way

20. According to the substitution effect, a fall in the price of apples results in

  a. an increase in the purchases of apples because other goods have become cheap relative to apples
  b. an increase in the purchases of apples because apples have become less expensive relative to other goods
  c. a decrease in the purchases of apples because apples have become less expensive relative to other goods
  d. a decrease in the purchases of apples because the buyer's real income has risen
  e. an increase in the purchases of apples because the buyer's real income has risen

EXERCISES

1a. If the price for the product shown in Figure 22.1 below is $7, then _____ units will be purchased, because this is the quantity where marginal benefit, as given by the height of the _____ curve, is equal to _____. There are two interpretations of any point such as R on an individual's demand curve. The first is that R indicates the quantity that will be purchased at a certain price of, say, $7. This interpretation is shown by arrow _____. The second is that R indicates, at a given quantity, the maximum price that the buyer is willing to pay for the marginal unit—in this case, the 100th unit. This second interpretation is shown by arrow _____. Since this arrow indicates how much the consumer will be willing to pay to acquire that 100th unit, it measures the value the consumer puts on that unit—that is, the (total value of all 100 units, marginal benefit of that 100th unit).

1b. The total benefit the consumer gets from all 100 units purchased is area _____, which is the sum of all the (horizontal, vertical) marginal benefit arrows like

_____ enclosed beneath the _____ curve throughout the range of quantities between _____ and _____. However, this purchase costs the consumer area _____, which is the quantity of _____ units multiplied by the $_____ price. Therefore, the net benefit to the consumer of this purchase is area _____, which is sometimes called _____.

2. If price increases to $10, the new equilibrium is at _____, where the quantity purchased is _____ units. The demand curve between R and T is (elastic, inelastic) because the % change in quantity is (less, more) than the % change in price. The total benefit from this smaller purchase is area _____. However, the cost is area _____, which is the quantity of _____ units times the $_____ price. Therefore, the net benefit to the purchaser when price is $10 is area _____.

3a. Since the net benefit to the purchaser when the price was $7 was area _____, and that benefit was reduced to area _____ when the price rose to $10, the burden of this price increase on the consumer is area _____, which is the area enclosed to the (left, right) of the _____ curve between the old price and the new price.

3b. Let's look at this from another point of view. Because price has risen, the consumer is buying _____ units less. The total benefit the consumer used to get on these units—and has now lost—is area _____. However, the consumer is no longer incurring the cost, shown by area _____, of purchasing these units, since they are no longer being bought. Therefore, the net loss of the consumer on these units that are no longer purchased is area _____. In addition, the consumer is hurt because of the greater price that has to be paid on the first 40 units (that continue to be purchased). The higher cost to the consumer on these units is area _____, which is the $_____ increase in price times those 40 units.

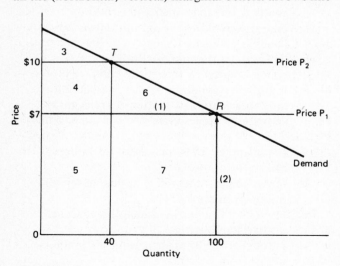

Figure 22.1

Thus, in summary, we confirm that the loss to the consumer because of the price increase is area _____. This is made up of a loss of area _____ because purchases are reduced, plus a loss of area _____ because of the higher price that must be paid on purchases that continue to be made.

ESSAY QUESTIONS

1. People derive more benefit from the water they use than they do from all the champagne they drink. Yet champagne costs far more than water. Would champagne be more expensive than water if the two had the same supply curve and were thus equally scarce? Explain your answer.

2. To judge by the amount of time spent, most people seem to derive more utility from watching television than from going to movies. Yet they will pay $4 or $5 to go to a movie, when they could stay home and watch television for nothing. Can you explain this?

3. When Henry Ford invented the mass production of automobiles, what effect do you suppose this had on the typical marginal benefit schedule for horse-drawn carriages? What do you suppose it did to the price and sales of horse-drawn carriages?

4. Heroin addicts find that the more they consume, the more they want. Does this contradict or illustrate diminishing marginal utility? Can you use this heroin example to illustrate the law of diminishing marginal utility?

ANSWERS

Important Terms: **1**h, **2**a, **3**c, **4**b, **5**f, **6**d, **7**e, **8**g, **9**j, **10**i
True-False: **1**T, **2**T, **3**T, **4**F, **5**T, **6**F, **7**F, **8**F, **9**T, **10**F
Multiple Choice: **1**c, **2**a, **3**e, **4**e, **5**b, **6**e, **7**b, **8**e, **9**d, **10**d, **11**b, **12**d, **13**c, **14**b, **15**b, **16**b, **17**d, **18**e, **19**a, **20**b
Exercises: **1a.** 100, demand, price, (1), (2), marginal benefit of that 100th unit **1b.** 3 + 4 + 5 + 6 + 7, vertical, (2), demand, zero, 100, 5 + 7, 100, $7, 3 + 4 + 6, consumer surplus **2.** *T*, 40, elastic, more, 3 + 4 + 5, 4 + 5, 40, $10, 3 **3a.** 3 + 4 + 6, 3, 4 + 6, left, demand **3b.** 60, 6 + 7, 7, 6, 4, $3, 6 + 4, 6, 4

ANSWERS TO SELECTED REVIEW QUESTIONS FROM THE TEXT

22-1. Unit elasticity. Market demand is constructed as in Figure 22-1 in the text. It is flatter than the individual demand, but not more elastic. (Flatness indicates elasticity only if we are comparing demand curves that pass through the same point—and these do not.)

22-4.

Unit	Hamburgers (price = $2) MU	Hamburgers (price = $2) MU per $	Novels (price = $2) MU	Novels (price = $2) MU per $
1	12	6	16	8
2	10	5	12	6
3	8	4	8	4
4	6	3	4	2
5	4	2	2	1

(i) With income of $10, buy 3 hamburgers and 2 novels, or vice versa.
(ii) Increases from 1 to 2 (or 3).
(iii) Three of each

22-5. You can illustrate how this conclusion could be incorrect with a diagram like Figure 22-5 in the text (with water representing food and diamonds entertainment).

Note, of course, that you are now comparing not the utility areas but, instead, the spending areas ($P \times Q$). Draw the demand curve for entertainment in panel (*b*) a bit farther to the right and have supply intersect it at, say, 1/4 the price shown for diamonds. (Entertainment is less expensive to produce than diamonds.) Then, the rectangular ($P \times Q$) value area for entertainment can exceed food. But food is more important, because of its very large (shaded) total utility area (most of which lies above the diagram).

22-7. Demand is likely to become more elastic because people know more about quality and price and, therefore, will not allow retailers to charge a higher price than their competitors. For example, when a salesperson tells them they "get what they pay for," they will recognize instances when the salesperson is trying to sell them less than what they're paying for.

22-8. The answer isn't clear. The manufacturer earns a profit on the car above its cost of production, but you acquire consumer surplus above the cost of the purchase to you.

Across

7. benefit of consumers in excess of what they pay
8. Beef and leather are examples of _____. (2 words)
10. laissez-_____
13. indefinite article
16. a means of travel
18. benefit from consuming one more unit (2 words)
23. When the price of one increases, the demand for the other increases.
24. where people skate
25. sound of disgust
26. first person possessive
28. unresponsive to a change in price
31. bounder
32. An important economic objective is to reduce this.
34. Price is likely to be _____ when both demand and supply are inelastic.
37. member of one of the British Houses of Parliament
38. fundamental reason for study of economics
39. If demand is elastic, total _____ increases when price is reduced.

Down

1. This joins all points that provide equal satisfaction. (2 words)
2. oxidized iron
3. close
4. area just outside a city
5. measure of how much quantity responds to a change in price
6. a continent
8. what an unemployed person wants
9. official price of a currency under pegged exchange rate system
11. part of the eye
12. an appointment to meet made by lovers
13. in addition
14. a fruit covered with a woody shell
15. very successful movie or song
17. devoured
18. The _____ tax rate is the tax rate on additional income.
19. central idea
20. all around
21. game without a winner
22. a small piece
27. passing fashions
29. one of the factors of production
30. one of the objectives of economic policy
32. This is used in producing many manufactured goods.
33. low business activity
35. ripped
36. The _____ year is the year from which price changes are measured.

Chapter 23

■ ■

Business Organizations: Proprietorships, Partnerships, and Corporations

MAJOR PURPOSE

The major purposes of this chapter are to (1) explain the three forms of business organization, (2) describe how businesses finance expansion, and (3) describe some of the problems that arise in the financial markets.

For big business, the major legal form is the corporation. This provides owners with the protection of *limited liability*. Stockholders are not responsible for the debts of their business, and can lose only the funds they have spent to acquire a share of ownership. Limited liability is one of the reasons there is such a broad market in common stock and why it is relatively easy for corporations to raise funds by selling additional stock.

One of the major functions of the markets for financial capital—such as the stock market and the bond market—is to provide funds to new and expanding companies. People have an incentive to buy the securities of rapidly growing, profitable, and financially sound corporations. The capital markets do a fairly good job of providing resources to the most profitable and promising corporations.

The appendix to the chapter explains the two basic types of business accounts—the balance sheet and the income statement.

LEARNING OBJECTIVES

After you have studied this chapter in the textbook and study guide, you should be able to
- Describe the three major types of business organization, and explain the major advantages and disadvantages of each
- Describe the ways in which a corporation can raise funds for expansion
- Explain the advantages and disadvantages to the corporation of issuing common stock (shares) rather than bonds
- Explain the advantages and disadvantages of buying common stock (shares) rather than bonds
- Explain what the concept of leverage means
- Explain how greater leverage can create risks for both corporations and bondholders
- Describe the major motives of the people who buy securities, and the major motives of those who issue securities

HIGHLIGHTS OF THE CHAPTER

There are three major types of business organization:

1. The *single proprietorship*, owned and operated by an individual. Many small businesses are single proprietorships.

2. The *partnership*, which is quite similar to the single proprietorship, except that there are several owners and operators. With a few exceptions, partnerships are quite small businesses.

3. The *corporation*, which is the standard organization for large businesses. The corporation provides *limited liability* to the shareholder-owners. This is a great advantage, because the shareholder-owners don't have to worry about being stuck with the obligations undertaken by the corporation. (In contrast, a partner is liable for the obligations undertaken by the partnership.) Because of limited liability, a large, well-known corporation may be able to sell shares of common stock (that is, shares of ownership) to a wide variety of people. Thus, the corporate form of organization has the advantage of making it *easier to finance growth*. A third advantage of the corporation is that it has automatic continuity. When one of the stockholder-owners dies, the stock goes to the heirs. The corporation continues uninterrupted. Because of the protection offered by limited liability, an heir need not be concerned about accepting the stock.

Many small corporations are not well-known, and the desire to raise funds is not the reason for incorporation. For many small businesses, tax considerations are important in the decision whether to incorporate or not. The income of a proprietorship or partnership is taxed as personal income of the owner or owners. Corporate profits are taxed differently; they are subject to the corporation income tax. For small corporations, the corporate tax rate is relatively low, and may be substantially less than the rate at which the owner's personal income is taxed. Thus, there may be an advantage in incorporating, especially if most of the corporation's profits will be reinvested rather than paid out to the owner as dividends. (Profits paid out as dividends are taxed as part of the owner's personal income, just like the profits from a proprietorship or a partnership. However, under Canadian tax law, shareholders who receive dividends from Canadian corporations are given credit for the corporate income tax that has already been levied on the profits from which the dividends are paid.)

Ways in which the corporation can raise funds include (1) issuing additional shares of *common stock*, each representing a fraction of the ownership of the corporation; (2) *selling bonds*, which is a way of borrowing money for a long period of time from the person who buys the bond; (3) *issuing shorter-term debt*, such as notes or commercial paper; and (4) *borrowing from a bank* or other financial institution.

Each of the first three items can normally be bought and sold in markets. For example, a person who owns stock or bonds of a corporation may sell them to anyone who is willing to buy. Transactions in such securities are usually facilitated by brokers or investment dealers. (Brokers bring buyers and sellers together. A dealer may be the actual buyer or seller of a bond.) Similarly, government bonds and shorter-term securities may be sold by the present holder to someone else. Thus, if the government or corporation issues long-term bonds, it has a guaranteed use of the funds for a long period of time. But the buyer is not necessarily tying up funds for a similar long period: the bond may be sold at any time. Thus, the financial markets provide *liquidity* to bondholders.

The prices of securities in the financial markets are determined by supply and demand; the prices of common shares, bonds, and other financial assets can fluctuate as conditions change. The major determinant of the price of common stock is the *expected profitability* of the corporation. The person who buys the share will participate in the good fortune (if any) of the corporation. Even though bonds provide a fixed contract—for, say $12,000 in interest payments each year over 20 years—they may nevertheless fluctuate in value. In the marketplace, people have the choice of buying new bonds or old bonds. If a new bond will pay more interest—say $14,000—then the amount people will be willing to pay for the old bond (with $12,000 interest per year) will go down.

Although interest payments on bonds are set by the bond contract, the payment of interest is not guaranteed. If the issuing corporation runs into trouble, it may not have the funds to pay interest. In this case, the bondholder has the legal right to sue, and may push the corporation into the bankruptcy courts. Even then, there is no assurance that the bondholder will be paid, because the corporation may simply not have enough assets to cover its liabilities. If a corporation is in difficulty, there may be an agreement among bondholders and other creditors to give it more time to pay, and perhaps take smaller interest payments.

Because bondholders are not guaranteed payment, they must be concerned with the prospects that the issuer will, in fact, be able to make interest payments on schedule, and repay the principal when the bond reaches maturity. If a corporation is shaky, people will avoid its bonds unless they offer an extra amount of interest to compensate for the risk—the so-called *risk premium*. Because of differences in risk, some bonds offer substantially higher interest rates than others.

In deciding which securities to buy, potential bond buyers weigh a number of factors—risk, return, and liquidity. Issuers of securities also have a number of factors to consider. One of their most important decisions is whether they will issue additional common stock or additional bonds. If they issue stock, they will be taking on additional part-owners. Thus, they will have to share their future profits among more people. If they issue additional bonds, they will be increasing the *leverage* of the corporation. If the business does well, the owners will only have to pay the interest; they will not have to share their profits with the bondholders. But they will be legally committed to pay the interest, whether the firm does well or not. Thus, leverage can add to the risks that the company may fail in the future.

The major function of financial markets is to allocate the saving of society to the various investment projects that can be undertaken. On the whole, the financial markets do a fairly good job in allocating funds among various projects. People who buy bonds or stocks have an incentive to put their funds into the corporation with the best prospects. Nevertheless, major mistakes are made. Some mistakes are inevitable in a risky and uncertain world—the best buggy whip manufacturer in North America became obsolete with the invention of the motor car. But some mistakes can be avoided if people have more information. This is where government regulation of financial markets plays an important role. It requires corporations to disclose their financial condition. By enforcing a reasonable rule—that information be disclosed—the government can help the private capital markets work better.

IMPORTANT TERMS: MATCH THE COLUMNS

Match each term in the first column with its corresponding phrase in the second column.

_____	1. Proprietorship	**a.** Chief advantage of forming a corporation
_____	2. Limited liability	**b.** A short-term debt
_____	3. Double taxation	**c.** Representative of a buyer or seller
_____	4. Common stock	**d.** Net worth divided by number of shares
_____	5. Bond	**e.** Unincorporated enterprise
_____	6. Commercial paper	**f.** Debt divided by net worth
_____	7. Net worth	**g.** Yield on less safe bonds minus yield on particularly safe bonds (such as those issued by the Government of Canada)
_____	8. Leverage	**h.** Represents ownership in a corporation
_____	9. Book value	**i.** Assets minus liabilities
_____	10. Risk premium	**j.** Long-term debt
_____	11. Broker	**k.** More of a problem for U.S. corporations than for Canadian corporations

TRUE-FALSE

T F 1. Partnerships have "unlimited liability." This means that there is no limit to the amount of bonds and other liabilities they can issue.

T F 2. A partnership with two partners (A and B) has its income taxed twice—once as the income of A, and once as the income of B.

T F 3. Under Canadian income tax rules, income received as dividends from a Canadian corporation is taxed at a lower rate of personal income tax than other types of income.

T F 4. A government bond is generally more liquid than a house.

T F 5. Issuing additional common stock increases the leverage of a corporation.

T F 6. Issuing more bonds increases the leverage of a corporation.

T F 7. Businesses that increase their leverage usually do so to reduce the risk of bankruptcy.

T F 8. A corporation's balance sheet shows its sales and costs over a period of time.

MULTIPLE CHOICE

1. In a standard partnership, each partner
    a. must pay personal income tax on all the income of the partnership
    b. has unlimited liability, but only for the debts which he or she undertook personally
    c. has unlimited liability, but only for his or her share of the debts of the corporation
    d. has unlimited liability for all the debts of the partnership, including those undertaken by the other partners
    e. can lose the amount of his or her initial investment, but no more

2. The partnership form of business organization
    a. provides each partner with a liability limited to his or her share of the business
    b. normally issues common stock to raise the funds for expansion
    c. can have a maximum of five partners (since any larger number means that incorporation is required)
    d. does not provide the automatic continuity that a corporation does in the event of the death of one of the owners
    e. is generally used by banks

3. Corporations provide "limited liability." This means that
    a. the stockholder-owners are not personally liable for debts of the corporation
    b. the corporation is not legally liable for debts of more than one-half its net worth in any one year
    c. officers of the corporation cannot be held legally liable for any fraudulent activities of the corporation
    d. the corporation is legally required to make contributions to the pension fund of its employees only in the years when it is profitable
    e. all of the above

4. The profits earned by a partnership
    a. are taxed twice
    b. are often retained by the firm, in which case, they escape taxation
    c. are treated as personal income of the partners, and are, therefore, subject to personal income tax
    d. are treated as capital gains for tax purposes
    e. are never taxed

5. Under Canadian tax law, shareholders who receive dividends from a Canadian corporation
    a. receive a tax credit representing their share of the income tax already paid by the corporation
    b. do not have to include the dividend income in their taxable income
    c. are taxed at double the rate on income from a partnership
    d. must report their dividend income to a provincial securities commission
    e. receive a tax credit that reduces the corporation's income tax the following year

6. Profits earned by a small Canadian corporation
    a. are subject to both corporation income tax and personal income tax if they are paid out as dividends to shareholders
    b. are taxed at a lower rate than profits from large corporations
    c. are not treated as taxable income of the shareholders if they are reinvested in the business
    d. do not add to retained earnings if they are paid out as dividends
    e. all of the above

7. Each share of common stock represents
    a. a debt of the issuing corporation
    b. an asset of the issuing corporation
    c. a fraction of the ownership of the corporation
    d. a claim on the stocks of inventories held by the corporation
    e. a right to receive dividends, even if interest cannot be paid on bonds

8. Normally, the riskiest type of security to buy is a
    a. federal government bond
    b. short-term debt of the federal government
    c. provincial government bond
    d. corporate bond
    e. common share

9. A major purpose of provincial government commissions that regulate financial markets is to require corporations to
    a. issue stock periodically so as to decrease leverage
    b. issue stock periodically so as to increase leverage
    c. issue bonds periodically so as to decrease leverage
    d. issue bonds periodically so as to provide bondholders a stable source of income
    e. make information available to the public

10. Financial leverage is measured by
    a. the trend in net worth, measured in dollars
    b. the trend in debt, measured in dollars
    c. the trend in debt, after adjustment for inflation
    d. the ratio of debt to net worth
    e. the price-earnings ratio

11. Leverage generally adds to the risks faced by
    a. the stockholders of the leveraged company
    b. the bondholders of the leveraged company
    c. suppliers to whom the leveraged company owes money
    d. the banks which have made loans to the leveraged company
    e. all of the above

12. The net worth of a company is equal to
    a. assets minus liabilities
    b. liabilities minus assets
    c. profits minus costs
    d. costs minus profits
    e. profits minus taxes

13. A commitment by a bank to lend up to a predetermined limit to a specific customer is known as a
    a. form of leverage over the bank
    b. stock option
    c. commercial paper
    d. line of credit
    e. illegal overdraft

14. Whenever a corporation issues bonds, rather than raising funds by issuing new common stock, it
    a. increases its leverage
    b. decreases its leverage
    c. decreases the risks faced by stockholders
    d. decreases the risks faced by bondholders
    e. increases the tax it has to pay

15. The book value of a share of common stock is equal to
    a. the value of the share when it was initially issued by the corporation
    b. today's price of a share on the books of investment dealers
    c. the market price of a share when the books were closed at the end of the most recent fiscal year
    d. retained earnings of the company divided by the number of shares outstanding
    e. net worth of the company divided by the number of shares outstanding

16. In the 1930s, the yield on many high-grade corporate bonds was as low as 5%, while the yield on lower grade corporate bonds was as much as 10% or more. The difference was
    a. a tax premium
    b. a risk premium
    c. an inflation premium
    d. an incentive for risky businesses to borrow
    e. a sign of the breakdown of capital markets

17. Interest rates on bonds of private corporations are normally several percentage points higher than the rates on Government of Canada bonds of comparable term to maturity. The difference represents
    a. a tax premium
    b. a risk premium
    c. an inflation premium
    d. an incentive for risky businesses to borrow
    e. a sign of the breakdown of capital markets

18. Interest rates on government bonds are most likely to rise during
    a. recessions
    b. depressions
    c. deflationary periods
    d. periods of rising inflation
    e. the period just prior to income tax time in April of each year

Note: The next two questions are based on the appendix to Chapter 23.

19. In the balance sheet of a corporation
    a. net worth = assets + liabilities
    b. assets = net worth − liabilities
    c. assets = liabilities − net worth
    d. assets = liabilities + net worth
    e. profits = sales − depreciation

20. What appears on the income statement of a corporation?
    a. depreciation
    b. income before taxes
    c. income after taxes
    d. all of the above
    e. none of the above

EXERCISE

This exercise is based on the appendix to Chapter 23.

1a. The following numbers apply to the XYZ Corporation. Prepare a balance sheet for the XYZ Corporation in Table 23.1. There are no assets and liabilities other than those listed below. However, not all items should be included in the balance sheet: USE ONLY THE ONES THAT BELONG.

Accounts payable	$800,000
Sales during year	$1,900,000
Accounts receivable	$900,000
Wages paid during year	$850,000
Long-term bonds of XYZ Corp. outstanding	$1,000,000
Plant and equipment (current value, after depreciation)	$2,000,000
Inventory on hand	$300,000
Revenue from service contracts	$250,000
Bank deposits and other cash items	$200,000
Depreciation during year	$300,000
Net interest paid	$150,000
Other costs	$250,000
Accrued liabilities	$150,000
Number of shares of common stock outstanding	100,000
Holdings of notes issued by ABC Corp.	$50,000

1b. Some of the numbers not used in part **a.** belong in the income statement. Use them to complete the income statement in Table 23.2. Assume that this corporation pays 30% of its income in taxes.

1c. The book value of each share of stock of the XYZ Corp. is ($15, $19.50, $20.00, $34.50).

Table 23.1 (thousands of dollars)

Assets	Liabilities
	Net Worth
Total Assets =	Total Liabilities and Net Worth =

Table 23.2 Income Statement (thousands of dollars)

1. Revenues:

   Total:

2. Costs:

   Total:

3. Profit before taxes:
4. Tax:
5. Net profit:
6. Addendum: profit per share:

ESSAY QUESTIONS

1. To find net worth, what do we subtract from assets? Is it possible for the net worth of a corporation to be negative? If so, what could we say about the book value of each share of common stock of a corporation with a negative net worth? Would it ever pay to buy shares in a firm with a negative net worth? If it is not possible, explain why not. Specifically, explain what will happen as the net worth of the corporation shrinks toward zero.

2. Suppose that you are in charge of finance for a large corporation. How would you go about raising funds to (a) finance the construction of a large plant, with an expected useful life of 25 years, (b) acquire larger inventories of raw materials, and (c) meet a temporary shortage of cash resulting from a decision by your customers to wait an extra month before paying their bills? Under what circumstances might you issue new common stock rather than borrow? Might it ever be a good idea to cut the dividend by, say, 50% to pay for any of the above? Explain why or why not. Might it ever be a good idea to cut the dividend for other reasons? Explain.

ANSWERS

Important Terms: **1e, 2a, 3k, 4h, 5j, 6b, 7i, 8f, 9d, 10g, 11c**
True-False: **1F, 2F, 3T, 4T, 5F, 6T, 7F, 8F**
Multiple Choice: **1d, 2d, 3a, 4c, 5a, 6e, 7c, 8e, 9e, 10d, 11e, 12a, 13d, 14a, 15e, 16b, 17b, 18d, 19d, 20d**
Exercises:

1a.

Table 23.1 completed
(thousands of dollars)

Assets		Liabilities	
Cash	$200	Accounts payable	$800
ABC note	50	Accrued liabilities	150
Accounts receivable	900	XYZ bonds	1,000
Inventory	300	(Total liabilities 1,950)	
Plant & equip.	2,000	Net Worth	1,500
		Total Liabilities	
Total Assets =	3,450	and Net Worth =	3,450

1c. $15.

1b.

Table 23.2 Income Statement completed
(thousands of dollars)

1. Revenues:		
	Sales	$1,900
	Service contracts	250
	Total:	$2,150
2. Costs:		
	Wages	$850
	Depreciation	300
	Net interest	150
	Other	250
	Total:	$1,550
3. Profit before taxes:		$600
4. Tax:		$180
5. Net profit:		$420
6. Addendum: profit per share:		$4.20

ANSWERS TO SELECTED REVIEW QUESTIONS FROM THE TEXT

23-3. No clearly right answer. Standard advice for the 50-year-old involves a combination of stocks and longer-term bonds. Because of the large increases in interest rates and corresponding fall in the prices of bonds, longer-term bonds turn out to have been a bad investment in the past. The combination depends in part on the tax bracket of the individual. Those in high tax brackets should avoid corporation bonds, and choose instead stocks whose gain is likely to come in the form of appreciation rather than high current dividends. For the future home buyer, liquidity is important. Money market funds give a combination of high liquidity, a reasonably good return, and safety.

23-4. (a) The owner of a share gains additional leverage. This means the potential of higher earnings if the company does well; the stockholder will own all the returns from the borrowed funds in excess of the interest payments. But if the company does not prosper, leverage can hurt the stockholder: The payment of interest may leave little or no profit for the stockholder.

(b) Additional bond sales are generally against the interest of the present bondholders, since they can increase the risk of bankruptcy. However, if additional bonds help the corporation to expand in a healthy way, they can improve the security of present bondholders by strengthening the company. (Also, the bonds of a large corporation are generally more liquid than those of a smaller company.)

23-5. (a) Probably by issuing 20-year bonds (unless the corporation already has such a large debt load that it would have to pay a very high interest rate). If you are right and the total value of the company rises as investors discover how profitable the mine is, the increase in the value per share is larger the fewer the number of shareholders. (Bondholders, of course, do not share in the increased value of the company.)

(b) If other people expected the mine to be very profitable, they would be willing to pay a relatively high price for the company's shares. As an existing shareholder, you would benefit from this. By the same token, if you are right and the mine is not very profitable, the total value of the company will fall as investors discover this. The reduction in the value per share will be smaller if there are many shareholders.

Chapter 24

■■■■■■■■■■■■■■■■■■■■■■■■■■■■■■■■■■■■■

The Costs of Production

MAJOR PURPOSE

Businesses make profits by selling at a price that exceeds costs. Price depends on the type of market in which they sell. (We will consider several types later in Chapters 25 through 28.) Now, in Chapter 24, we examine costs with special reference to how they differ in the short run and the long run.

In the short run—the period in which the firm's capital stock is fixed—the key decision is: How much will it cost to increase output when only labour and other variable inputs can be increased, but fixed inputs such as capital cannot? The first half of this chapter is devoted to this question, and we derive a number of measures of cost—such as marginal cost, MC, and average total cost, ATC—that will eventually in later chapters become important tools in examining how firms maximize profits.

Then, we turn to costs in the long run when the firm can vary not only its labour input, but also those factors of production, such as capital, that are fixed in the short run. Thus, in the long run, all costs become variable. Now, the picture of how costs vary when the firm changes its output is quite different. In particular, we focus on the quite different way in which its average cost changes. How does its long-run average cost compare to its short-run average cost?

We also show how the economist's definition of a firm's cost is far broader than an accountant's. For an economist, costs include not only the out-of-pocket costs that accountants take into account, but also implicit costs such as the opportunity costs of the owner's time and capital invested in the firm. Because the opportunity cost of the owner's capital—that is, normal profit—is included by an economist in calculating a firm's costs, any additional (excess or economic) profit is a return that can be earned in this industry above and beyond the return that can be earned elsewhere. Therefore, it is an incentive for more resources to move into the industry.

LEARNING OBJECTIVES

After you have studied this chapter in the textbook and the study guide, you should be able to

- Explain why, in the short run, some costs are fixed and some are variable while, in the long run, all costs are variable
- Define total, variable, fixed, and marginal costs; also average total cost, average variable cost, and average fixed cost
- Explain the law of (eventually) diminishing returns, and why this law means that marginal costs must eventually rise
- Explain, using a diagram, why a firm's average cost curve is cut, at its minimum point, by its marginal cost curve
- Show in a diagram how long-run and short-run average cost curves are related to each other by an envelope relationship
- Define economies of scale and diminishing returns, clearly distinguishing between the two. You should also be able to explain why a firm may face both
- Explain the difference between accounting costs and economic costs, and why opportunity costs must be included in economic costs
- Explain why an economist defines costs to include normal profit, but not excess profit

HIGHLIGHTS OF THE CHAPTER

In this chapter, we first focus on the short run—the period in which the firm cannot change the amount of plant and equipment it is using. Then, in a later part of the chapter, we turn to the long run, when the firm is able to vary the amount of capital and equipment it uses.

The Long Run vs. the Short Run

In the short run, one or more inputs are fixed. The capital the auto producer has is fixed. The land a farmer has is set. The decision is a narrow one: How much should the firm use of the variable inputs? In this simplified treatment, we consider only one variable input: labour.

In the long run, all inputs are variable. The firm now has to decide not only how much labour it should use, but also how much land and capital it should use. (In this simplified analysis, we assume that there is only one of these inputs—capital.)

The short run when capital is fixed isn't specified in number of years. For a college entrepreneur typing term papers, it may take only a matter of days to acquire more capital—that is, a small computer. But, for the company generating electrical power, the short run may be 10 years or more—the time necessary to build a new power generating plant.

Costs in the Short Run

To understand short-run costs, there is no substitute for working your way across Table 24-1 in the text—at least the first three rows for outputs 0, 1, and 2. Thus, in the first row, at an output of zero (in column 1) there is no variable cost (in column 3); since the firm is producing nothing, it hires no labour and, therefore, has no variable costs. But it does have that $35 of fixed cost (in column 2) that it cannot escape—for example, its capital equipment will depreciate and will have to be insured against fire even if it's producing nothing. Since such charges are incurred regardless of the firm's output, this $35 always remains the same as you go down column 2. However, in column 3, variable costs do rise to $24, then $40, and so on, as the firm increases its output and hires more labour.

With this in hand, you can now finish working your way across the first three (or more) rows, showing how each of the figures you calculate appears in Figure 24-1. As you proceed, you cover all the definitions of various concepts of cost in the text.

The Relationship Between Average and Marginal Costs

MC intersects ATC at the lowest point on ATC. The reason is that initially the marginal value (MC) is below the average value (ATC), so it's dragging the average value down. But when MC rises above ATC (as it does after output 5 in this example) MC begins to pull ATC up. If you follow baseball at all, Box 24-1 will make this idea transparent.

The Short-Run Production Function: Marginal Product and Marginal Cost

The *law of eventually diminishing returns* guarantees that the short-run marginal cost curve, MC, will ultimately rise—as indeed it does in Figure 24-1(*b*). To understand this law, consider the short-run situation of a firm producing bicycles with a given stock of capital and only one variable factor, labour. As the firm initially hires more labour, each additional worker increases the firm's output by a substantial amount. But, ultimately, as its labour force grows and its capital equipment is operated closer and closer to capacity, an additional worker will add only a small amount to the firm's output. All the new employee can do is work on odd jobs or stand around waiting for one of the machines to be free. In other words, the *marginal product* of labour—that is, the number of additional units of output (bicycles) which result from using one more worker—must eventually decrease. This illustrates the law of (eventually) diminishing returns: If more of one factor (labour) is employed while all other factors (capital, etc.) are held constant, eventually the marginal product of that one factor (labour) must fall.

In Part 9 of the text, it will become clear that the law of diminishing returns is a key to explaining wages and other income payments. For now, it is important because it explains why marginal costs must ultimately rise. In our example, the law of diminishing returns means that eventually an extra worker in the bicycle factory is able to do only odd jobs and produce very little. Most of his time is wasted. True, the firm can still produce another unit of output; but when it's done by a worker like this who is wasting most of his time, this unit of output comes at a very high marginal cost. Thus, the law of diminishing returns ensures that marginal costs must eventually rise.

Costs in the Long Run

In the short run, labour is variable but capital is fixed. However, in the long run, both labour and capital are variable. The firm now has to decide how much capital it should install.

Describing this decision by a firm requires knowledge of its cost curves, and Figure 24-4 in the text shows how a firm's long-run average cost curve (LAC) can be derived from its short-run average cost curves (SAC). (Each of its SAC curves applies to a specific amount of capital.) Note in that diagram how the firm's LAC curve is the envelope curve enclosing all the SAC curves from below. LAC shows how a firm wishing to produce any specified level of output—say q_4—can select the appropriate amount of capital. Specifically, the firm minimizes its average cost of producing q_4 at point J by selecting capital stock 4. (SAC_4, of course, is the short-run average cost curve that applies if the firm has capital stock 4.) Alternatively, if the firm wished to produce output q_2, it would do so at minimum average cost by producing at G using capital stock 2. Thus, the LAC "planning curve" tells the firm what its minimum average cost will be for each level of output when, in the long run, it is free to select any capital stock.

This, then, sets the stage for comparing two important economic phenomena.

Economies of Scale and the Law of (Eventually) Diminishing Returns

Economies of scale exist when a 10% increase in output requires less than a 10% increase in all inputs—in other words, when input costs increase less rapidly than output. In this situation, the average cost of producing output falls as output increases; LAC slopes downward and to the right. An important conclusion follows: When there are economies of scale, the LAC slopes downward.

Figure 24-6 shows how a firm facing economies of scale—with a downward-sloping LAC shown by arrow e—can also be facing diminishing returns (arrow f). The reason is that diminishing returns occur when the short-run marginal cost curve SMC_1 rises. Although economies of scale refer to falling costs (specifically, a downward-sloping LAC) and diminishing returns refer to rising costs (an upward-sloping marginal cost curve), the two are not in contradiction. Diminishing returns apply to the short run, when the firm cannot change its capital stock. On the other hand, economies of scale apply to the long run, when the firm is not constrained in this way and can do better—that is, achieve lower costs—by changing its capital stock. To see this in more detail in Figure 24-6, note that in the short run the firm cannot change its fixed capital stock. Increasing only its labour results in rising marginal cost (SMC_1)—that is, diminishing returns. However, in the long run, when the firm can vary both labour and capital, it can operate on LAC. Because this is falling, the firm enjoys economies of scale.

The Economist's Concept of Cost: Opportunity Cost

The final important topic covered in this chapter is the difference between economic cost and accounting cost. While the accountant looks only at explicit, out-of-pocket costs, the economist also considers implicit costs, such as the opportunity costs of the owner of a firm. One of these opportunity costs is the salary the owner could have earned in another job; another is the interest income or dividends that the owner could have earned by investing her capital elsewhere. This alternative possible income on capital—that is, the opportunity cost of capital—is called the firm's *normal profit*; it is the amount that is necessary to keep capital in that firm. Because economists thus include normal profit as a cost, when they speak of "profit" they mean *excess* profit—that is, additional profit above and beyond normal profit. Such above-normal or excess profit is important for the operation of the market system because, whenever it exists, it acts as a signal to attract resources into that industry.

IMPORTANT TERMS: MATCH THE COLUMNS

Match each term in the first column with its corresponding phrase in the second column.

_____   **1.** Short run

_____   **2.** Long run

_____   **3.** Short-run production function

_____   **4.** Marginal product

_____   **5.** Law of (eventually) diminishing returns

_____   **6.** Fixed costs

_____   **7.** Variable costs

_____   **8.** Total cost

_____   **9.** Average total cost

_____   **10.** Marginal cost

_____   **11.** Opportunity cost

_____   **12.** Economic cost

_____   **13.** Economic profit

_____   **14.** Economies of scale

a. The income an input could earn in its best alternative use

b. The sum of both fixed and variable costs

c. Costs that do not vary as output increases in the short run

d. If more of one factor is employed while all other factors are held constant, the marginal product of that factor must eventually fall

e. The time period over which the firm's capital stock is variable

f. The relationship between the amount of variable inputs used and the amount of output that can be produced, when the amount of capital is constant

g. Explicit accounting costs, plus implicit opportunity costs

h. Income above normal profits

i. Doubling all inputs more than doubles output

j. In the long run, all costs

k. Cost per unit

l. The increase in total cost when output is increased by one unit

m. The time period over which the firm cannot vary its capital stock

n. The additional output the firm can produce by using one more unit of an input

TRUE-FALSE

T   F   **1.** If output is zero, variable costs must be zero.

T   F   **2.** The law of diminishing returns states that the marginal product of any factor must eventually fall if other factors are held constant.

T   F   **3.** In a firm's short-run production function, the firm's labour and plant are held constant, while its machinery is allowed to vary.

T   F   **4.** The law of diminishing returns is unrealistic because it implies that we could feed the world from our back garden.

T   F   **5.** When existing firms earn economic profit, then that industry is attractive for new firms.

T   F   **6.** Economic profit is the profit that remains after account is taken of all explicit and implicit costs, including normal profit.

T   F   **7.** Diseconomies of scale exist if a 15% increase in output requires a 16% increase in all inputs.

T   F   **8.** It is not possible for a firm to be facing diminishing returns if its long-run average cost curve is falling.

T   F   **9.** In the long run, there are no variable costs.

T   F   **10.** The law of eventually diminishing returns describes a short-run situation in which labour varies but fixed factors do not.

For those who have studied the appendices to Chapters 22 and 24:

T   F   **11.** Whereas each indifference curve of a consumer represents a specific number of units of satisfaction, each isoquant in a production function represents only a "higher" or "lower" level of output.

MULTIPLE CHOICE

1. An example of a variable cost is:
   a. wage payments
   b. rental payments on a long-term lease
   c. interest payments on a mortgage
   d. depreciation costs
   e. all of the above

2. As output increases in the short run:
   a. fixed costs increase, but variable costs do not
   b. fixed costs decrease, but variable costs do not
   c. both fixed costs and variable costs change
   d. neither fixed costs nor variable costs change
   e. variable costs increase, but fixed costs do not

3. As output increases in the short run:
   a. fixed cost falls
   b. fixed cost rises
   c. fixed cost has less and less influence on average total cost
   d. fixed costs has more and more influence on average total cost
   e. average fixed cost rises

4. A firm's costs are related in the following way:
   a. average cost ATC cuts marginal cost MC at the minimum point of MC
   b. average cost ATC cuts average variable cost AVC at the minimum point of AVC
   c. MC cuts ATC at the minimum point of ATC
   d. MC cuts total cost at the minimum point of total cost
   e. AVC cuts ATC at the minimum point of ATC

5. If total costs are rising, then marginal cost must be:
   a. rising
   b. falling
   c. positive
   d. negative
   e. zero

6. The law of diminishing returns means that, as output increases in the short run,
   a. fixed cost will eventually fall
   b. fixed cost will eventually rise
   c. marginal costs will eventually rise
   d. marginal costs will eventually fall
   e. marginal costs will eventually become constant

7. In the long-run decisions of a firm:
   a. employment of labour is held constant, while its use of capital is allowed to increase
   b. employment of labour is held constant, while its use of capital is allowed to decrease
   c. use of capital is held constant, while its employment of labour is allowed to vary
   d. both are allowed to vary

   e. neither is allowed to vary

8. To calculate all the short-run costs of a firm with two inputs—labour and capital—all we need to know is:
   a. the firm's short-run production function
   b. the firm's short-run production function and its fixed costs
   c. the firm's short-run production function and its wage rate
   d. the firm's short-run production function, its wage rate, and its fixed costs
   e. none of the above is enough

9. If a firm's fixed cost is $100, and its total cost is $200 to produce one unit and $310 to produce two, then the marginal cost of the second unit is:
   a. $100
   b. $110
   c. $200
   d. $210
   e. $310

10. If a firm's fixed cost is $100, and its total cost is $200 to produce one unit and $310 to produce two, then its average variable cost for each of the two units is:
    a. $50
    b. $100
    c. $105
    d. $110
    e. $155

11. If a firm's fixed cost is $100, and its total cost is $200 to produce one unit, and $310 to produce two, the firm is:
    a. already facing diminishing returns
    b. not yet facing diminishing returns
    c. not yet facing constant returns
    d. already facing increasing returns
    e. facing constant returns

12. If there are economies of scale:
    a. short-run average cost rises
    b. short-run average cost is constant
    c. short-run average cost falls
    d. long-run average cost falls
    e. long-run average cost rises

13. If there are diminishing returns:
    a. short-run marginal cost falls
    b. short-run marginal cost rises
    c. short-run marginal cost is constant
    d. long-run marginal cost falls
    e. long-run marginal cost is constant

14. Fixed costs are:
    a. fixed only in the short run
    b. fixed only in the long run
    c. fixed in both the long and short run
    d. fixed in neither the long nor the short run
    e. variable in the short run

15. In the long run, a firm has to decide on:
  a. how much plant and equipment it uses, but not how much labour
  b. how much plant it uses, but not how much equipment and labour
  c. how much equipment and labour it uses, but not how much plant
  d. how much labour it uses, but not how much plant and equipment
  e. how much of all three it uses

16. A firm's long-run average cost curve is the envelope of its short-run:
  a. marginal cost curves
  b. fixed cost curves
  c. average variable cost curves
  d. average cost curves
  e. total cost curves

17. The long-run average cost curve is constructed by:
  a. joining the minimum points on all the short-run marginal cost curves
  b. joining the minimum points on all the short-run average cost curves
  c. joining the minimum points on all the short-run average variable cost curves
  d. joining the minimum points on all of the firm's planning curves
  e. none of the above

18. If a firm is simultaneously facing diminishing returns and economies of scale, then:
  a. its long-run average cost curve is falling, while its short-run marginal cost curve is rising
  b. its long-run average cost curve is rising, while its short-run marginal cost curve is rising
  c. its long-run average cost curve is rising, while its short-run marginal cost curve is falling
  d. its long-run average cost curve is falling, while its short-run marginal cost curve is falling

  e. its long-run average cost curve is neither rising nor falling, while its short-run marginal cost curve is rising

19. In reading a long-run production function table, any evidence of:
  a. economies of scale would be found along a row, with diminishing returns along a diagonal
  b. economies of scale would be found along a diagonal, with diminishing returns along a row
  c. both economies of scale and diminishing returns would be found along a row
  d. both economies of scale and diminishing returns would be found along a diagonal
  e. economies of scale would be found along a column

For those who have studied the appendix to Chapter 24:

20. At the long-run equilibrium for the firm:
  a. an isoquant of the long-run production function is tangent to an equal-cost line
  b. an isoquant of the short-run production function is tangent to an equal-cost line
  c. an isoquant of the long-run production function intersects an equal-cost line
  d. an isoquant of the short-run production function intersects an equal-cost line
  e. an indifference curve is tangent to an equal-cost line

21. The opportunity cost of an input is:
  a. the most it could earn in its least productive alternative use
  b. the least it could earn in its least productive alternative use
  c. the most it could earn in its most productive alternative use
  d. **a.** or **c.**
  e. **b.** or **c.**

EXERCISES

1a. Table 24.1 shows 2 short-run production functions for a firm that uses only 2 factors: labour and capital. Each production function describes the amounts of labour the firm would require to produce various amounts of output. The left panel shows the short-run production function if the firm has 20 units of capital; the right panel shows its short-run production function if it has 40 units of capital.

The cost of labour to the firm is $500 per unit and the cost of capital is $250 per unit. Thus, producing, say, 3

Table 24.1 Two Short-run Production Functions

20 units of capital			40 units of capital		
Output	Capital	Labour required	Output	Capital	Labour required
0	20	0	0	40	0
1	20	8	1	40	7
2	20	14	2	40	12
3	20	28	3	40	20
4	20	45	4	40	30
5	20	65	5	40	46
6	20	90	6	40	66

units of output with 20 units of capital cost would total $19,000; that is, $5,000 in fixed costs (20 units of capital at $250 per unit) plus $14,000 in variable costs (28 units of labour at a $500 per unit wage rate). This $19,000 is entered in Table 24.2 below. Fill in the rest of this table.

1b. If the firm is making a long-run decision and wishes to produce 2 units of output, how much capital should it acquire—20 units or 40? Why?

1c. Answer question **1b.** if the firm wishes to produce 5 units of output.

Table 24.2   Costs Calculated from the Two Short-run Production Functions in Table 24.1 Given a Wage of $500

Out-put	Total cost	Fixed cost	Variable cost	Average cost	Average variable cost	Marginal cost	Total cost	Fixed cost	Variable cost	Average cost	Average variable cost	Marginal cost
0				——	——	0				——	——	0
1												
2												
3	19,000	5,000	14,000	6,333	4,667							
4												
5												
6												

2.   Table 24.3 presents average cost figures for 4 of the large number of plant sizes that a firm can select in the long run. (Note that plants B and C have costs similar—but not identical—to those you calculated for the 2 plants in Table 24.2.) In Figure 24.1, graph the 4 average cost curves. Label them A, B, C, and D and mark the minimum point of each M_A, M_B, M_C and M_D. Sketch in a rough long-run average cost curve (LAC) for this firm. Does it pass through all the minimum points? In particular, does it pass through M_A and M_D? Through M_C? Why?

Table 24.3

	Average cost, if fixed cost is:			
	$2,000	$5,000	$10,000	$15,000
Output	Plant A	Plant B	Plant C	Plant D
1	$ 7,100	$9,000	$13,500	$13,900
2	6,700	7,000	8,000	8,500
3	6,800	6,300	6,700	6,900
4	8,000	6,900	6,200	6,600
5	9,600	7,600	6,600	6,500
6	12,000	8,700	7,200	6,600

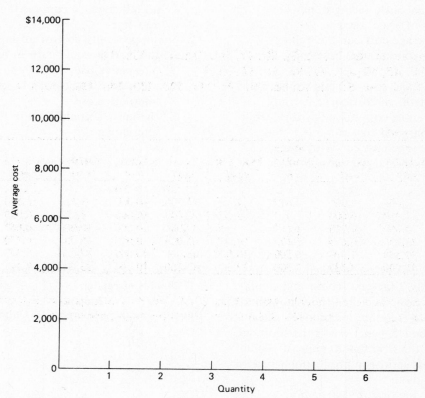

Figure 24.1

3. Fill in a table similar to Table 24-3 in the textbook, showing how an accountant and an economist would describe the costs and profit of Peter Davidson, who owns and operates a farm. His total revenue in this particular year is $180,000. His expenses include $27,000 to hire farm labour, $12,000 for fertilizer and seed, $10,000 rent for an adjacent farm, and $20,000 for gas and other costs. Although his accountant tells him that, relative to his neighbours, he's extremely successful, he sometimes con-siders giving up farming to take a job managing a farm supply business nearby where he has been offered a $65,000 salary. If he did so, he would sell his farm and invest the proceeds in government bonds that would yield a $62,000 per year interest income.

What is his accounting profit and his economic profit? Assuming that he finds farming and managing the farm supply business equally attractive, what would you recommend that he do? Why?

ESSAY QUESTIONS

1. Draw a U-shaped average cost curve. Then, draw in the corresponding MC curve and, finally, the AVC curve. In red, show the new curves after a cost-cutting technological innovation. What effect do you think this would have on the firm's supply curve?

2. Would you expect the short run to be longer for a gardening service or a steel company? Explain.

3. In Figure 24-2(b) in the text, the marginal product curve cuts the average product curve at the highest point on the average product curve. Explain why this must be so, using an argument similar to the one used to estab-lish that the MC curve intersects the AC at the lowest point on the AC curve.

4. "The law of diminishing returns ensures a dismal economic future, because it tells us that as the labour force grows, it will eventually produce a lower and lower marginal product." Do you agree? Why or why not?

5. Do you agree with the following statement? Explain why. "If a firm producing 1000 units of output is on its long-run average cost curve, then the combination of cap-ital and labour that it is using costs less than any alterna-tive combination which could be used to produce 1000 units of output." Illustrate your answer with a diagram, showing two or three of the other combinations.

6. Are either normal profit or economic profit—or both—included in costs? Explain why.

ANSWERS

Important Terms: **1m, 2e, 3f, 4n, 5d, 6c, 7j, 8b, 9k, 10l, 11a, 12g, 13h, 14i**
True-False: **1T, 2T, 3F, 4F, 5T, 6T, 7T, 8F, 9F, 10T, 11F**
Multiple Choice: **1a, 2e, 3c, 4c, 5c, 6c, 7d, 8d, 9b, 10c, 11a, 12d, 13b, 14a, 15e, 16d, 17e, 18a, 19b, 20a, 21c**
Exercises:

1a. Table 24.2   completed

Out-put	Total cost	Fixed cost	Variable cost	Average cost	Average variable cost	Marginal cost	Total cost	Fixed cost	Variable cost	Average cost	Average variable cost	Marginal cost
0	5,000	5,000	0	___	___	0	10,000	10,000	0	___	___	0
1	9,000	5,000	4,000	9,000	4,000	4,000	13,500	10,000	3,500	13,500	3,500	3,500
2	12,000	5,000	7,000	6,000	3,500	3,000	16,000	10,000	6,000	8,000	3,000	2,500
3	19,000	5,000	14,000	6,333	4,667	7,000	20,000	10,000	10,000	6,667	3,333	4,000
4	27,500	5,000	22,500	6,875	5,625	8,500	25,000	10,000	15,000	6,250	3,750	5,000
5	37,500	5,000	32,500	7,500	6,500	10,000	33,000	10,000	23,000	6,600	4,600	8,000
6	50,000	5,000	45,000	8,333	7,500	12,500	43,000	10,000	33,000	7,167	5,500	10,000

1b. 20 units; its average cost will be $6,000, rather than $8,000 **1c.** 40 units; its average cost will be $6,600, rather than $7,500 **2.** no, no, yes, because M_C is the lowest of all the minimum values

Figure 24.1 completed

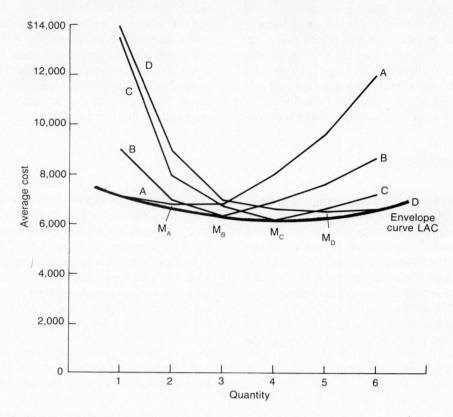

3. The table you derive should look like this:

Table 24.4   completed

Costs and profits, evaluated by:			
1. An accountant		**2. An economist**	
Total revenue	$180,000	Total revenue	$180,000
		Costs:	
Costs:		Explicit:	
Labour	27,000	Labour	27,000
Fertilizer, seed	12,000	Fertilizer, seed	12,000
Rent	10,000	Rent	10,000
Gas, etc.	20,000	Gas, etc.	20,000
Total costs	69,000	Implicit:	
		Owner's salary	65,000
		Normal profit	62,000
		Total costs	196,000
Accounting profit	111,000	Economic (above-normal) profit	−16,000

His accounting profit is $111,000, but his economic profit is −$16,000.

His best course of action is to sell the farm, buy bonds with the proceeds, and take the other job, since he is now earning $16,000 less in farming than he could if he followed this alternative course of action. That is, his economic loss in farming is $16,000; his $111,000 of accounting profit is $16,000 less than his opportunity cost of $65,000 + $62,000 = $127,000.

ANSWERS TO SELECTED REVIEW QUESTIONS FROM THE TEXT

24-1. Yes. Yes.

24-2. The calculations follow the same pattern as in Table 24-1. Note that $500 replaces $35 throughout column 2.

(a) No. Because variable cost remains the same, so does marginal cost. (Marginal cost is the increase in either total cost or variable cost.)

(b) While nothing happens to MC, AC shifts up dramatically. Its minimum point—the point where it passes through MC—will be at a greater quantity of output (as long as MC slopes up to the right).

24-3. Yes. Use exactly the same argument as before. When marginal cost is below AVC, it is pulling AVC down. When marginal cost is above AVC, it is pulling AVC up.

24-4. (a) False. MC could be rising, but still be below ATC, and therefore pulling ATC down.

(b) This statement is false for AVC, just as it was for ATC in part (a). MC could be rising, but still be below AVC, and therefore pulling AVC down.

(c) True. Since MC is higher than ATC, it is pulling ATC up.

(d) True. Since MC is higher than AVC, it is pulling AVC up.

(e) False. AFC always falls. MC is not related to fixed costs.

(f) False. No reason it should. For example, see falling MC on the left of Figure 24-1(*b*), even though ATC is above it.

24-6. Not necessarily. For example, see the second last row of the production function in Table 24-4 on page 471. When the capital stock is 2, the MPL starts declining when the second worker is added. (This is, of course, the long-run production function from which, in the last row, the short-run production function in Table 24-2 is taken.)

24-8. $350 because that is their opportunity cost.

24-9. Normal profit is the opportunity cost of equity capital. It must be included in costs, because only then will this give a true picture of all the resources being used by an industry. If existing firms are earning above-normal profit, then there is an incentive for new firms to move into this industry.

Part Seven

Market Structure and Economic Efficiency

Chapter 25

■ ■

Supply in a Perfectly Competitive Market

MAJOR PURPOSE

In Chapter 22 we saw how a demand curve reflects the desire of buyers to acquire a good. In this chapter, our attention turns to supply. It will be shown that, in a perfectly competitive market, a supply curve reflects the marginal cost of producing a good. Specifically, just as you can visualize a whole set of marginal benefit arrows rising up to a demand curve, you can also visualize a whole set of marginal cost arrows rising up to a supply curve. To establish this important conclusion, we analyse a profit-maximizing firm's response to various market prices. At each price, the firm will supply a quantity determined by its marginal cost curve (provided its variable costs are covered). Therefore, supply reflects marginal cost. We also show the importance in the long run of free entry of new firms into an industry—and free exit by existing firms. Thus, for example, the long-term adjustment of a perfectly competitive industry to an increase

in demand will involve not only an increase in the output of existing firms but also an increase in the number of firms. This is one of the reasons that the long-term supply response by an industry will be more elastic than its short-term response.

The final objective in this chapter is to show how the profit position of perfectly competitive producers is affected by a change in market price. We will show that, just as a price increase in Chapter 22 hurt consumers by the area to the left of the demand curve (between the old and new price), a price increase will benefit producers by the area to the left of the supply curve (between the old and new price). With this knowledge of how both producers and consumers are affected, we are now in a position to analyse the winners and losers when, say, government intervention affects a market price. The example given is the imposition of a sales tax.

LEARNING OBJECTIVES

After you have studied this chapter in the textbook and the study guide, you should be able to

- Define perfect competition, explaining each of the five important requirements
- Show why the condition for profit maximization by any firm is to produce until "marginal cost = marginal revenue"
- Show, as one specific case of this general principle, that the condition for profit maximization by a perfectly competitive firm is to produce until "marginal cost = price"
- Demonstrate why the short-run supply curve of a perfectly competitive firm is its marginal cost curve (above its average variable cost curve)
- Analyse the long-run effect of the entry of new firms on an industry's supply
- Describe how an industry adjusts to an increase in demand, clearly distinguishing between the short-run increase in price, and the long-term drift of that price back down toward its original level as new firms enter the industry
- Distinguish between case A where, in the long run, price falls all the way back to its original level and case B where it falls back only part way
- Explain the underlying conditions that give rise to each of these two cases

• Restate this analysis to describe what happens when demand decreases, rather than increases
• Show how the gain to producers from a price increase can be read off a supply curve, just as a change in consumer surplus can be read off a demand curve

HIGHLIGHTS OF THE CHAPTER

In our examination in this chapter of what underlies the cost curve—just as in our parallel examination in Chapter 22 of what underlies demand—we assume that rational self-interest is pursued. Specifically, in this chapter, we assume that firms will produce the quantity of a good that will maximize their profit.

First, recall that our description of costs in Chapter 24 equally well describes the costs of a firm producing in perfect competition or in any other form of market. However, the important question "How much will the firm produce?" cannot be answered without specifying the market form. In the text, the market is assumed to be perfectly competitive, and a more complete definition of this market form is now required. So far, we have emphasized only that it is a market in which there are so many buyers and sellers that none can influence price. Now we recognize several further conditions—in particular, the requirements that the product is standardized and that there are no barriers to the entry of new firms or the exit of existing firms.

Supply in the Short Run

The stage is now set for addressing the question: Given the firm's marginal cost (MC) and other cost schedules described in Chapter 24, how much will the firm supply at any given price? The rule for any profit-maximizing firm is to produce until its MC equals its marginal revenue MR, where MR is its additional revenue earned from producing one more unit of output.

This general rule—that a firm will produce until MC = MR—can be stated in an alternative way for a perfectly competitive firm: Such a firm will produce until its MC = price. The reason is that such a firm takes the price of its output as given. Therefore, its MR is just the price that it faces. For example, if it sells apples for a price $P = \$2$ a basket, then each additional basket provides \$2 of extra revenue MR. This conclusion that a competitive firm continues to produce until MC = P is important. It means that when it is faced with any given market price P, it will supply a quantity of output that can be read off its MC curve; in other words, the firm's supply curve depends on its MC curve. Be sure that you fully understand Figure 25-2 and Table 25-1 in the text-

book. These most clearly demonstrate why the firm will produce until MC = P and why, therefore, the firm's supply curve is the same as its marginal cost curve.

In making this statement about the firm's supply, however, we must recognize one important reservation. Price must be above a certain minimum level or the firm won't supply anything at all. This minimum level is the price that will generate enough revenue to cover the firm's variable costs. More specifically, price must be at least as high as the firm's "shutdown point" on its average variable cost (AVC) curve—that is, at least as high as point K in Figure 25-3 in the textbook. As long as price is at least this high, then in the short run the firm will supply this product. This is true, even if the price is still below the "breakeven point" (H in the same diagram) where the firm is just barely able to cover its total cost, including both its variable costs and its fixed costs. Even though a firm operating between these two points is incurring a loss, it is still able to cover part of its variable costs and have at least something left over to cover its fixed costs. Therefore, it is better to continue to operate than to close down altogether. (If it were to close down, it would be worse off because it would be unable to cover any of its fixed costs.)

This, then, leads to the conclusion that, as price falls, the firm's short-run supply curve will follow its MC curve down until it reaches the shutdown point where MC intersects AVC.

The short-run industry supply curve is the horizontal summation of the short-run supply curves of all of the individual firms, as shown in Figure 25-4.

Supply in the Long Run

In the long run (unlike the short run) the firm can escape from its fixed costs, because all costs are variable. Therefore, it can operate on its flatter long-run ATC (envelope) curve. And there is another important difference: In the long run, firms can enter or leave the industry.

In deriving long-run supply, two cases should be distinguished.

Case A: Long-run supply is completely elastic. (Figures 25-6 and 25-7 in the text.) Suppose new firms can produce at the same cost as old firms. (For this to happen, inputs acquired by new firms would have to be as productive as those used by existing firms; and the industry would have to be small enough so that new firms can purchase inputs without bidding up their price.) In such circumstances, an increase in demand for this industry's output can, in the long run, be met entirely by new firms entering the industry and selling at the same cost and price as old firms. Since supply can increase without any increase in price, the long-run supply is completely elastic; an example is S_L in Figure 25-6.

It is true that when demand initially increases, price does rise in the short run before new firms can enter. It is this increase in price and, hence, profit to existing firms that becomes the incentive for new firms to enter the industry. As new firms enter, supply shifts to the right. As a result, profit is reduced. This process continues until price falls back all the way to its original level, above-normal profit is eliminated, and there is therefore no incentive left for new firms to enter.

Case B: A rising long-run supply curve. (Figure 25-8 in the text.) In this case, price does not fall all the way back to its original level. The reason is that, as the number of firms in the industry increases, costs rise. This may happen because new firms cannot purchase inputs without bidding up their price, or because these firms cannot acquire inputs of the same quality as those used by existing firms. (For example, new entrants into farming may find that the only available land is less productive.) Because new firms are incurring higher costs, their profits will disappear before price falls all the way back to its original level. At this point, there will be no incentive left for more firms to enter; thus, the new equilibrium price will be higher than its original level. In this case, there-fore, the long-run supply curve slopes up; an example is S_L in Figure 25-8.

The Benefit to Producers from a Higher Price

When, in response to a higher price, producers move from E_1 to E_2 in Figure 25-9, they acquire two benefits:

1. They get a higher price on their original 30 units of sales; thus, their profit increases by area 1.

2. On the additional 20 units they now sell, their costs are given by the height of the supply curve. But they receive the higher $700 price. Thus, profit increases by the difference between the two—area 2. Therefore, when price rises, producers benefit by the area to the left of the supply curve between the old and new price.

Reprise: The Burden of an Excise Tax

A $1 tax in Figure 25-10 shifts the S curve up from S_1 to S_2, with consumer equilibrium moving from E_1 to E_2.

Consumers lose areas 1 + 2, the area to the left of the demand curve between the old and new price.

Producers must take a price reduction (after tax) from $2 to $1.60. Thus, they lose areas 3 + 4 to the left of the supply curve.

The government gains 1 + 3 of tax revenue—a $1 tax on each of the 3000 units sold.

Thus, there is a transfer of 1 + 3 from consumers and producers to the government (i.e., to taxpayers). The rest of the loss (area 3 + 4) is a deadweight loss that goes to no one. It's a loss because a tax has distorted this market—in particular, has reduced the quantity bought and sold from 5000 to 3000.

IMPORTANT TERMS: MATCH THE COLUMNS

Match each term in the first column with its corresponding phrase in the second column.

_____ **1.** Perfect competition	**a.** Income in excess of opportunity cost
_____ **2.** Short-run supply	**b.** A market where there are no barriers to entry or exit, and there are so many buyers and sellers of a standardized product that none has any influence over its price
_____ **3.** Long-run supply	
_____ **4.** Marginal revenue	
_____ **5.** Break-even point	**c.** The quantity sold in the time period during which the capital stock is variable
_____ **6.** Shutdown point	
_____ **7.** Increase in producer surplus	**d.** The increase in total revenue from the sale of one more unit. In perfect competition, this is the same as market price.
_____ **8.** Above-normal profit	
	e. The point at which the marginal cost curve intersects the average variable cost curve. If the price falls below this, the firm will cease operating even in the short run.

f. The point at which the marginal cost curve intersects the average cost curve, and the firm makes a zero profit

g. The quantity sold in the time period during which the capital stock is fixed

h. The area to the left of the supply curve between the old and new price

TRUE-FALSE

T   F   **1.** Marginal revenue is total revenue less the cost that results when one more unit is produced.

T   F   **2.** If a competitive firm is producing slightly less than the profit-maximizing amount, then price is greater than marginal cost.

T   F   **3.** In the short run, the firm stops producing if price falls below its minimum average total cost.

T   F   **4.** As you move up a firm's short-run marginal cost curve to the right, you reach the shutdown point before the break-even point.

T   F   **5.** A firm maximizes its profits where the vertical distance between its total cost and total revenue curves is minimized.

T   F   **6.** If a firm is operating at capacity—that is, with a completely inelastic supply (MC) curve—then an increase in market price will result in no increase in its total revenue or output.

T   F   **7.** In the short run, a firm that is operating at its shutdown point is earning no economic profit or loss.

T   F   **8.** Unless there are economies of scale, a perfectly competitive firm's short-run supply curve cannot slope upward to the right.

T   F   **9.** An increase in demand for a perfectly competitive good will result in a short-run increase in the output and profit of existing firms.

T   F   **10.** If new entrants to an industry can obtain the same quality of inputs as existing firms, and inputs are available at stable prices, then the long-run industry supply will be upward sloping.

MULTIPLE CHOICE

1. For a perfectly competitive firm, marginal revenue is
  a. less than the price of its output
  b. equal to the price of its output
  c. greater than the price of its output
  d. greater than the price of its output if the elasticity of demand for its output is greater than 1
  e. not related to the price of its output

2. The short-run supply curve slopes upward because of
  a. the law of eventually diminishing returns
  b. economies of scale
  c. the upward slope of the marginal cost curve
  d. a. and c.
  e. b. and c.

3. In a perfectly competitive industry, there are
  a. so few buyers and sellers that each one can influence price
  b. so few buyers and sellers that none can influence price
  c. so many buyers and sellers that none can influence price
  d. so many buyers and sellers that each one can influence price
  e. just the right number of buyers and sellers so that each can influence the price

4. In a perfectly competitive market, an individual consumer determines
  a. price but not the quantity to purchase
  b. quantity to purchase, but not price
  c. neither the quantity to purchase, nor price
  d. both the quantity to purchase, and price
  e. both the quantity to purchase and price, but only if the product is standardized

5. In perfect competition, the demand by individual buyers is
  a. perfectly elastic while the demand facing individual sellers is not
  b. perfectly elastic like the demand facing individual sellers
  c. not perfectly elastic while the demand facing individual sellers is perfectly elastic

d. not perfectly elastic, nor is the demand facing individual sellers

e. perfectly elastic while the demand facing individual sellers can be either elastic or inelastic

6. In perfect competition, the per unit profit of an individual firm is

a. its total cost minus its total revenue

b. its total revenue minus its total cost

c. its average total cost minus the price at which it sells

d. its average total cost plus the price at which it sells

e. its selling price minus its average total cost

7. In perfect competition, total profit of an individual firm is its

a. marginal revenue minus its average total cost

b. total revenue minus its average total cost

c. total revenue minus its total cost

d. marginal revenue minus its total cost

e. marginal revenue minus its marginal cost

8. Consider a perfectly competitive industry, where there are many identical firms initially producing with zero (excess) profit. If demand decreases, then in the short run

a. each firm will produce more and operate at a loss

b. each firm will produce more and operate at a profit

c. each firm will produce more and continue to operate with zero profit

d. each firm will produce less and operate at a profit

e. each firm will produce less and operate at a loss

9. The shutdown point is

a. the minimum point on the average total cost curve

b. the minimum point on the average variable cost curve

c. the minimum point on the marginal cost curve

d. the minimum point on the average fixed cost curve

e. the point where marginal cost cuts the average fixed cost curve

10. Beneath a supply curve, you can visualize a set of vertical

a. marginal revenue arrows

b. marginal benefit arrows

c. marginal cost arrows

d. average cost arrows

e. average benefit arrows

11. In the short run, the break-even point is

a. at the intersection of the marginal cost curve and the average fixed cost curve

b. below the intersection of the marginal cost curve and the average fixed cost curve

c. the same as the shutdown point

d. above the shutdown point

e. below the shutdown point

12. In the short run, the perfectly competitive firm's break-even point occurs at

a. a greater quantity of output than the shutdown point

b. a smaller quantity than the shutdown point

c. the same quantity as the shutdown point

d. a lower price than the shutdown point

e. the same price as the shutdown point

13. If a firm's total cost and total revenue curves (TC and TR) are plotted, the firm can earn a profit and maximizes it where

a. its TC cuts its TR from above

b. its TC cuts its TR from below

c. its TC is parallel to and above its TR

d. its TC is parallel to and below its TR

e. its TC is horizontal

14. Removing restrictions on entry by new firms will

a. shift the industry's supply curve to the left

b. shift the industry's demand curve to the left

c. shift the industry's supply curve to the right

d. have no affect on the industry's supply curve

e. have no affect on the industry's supply and demand curves

15. If demand decreases in a perfectly competitive industry, then price will

a. rise in the short run and fall in the long run

b. rise in the short run and rise further in the long run

c. fall in the short run and fall further in the long run

d. fall in the short run and rise back towards the original price in the long run

e. fall in the short run and thereafter remain constant at that level

16. Suppose demand has increased in a perfectly competitive industry, and each firm has moved to a new short-run equilibrium. Then, in the further process of long-run adjustment, the individual firm will face

a. falling price and decreasing profit

b. falling price and increasing profit

c. falling price and constant profit

d. increasing price and decreasing profit

e. increasing price and increasing profit

17. For long-run industry supply to be completely elastic (horizontal)

a. the industry must be large enough so that it can influence the price of its inputs

b. inputs of uniform quality must be available to old and new firms alike

c. both of the above

d. neither of the above

e. It is not possible for an industry supply curve to be completely elastic

18. The long-run supply curve for an industry will be upward sloping if

a. new firms bid up the price of inputs

b. the quality of inputs deteriorates as new firms purchase more

c. **a.** or **b.**

d. neither **a.** nor **b.**

e. It's impossible for a long-run supply curve to be upward sloping

19. If price rises and output increases, then the gain to the producing firm is

a. the increase in the firm's revenue, plus the increase in its costs

b. the increase in the firm's revenue, minus the increase in its costs

c. the increase in the firm's revenue

d. the increase in the firm's costs, minus the increase in its revenue

e. the decrease in the firm's costs

20. If price falls, then producers

a. benefit by the area to the left of the supply curve between the old and new price

b. benefit by the area to the left of the demand curve between the old and new price

c. are worse off by the area to the left of the demand curve between the old and new price

d. are worse off by the area to the left of the supply curve between the old and new price

e. are not affected

21. When the government imposes an excise tax on a product

a. the consumers' and producers' loss is less than the government's tax collections

b. the consumers' and producers' loss is the same as the government's tax collections

c. the consumers' and producers' gain is the same as the government's loss of tax collections

d. the consumers' and producers' gain is less than the government's loss of tax collections

e. the consumers' and producers' loss is greater than the government's tax collections

EXERCISES

1a. If the price is P_1 in Figure 25.1 below, the quantity supplied will be _____, total revenue will be area _____, average cost will be _____, and multiplying this by the number of units sold yields a total cost of area _____. Thus economic profit will be area _____.

1b. Alternatively, we can arrive at this same profit by noting that the firm's average revenue is its price P_1, its average cost is _____ and, therefore, its average profit is _____. Multiplying this by its quantity of output yields its total profit of area _____.

1c. If the price is P_2, the firm will supply quantity _____, total revenue will be _____, average cost will be _____, total cost will be _____, and economic profit will be _____. Therefore, the (breakeven, shutdown) point is _____.

1d. If the price is P_3, the firm will supply _____, total revenue will be _____, average cost will be _____, and total cost will be _____. Therefore, total economic (profit, loss) will be _____. If price stays at P_3, then the firm will continue to operate in the _____ run, but not in the _____ run. Despite its loss, it makes this short-run decision because price P_3 is still above the firm's (shutdown, breakeven) point at _____. Another way of viewing this decision is that the firm is operating above its (MC, AC, AVC) curve. Therefore, it can more than cover its _____ costs and, thus, have some left over partly to cover its _____ costs. Shade in and mark for future reference the firm's profit when its price (in this case, P_1) is above the minimum point K on its AC curve; and its loss when its price (in this case, P_3) is below K.

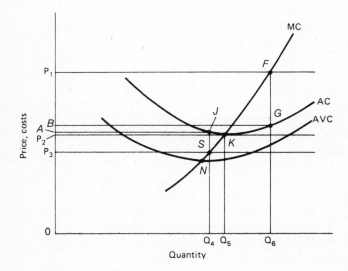

Figure 25.1

2. Table 25.1 describes some of a firm's long-run costs. Fill in the rest of this table. Note, in particular, that column 3 is to show its envelope curve LAC.

When the price of this firm's output is $70, the firm's long-run profit-maximizing output is _____, and its economic profit is _____. When the price is $85, the firm's profit-maximizing output is _____, and its profit is _____.

When price rises from $70 to $85, there is a (gain, loss) to this firm of _____.

3. In Figure 25.2, supply is S$_1$ in panel (b). When D$_1$ decreases to D$_2$, price falls from _____ to _____ as the short-run equilibrium of the industry shifts from _____ to _____. Each firm in panel (a) responds by moving along its supply curve from _____ to _____. Each firm now has a (profit, loss) of _____. As firms therefore (enter, leave) the industry, the industry supply in panel (b) shifts from _____ to _____, and industry equilibrium moves from _____ to _____. The initial 30% leftward shift in demand has been offset by a _____% shift in supply, and price (moves to, returns to) _____. Long-run supply is constructed by joining all points such as _____ and _____. It is (completely elastic, unit elastic, inelastic).

4. If price is P$_1$, the total revenue of the perfectly competitive industry shown in Figure 25.3 is _____. If price falls to P$_2$, its total revenue is _____, for a (decrease, increase) in revenue of _____. However, this is partially offset by a decrease in _____ of _____. Therefore, the reduction in producer surplus is _____.

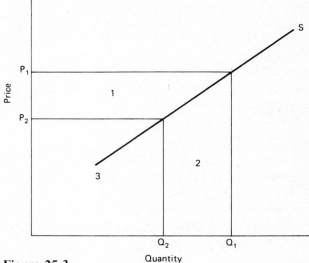

Figure 25.3

Table 25.1 A Firm's Long-run Costs

Output	Total cost	Average cost (LAC)	Marginal cost	Total revenue if price equals $70	Economic profit if price equals $70	Total revenue if price equals $85	Economic profit if price equals $85
1	$120		$120				
2	150						
3	200						
4	270						
5	350						
6	440						

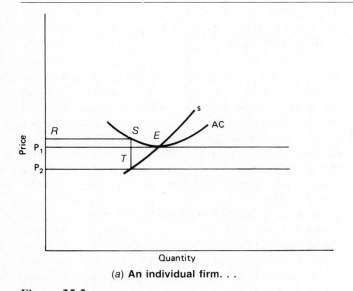

(a) **An individual firm. . .**

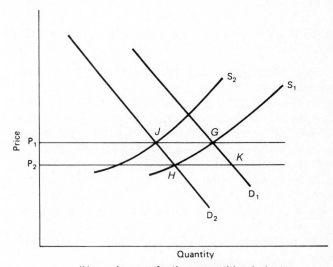

(b) **. . . in a perfectly competitive industry**

Figure 25.2

ESSAY QUESTIONS

1. "If a firm's overhead costs increase by, say, 20% because of an increase in its property taxes, its output will not be affected." Evaluate this statement, clearly distinguishing between the short and long run.

2. Draw a U-shaped average cost curve. Then, draw in the corresponding MC curve and, finally, the AVC curve. Show the new curves after a cost-cutting technological innovation. What effect does this have on the firm's supply curve?

3. "In the short run, a perfectly competitive firm will not produce at any point where its average cost is still falling." Do you agree? Why or why not?

4. "If demand for a perfectly competitive product shifts downward, price must fall." Do you agree? Explain, clearly distinguishing between the long and short run.

ANSWERS

Important Terms: **1**b, **2**g, **3**c, **4**d, **5**f, **6**e, **7**h, **8**a
True-False: **1**F, **2**T, **3**F, **4**T, **5**F, **6**F, **7**F, **8**F, **9**T, **10**F
Multiple Choice: **1**b, **2**d, **3**c, **4**b, **5**c, **6**e, **7**c, **8**e, **9**b, **10**c, **11**d, **12**a, **13**d, **14**c, **15**d, **16**a, **17**b, **18**c, **19**b, **20**d, **21**e
Exercises: **1a.** Q_6, P_1FQ_60, B, BGQ_60, P_1FGB **1b.** B, BP_1, P_1FGB **1c.** Q_5, P_2KQ_50, P_2, P_2KQ_50, zero, breakeven, K **1d.** Q_4, P_3SQ_40, A, AJQ_40, loss, $AJSP_3$, short, long, shutdown, N, AVC, variable, fixed

2. Table 25.1 completed

Output	Total cost	Average cost (LAC)	Marginal cost	Total revenue if $P = \$70$	Profit if $P = \$70$	Total revenue if $P = \$85$	Profit if $P = \$85$
1	$120	$120	$120	$ 70	$-50	$ 85	$-35
2	150	75	30	140	-10	170	20
3	200	66 $^2/_3$	50	210	10	255	55
4	270	67 $^1/_2$	70	280	10	340	70
5	350	70	80	350	0	425	75
6	400	73 $^1/_3$	90	420	-20	510	70

4, $10, 5, $75, gain, $65

3. P_1, P_2, G, H, E, T, loss, $RSTP_2$, leave, S_1, S_2, H, J, 30%, returns to, P_1, G, J, completely elastic

4. 1 + 2 + 3, 3, decrease, 1 + 2, costs, 2, 1

ANSWERS TO SELECTED REVIEW QUESTIONS FROM THE TEXT

25-1. Yes, because its profit from this additional unit would be $90 − $50 = $40.

25-2. Add 2 columns to the right of Table 25-1, just like the last two columns of Table 25-2, except that they are headed "Price = $55 = MR." The profit-maximizing output is 7 units, where MC = MR = $55. Profit is 7($55) − $245 = $140.

25-3. 6 units. Nothing. Price must be at least as high as MC = $55 before the 7th unit will be justified.

25-4. **(a)** Add $35 to each item in column (2) and follow exactly the same calculations as before.

(b) Nothing happens to MC, but ATC shifts up. Profit falls.

(c) Because ATC shifts up you can visualize its minimum point shifting up along the MC curve to a greater level of output. (The MC curve slopes upward to the right.) Therefore, it is generally true that heavier fixed cost makes ATC fall over a wider range of output—although, in this particular case, this effect isn't quite strong enough to trigger a change; minimum ATC still occurs at 5 units of output. (To clearly see ATC falling through a wider range, increase fixed costs to $1,000.)

(d) AVC remains unchanged. (It has nothing to do with fixed cost.)

(e) Since fixed cost is included in ATC, ATC is affected by it. But AVC is not; fixed costs are not included in AVC.

(f) In columns 5 and 7 of Table 25-2, we see that AVC = MC = $20 at 3 units of output. This is the shutdown point whether fixed cost is $30, $70, or any other amount.

It doesn't matter how you change fixed costs, AVC and MC are both unaffected; therefore, so is the shutdown point. (However, the break-even point is affected because that is on ATC which is influenced by fixed cost.)

25-6. (a) Yes. Its short-run supply extends down its short-run marginal cost curve SMC until SMC intersects its short run AVC curve. The firm won't supply at a price below this because it is the shutdown point.

(b) Since its price has fallen below its break-even point at H, the firm would view its original decision to get into this industry as a mistake. In the short run it would continue to produce (as long as price is at least as high as the shutdown level). However, in the long run it won't produce at all. This makes long-run supply more elastic because it reflects firms leaving the industry, while short-run supply does not.

25-7. (a) In the long run nothing, because price doesn't rise. Each firm ends up back again at H with zero above-normal profit. (In the short run, there can be rent because price does rise—but that's another story.)

(b) Corn, since cranberry land is more specialized and scarcer. (Cranberries are more likely to be like Figure 25-8.)

(crossword grid)

Across

1, 5. When you know these, you can calculate marginal costs.
7. head of a corporation (abbrev.)
9. be (first person singular)
11. in the past
13. the amount an input could earn in its best alternative use (2 words)
15. grows in damp cool places
16. The federal government has had a large deficit in its _____ in recent years.
18. preposition
19. professional degree (abbrev.)
21, 23. the relationship of the long-run cost curve to a series of short-run cost curves
25. At this point, losses equal fixed costs.
26. sign of affection
29. third person singular (impersonal pronoun)
30. overrun and inhabit
34. the sum of fixed and variable costs (2 words)
37. This elasticity is measured between two points on a curve.
38. compulsive saver
39. more than a few
42. To maximize profits, a firm equates this with marginal cost. (2 words)
44. indefinite article preceding vowel
45. With this type of exchange rate float, governments don't accumulate foreign exchange reserves.

Down

1. forbid, prohibit
2. harvest (verb)
3. what Toronto wants to do to Montreal in football and hockey
4. a reason why there are gains from specialization (3 words)
5. expenses
6. systematic statement of principles or propositions
8. A barrier to _____ reduces competition.
10. Things are dead around here.
12. Please don't chew this in class.
14. be (third person singular)
16. At the _____-even point, profits are zero.
17. a number
18. Shakespeare is often called this.
19. sever
20. When night falls, so does this.
22. go to see
23. hints, signals
24. expression of choice
27. German concentration camp
28. a size of type
31. Economists consider this type of profit to be a cost.
32. main character in 1983 movie
33. Elasticity of demand and supply determines who bears the _____ of a sales tax.
35. Your liver is one.
36. This type of cost does not affect marginal cost.
40. U.S. gun lobby (abbrev.)
41. Japanese currency
42. post-graduate degree
43. gratis (abbrev.)

Chapter 26

■ ■

Perfect Competition and Economic Efficiency

MAJOR PURPOSE

The primary objective in this chapter is to demonstrate that, under certain conditions, a perfectly competitive market provides an efficient outcome. Thus perfect competition must be studied carefully, even though it doesn't describe a large part of the economy; most products are produced in some other type of market. Specifically, they are produced most frequently in markets between monopoly and perfect competition. Such markets are not efficient, and we will be able to see why in later chapters only if we now develop a full understanding of the conditions under which perfect competition is efficient.

Another important topic of later chapters will be those instances in which even perfect competition is not efficient. So, efficiency is seldom completely achieved. But it must be understood to ensure that policies to cure inefficiency do indeed move the economy in that direction, rather than making matters worse. Thus, understanding what efficiency means and why it is sometimes achieved in perfectly competitive markets is our major task in this chapter.

LEARNING OBJECTIVES

After you have studied this chapter in the textbook and the study guide, you should be able to
* Explain why the condition "marginal cost to society = marginal benefit to society" is necessary for allocative efficiency
* Explain why perfect competition results in allocative efficiency when there are no externalities
* Show how perfect competition tends to promote technical efficiency
* Demonstrate, in a diagram similar to Figure 26-3 in the text, that a deadweight loss to society results if either more or less than the efficient quantity of output is produced
* Explain why perfect competition tends to promote dynamic efficiency in certain ways; but why, in some other ways, other types of markets may provide greater dynamic efficiency
* Show not only the great virtues of a perfectly competitive market, but also its limitations; in particular, be able to explain why an efficient outcome is not necessarily best, and why there are many possible efficient outcomes
* Explain why speculation sometimes benefits society, and why it sometimes damages society
* Explain why government agricultural support programs may improve efficiency by stabilizing prices, but may reduce efficiency if they stabilize prices and quantities at the wrong levels

HIGHLIGHTS OF THE CHAPTER

You sometimes hear it said that we should learn to cooperate more with each other rather than compete. But the economist will say that, on the contrary, competition is often the best method of ensuring harmony. This is the message of Adam Smith's "invisible hand," as described in Chapter 1. In pursuing our own self-interest, each of us is led by market forces—as if by an invisible hand—to promote the interests of others as well. In this chapter we show how this does indeed often happen in perfectly competitive markets. (In other markets, it often does not.) We also show that, even when they are efficient, perfectly competitive markets do have some shortcomings.

Perfect Competition and Allocative Efficiency

The core idea of this chapter is that, under certain conditions, perfectly competitive markets produce an efficient outcome. Consider first the concept of allocative efficiency, defined in Chapter 1. This requires that the marginal social cost of any activity be equal to its marginal social benefit—otherwise, a net gain can be acquired by changing the level of that activity. For example, if the marginal benefit of producing wheat is less than its marginal cost—that is, if the benefit of one more bushel of wheat exceeds its cost—then there is a net benefit from producing that additional bushel. The output of wheat should be increased. Moreover, it should continue to be increased until marginal benefit and cost are equal. Only then will the incentive for increasing output disappear; this output is efficient.

Under perfect competition, output is efficient because marginal social benefit (MB_S) and marginal social cost (MC_S) are equalized. The reason is that under perfect competition, supply equals demand. Supply reflects the marginal cost of producers and demand reflects the marginal benefit to consumers. Therefore, the equality of supply and demand means that the marginal cost of producers is equal to the marginal benefit to consumers. Provided these are the only benefits and costs—as carefully assumed in equations 26-1 and 26-2 of the text—it follows that the marginal cost to society is equal to the marginal benefit to society, and an efficient outcome results. Thus, in a perfectly competitive market, the pursuit by producers and consumers of their own private interest promotes the interest of society as a whole.

Figure 26-2 is particularly useful in clarifying this. In panel (*a*), consumers pursue their self-interest by responding as perfectly competitive price takers to the $10 market price. In panel (*b*), perfectly competitive producers pursue their self-interest by also responding as price takers

to the same $10 market price. The result in panel (*c*) is an efficient outcome for society as a whole. We emphasize that this occurs in perfect competition, because both producers and consumers are price takers, who respond to the same market price.

In succeeding chapters we will examine markets that, for one reason or another, are not efficient. One possible reason is that producers are not perfectly competitive price takers. A second reason is that consumers are not perfectly competitive price takers. In either case, the market is not perfectly competitive and, therefore, is inefficient. But sometimes a market is inefficient, even though it is perfectly competitive. There are two reasons. The first is that consumers are not the only ones to benefit from a good; there are benefits that go to others in society as well. (When you have landscaping done around your home, the benefits may go not only to you, but also to your neighbours, since they too will enjoy the improved appearance of your garden.) The second reason is that producers may not be the only ones who face a cost when a good is produced. (For example, those living downstream from a chemical factory face a cost when the factory dumps waste into a river.) Note that, in each case, inefficiency arises because of the violation of one of the key assumptions made in this chapter.

Perfect Competition and Other Kinds of Efficiency

Perfect competition also tends to promote technical efficiency. Technically inefficient firms that are operating above their AC curves aren't likely to survive competition with technically efficient firms that are operating on their AC curves.

The situation is different with respect to dynamic efficiency. Discovering innovations that generate economic growth is usually very expensive. The perfectly competitive firm may be too small to be able to afford such expenditures. Moreover, it has less incentive to undertake them; a farmer who discovers a new strain of wheat would find that most of the benefit would go to the millions of other farmers.

However, when innovations are discovered, they will be quickly adopted by perfectly competitive firms. These firms have no choice: If they don't make these changes, their competitors will drive them out of business.

Other Reservations about Perfect Competition

Efficiency isn't everything. There are problems that the perfectly competitive market doesn't solve. One is how the nation's income should be distributed. Perfect competition provides no answer here. The reason is that for every possible distribution of income there is a different perfectly competitive equilibrium. While each is efficient, the economist has no objective way of deciding which of these efficient outcomes is "best." This is an important point: Make sure you can explain it using Figures 26-1 and 26-6 in the textbook.

Another possible drawback of a perfectly competitive market is that it may be subject to severe fluctuations in price and quantity—especially when there is a time lag between the production decision and the delivery of the product to the market. In the case of the hog cycle, the text shows how the expectation that future price will be the same as today's price leads to cyclical fluctuations in price and quantity.

Speculation

The text describes how price fluctuations may be reduced by speculators. For example, if private speculators make accurate forecasts they will tend to iron out fluctuations in the market. They do this by buying when there is an oversupply (and thus keeping price from falling even more) and by selling when there is a scarcity (and thereby keeping the price from rising even higher).

A speculator who succeeds in this strategy will not only make a personal profit, but will also benefit society by helping to iron out the instability in this market. On the other hand, a speculator who gets it wrong—for example, one who buys when the good is cheap and is forced to sell when it is even cheaper—will lose money and will

damage society as well. But such individuals typically go out of business.

Another type of speculation that is against the public interest is the attempt to corner a market in order to reduce sales and thus raise price. The resulting contrived scarcity is damaging to society. There may also be costs to society even if those who are trying to corner a market don't succeed, if their purchases trigger severe price fluctuations. An example was the apparent attempt by the Hunt brothers to corner the silver market.

Farm Programs

Ideally, a government price-support policy can be viewed as playing the same socially desirable role that speculators play—that is, stabilizing by buying when the item is in oversupply and selling when it is scarce. In practice, it is not that simple. Just as speculators damage society when they err in their predictions, so, too, can the government. (Some would say that this problem is more serious for a government, since its decisions may sometimes be made by those without experience or talent in predicting the future.) Government price-support policies are also complicated because they are often used not just to stabilize price, but also to raise it. In this case, farmers may respond to an artificially high price by increasing their output above the efficient level (and the government may have to dispose of a surplus at bargain-basement prices in the world market). Alternatively, if the government limits the amount that each producer is allowed to put on the market, the result may be an output *below* the efficient level.

IMPORTANT TERMS: MATCH THE COLUMNS

Match each term in the first column with its corresponding explanation in the second column.

_____ 1. Allocative efficiency	**a.** The activity of buying and selling commodities with a view to profiting from future price changes. In perfectly competitive commodity markets, this tends to stabilize prices if forecasts are reasonably good.
_____ 2. Efficiency loss	
_____ 3. Speculation	
_____ 4. Cornering a market	
_____ 5. *Pareto optimum	**b.** Buying up enough of a commodity to become the single (or at least dominant) holder, and thus acquire the power to resell at a higher price
_____ 6. *Pareto improvement	
_____ 7. Technical inefficiency	
_____ 8. Moral hazard	**c.** A situation in which it is impossible to make anyone better off without making someone else worse off
_____ 9. Dynamic efficiency	
	d. The loss from producing an amount that is not efficient

* Starred terms are drawn from boxes, appendices, or optional sections of the text.

e. Any change that benefits someone, without making anyone else worse off

f. Running an activity at a level where marginal social cost equals marginal social benefit

g. Changes taking place at the best rate over time

h. Waste in the production process

i. The problem that arises when people who get insurance take less care in avoiding risk

TRUE-FALSE

T F   1. Perfect competition guarantees an efficient solution.

T F   2. For a good with external benefits, marginal benefit to buyers is less than marginal social benefit.

T F   3. The typical firm in perfect competition must strive to eliminate technical inefficiency because it could be driven out of business otherwise.

T F   4. For each distribution of income, there is a different efficient solution.

T F   5. The best possible distribution of income is the only distribution that can lead to an efficient outcome.

T F   6. The only efficient outcome is the one in which everyone receives the same income.

T F   7. The greater the cost of storing a good, the greater will be the gap in its price between two years.

T F   8. A speculator may try to corner a market in order to be able to create a future shortage and thus raise the price.

T F   9. For a good with external costs, marginal cost to producers is greater than marginal cost to society.

For those who have studied the appendices to Chapter 26:

T F   10. Canadian farm price supports provide a subsidy that is larger in dollar terms to the poor farmer than to the rich farmer.

T F   11. Producers maximize their income by producing at a point of tangency between their production possibilities curve and the highest income line they can reach.

MULTIPLE CHOICE

1. In a perfectly competitive market where supply equals demand, the marginal benefit of each consumer will

a. be greater than the marginal cost of each producer

b. be equal to the marginal cost of each producer

c. be less than the marginal cost of each producer

d. be less than the average variable cost of each producer

e. be less than the average fixed cost of each producer

2. A perfectly competitive market generates an efficient outcome if all but one of the following conditions holds. Which of the conditions below does not hold?

a. social costs are the same as private costs

b. social benefits are the same as private benefits

c. consumers equate marginal benefit and price

d. producers equate marginal cost and price

e. consumers equate marginal benefit and total cost

3. If more than the efficient output is being produced, then

a. marginal social benefit MB_S is equal to marginal social cost MC_S

b. MB_S is less than MC_S

c. MB_S is more than MC_S

d. MB_S is zero

e. MC_S is zero

4. To be efficient, a perfectly competitive market requires that

a. benefits from the good are widely dispersed among buyers and non-buyers

b. all benefits of the good go to its purchasers, with none going to others

c. costs of the good are borne by all producers and some non-producers

d. all costs of the good are borne by non-producers

e. costs of the good are borne by all members of society

5. If a firm is prevented from entering an industry

because of failure to obtain a government licence, then

  a. more will be produced at a higher price
  b. more will be produced at a lower price
  c. less will be produced at a lower price
  d. less will be produced at a higher price
  e. less will be produced at the same price

6. In a perfectly competitive market

  a. price is a rationing device that determines which buyers will acquire a good, and which sellers will produce it
  b. price is a rationing device that determines only which buyers will acquire a good
  c. price determines only which sellers will produce a good
  d. price determines neither the buyers nor the sellers of a good; price determines only how wealthy sellers will be
  e. none of the above

7. Perfect competition is superior to monopoly in terms of

  a. dynamic efficiency, but not necessarily allocative efficiency
  b. allocative efficiency, but not necessarily dynamic efficiency
  c. allocative efficiency, but not technical efficiency
  d. dynamic and technical efficiency
  e. dynamic and allocative efficiency

8. It is sometimes argued that perfect competition is inferior to other market forms in creating innovation because the typical small firm

  a. has an incentive, but not the funds to finance large R&D expenditures
  b. has lots of funds, but doesn't have an incentive to spend them on R&D, since it would gain only a small share of the benefits
  c. has neither the funds nor the incentive to spend them on R&D
  d. has both the funds and the incentive to spend them on R&D, but it is just mismanaged
  e. knows that once it has created an innovation, the government will not allow it to be widely applied

9. If we are initially in an efficient, perfectly competitive equilibrium, and we take income from Smith and give it to Jones, then

  a. the quantities of goods that each will acquire will remain unchanged
  b. there will be a move to a new, efficient equilibrium where Smith acquires fewer goods and Jones more
  c. there will be a move to a new, efficient equilibrium where Jones acquires fewer goods and Smith more

  d. there will be a move to a new, inefficient equilibrium where Smith acquires fewer goods and Jones more
  e. there will be a move to a new, inefficient equilibrium where Jones acquires fewer goods and Smith more

10. If the price in a hog cycle is

  a. low this year, then there will be decreased production, and price will be even lower next year
  b. low this year, then there will be increased production, and price will be even lower next year
  c. high this year, then there will be reduced production, and price will be even higher next year
  d. high this year, then there will be increased production, and price will be even higher next year
  e. high this year, then there will be increased production, and price will be lower next year

11. In a market with only a few sellers (when some have influence over price) which of the following efficiency conditions for perfect competition is violated?

  a. there are costs of a product to others than producers
  b. there are benefits of a product to others than buyers
  c. sellers equate their marginal cost and price
  d. buyers equate their marginal benefit and price
  e. none of the above

12. Speculation will be most effective in moderating a hog cycle if

  a. speculators buy pork when it is cheap and sell it when it is dear
  b. speculators sell pork when it is cheap and buy it when it is dear
  c. speculators buy pork when it is cheap and buy it again when it is dear
  d. speculators sell pork when it is cheap and sell it again when it is dear
  e. speculators lose money on the transaction

13. Suppose speculators buy in the first year and sell in the second. Then

  a. if price is higher in the second year, this speculation results in an efficiency loss for society, but a profit for speculators
  b. if price is higher in the second year, this speculation results in an efficiency gain for society, but a loss for speculators
  c. if price is lower in the second year, this speculation results in an efficiency loss for society, and a loss for speculators
  d. if price is lower in the second year, this

speculation results in an efficiency loss for society, but a profit for speculators

  e. if price is lower in the second year, this speculation results in an efficiency gain for society, but a loss for speculators

14. Speculation that stabilizes price and quantity
  a. is beneficial to society because goods are moved from a year of glut to a year of scarcity when they are valued more highly
  b. is beneficial to society because goods are moved from a year of scarcity to a year of glut when they are valued more highly
  c. is damaging to society because goods are moved from a year of glut to a year of scarcity when they are valued more highly
  d. is damaging to society for other reasons; supplies are not moved from one year to another
  e. has no effect on society

15. A perfectly competitive market is likely to rank
  a. high in developing new technology but low in adopting it
  b. low in developing new technology but high in adopting it
  c. low in both
  d. high in both
  e. high in neither

16. British deregulation of the London financial markets in 1986
  a. raised the cost of financial services
  b. left the cost of financial services unchanged
  c. made entry of new firms easier
  d. made entry of new firms more difficult
  e. had no effect on the entry of new firms

17. For a good with an external cost, the
  a. marginal benefit to society is more than the marginal benefit to buyers
  b. marginal benefit to society is less than the marginal benefit to buyers
  c. marginal cost to society is the same as the marginal cost to sellers
  d. marginal cost to society is greater than the

marginal cost to sellers
  e. marginal cost to society has an unknown relationship to the marginal cost to sellers

18. At a Pareto optimum
  a. it is possible to make someone better off without hurting someone else
  b. it is impossible to make someone better off without hurting someone else
  c. many Pareto improvements can still be made
  d. a few Pareto improvements can still be made
  e. none of the above

19. According to economists, moral hazard occurs when
  a. people stop celebrating religious holidays
  b. those who are insured become more careful in protecting themselves against risk
  c. those who are insured become less careful in protecting themselves against risk
  d. those who are insured don't change their attitude toward risk
  e. **a.** and **b.**

20. Cornering a market is
  a. selling a whole block of city property
  b. selling a large block of the common stock of a company
  c. selling enough of a good to be able to raise its price in the future
  d. none of the above
  e. all of the above

21. Marketing board quota systems
  a. are used primarily in deficiency payment programs
  b. are used primarily in price-support programs to ensure that there is enough production to meet export demand
  c. are used primarily in price-support programs to avoid costly surplus disposal
  d. require minimum production levels from each participating farmer
  e. are used to ensure that each province gets an equal share of total farm exports

EXERCISES

1a. Figure 26.1 shows the supply and demand for wheat. (This question also draws on Chapter 25.)

If the market supply curve is S, the equilibrium price is _____, and the equilibrium quantity is _____. Now suppose that the government imposes a sales tax t = JK = LM. The new equilibrium price is _____ and quantity is _____. The efficiency (gain/loss) is 10 + _____ because output has been (increased above/reduced below) its efficient level. Consumers (gain, lose) area _____, while producers

(gain/lose) area _____. The government (gains/loses) area _____. The difference between all the losses and all the gains is a (gain/loss) of area _____, which is recognized to be the _____.

1b. Now suppose that, instead of this tax, the government sets a floor price on wheat. It stands ready to buy whatever amount of wheat may be necessary to keep its price from falling below P_2. The new equilibrium price and quantity sold are _____ and _____. The public purchases quantity _____ while the govern-

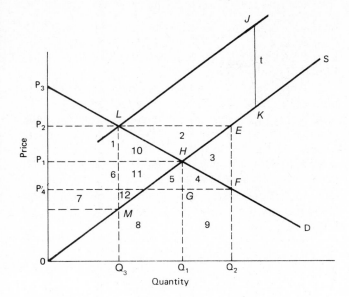

Figure 26.1

ment (buys/sells) quantity _____. The efficiency (gain/loss) is _____ because output has been (increased above/reduced below) its efficient level _____. The cost to the government of (increasing/decreasing) its stockpile of wheat is the rectangle with base _____ and height _____.

1c. Repeat question **b.**, assuming the government imposes a price floor at P_4.

2a. The purpose of this next exercise is to demonstrate the social benefit that can be produced by the existence of markets. Figures 26.2 and 26.3 represent the markets for a manufactured good in New Brunswick and Quebec.

Suppose that initially there was no trade between the two provinces; that is, no market in which people from one province could trade with people from the other. Then the equilibrium price in New Brunswick would be _____ and the equilibrium price in Quebec would be _____.

2b. Next, suppose that a group of traders organized a market in which Quebeckers could trade with New Brunswickers. Suppose that there were no transportation costs or any other kind of cost to separate the market of the two provinces. Then, there would be only one market that included both provinces. A single equilibrium price would be established such that the total amount supplied in the two provinces together was just equal to the amount demanded in the two provinces together (suppose no other provinces are involved). Therefore, the excess of supply over demand in one province must equal the shortfall in the other. In Figures 26.2 and 26.3 this equilibrium price is _____. At that price New Brunswick has an excess (demand, supply) of _____. This is an equilibrium price because the excess (supply, demand) of Quebec is _____, which is equal to the excess (supply, demand) of New Brunswick.

2c. As a result of trade between the two provinces, consumers in New Brunswick have realized a (gain, loss) of _____, producers in New Brunswick are (worse, better) off by _____ ; so the net (benefit, loss) to New Brunswick is _____.

2d. Consumers in Quebec have realized a (gain, loss) of _____, and producers in Quebec are (better, worse) off by _____. Therefore, the overall (gain, loss) to Quebec is _____.

These two triangles provide estimates of the gains to the two provinces from creating a market in this good.

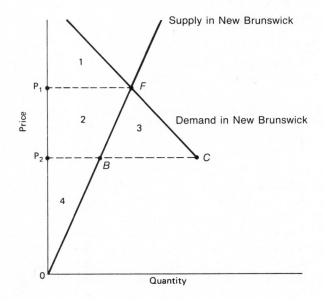

Figure 26.2

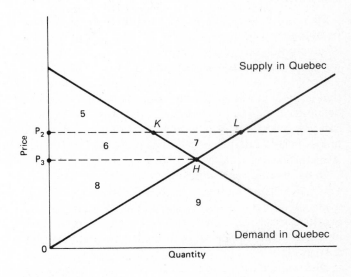

Figure 26.3

ESSAY QUESTIONS

1. In exercise **2.** immediately above, who would be the winners and who would be the losers from the opening up of trade between the two provinces? What sort of arguments do you suppose the losers might propose in favour of a government prohibition of such trade? How could these arguments be countered? Can you imagine any way in which the winners might compensate the losers? Would the total gain in each province be enough so that after such compensation everybody could end up a winner? Would this then be a Pareto improvement?

2. According to the economist's theory of how markets work, butchers provide the public with meat in an economically efficient manner, not because they hate to see people go hungry, but because they are interested in making as large a profit as possible. In this chapter we have seen that this is true in perfect competition where there are so many buyers and sellers that none can affect price. But is it true if there is a monopoly—that is, a single seller with power to raise price? Specifically, suppose there is a monopolist who raises price from P_1 to P_2 in

Figure 26.1 above. Is the outcome then an efficient one? Explain your answer.

3. Argue the case that perfect competition tends to promote at least two different kinds of efficiency.

4. Apply the analysis of this chapter to show in a diagram the triangular efficiency loss from a rent control policy.

5. Earlier we stated that the demand and supply of a product are defined in terms of a certain time and certain place. What is the "place," that is, the geographical extent of the market for the firms supplying the following items?

a. pastries

b. haircuts

c. copper

6. The text gave reasons that a perfectly competitive firm would not engage in much R&D expenditure. Is the same true of advertising expenditure? Explain why. Do you think it might make sense for all perfect competitors in an industry to advertise?

ANSWERS

Important Terms: **1**f, **2**d, **3**a, **4**b, **5**c, **6**e, **7**h, **8**i, **9**g

True-False: **1**F, **2**T, **3**T, **4**T, **5**F, **6**F, **7**T, **8**T, **9**F, **10**F, **11**T

Multiple Choice: **1**b, **2**e, **3**b, **4**b, **5**d, **6**a, **7**b, **8**c, **9**b, **10**e, **11**c, **12**a, **13**c, **14**a, **15**b, **16**c, **17**d, **18**b, **19**c, **20**d, **21**c

Exercises: **1a.** P_1, Q_1, P_2, Q_3, loss, 10 + 11 + 12, reduced below, lose, 1 + 10, lose, 6 + 7 + 11 + 12, gains, 1 + 6 + 7, loss, 10 + 11 + 12, efficiency loss **1b.** P_2, Q_2, Q_3, buys, Q_3Q_2, loss, 3, increased above, Q_1, increasing, Q_3Q_2, Q_3L **1c.** This floor has no effect because the market price is already above it **2a.** P_1, P_3 **2b.** P_2, demand, *BC*, supply, *KL*, demand **2c.** gain, 2 + 3, worse, 2, benefit, 3 **2d.** loss, 6, better, 6 + 7, gain, 7

ANSWERS TO SELECTED REVIEW QUESTIONS FROM THE TEXT

26-1. Regardless of which of the three firms reduces its output, it will move to the left along its supply curve where marginal cost is less than $10. Thus, the cost saving will be less than $10 per unit.

Regardless of the individual reducing consumption, that individual will have to move to the left up his or her demand curve. The loss in benefit, therefore, will exceed $10 per unit. Thus, this reduction in output will result in lost benefits that exceed cost savings. The difference is the efficiency loss.

26-4. New entrants will come in to produce at *G*, with a per unit economic profit of *GF* (since the price is *F*, while per unit cost is *G*). Industry supply increases, driving down price to *G*. Old firms can't remain in business unless they adopt the new technology, reducing their unit cost to *G*.

26-5. There would be a loss to speculators (since they would be selling it more cheaply than they bought it).

There would also be an efficiency loss.

26-6. (a) Inadequate fireproofing when houses are built, and insufficient fire protection once they are occupied.

(b) Inadequate stormproofing when houses are built, and they may be constructed in areas where the risks from storm damage (due to, say, flooding) is high.

(c) Inadequate care by the insured to avoid health risks to themselves and to their families.

(d) It appears that there would be very little moral hazard here. Who is going to risk his life to get insurance that he won't be around to spend?

An example of a case where insurance reduces the chance of an unfavourable outcome may be health insurance that encourages individuals to have regular checkups; this may lead to early detection and cure of disease that otherwise might have become serious.

Chapter 27

■ ■

Monopoly

MAJOR PURPOSE

We have now completed our analysis of one extreme of the market spectrum—perfect competition, where there is free entry and so many buyers and sellers that none can influence price. Our focus now turns to the other extreme: monopoly, where a single seller not only can influence price, but can actually determine it, subject only to demand conditions. The following questions will be addressed: Under what conditions does monopoly arise?

How does the monopolist's price and quantity compare with the perfect competitor's? How efficient is monopoly? What are the government's methods of controlling monopoly? Are there conditions under which a monopoly should be free not just to set its price, but to go beyond this to set several prices that discriminate between buyers?

LEARNING OBJECTIVES

After you have studied this chapter in the textbook and the study guide, you should be able to
- Explain four reasons that monopolies exist
- Describe the cost conditions that lead to a natural monopoly, and explain how, in these circumstances, competition will eliminate all firms but one
- Show why a monopolist's demand and marginal revenue are quite different from a perfect competitor's
- Explain how a monopoly can select its profit-maximizing output by equating its marginal cost and marginal revenue
- Demonstrate the alternative method of selecting this output by maximizing the rectangle defined between the firm's average cost and demand curves
- Show why a monopoly produces too low a level of output to achieve allocative efficiency
- Explain why the appropriate government policy toward collusive monopoly is to break it up or prevent it from being formed in the first place
- Demonstrate why marginal cost pricing is the appropriate government policy toward natural monopoly, provided it is feasible; and why, if it is not feasible, average cost pricing may be used
- Show why, in very special circumstances, price discrimination by a monopolist may benefit all concerned—both the producer and consumers of the product

If you have studied the appendix to Chapter 27, you should be able to
- Explain why, in some sectors of agriculture, the government has *helped* organize monopolistic marketing boards, and also describe some of the problems that this has created

HIGHLIGHTS OF THE CHAPTER

Discussion of the key questions follows:

Why Does Monopoly Exist?

Monopolies exist for any or all of the following reasons: (1) the monopoly may possess something valuable that is not available to a potential competitor (for example, some talent, property, or patent); (2) government may have created the monopoly by making competition illegal, as in the case of certain kinds of mail carried by the post office, or in some sectors of agriculture; (3) there may be a natural monopoly; or (4) the existing sellers may have colluded—that is, agreed to act in cooperation rather than competition.

The case of natural monopoly is perhaps the most important. It exists whenever there are economies of scale through a wide range—that is, whenever a firm has an average cost curve that continues to fall until its output becomes about large enough to satisfy the entire industry demand. (See panel (*b*) in Figure 27-1 in the textbook.)

How Does a Monopoly Maximize Its Profit, and How Do Its Price and Output Compare with a Perfect Competitor's?

A monopoly, just like a perfectly competitive firm, maximizes profit by choosing the level of output where its marginal revenue (MR) equals its marginal cost (MC). But, whereas the perfect competitor's MR equals the market price, the monopoly's MR is less than the market price; that is, its MR curve lies below its demand curve. This is because the perfectly competitive firm is so small in relation to the entire market that it doesn't have to take into account the minute effect that any increase in its own sales will have on the market price. Thus, such a firm effectively faces a horizontal demand curve. When the firm sells one more unit, its extra revenue MR is just the existing market price. Compare this to a monopoly, which is the only seller in the market: It has to recognize that the demand curve for its good slopes downward to the right. When this firm sells one more unit, it has to recognize that the price doesn't stay the same. Thus, the monopoly's extra revenue (MR) is the price that it receives from selling the extra unit, minus the loss it incurs because selling this extra unit lowers the price it receives for all the other units it sells in the market.

Since the monopoly's MR curve lies below its demand curve, it intersects the MC curve at a smaller output, as you can see in Figure 27-6 in the textbook. Thus, the monopoly exploits its advantage by reducing its output.

By making the product scarce, it is able to raise price.

Like the perfectly competitive firm, the monopoly produces where MR = MC only if it is able to cover its costs. This requires that the demand curve overlap the AC curve; that is, the demand curve must not always be below the AC curve.

Is Monopoly Efficient?

The efficient output is the one under perfect competition, where supply (MC) equals demand (the marginal benefit of this good). When competitors collude to form a monopoly, output is reduced because the new monopoly is equating MC, not with price, but instead with MR which is below the price (that is, below the demand curve). Because this reduces output below the efficient, perfectly competitive level, monopoly is inefficient. This is the main disadvantage of monopoly. But a complete verdict on any particular monopoly is not possible without also taking into account other factors such as the technical inefficiency that may exist because there is no competition to force the monopoly to fight rising costs. It is also necessary to take into account the transfer of income from consumers to the monopoly that results from the monopoly's higher price. Strictly speaking, we can't be sure whether this transfer is desirable or undesirable, because there is no objective way of comparing one person's gain with another's loss. However, it is often reasonable to assume that these transfer effects cancel; that is, each dollar transferred is valued as highly by the person losing it as the person receiving it. If this assumption is reasonable, then the efficiency loss of monopoly implies a welfare loss.

In the appendix, we discuss the case of agricultural marketing boards. To their critics, these boards should simply be interpreted as government-sanctioned collusive monopolies that keep farm prices high by restricting supply. Supporters of marketing boards claim that their principal effect is to *stabilize* the prices of agricultural commodities, not to raise them toward the level that an unregulated monopolist would set. Moreover, they often argue that marketing boards have favourable transfer effects, since they make it possible for smaller family-based farm operations to remain in business.

What Should Government Policy Be toward Monopoly?

To answer this question, it is first necessary to specify what sort of monopoly is being considered. If it is a collusive monopoly of firms that would otherwise be highly competitive, then the solution is to break up the monopoly—or, better still, prevent it from being formed in the first place. This is a problem of competition policy that is discussed in Chapter 29. On the other hand, if it is a natural monopoly because of extended economies of scale, then breaking it up is no longer a simple solution. The reason is that this policy would create smaller-volume firms, thereby raising costs of production; this would impose an unnecessary cost on society. The preferred approach in this case is to leave the firm as a monopoly and continue to benefit from its relatively low costs of production; at the same time, impose a government policy that forces the monopoly to act as though it were a price-taking perfect competitor. That is, take away its market power to raise its price by imposing a ceiling on that price.

The question is, at what level should that price be set? The simple answer is marginal cost pricing, shown in Figure 27-7 of the text; set the price at the efficient level where the marginal cost of producing this good (MC) equals the marginal benefit it provides—that is, the market demand.

Unfortunately, in many instances this policy is not feasible because forcing the price down this much would turn the monopoly into a money-loser, and drive it out of business in the long run. This is the case examined in Box 27-2, where the government would have to supplement marginal cost pricing with whatever subsidy would be necessary to keep the firm in business; or, equivalently, put the firm under government ownership and subsidize its operations in this way. A final often-used alternative is average cost pricing: Instead of driving the price all the way down to the level required by marginal cost pricing, drive it down only part way—specifically, to the level where demand intersects *average* cost rather than mar-

ginal cost. Because price equals average cost, the firm breaks even. It is not turned into a money-loser, and the problem of going out of business does not arise.

However, since price is reduced only part way, monopoly inefficiency is only reduced part way; it is not eliminated. There is also a problem which applies not only to average cost pricing, but also to marginal cost pricing—and indeed to any government policy to control natural monopoly. Firms lack adequate incentive to keep costs down: If their costs rise, they know that the government-administered price will rise, because price is tied to costs.

Price Discrimination

So far we have assumed that the monopoly charges a single price to all consumers. But the firm will usually find it more profitable if it can charge different customers different prices—that is, if it can divide its market and charge a higher price to the group of customers with less elastic demand than to those with more elastic demand. Such a pricing policy by a monopoly may be beneficial to all concerned if the firm would not otherwise exist. In that case, allowing the firm to discriminate may not only allow the firm to cover its costs, but also provide a benefit to consumers who would not otherwise be able to buy this product.

On the other hand, if a monopoly quoting a single price can exist, then price discrimination can no longer be defended in this way. In this case, it may be justified on other grounds, or it may not. A justified case is charging a higher toll on a highway in rush-hour periods of congestion. An unjustified case arises when a nationwide firm cuts its price in a region to bankrupt a small, emerging competitor in that region.

IMPORTANT TERMS: MATCH THE COLUMNS

Match each term in the first column with its corresponding explanation in the second column.

_____	1.	Natural monopoly
_____	2.	Market power
_____	3.	Marginal revenue
_____	4.	Price discrimination
_____	5.	Marginal cost pricing
_____	6.	Theory of the second best
_____	7.	Average cost pricing
_____	8.	Marketing board
_____	9.	Price maker
_____	10.	Economies of scope

a. A government-sanctioned agency set up to stabilize and/or raise the price of agricultural products

b. The theory of what constitutes an efficient level of output in one industry when, due to monopoly or for other reasons, the level of output in other industries is not efficient

c. The policy of regulating a monopoly's price by setting it at the level where the firm's average cost curve intersects the market demand curve

d. The ability of a seller or buyer to influence price

e. The practice of charging different prices to different customers for the same good; this is one method a monopoly may use to increase its profits or avoid a loss

f. A situation in which there are economies of scale (falling average costs) over such an extended range of output that one firm can produce the total quantity sold at a lower average cost than could two or more firms

g. The policy of regulating a monopoly's price by setting it at the level where the firm's marginal cost curve intersects the market demand curve

h. The additional revenue from selling one more unit of output

i. A monopoly firm that does not have to take price as given, but can instead set it

j. Reduced cost of existing products when new products are added to a firm's line

TRUE-FALSE

T F 1. An unregulated profit-maximizing monopoly will set a price where marginal cost intersects the demand curve.

T F 2. Oligopoly—a market dominated by a few sellers—is very rare compared to monopoly.

T F 3. A profit-maximizing monopolist will set a price above marginal cost.

T F 4. One cannot be certain that monopoly, with its efficiency loss, is damaging to society without taking into account the monopoly transfer of income.

T F 5. A likely disadvantage of breaking up a natural monopoly is that it will raise costs of production.

T F 6. One problem with government ownership or price regulation of a monopoly is this: Once the firm knows that the government will ensure that its costs are covered, the firm will have a reduced incentive to keep its costs down.

T F 7. If marginal cost pricing is feasible, it will eliminate the efficiency loss from a monopoly.

T F 8. Government fixing of a free market price may increase efficiency in one set of circumstances, but decrease it in another.

T F 9. Price discrimination is justified only if the monopolist is already earning at least a normal profit.

T F 10. If a monopoly is formed in a perfectly competitive industry, the resulting monopoly firm will act like a competitive firm.

MULTIPLE CHOICE

1. An example of a monopoly is
   a. the auto industry, while an example of an oligopoly is the steel industry
   b. the auto industry, while an example of an oligopoly is the local natural gas supplier
   c. the steel industry, while an example of an oligopoly is the local natural gas supplier
   d. the local natural gas supplier, while an example of an oligopoly is wheat production
   e. the local natural gas supplier, while an example of an oligopoly is the auto industry

2. A firm's minimum cost is $30, achievable at 1000 units of output. This firm will be a natural monopoly if the quantity demanded at a $30 price is about
   a. 1 million units
   b. 100 000 units
   c. 10 000 units
   d. 2000 units
   e. 1000 units

3. Economists define market power as
   a. the ability of a firm to influence federal anti-pollution legislation
   b. the ability of a firm to influence tax legislation in its home province
   c. the ability of consumers to purchase imports rather than domestically produced goods
   d. the ability of a firm to influence Supreme Court decisions
   e. none of the above

4. A monopoly's marginal revenue is
    a. always positive
    b. always above average cost
    c. equal to the height of its demand curve
    d. less than the height of its demand curve
    e. greater than the height of its demand curve
5. Which of the following faces a completely elastic demand?
    a. Ontario Hydro
    b. an individual apple grower
    c. General Motors
    d. Air Canada
    e. an urban transit company that is not subject to government price regulation
6. The demand facing a monopoly is
    a. the same as the total market demand
    b. to the right of total market demand
    c. to the left of total market demand
    d. completely elastic
    e. more elastic than the total market demand
7. At the equilibrium output of an unregulated monopoly, marginal revenue is
    a. less than marginal cost
    b. more than marginal cost
    c. more than market price
    d. equal to market price
    e. less than the market price
8. An unregulated monopoly is inefficient because it equates
    a. marginal cost with demand rather than with marginal revenue
    b. marginal revenue with demand rather than with marginal cost
    c. marginal revenue with average cost rather than with marginal cost
    d. average cost with demand rather than with marginal revenue
    e. marginal cost with marginal revenue rather than with demand
9. If the monopolist is producing more than the profit-maximizing amount, then
    a. marginal revenue will exceed price
    b. marginal cost will exceed price
    c. marginal cost will exceed marginal revenue
    d. average cost will exceed price
    e. marginal revenue will exceed average cost
10. If a monopoly is maximizing profit, then the marginal cost of producing one more unit is
    a. equal to its marginal benefit to society
    b. more than its marginal benefit to society
    c. less than its marginal benefit to society
    d. less than its marginal benefit to the monopoly firm
    e. more than its marginal benefit to the monopoly firm

11. If a perfectly competitive industry is monopolized, the result is
    a. higher output and lower price
    b. higher output and the same price
    c. higher output and higher price
    d. lower output and higher price
    e. lower output and lower price
12. The profit rectangle for a monopoly is its quantity of output times
    a. the monopoly's average cost
    b. its price
    c. its price less its average cost
    d. its marginal cost
    e. its price less its marginal cost
13. Monopoly often results in
    a. allocative efficiency
    b. technical inefficiency
    c. allocative inefficiency
    d. a. and b.
    e. b. and c.
14. When a regulatory agency controls a monopoly by marginal cost pricing, the monopoly's
    a. price is reduced
    b. output is reduced
    c. profit is eliminated
    d. level of efficiency remains the same
    e. all of the above
15. Which of the following makes zero profit?
    a. an unregulated monopoly charging a single price
    b. an unregulated, price-discriminating monopoly
    c. a monopoly regulated by marginal cost pricing
    d. a monopoly regulated by average cost pricing
    e. a monopoly regulated by variable cost pricing
16. The theory of the second best tells us that monopolizing one industry in an economy where monopoly exists elsewhere will
    a. reduce efficiency
    b. increase efficiency
    c. have no effect on efficiency
    d. have an uncertain effect on efficiency
    e. lower price in that industry
17. Government marginal cost regulation of monopoly is designed to induce the firm to
    a. act like a perfect competitor by reducing output
    b. act like a perfect competitor by taking price as given
    c. produce to the point where above-normal profit finally disappears
    d. produce to the point where normal profit finally disappears
    e. reduce price while holding its output constant

18. A product is not being provided because the potential producer is a monopoly whose demand lies below its average cost curve AC. This problem may be solved by permitting the firm to discriminate and thus
   a. at least cover its costs
   b. shift its demand above its marginal cost curve
   c. shift its demand above its average variable cost curve
   d. shift its AC curve down so it overlaps demand
   e. shift its demand above its AC curve

19. A government-sanctioned marketing board that is introduced into a competitive agricultural industry will
   a. typically set quotas to ensure that producers will increase their sales
   b. typically set quotas to ensure that producers will reduce their sales
   c. typically set quotas to ensure that producers will maintain their previous sales levels
   d. not set quotas, but will encourage producers to sell more
   e. encourage the entry of new firms

20. If a discriminating monopolist charges a higher price to the group with the more elastic demand than to the group with the less elastic demand
   a. its profit will increase
   b. its profit will decrease
   c. its profit will remain unchanged
   d. its profit will be zero
   e. **c.** and **d.**

EXERCISES

1a. If the monopoly shown in Figure 27.1 is unregulated, it will maximize profits by selecting output _____ where _____ equals _____. The price it will quote is _____, the highest price at which this output can be sold. Its profit will be _____ for each of the units it sells, that is, a total profit of area _____. An alternative view of its decision is that it selects the point _____ on the _____ curve that maximizes this profit rectangle. The efficiency (gain, loss) is _____.

1b. A government regulatory agency that uses marginal cost pricing will set price equal to _____. The firm will respond in the short run by producing _____ output because this is where its _____

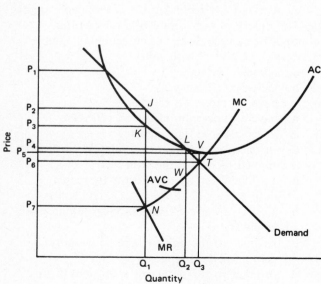

Figure 27.1

curve cuts the price line at P_6. However, in the long run, the firm would produce an output of _____ because at equilibrium T it is operating at a (profit, loss) of _____. To keep it in business the government would have to (provide a subsidy, impose a tax) of _____. This policy would (reduce, increase, eliminate) the previous efficiency loss of _____ ; that is, it would improve efficiency by _____.

1c. If the agency were instead to use average cost pricing, it would set price at _____. The monopolist would produce output _____ and earn a profit of _____. The subsidy now necessary to keep this firm in business would be _____. This policy would reduce the efficiency loss from the original JTN to _____, that is, it would improve efficiency by _____. Compared to marginal cost pricing, this average cost pricing policy improves efficiency (more, less); but it avoids the government problem of having to (subsidize, tax) this firm.

1d. With either form of regulation, the monopoly is forced to act like a (perfect competitor, oligopolist, natural monopolist) facing a fixed price.

2a. A monopoly has the demand and total cost figures shown in Table 27-1. Fill in this table, ignoring for now the last three columns.

The monopoly's fixed cost is _____. It will choose to produce a level of output equal to _____ and charge a price equal to _____. Its maximum attainable profit is _____.

2b. Suppose that, in an attempt to capture some of this monopoly's profits for the taxpayer's benefit, the government imposes a lump-sum tax of $5. This tax may be regarded by the monopoly as a fixed cost, because it must be paid no matter how much output is produced. After the imposition of this tax, the monopoly's fixed

Table 27.1

P	Quantity demanded	Total revenue	Marginal revenue	Total cost	Average cost	Marginal cost	Profit	(1) Net profit with lump-sum tax	(2) Net total revenue with ex-cise tax	(3) Net profit with ex-cise tax
$10	0	$0	$0	$ 2	$ -	$0	$	$	$	$
8	1	8		3						
6	2			6						
4	3			11						
2	4			18						

cost is _____. Fill in (1), the third-last column, that indicates the monopoly's after-tax profit. After imposition of the tax, the monopoly will choose to produce an output equal to _____ and to charge a price equal to _____. Its maximum attainable after-tax profit will be _____.

2c. Suppose that instead of the lump-sum tax, the government decides to impose a 50% excise tax on the monopoly. In other words, the monopoly must now pay the government 50% of its total revenue. In this case, the monopoly's fixed cost is _____. Fill in the second-last column (2), showing the monopoly's after-

tax total revenue, and the last column (3), showing its after-tax profit. In this case, the monopoly will choose to produce an amount of output equal to _____, and to charge a price equal to _____. Its maximum attainable after-tax profit will be _____. The amount of excise tax collected from this monopoly will be _____.

2d. From the point of view of economic efficiency the (lump-sum, excise) tax is preferable. From the point of view of maximizing the amount of tax revenue collected from the monopoly, the (lump-sum, excise) tax is preferable.

ESSAY QUESTIONS

1. Are economies of scale a barrier to entry? Explain. Is IBM a monopoly? A perfect competitor? Or in a dominant position somewhere in between? Do you think economies of scale give it an advantage over potential competitors?

2. Compare a monopoly and a perfectly competitive firm in terms of (1) their demand and marginal revenue schedules, (2) their market power, (3) their efficiency, and (4) the appropriate government policy in dealing with each.

3. "Allowing a monopolist to charge some customers more than others is not appropriate because it is unfair to those who have to pay the higher price." Evaluate this statement. Are there any circumstances in which those who pay the higher price could actually benefit?

4. Suppose the only two firms in an industry are considering a merger that would result in a reduction in costs of production through the elimination of wasteful dupli-

cation. Is it possible to argue that this government action could increase efficiency? If so, how? Might it decrease efficiency? If so, how?

5. A perfectly competitive firm can sell all it wants at the existing price. Can a monopoly do that? If it tried to, what would happen? Does that mean that a monopoly is more constrained in its decision making than a perfect competitor?

6. Recall our discussion of the elasticity of demand from Chapter 21. If a monopoly's demand function is elastic, then what happens to its total revenue as its output increases? In this case, what can be said about the monopoly's marginal revenue? If the market demand is inelastic, what can be said about the monopolist's marginal revenue? In view of this, explain why a monopoly that has discovered that its demand curve is inelastic would want to change its output.

ANSWERS

Important Terms: **1**f, **2**d, **3**h, **4**e, **5**g, **6**b, **7**c, **8**a, **9**i, **10**j
True-False: **1**F, **2**F, **3**T, **4**T, **5**T, **6**T, **7**T, **8**T, **9**F, **10**F
Multiple Choice: **1**e, **2**e, **3**e, **4**d, **5**b, **6**a, **7**e, **8**e, **9**c, **10**c, **11**d, **12**c, **13**e, **14**a, **15**d, **16**d, **17**b, **18**a, **19**b, **20**b
Exercises: **1a.** Q_1, MC, MR, P_2, JK, P_2JKP_3, J, demand, loss, JNT **1b.** P_6, Q_3, MC, zero, loss, P_5VTP_6, provide a subsidy, P_5VTP_6, eliminate, JNT, JNT **1c.** P_4, Q_2, zero, zero, LWT, $JLWN$, less, subsidize **1d.** perfect competitor

Table 27.1   completed

P	Quantity demanded	Total revenue	Marginal revenue	Total cost	Average cost	Marginal cost	Profit	(1)	(2)	(3)
$10	0	$ 0	$ 0	$ 2	$ -	$0	$ − 2	$ − 7	$0	$ − 2
8	1	8	8	3	3	1	5	0	4	1
6	2	12	4	6	3	3	6	1	6	0
4	3	12	0	11	$3^{2}/_{3}$	5	1	− 4	6	− 5
2	4	8	− 4	18	$4^{1}/_{2}$	7	− 10	− 15	4	− 14

2a. $2, 2, $6, $6 **2b.** $7, 2, $6, $1 **2c.** $2, 1, $8, $1, $4 **2d.** lump-sum, lump-sum

ANSWERS TO SELECTED REVIEW QUESTIONS FROM THE TEXT

27-1. (a) Rolls Royce. It's easy to find a substitute for a Volkswagen, but much more difficult to find a substitute for a Rolls Royce.

(b) The small town producer. In the absence of much competition, this firm may exercise considerable influence over price. The wheat farmer can exercise none.

27-3. (a) Not necessarily. If there is a labour union, it may well acquire some of this profit by negotiating for a higher wage; and the owners of a resource this firm requires may be able to increase the price they charge.

(b) Regulate price where MC intersects demand. This is best because MC = D, the marginal benefit to society.

27-4. Profit maximization involves maximizing the difference between TR and TC—that is, maximizing the vertical distance between the TR and TC curves. This is accomplished at the output where the two curves have the same slope. Since the slope of TR is MR, and the slope of TC is MC, the firm will therefore equate MR and MC.

27-6. (a) P_1

(b) P_3 where AC intersects D. Profit is zero because AC is equal to P_3.

(c) P_2 (See Figure 27-7 in the textbook.)

P_1 is not efficient, because it generates output Q_1, which is less than the efficient output Q_2. P_3 is not efficient, because it corresponds to output Q_3, which is more than the efficient output of Q_2.

27-7. No. By reducing output slightly, the monopoly can increase its per unit profit. However, total profit will shrink, because fewer units will be sold.

27-8. We agree with the first two sentences. We disagree that the government should control rents because apartment units are sold in a highly competitive market (almost perfect competition, but not quite).

27-9. Condition (26-4) is violated because price is Q_1E_1 while marginal cost is the much smaller Q_1T.

27-10. (a) The firm's loss L is minimized in Figure 27.2 below by setting price at P_A and selling Q_A.

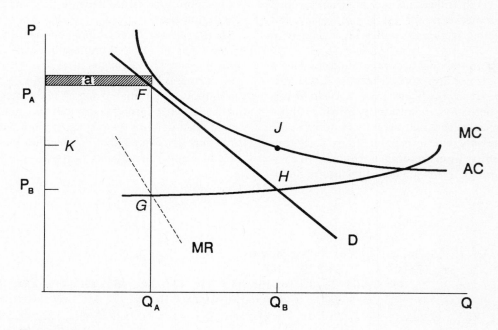

Figure 27.2

(b) No; it results in efficiency loss *FGH* because the firm is equating marginal cost MC to its own marginal benefit (MR), rather than to society's marginal benefit (*D*). The most efficient output level is Q_B, where marginal benefit to society (*D*) equals marginal cost (MC). While this eliminates the efficiency loss, it raises a problem: To reach this quantity of output, the firm would have to set price at P_B and incur an even greater loss (P_B *HJK*) than before.

(c) In Figure 27.3 below, it sets price of P_C on the first Q_C units it sells, and P_B on the rest. It sells the efficient quantity Q_B; but, because it is charging a higher price for the first Q_C units than before, it has increased its revenue by P_C *LMP*$_B$. This reduces its loss, or perhaps even provides it with a profit.

(d) Yes; it is the way to get an efficient output level, while cutting down the cost to the taxpayer of subsidizing the utility.

(e) In theory, public utilities could discriminate between buyers in, say, a wealthy area and a poor one. In practice, the electrical firm may discriminate in its dealings with each customer by charging a high rate on initial purchases, and a lower rate on purchases above a certain volume. Or, it may discriminate by charging all customers a higher price during periods of high demand.

27-11. Price should be set in each case where MC intersects demand. This yields a profit for the firm in Figure 27-7 in the text, and a loss in Figure 27-8. This profit and loss could cancel; it's not clear that any subsidy would be required if the two firms are merged into one.

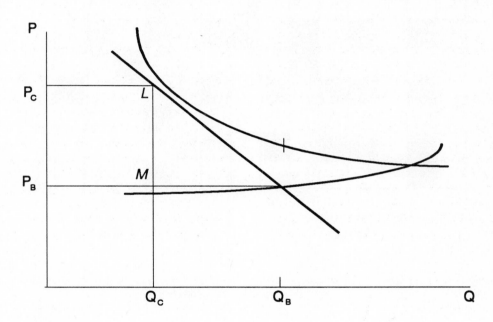

Figure 27.3

Across

1, 4. If perfect competition is to be efficient, this must equal the benefit to consumers.

7. indefinite article preceding vowel

8. _____ what?

9. major department store chain

10. business owned by a group of consumers or producers (abbrev.)

12. something that is true

14. king (French)

15. A dry _____ consists mostly of gin.

19. To maximize profits, a firm equalizes this and marginal cost. (2 words)

21. southern American state (abbrev.)

22. fate

24. university degree

25. muse of history

26. preposition

27. poor

28. really great!

31. conjunction

33. not just apparent

35. industries with only one seller

36. to keep flowers in

38. written reminders

39, 40. the increase in variable cost when one more unit is produced

Down

1. buy or sell in the hope of profiting from a change in price

2. automobile

3. Monetary and fiscal policy should be used to avoid this in our economy.

4. sound of disapproval

5. This exists when we get the most out of our resources.

6. explosive substance (abbrev.)

8. Marginal private benefit is not always the same as marginal _____ benefit.

11. With perfect competition, this is what all buyers and sellers are. (2 words)

13. when sellers get together to fix price

17. natural logarithm (abbrev.)

18. the best we can do when there are immutable imperfections in the market (2 words)

20. a very deep hole

22. a type of efficiency

23. breastbone

29. association of workers

30. thing (Latin)

31. A famous battle took place here during the Mexican-American War.

32. last name of famous Swedish tennis player

34. with (French)

37. signal for help (abbrev.)

Chapter 28

■ ■

Markets Between Monopoly and Perfect Competition

MAJOR PURPOSE

The last two chapters have described the two extremes in the spectrum of markets: perfect competition, where there are so many sellers that none has any influence over price; and monopoly, where the single firm is free to set any price it chooses, since it has no competitors to worry about. (A monopoly is restrained only by consumer demand and the possibility of government intervention.) Most Canadian industries do not conform to either of these two extremes, but lie somewhere in between where individual firms have *some* influence over price. The objective in this chapter is to analyse some of the market forms that lie within this intermediate range. We begin with monopolistic competition, the market closest to perfect competition, and then work our way toward monopoly by considering markets with fewer and fewer firms. Thus, we describe oligopoly, a market with several firms, and then duopoly, a market with only two.

In monopolistic competition—as in perfect competition—there are a large number of sellers and free entry into the market. However, monopolistic competition differs from perfect competition because each firm produces a differentiated product, and this gives each firm some small degree of influence over price.

Oligopoly is a market dominated by a few sellers, in which (in the absence of government intervention) there is a strong incentive for firms to collude in order to act like a monopolist and raise price. The most prominent example of such collusive behaviour is described in this chapter: the Organization of Petroleum Exporting Countries (OPEC) which raised oil prices by more than ten times in less than a decade.

In duopoly, there are only two firms. The importance of how your competitor may react becomes paramount, and game theory will be used to highlight that issue.

LEARNING OBJECTIVES

After you have studied this chapter in the textbook and the study guide, you should be able to
- Clearly distinguish between perfect competition, monopolistic competition, oligopoly, duopoly, and monopoly
- Explain why the run-of-the-mill firm earns no above-normal profits in the long run in monopolistic competition, and why this market form is not necessarily inefficient, even though fewer firms could produce the same output at lower costs
- Give two reasons why oligopoly may arise
- Describe why economies of scale and advertising create barriers to entry
- Explain why oligopolists have an incentive to collude, and the effect such collusion will have on efficiency
- Explain why the OPEC countries were able to collude to raise the price of oil during the 1970s without imposing formal production quotas and why they at least tried to set formal production quotas in the 1980s
- Describe the kinked demand curve with a diagram
- Explain why the kinked demand curve would discourage an oligopolist from changing price frequently

• Explain the concept of price leadership, how it relates to the analysis of kinked demand, and why it is often viewed as "tacit collusion"
• Give three examples of non-price competition
• Summarize the arguments for and against advertising
• Describe game theory and explain why it may be useful in analysing duopoly
• Explain why the outcome of a game may be influenced by such factors as (i) how easy it is for a player to cheat on a prior understanding and (ii) whether or not the game is repeated
• Describe a contestable market and why this concept is important

HIGHLIGHTS OF THE CHAPTER

In this chapter we discuss monopolistic competition, oligopoly, and duopoly—three of the "imperfectly competitive" market forms that lie between the extremes of monopoly and perfect competition.

Monopolistic Competition

This is closest to perfect competition. In monopolistic competition, as in perfect competition, there is a large number of firms. There is also free entry of firms into the industry, which means that any short-run excess profit for the run-of-the-mill firm will be eliminated in the long run. The important difference between the two market forms is this: Under monopolistic competition, a firm produces a differentiated product and, therefore, faces a downward-sloping demand curve. Under perfect competition, the firm produces a standardized product and faces a completely horizontal demand curve. Because the sloping demand curve gives a firm in monopolistic competition some influence over price, the firm quotes a higher price and, therefore, produces a smaller output than a perfectly competitive firm that cannot raise its price. This restricted output suggests that monopolistic competition is inefficient, but this is not necessarily the case. Lower output by each firm means more firms are satisfying total market demand. Thus, the consumer can choose from a wider range of differentiated products. This wider choice may more than make up for the disadvantage of lower output by each firm.

Oligopoly: A Market with a Few Sellers

The smaller the number of sellers, the greater the market power (the influence over price) that can be exercised by each firm. Thus, the first task is to define the degree of concentration of the industry. This has traditionally been measured by the proportion of the industry's output produced by the four largest firms. More recently,

another measure, called the Herfindahl-Hirschman index, often is used instead because it takes into account all firms in the industry—not just the four largest.

An oligopoly can arise because an industry is a "natural oligopoly" in which the lowest-cost way of satisfying market demand is with a small number of firms. Alternatively, firms may combine or grow large, not because of cost conditions but, instead, because they seek to acquire market power.

Because there are few clear-cut principles governing the behaviour of oligopolists, the theoretical analysis is not as straightforward for oligopoly as it is for many other market forms. But the following points are important:

1. There is a tendency for oligopolists to collude—that is, to act like a monopolist and raise price so as to maximize the total profits of the industry. To maintain the high price, the product must be made scarce. Therefore, each colluding firm is required to restrict its output to a certain quota level. This reduction in output leads to the same sort of efficiency loss as in the case of monopoly. However, it is precisely this reduction in the output of each firm that creates a tendency for collusive arrangements to break down; each firm is asked to reduce its output when it has an incentive to produce more. The reason the individual firm would like to produce more is that, at its restricted level of output, the firm's marginal cost is still below its price. Therefore, it has an incentive to increase its output, if it can get away with such cheating. But if firms do cheat by producing more than their quota of output, the high price cannot be maintained, and the collusive arrangement comes apart.

2. When the oligopolistic firm makes a change in, say, its price, it must take into account the possible reaction of its rivals—something that need not even be considered by a monopolist (with no rivals) or a perfectly competitive firm (whose rivals don't even notice what it's doing). This sort of complicated decision making is what makes the theory of oligopoly so interesting and difficult.

3. Oligopolistic firms sometimes face a *kinked demand curve*. If one firm raises its price, its rivals won't. Instead, they'll hope to capture some of its sales. But if the firm lowers its price, its rivals will follow suit to avoid being undersold. In such circumstances, the firm is facing the kinked demand curve shown in Figure 28-6 of the textbook; it is unlikely to change its price from the kinked level unless underlying cost conditions change a great deal. While the theory of kinked demand is controversial as an explanation of how firms behave, it is very useful in making clear the issues that firms must deal with in making their decisions. For example, the kinked demand analysis in Figure 28-6 can be modified slightly to explain price leadership.

4. In an industry with price leadership one firm takes on the role of being the leader in announcing a price change, on the understanding that other firms will follow. This sort of "gentlemen's agreement" has often been criticized as a collusive arrangement, with the price leader setting the price at about the level that a monopolist would select. However, it is only "tacit collusion" because there is no communication between the firms and it is, therefore, very difficult or impossible to prove that collusion has taken place. (Selling at the same price is not proof of collusion because, after all, that is what perfectly competitive firms do.)

5. Oligopolists who wish to avoid potentially destructive price competition have other options (in addition to tacit collusion in the form of price leadership). They can attempt to increase their market share by various forms of *non-price competition*, such as advertising or R&D expenditure to improve product quality. Advertising, in particular, is controversial. On the one hand, it may involve wasteful competition, distort people's values, and mislead consumers. On the other hand, it may make consumers better informed and help to promote product quality by making firms fearful of losing the good will that they achieve through advertising. Moreover, it provides financial support for the media.

6. Oligopolists often succeed in erecting barriers to entry against new competitors. One such barrier is advertising, which creates a favourable image of an existing firm that is difficult for new firms to overcome. But the most important barrier to entry may be economies of scale that leave room for only a few low-cost firms in the industry.

OPEC: An Example of Oligopoly Collusion

In many ways, the most interesting and far-reaching example of a collusive oligopoly has been the Organization of Petroleum Exporting Countries, OPEC. This collusive arrangement succeeded in quadrupling oil prices in 1973/74, and again doubling them in 1979/80. This was even more remarkable because, during the 1970s,

OPEC did not have to rely on the formal quotas on output that are typically required to keep price up and ensure that the collusive arrangement won't come apart. One of the reasons for this was the dominant role of the Saudi Arabians in producing world-traded oil. For many years they could keep the price up by restricting just their own very large output.

However, by 1985 the Saudis' production had been so far reduced in the attempt to maintain price, that they were unwilling to continue to do this. They turned up their pumps and the price of oil fell sharply, to less than $10 a barrel, compared to the high of $32 a barrel three years earlier. This made other OPEC countries recognize the importance of abiding by quotas. The question is: Will they?

Duopoly: The Insights of Game Theory

In most oligopoly markets, a key issue is "How will competing firms react?" In duopoly, this becomes of paramount importance. Game theory is designed to deal with this issue, and the text provides an example of how it can be applied. In this example, the two firms are both far worse off if they both cut their price than if they both do not. It's in their collective interest not to. The problem is that it's in the individual interest of each of the firms to cut price and capture market share from the competitor. Game theory describes the possible outcomes, which depend on such questions as:

1. Is the game repeated? If it is, then the best strategy may be to "stand pat." Avoid price cutting on the first play of the game, in order to increase the chance of avoiding a mutually destructive price war. Stand pat in the hope your competitor will do the same; don't cut your price until your competitor does.

2. How much can each firm trust the other? The more trust there is (that is, the more each firm can trust the other not to cut price) the more reasonable it is for each to refrain from price cutting.

3. How long does it take for cheating (price cutting) to be detected and for the other firm to retaliate? The shorter the time period, the less likely it is for either firm to cheat.

Don't Just Count Numbers: The Concept of Contestable Markets

Even if there is only one firm in an industry, it cannot act like a monopolist if the market is *contestable*, and new firms can freely enter and leave. Then any attempt by the firm to increase price and profit will be met by the free entry of new competitors, and any new excess profit will be competed away.

IMPORTANT TERMS: MATCH THE COLUMNS

Match each term in the first column with its corresponding explanation in the second column.

_____ 1. Oligopoly
_____ 2. Concentration ratio
_____ 3. Natural oligopoly
_____ 4. Product differentiation
_____ 5. Cartel
_____ 6. OPEC
_____ 7. Kinked demand curve
_____ 8. Price leadership
_____ 9. Barrier to entry
_____ 10. Monopolistic competition
_____ 11. Contestable market
_____ 12. Payoff matrix

a. The practice in some oligopolistic industries of having one firm announce its price change first, on the unspoken understanding that other firms will follow suit
b. The ability of each firm to distinguish its product from those of its rivals. Such distinctions may be real or imagined
c. A market dominated by only a few sellers
d. A market in which there is (a) a large number of firms, (b) free entry of new ones, and (c) differentiated products. The demand curve facing each seller is quite elastic, but not completely so.
e. The proportion of an industry's output produced by the four largest firms (or, using an alternative measure, by the eight largest firms)
f. Anything that makes it difficult for new firms to enter an industry to compete against existing firms
g. Any formal agreement among firms to collude in order to set price and/or determine market shares
h. An industry in which total market demand can be satisfied at lowest cost by a few firms
i. The demand curve that will face an oligopolist if its rivals will follow it if it cuts its price, but will not follow it if it increases its price
j. A specific example of a cartel
k. Table showing the outcomes of a game
l. A market in which free entry makes even a monopolist act like a perfect competitor

TRUE-FALSE

T F 1. Monopolistic competition is similar in many respects to perfect competition; but one important difference is that the product is differentiated.
T F 2. Because consumers like variety, we cannot conclude that monopolistic competition is inefficient.
T F 3. The concentration ratio is relatively low in the auto industry.
T F 4. Colluding firms in a cartel typically have an incentive to cheat by producing less than their quotas.
T F 5. All cartels, regardless of where they may exist, are illegal.
T F 6. A large firm, acting as a price leader, may decide not to retaliate against a small firm that has cut price, for fear that this may initiate a price war with other large firms.
T F 7. Price leadership may be a disguised method of collusion.
T F 8. The kinked demand curve arises mainly in monopolistic competition.
T F 9. The theory of the kinked demand curve doesn't predict the price where the kink will occur.
T F 10. All barriers to entry take the form of economies of scale.
T F 11. Duopoly firms have an individual and collective interest in cutting price if their situation is similar to the prisoners' dilemma.
T F 12. A stand-pat, collusive outcome becomes more likely if a duopoly game is repeated.

MULTIPLE CHOICE

1. Product differentiation by a firm occurs:
   a. only in perfect competition
   b. only in monopoly
   c. in monopoly and perfect competition
   d. in monopolistic competition
   e. in all market structures

2. In the long run, a firm in monopolistic competition will:
   a. face a perfectly elastic demand curve
   b. produce more than the amount that minimizes average cost
   c. produce less than the amount that minimizes average costs
   d. produce the amount that minimizes average costs
   e. earn an above-normal profit

3. In monopolistic competition:
   a. there is a standardized product, just as in perfect competition
   b. there is a standardized product, unlike the differentiated product in perfect competition
   c. entry of new firms is restricted, unlike the free entry that exists in perfect competition
   d. entry of new firms is restricted, just as in perfect competition
   e. there is a large number of sellers, just as in perfect competition

4. In monopolistic competition:
   a. there are very few sellers
   b. it is impossible for new firms to enter the market
   c. firms sell differentiated products
   d. all of the above
   e. none of the above

5. The feature of monopolistic competition that drives a firm's profits to zero in the long run is:
   a. production differentiation
   b. price leadership
   c. market power
   d. free entry
   e. collusion by sellers

6. A firm's minimum cost is $10, achievable at 20 000 units of output. The industry will be perfectly competitive if the total quantity demanded of this product at a $10 price is:
   a. 1 million units
   b. 100 000 units
   c. 40 000 units
   d. 20 000 units
   e. 10 000 units

7. If oligopolistic firms collude to raise price:
   a. each benefits, while there is an overall loss to the economy as a whole
   b. the price leader benefits, while the other firms and the economy as a whole lose
   c. each firm and the economy as a whole benefit
   d. each firm benefits, while the economy as a whole is not affected
   e. each firm and the economy as a whole lose

8. In the North American market for passenger vehicles, General Motors is a:
   a. monopolist
   b. duopolist
   c. oligopolist
   d. monopolistic competitor
   e. perfect competitor

9. A high concentration ratio in an industry typically indicates that:
   a. the dominant firms in the industry have a great deal of market power
   b. no firms in the industry have much market power
   c. no firms in the industry have any market power
   d. the industry is monopolistically competitive
   e. the industry is perfectly competitive

10. Between 1975 and 1985, Canadian industry became:
    a. less competitive, because of the decline in international trade
    b. more competitive, because of the decline in international trade
    c. less competitive, because of the growth in international trade
    d. more competitive, because of the growth of international trade
    e. more competitive, despite the decline in international trade

11. The Herfindahl-Hirschman index for an industry where one firm produces 80% of the industry output and the other two produce 10% each is:
    a. 0.84
    b. 6600
    c. 0.88
    d. 8800
    e. 1.0

12. The biggest surprise about OPEC is that it:
    a. survived for many years without a formal set of production quotas
    b. did not increase the price of oil when it had an opportunity to do so in 1973/74
    c. has made no further price increases since its spectacular success in 1973/74
    d. has been able to prevent any price reduction since 1973
    e. includes only countries from the Middle East

13. The success of the OPEC cartel in the 1970s and early 1980s was in substantial part due to:
  a. strong cultural ties among the member countries
  b. the strong sense of political unity among the member countries
  c. close social ties among the member countries
  d. all of the above
  e. the willingness of the Saudis to cut back their production

14. If a firm is at the kink in its demand curve and it raises its price, then:
  a. it will lose market share, but only to those competitors that follow its price increase
  b. it will lose market share to those competitors that don't follow its price increase
  c. its market share will not be affected
  d. its market share will increase
  e. its market share will increase, but only at the expense of those competitors that follow its price increase

15. If all firms sell at the same price:
  a. there must be price leadership
  b. there must be some other form of collusion
  c. the industry must be perfectly competitive
  d. the industry must be an oligopoly
  e. none of the above

16. The growing importance of international trade has:
  a. made Canadian firms more competitive
  b. made Canadian firms less competitive
  c. not affected the competitiveness of Canadian firms
  d. made domestic concentration ratios more meaningful
  e. **b.** and **d.**

17. Price leadership:
  a. only occurs when there is heavy advertising in an industry
  b. is a means of achieving "orderly" price changes in an oligopolistic industry
  c. indicates which senior executive within a firm will make pricing decisions
  d. frequently occurs in perfect competition
  e. frequently occurs in a monopolized industry

18. The kinked demand curve:

  a. helps to explain why oligopoly price has some degree of stability
  b. leaves unanswered the question of how price is established in the first place
  c. is based on the assumption that if a firm lowers its price, its competitors will follow
  d. is based on the assumption that if a firm raises its price, its competitors won't follow
  e. all of the above

19. Which of the following is not true about advertising?
  a. it may involve waste
  b. it may mislead consumers
  c. it provides financial support for the media
  d. it may help to promote product quality by making firms fearful of losing good will
  e. it is often undertaken by single firms in a perfectly competitive market

20. In a contestable market:
  a. there is a single firm which can act as a monopolist
  b. there is no free entry
  c. the potential entry of new firms increases the market power of the existing firm
  d. the potential entry of new firms has no effect on the market power of the existing firm
  e. if there is a single firm, it cannot act as though it is a monopolist

21. A payoff matrix shows:
  a. the difference between duopoly and oligopoly
  b. the difference between duopoly and monopolistic competition
  c. the difference between oligopoly and monopolistic competition
  d. the definition of duopoly
  e. how the outcome in duopoly depends on the policy selected by each firm

22. Once firms recognize that a game is to be repeated:
  a. the chance of a collusive, stand-pat outcome decreases
  b. the chance of a collusive, stand-pat outcome increases
  c. the chance of a collusive, stand-pat outcome is left unchanged
  d. both firms will lower their price
  e. both firms will increase their output

EXERCISES

1a. In Figure 28.1, D represents the total market demand for an industry, with MR_I being the marginal revenue curve that corresponds to D. (For any demand curve, there exists a marginal revenue curve.) MC_A and AC_A are the cost curves for firm A, one of the 5 identi-

cal firms in this industry. Draw in the marginal cost curve for the industry, and label it MC_I. Label point R, where MC_I and D intersect, and point S, where MC_I and MR_I intersect. Label as Z the point directly above S on the demand curve.

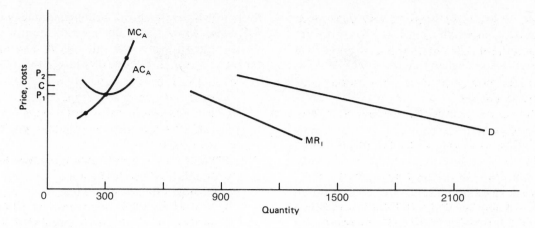

Figure 28.1

If these firms act like perfect competitors and take price as given, then MC_I becomes the industry (demand, supply) curve, and the industry equilibrium is at point _____. _____ units are sold at price _____, with each firm earning a profit of _____.

1b. Now suppose these firms collude to maximize their collective profit, which they will do by equating MC_I and _____, at an output of _____ units. They will sell this output for price _____. That is, the industry will select its profit maximizing point _____ on the demand curve D. Since industry output has been reduced from _____ to _____ units, the output of each individual firm, such as A, must be reduced by the same proportion, from _____ units to _____. Draw in point T, which is the equilibrium for firm A, where this firm is now selling _____ units at price _____. Label as V the point on AC_A directly below T. Shade in the new profit area _____ of firm A.

By colluding, these 5 firms have each (increased, decreased) their profit from _____ to _____. At the same time, the nation as a whole has (lost, gained) because of the efficiency (loss, gain) of area _____ that results because output has been (reduced, increased) to the (efficient, inefficient) level of _____ units from the (efficient, inefficient) level of _____ units where the marginal benefit to society shown by curve _____ equals the marginal cost to society shown by curve _____.

2a. Figure 28.2 shows an oligopoly which, along with all its rivals, is currently charging price P and producing quantity Q. This firm faces the kinked demand curve that consists of the segment of D_A above the existing price P and the segment of D_B below the price P. The respective marginal revenue curves are MR_A and MR_B.

If the firm increases its output to more than Q, it faces demand curve _____, and its MR curve is therefore

(MR_A, MR_B). But if it decreases its output to less than Q, if faces demand curve _____, and its MR curve is therefore (MR_A, MR_B). Therefore, its complete MR curve is (MR_A, MR_B, *WXYZ*).

2b. If its MC is MC_1, then it will charge a price that is (more than, less than, the same as) P, and it will choose a quantity that is (more than, less than, the same as) Q.

2c. If its MC is MC_2, then it will charge a price that is (more than, less than, the same as) P, and choose a quantity that is (more than, less than, the same as) Q.

2d. If its MC is MC_3, then it will charge a price that is (more than, less than, the same as) P, and choose a quantity that is (more than, less than, the same as) Q.

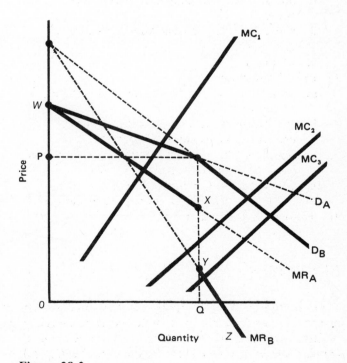

Figure 28.2

2e. If its MC is MC$_2$, we now see why the kinked demand curve results in a stable price. If MC$_2$ shifts up, but still intersects the vertical segment XY, then the firm will (raise, lower, leave unchanged) the price. Alterna-tively, if MC$_2$ shifts down, still intersecting XY, the firm will (raise, lower, leave unchanged) the price. In other words, marginal cost can shift up or down within the range _____ without affecting price at all.

ESSAY QUESTIONS

1. Firms in monopolistic competition have some influence over price. Why don't they use this influence to raise price above average costs and, therefore, make an above-normal profit in the long run?

2. Will firms in an industry with a high concentration ratio be more or less likely to engage in collusive activity than those in an industry with a low concentration ratio? Why?

3. Oligopoly is a market with a few sellers. But how many is a few? Does it matter if there are 4 or 14? Why? To be specific, compare the situation of an individual Canadian firm if

(a) it has only 3 Canadian competitors, versus

(b) a situation in which it has the same 3 Canadian competitors, plus 2 Japanese competitors, 4 U.S. competitors, and 2 other foreign competitors.

Would the Canadian firm have the same market power in either case? Would firms be equally able to collude, tacitly or explicitly?

4. Explain why a group of oligopolists might have trouble establishing a collusive price agreement, and then have trouble keeping the agreement from coming apart.

5. It is often argued that advertising increases sales, and this permits lower prices to consumers. Explain the circumstances in which this could occur. Also explain the circumstances in which advertising would increase prices to consumers.

6. What industry characteristics distinguish oligopoly from monopoly? from perfect competition?

7. Explain some of the techniques oligopolists use to avoid price competition.

8. If it is in the collective interests of 2 duopoly firms to avoid price cutting, how can it be in the individual interest of each to engage in price cutting?

ANSWERS

Important Terms: 1c, 2e, 3h, 4b, 5g, 6j, 7i, 8a, 9f, 10d, 11l, 12k

True-False: 1T, 2T, 3F, 4F, 5F, 6T, 7T, 8F, 9T, 10F, 11F, 12T

Multiple Choice: 1d, 2c, 3e, 4c, 5d, 6a, 7a, 8c, 9a, 10d, 11b, 12a, 13e, 14b, 15e, 16a, 17b, 18e, 19e, 20e, **21e, 22b**

Exercises: **1a.** supply, R, 1500, P$_1$, zero **1b.** MR$_1$, 1000, P$_2$, Z, 1500, 1000, 300, 200, 200, P$_2$, P$_2$$TVC$, in-creased, zero, the shaded area, lost, loss, ZSR, reduced, inefficient, 1000, efficient, 1500, D, MC$_1$

Figure 28.1 completed

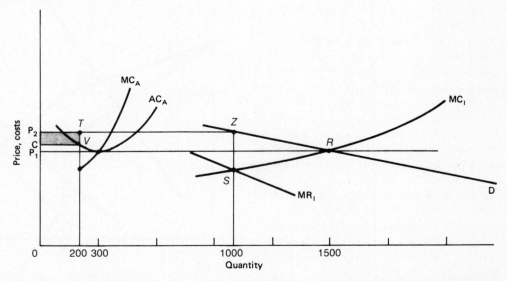

2a. D$_B$, MR$_B$, D$_A$, MR$_A$, $WXYZ$ **2b.** more than, less than **2c.** the same as, the same as **2d.** less than, more than **2e.** leave unchanged, leave unchanged, XY

ANSWERS TO SELECTED REVIEW QUESTIONS FROM THE TEXT

28-2.(a) (i) $^{100}/_{10\,000}$
    (ii) $^{100}/_{3333}$
    (iii) $^{100}/_{3750}$

(b) HHI is better because it takes account of all firms, not just the four largest. Moreover, in part (a) above, it is clear that it does a better job even when there are not more than four firms in an industry. The industry in (iii) is more concentrated than the industry in (ii) because it has a dominant firm. But you wouldn't know this from the four-firm concentration ratio, which is 100 in both cases.

28-4. (a) Again, see the pros and cons of advertising in the text. To the degree that advertising just shifts customers from one firm to another (and perhaps back again), it is a waste in either industry. In such circumstances, the information provided by either tobacco or liquor companies seems to have little or no value, unless you are prepared to argue that people feel better because they are using a brand that someone in the media has told them is highly desirable.

However, advertising also leads to greater total consumption, in the case of either tobacco or alcohol. It is here that advertising is costly, since greater consumption is related to higher health care costs.

The agreement among tobacco companies to voluntarily restrict advertising may have raised total industry profits, since it eliminated the need for each company to advertise in order to offset the impact of the others' advertising.

28-5. This regulation has had much the same effect from an economic point of view as past restrictions by organized medicine (the American Medical Association, Canadian Medical Association) on the supply of doctors. It holds the price of legal services up and, consequently, less than the efficient quantity of legal service is purchased. You can judge for yourself the argument that such a floor on fees has improved the quality of legal service. ("Lawyers who don't cut prices don't have to cut down on the services they provide.") In our view, there is something in this argument, but it tends to be overstated.

Lawyers are likely to approve of such a regulation because it keeps their fees up. They may also support it because they believe it improves the quality of legal services.

28-6. (a) This would reduce the OPEC supply onto the world market and thus drive price up.

(b) This would reduce the supply and drive price up.

(c) This would drive the world price down because OPEC would be under pressure to reduce its price.

(d) This would reduce the demand for OPEC oil and thus lower its price (that is, the world price). Indeed, it could make the price reduction even more severe if OPEC members felt under increasing pressure to engage in competitive price reductions.

(e) Far less effect on price, if any. Such discoveries might simply add to Saudi Arabia's already existing excess capacity. (But greater Saudi excess capacity would increase its ability in the future to hold back a rapid price increase by producing enough to create a glut.)

(f) It is possible that the Saudis might retain the role of residual supplier in order to maintain price. In this case, there might be little or no change in the price of oil. The other possibility is that the Saudis might abandon any attempt to keep world price up, and increase their supply. Then, world price would fall.

(g) The OPEC countries would have less incentive to keep a large quantity of their oil in the ground. (By 2010, it will no longer be as valuable a commodity.) In other words, they would want to sell more oil now, and this would be likely to lower its price.

(h) This would reduce U.S. demand for OPEC oil, with effects similar to those outlined in (d).

28-7. Confessed. If each can be convinced of this, he will have nothing to lose by confessing—and a gain in the form of a shorter jail term. Thus each will confess. (Another motive: each will feel he has been double-crossed, and will confess to get even.)

As long as each thinks the other has not confessed, then he will have at least some incentive to do the same, in the hope that if they can maintain their agreement, they will be able to keep the jail sentence to both down. (He may also not want to break an agreement. There may be, indeed, honour among thieves.)

28-9. They would jointly maximize profit if they could get an agreement to keep price up that each would stick with (quadrant I). The pressures that would make this difficult—and would almost certainly lead them to forget about the agreement and engage in price competition—are (1) the fact that such an agreement is against the law, and (2) each firm would have an economic incentive to cheat, even if the agreement were legal.

Part Eight

Economic Efficiency: Issues of Our Time

Chapter 29

■ ■

Government Regulation of Business

MAJOR PURPOSE

This chapter begins Part 8, in which a number of markets are examined to see how well they work. When they don't work well, what sort of government intervention is appropriate? For example, Chapter 29 describes government competition policy to safeguard the public interest when there is a threat by firms to collude in order to restrain trade or monopolize an industry. Chapter 30 demonstrates how a free market may do an inadequate job of protecting our health, safety, and the environment; and how the government is justified in intervening to provide such protection. Sometimes, government intervention also may be justified in order to prevent our resources from too rapid depletion (Chapter 31) and to provide public goods that free markets fail to provide (Chapter 32). Finally, the last two chapters in Part 8 (Chapters 33 and 34) deal with the great debate: What are the gains from international trade and should the government intervene to restrict that trade? Although there are some situations in which such intervention is justified, the broad conclusion is that, with some exceptions, international markets work reasonably well, and there has been too much government intervention in this area in the past. In this context, we also discuss an issue that has been at the centre of the Canadian economic policy debate in recent years: What the effects are likely to be of the Canada/United States free trade agreement.

Chapter 29, to which we now turn, deals with two broad types of government regulation of business:

1. Competition laws that prevent collusion and other restraints to trade. While such laws are necessary, their application is critically evaluated by posing such questions as: Should mergers between large firms be discouraged even though they may create economies of scale and reduce the average cost of production?

2. Regulation of naturally competitive industries, such as trucking and the airlines, where government regulation in the past has not *removed* restraints on trade, but instead has created them. Certain types of government intervention of this form have often been hard to justify, and there is now a trend, in both Canada and the United States, toward deregulation of these industries.

LEARNING OBJECTIVES

After you have studied this chapter in the textbook and the study guide, you should be able to
- Identify and briefly describe the legislative act that forms the cornerstone of Canada's competition policy
- Explain why it may be advantageous to have large-size firms, and why legal rules that discourage formation of large firms may involve costs as well as benefits
- Explain why competition from foreign sellers reduces the ability of large Canadian firms to exercise market power in the markets for Canadian-produced goods
- Show how economic efficiency may be promoted if the government on the one hand allows natural monopolies to exist (subject to international competition or price regulation), while on the other hand it uses competition policy to prevent the formation of collusive monopolies
- Give several reasons that "market-structure" regulation of naturally more competitive industries tends to be in the interest of the firms being regulated, rather than in the interest of consumers or the nation as a whole

- Explain the two important reasons that it is feasible for a government agency to cartelize an industry, but why it is not possible for a private group of producers to do so
- Explain how provincial trucking regulations have affected the interests of (1) established trucking firms, (2) the nation as a whole, (3) shippers on truck routes with high traffic volumes, and (4) shippers in small communities with low traffic volumes. (In explaining (3) and (4), use the concept of cross-subsidization.)

HIGHLIGHTS OF THE CHAPTER

This chapter focuses on several ways in which the government regulates business.

Competition Legislation

The first category of regulation consists of legislation designed to prevent business practices that reduce competition. This legislation, which was revised in the 1980s, is contained in the Competition Act, which has its roots in laws going back as far as 1889. The main provisions in the Act relate to:

1. *The prohibition of collusive agreements* among firms to fix prices or limit production. (Although agreements among firms that reduce competition are generally detrimental to the public interest, there are other kinds of agreements that can be beneficial. The Competition Act lists certain kinds of agreements that are permitted or even encouraged, such as agreements to share research and development (R&D) expenditures or to limit advertising and promotional expenditures.)

2. *Merger and abuse of dominant position.* The purpose of these sections, which were substantially revised in the mid-1980s, is to make it illegal for a firm to create a monopoly position for itself by various forms of cut-throat competition to drive its rivals out of the market or, in some cases, by buying out competing firms.

With respect to mergers between large firms, the Act specifies that they must first be approved by the *Competition Tribunal*, which must decide whether the merger would, on balance, be against the public interest, or whether factors such as improved scale economies and better international competitiveness are sufficiently important so that the merger should be allowed to go ahead, even though it may substantially increase a firm's share of the Canadian market.

3. The prohibition of *price discrimination*; that is, making it illegal for a seller to charge different prices to buyers who buy goods of like quality and in the same quantity.

4. Prohibiting *resale price maintenance*; that is, making it illegal for a manufacturer to force retailers to charge a minimum price for the manufacturer's product.

5. Outlawing *misleading advertising* and prohibiting certain forms of tied selling.

The primary objective of provisions (1) and (2) is to reduce restraint on trade and the abuse of market power by monopoly and oligopoly firms. The main tactic is to prevent a single firm or group of firms from attaining a dominant position in the market. However, a policy of preventing any one firm from becoming large enough to dominate the market may carry a cost, because size has advantages:

1. Large firms can better afford the (R&D) expenditures that generate growth and technological improvements. Large firms also have *more incentive* to undertake R&D expenditures, because their large market share allows them to capture a large share of the benefits from any new technique or product they may develop. For example, if Northern Telecom develops a superior office telephone system, it will acquire millions of dollars of benefits from this in its huge sales of telephone equipment, so it can justify this sort of R&D. However, a Manitoba farmer can't justify a similar R&D expenditure to develop a better strain of wheat; the benefits to him would be limited to a few thousand dollars, while the millions of dollars of additional benefit would be spread among thousands of wheat farmers.

2. Because of economies of scale, large firms may enjoy lower costs per unit than smaller firms; this point was demonstrated in the case of natural monopoly in Chapter 27.

In a country with relatively small domestic markets, these advantages of large firm size effectively compel the government to allow firms to have a relatively large share of many markets. However, there are some ways in which the government may lessen the ability of such firms to exploit their potential market power.

First, for goods that can be transported long distances relatively easily, the government may make sure that domestic firms are subject to competition from foreign firms by not restricting imports of foreign goods into Canada. For goods and services that cannot be transported as easily, the small size of the market may mean that the industry comes close to being a natural monopoly. In such industries, the government's best policy *may* be to let a single firm monopolize the market. The problem with this second solution, of course, is that despite its cost advantage, a natural monopoly left unregulated will produce the efficiency loss that we studied in Chapter 27. Consequently, the policy needs to be supplemented by price regulation (or by government ownership) of natural monopolies. As we have seen, this sort of regulation is imperfect, and government ownership may have problems of its own. Thus, in practice, it might even make sense sometimes to prevent the formation of a natural monopoly, despite its economies of scale, as a way of eliminating all these problems of regulation.

The enforcement of competition legislation is a very difficult task—in part, because it is not easy to distinguish anti-competitive efforts from the normal efforts of business firms to compete in the marketplace. Consider, for example, cut-throat competition—when firms set a price below cost in order to drive competitors out of business. A problem in trying to deal with cut-throat competition is that it is never clear whether a firm is setting its price below costs because it is trying to cut the throats of its competitors, or because it is just trying desperately to make sales in a weak market—perhaps in the face of stiff foreign competition.

A second example is the objective of preventing firms from colluding to "cartelize" an otherwise competitive industry. Collusion, like cut-throat competition, is difficult to establish in the courts. For example, the fact that all firms in an industry are charging the same price doesn't prove that there has been a conspiracy to fix prices, because uniformity of price occurs in a perfectly competitive market in which there is no collusion whatsoever.

The Canadian courts' interpretation of the restrictive wording in the "collusive agreements" and "monopoly and merger" sections in the Combines Investigations Act (the predecessor of the 1986 Competition Act), coupled with the fact that under earlier legislation, the burden of proof was mostly on the prosecution, made it hard for the government to get convictions in the past. However, under the terms of the Competition Act, enforcement is easier because most competition legislation has been put under the rules of civil law rather than criminal law.

Market Structure Regulation

The textbook discusses market structure regulation mostly in terms of the example of Canada's trucking industry, which has been regulated since the 1930s, even though it certainly is not an industry with a natural monopoly. (Why not?)

The regulation of trucking had its origin in the increasing competition that trucking firms were offering the (already regulated) railroads, as more efficient trucks and better roads were being built in the 1920s and 1930s. The government authorities who were regulating rail transport had required the railroad companies to maintain rail service to small, remote communities even though it was unprofitable for the railroads. In return, the authorities had allowed the railroads to charge high freight rates and earn high profits on short-haul, high-volume freight. (This illustrates the use of *cross-subsidization* as a regulatory technique; the authorities were forcing the railroads to use the high profits from the high-volume routes to subsidize the low-volume service they were forced to maintain in small communities. But the high rail freight rates on the high-volume routes made it easier for trucking firms to take business away from the railroads on those routes by offering lower rates.) For this reason, the railroad companies were campaigning vigorously for regulation of trucking. The trucking firms themselves also wanted regulation of their own industry, since they were now competing not just with the railroads but also with other trucking firms.

In the mid-1980s, all provinces except Alberta had extensive legislation regulating things like entry of new trucking firms, the routes that each firm might serve, the allowable frequency of service to various communities, and types of freight that firms were allowed to carry; some provinces also regulated the rates that trucking firms were allowed to charge. Studies undertaken for the Economic Council of Canada have shown that this type of complicated network of regulation was very costly. In addition to the costs of administering the system (which are borne by the provincial taxpayers), the licensing system sometimes forced the firms to operate in inefficient ways, with high freight rates to consumers and lower profits for the firms as a result.

Price and entry regulation in industries that by themselves would be relatively competitive is not confined to trucking. Other examples include the radio and television industry and the taxi industry. Another area where regulation has become very extensive is that of government licensing and certification requirements for specific occupations; government regulation of pricing and production in agricultural markets has also grown rapidly in recent years.

By the mid-1980s, many types of regulation were coming under increasing criticism in both Canada and the United States, and steps were taken to reduce the extent of regulation in a number of sectors. In the United States, the airline industry became deregulated as early as 1979; in the late 1980s, regulation of air travel was substantially reduced in Canada as well. Federal regulations of railroad freight rates were eased, and an agreement was struck between the federal and provincial governments providing for reduced regulation of trucking as well.

Not everyone was happy with these trends. For example, some argued that deregulation was leading to both crowded skies and crowded airport terminals, making air travel both less safe and less convenient. But the benefits to the public, in the form of lower air fares and freight rates, were also becoming evident and, in the early 1990s, there was little support for proposals to return to the restrictive regulatory regimes of earlier decades.

IMPORTANT TERMS: MATCH THE COLUMNS

Match each term in the first column with its corresponding explanation in the second column.

_____ 1. Cut-throat competition
_____ 2. Price leadership
_____ 3. Price discrimination
_____ 4. Tying contract
_____ 5. Resale price maintenance
_____ 6. Horizontal merger
_____ 7. Vertical merger
_____ 8. Conglomerate merger
_____ 9. Natural monopoly regulation
_____ 10. Entry regulation
_____ 11. Cross-subsidization

a. Charging one group of customers more in order to help finance service to another group of customers
b. The union of firms in the same competing activity
c. Fixing by a manufacturer of the price that retail stores can charge for its product
d. The practice in some oligopolistic industries of having one firm announce its price changes first, on the understanding that other firms will follow suit. Such a practice is sometimes suspected of being a form of "tacit" or silent collusion, in which the initial firm sets approximately the same price that a cartel would set.
e. The union of firms in unrelated activities
f. A contract which requires purchasers to buy other items in a seller's line in order to get the items they really want. (sometimes called full-line forcing)
g. Charging different prices to buyers who buy goods of like quality and quantity
h. Regulation of trucking is an example
i. Pricing below costs in order to drive competitors out of business
j. The union of a firm and its supplier
k. Setting the price that can be charged by an electric power company or a telephone company

TRUE-FALSE

T F 1. Following the introduction of the Competition Act in 1986, most of Canada's competition legislation has been made part of our criminal rather than civil law.

T F 2. Predatory or cut-throat pricing is defined as setting price above average cost, but still low enough to put competing firms under pressure.

T F 3. Preventing the merger of two firms in an industry that is a natural monopoly will help maintain lower average costs of production.

T F 4. Tied selling is the requirement that purchasers buy a whole line of items in order to get the one they really want. The Competition Act outlaws certain forms of tied selling.

T F 5. So long as the acquiring firm offers to buy the target firm's stock, the management of a target firm will support the merger.

T F 6. Free access of Canadian buyers to imported substitutes for domestically produced goods reduces the market power of large Canadian firms that have a large share of the domestic market.

T F 7. All takeover bids will be resisted by target companies.

T F 8. In merger cases, the rule followed by the Competition Tribunal is to disallow all mergers that would cause the Herfindahl-Hirschman index of the industry to rise above 1000.

T F 9. In the mid-1980s, the freight rates charged by trucking firms in Alberta (where there was no trucking regulation) were substantially higher than in other provinces.

T F 10. A merger that increases the market power of the new firm will automatically be disallowed by the Competition Tribunal.

T F 11. Under cross-subsidization, the price to one group is raised so that better service or reduced price can be provided to another group.

MULTIPLE CHOICE

1. In recent years, the market power of large Canadian corporations has
   a. decreased because of the growth of foreign competition
   b. decreased because of the decline of foreign competition
   c. increased because of the growth of foreign competition
   d. increased because of the decline of foreign competition
   e. been unaffected by changes in foreign competition

2. Cut-throat competition is
   a. pricing above cost to drive competitors out of business
   b. pricing at cost to drive competitors out of business
   c. pricing below cost to drive competitors out of business
   d. decreasing advertising in order to put pressure on competitors
   e. restricting sales in order to put pressure on competitors

3. Which of the following is *not* dealt with in the Competition Act?
   a. collusive agreements
   b. misleading advertising
   c. cross-subsidization
   d. resale price maintenance
   e. price discrimination

4. Under the rules of the Competition Act, a merger between two large firms
   a. can't be approved if the new firm's share of the Canadian market will be more than 15%
   b. requires approval by Parliament
   c. requires approval by Cabinet
   d. all of the above
   e. none of the above

5. Government action to prevent the formation of a natural monopoly may
   a. restrict benefits from economies of scale
   b. increase benefits from economies of scale
   c. increase benefits from the law of diminishing returns
   d. decrease benefits from the law of diminishing returns
   e. have no economies-of-scale effect

6. Under Canadian law, the prices charged by manufacturers and wholesalers when they sell their products to large retail chains
   a. are required to be higher than when they sell to small retailers, to offset the large chains' cost advantage
   b. are required to be lower than when they sell to small retailers
   c. are required to be the same as when they sell to small retailers
   d. are only allowed to be lower than when they sell to small retailers if the large chains are buying goods of lower quality
   e. none of the above

7. The increasing strength of foreign competition in Canada has meant that enforcement of the legal provisions relating to merger and "abuse of dominant position" in the Competition Act has become
   a. illegal
   b. more necessary
   c. less necessary
   d. neither more nor less necessary
   e. more necessary in some respects, but less in others

8. Under the Competition Act's rules concerning mergers, the Competition Tribunal is *least* likely to approve a merger between two firms
   a. when both firms are small
   b. when one of the firms is large and the other is small
   c. when the two firms face intense competition from imports
   d. when one of the two firms is threatened by bankruptcy
   e. if there are no significant scale economies in the industry

9. Even though the Competition Act prohibits firms in most industries from making agreements to limit production and fix prices, provincial egg marketing organizations are allowed to limit the amount that individual egg farmers may produce and to fix the price at which eggs are sold to retailers. This is legal because
   a. the Act does not apply to a regulated industry
   b. egg marketing boards have a natural monopoly in the egg production industry
   c. if egg production were not limited, the quality of rural life would suffer because of the overpowering smell of chicken manure
   d. Canadian courts have ruled that the egg marketing arrangements do not ''unduly'' limit competition
   e. the price fixing applies only to egg exports, not to eggs sold in the domestic market

10. An example of collusion is
    a. an agreement to fix price
    b. an agreement to restrict sales
    c. an agreement to rig bids
    d. all of the above
    e. none of the above

11. An example of collusion that is beneficial for society as a whole might be
    a. an agreement by producers to reduce sales
    b. an agreement by chemical firms to cooperate in developing pollution-control devices
    c. an agreement by buyers to rig bids
    d. an agreement by producers to fix price
    e. all of the above

12. The practice of price leadership
    a. makes tacit collusion difficult to detect
    b. is practised by monopolies
    c. is practised only under perfect competition
    d. is used primarily in cut-throat competition
    e. is never practised by oligopolists

13. A merger of a firm and its supplier is called
    a. a vertical merger
    b. a horizontal merger
    c. a conglomerate merger
    d. a direct merger
    e. an indirect merger

14. In a takeover bid by firm A for firm B
    a. both the management and stockholders of B are almost certain to welcome the bid
    b. both the management and stockholders of B are almost certain to oppose the bid
    c. the managers may oppose it, even though the stockholders welcome it
    d. the managers of firm A typically employ their golden parachutes
    e. firm A usually regards firm B as a black knight

15. Greenmail is
    a. the premium paid by a target firm to buy its own stock from a shark
    b. the premium paid by a shark to buy its own stock from a target company
    c. the price reduction a private firm enjoys when it buys its own stock from a shark
    d. the price reduction a shark has to accept when it sells the target firm's stock
    e. none of the above

16. Which of the following is an example of an industry or profession with price and entry regulation in most places in Canada?
    a. the market for legal services
    b. radio and television broadcasting
    c. the taxi business
    d. milk production
    e. all of the above

17. Regulation of radio and television broadcasting by the Canadian Radio-television and Telecommunications Commission
    a. encourages competition by restricting the entry of new firms
    b. encourages competition by allowing the entry of new firms
    c. discourages competition by allowing the entry of new firms
    d. discourages competition by restricting the entry of new firms
    e. has no effect on competition because it prevents new firms from entering cities that are already served by a radio or television station

18. A cartel organized by a regulatory agency is easier to operate than a cartel in an unregulated industry because in the regulated industry
    a. the quotas are imposed by law and the firms are immune from prosecution
    b. the firms are free to engage in non-price competition
    c. the interests of the public are being served when the industry is regulated
    d. regulated firms are not forced to cross-subsidize the consumers of unprofitable lines
    e. entry of new firms is encouraged

19. Regulation of trucking in most Canadian provinces tends to benefit
    a. the established trucking firm and the nation as a whole
    b. the nation, but not the established trucking firm
    c. the established trucking firm, but not the nation
    d. neither the established trucking firm nor the nation

e. potential new trucking firms and the economy as a whole

20. The American experience with airline deregulation suggests that the safety of all travellers taken together may have *increased* because

   a. it raised airline fares and thus induced Americans to switch from planes to safer cars

   b. it raised airline fares and thus induced Americans to switch from cars to safer planes

   c. it reduced airline fares and thus induced Americans to switch from cars to safer planes

   d. it reduced airline fares and thus induced Americans to switch from planes to safer cars

   e. it had no effect on airline fares

EXERCISES

This is a review of Chapter 29 and of marginal cost price regulation in Chapter 27.

1a. Suppose that the total cost for a firm producing widgets equals the fixed cost of $2 million plus a variable cost equal to $4 for every widget produced. Thus, the marginal cost of producing widgets is always (constant, increasing, decreasing), and average cost is always (constant, increasing, decreasing). The widget industry is a _____.

1b. Suppose this firm is being regulated using marginal cost pricing. Then its price would be $ _____. Suppose the firm sells 2 million units at this price. Its cost per unit would be $ _____, and its loss per unit would be $ _____. Therefore, the taxpayer would have to pay a total subsidy of $ _____ to keep the firm in operation.

1c. If the industry were broken up into two separate firms, each with the same cost structure as before, and each firm were to produce half of this quantity, then the cost per unit would be _____, which is (more than, less than, the same as) before. The loss per unit would be $ _____, which is (higher, lower, no different) than before. Therefore, the total subsidy required to keep the industry alive would be (higher, lower, no different) than before. Specifically, the total subsidy paid to both firms would be $ _____.

1d. After this monopoly is broken up and all necessary subsidies are paid, the firms would (gain, lose, be unaffected), the consumers would (gain, lose, be unaffected), and the taxpayers would (gain, lose, be unaffected). Thus, the nation as a whole would (gain, lose, be unaffected). What important principle is illustrated by this hypothetical example?

ESSAY QUESTIONS

1. Discuss the benefits and costs of breaking up a natural monopoly.

2. "Giant foreign and domestic companies such as General Motors, Canadian Airlines, and Great Lakes Paper still dominate the production of many goods. Thus, our competition policies cannot have been effective." To what extent do you agree with this statement? Explain your position.

3. "In restricting GM's use of its market power in the North American market, the competition from Japanese auto companies has been far more effective than our Canadian competition policy or U.S. antitrust laws." Do you agree? Explain your position.

4. Why do you suppose the unions representing truck drivers are likely to be strongly opposed to deregulation of the Canadian trucking industry?

ANSWERS

Important Terms: **1**i, **2**d, **3**g, **4**f, **5**c, **6**b, **7**j, **8**e, **9**k, **10**h, **11**a
True-False: **1**F, **2**F, **3**F, **4**T, **5**F, **6**T, **7**F, **8**F, **9**F, **10**F, **11**T
Multiple Choice: **1**a, **2**c, **3**c, **4**e, **5**a, **6**e, **7**c, **8**e, **9**a, **10**d, **11**b, **12**a, **13**a, **14**c, **15**a, **16**e, **17**d, **18**a, **19**c, **20**c
Exercises: **1a.** constant, decreasing, natural monopoly **1b.** $4, $5, $1, $2 million **1c.** $6, more than, $2, higher, higher, $4 million **1d.** be unaffected, be unaffected, lose, lose. From the point of view of efficiency, natural monopolies should be regulated rather than broken up.

ANSWERS TO SELECTED REVIEW QUESTIONS FROM THE TEXT

29-2. (a) and (b) are undesirable, because either agreement is a means whereby producers exercise market power to raise price. The result is an inefficient allocation of resources. (c) is more desirable because it is introduced for a different reason: It lowers costs to railroads of providing transport services. (In its early history, Australia had more than one size track. This raised the cost and inconvenience of running a railroad system.)

29-3. The brief from the industry would argue that the effect of the existing price regulation was not an increased level of industry profits, but instead a possibility for the companies to divert some of their net earnings from the big-city hotels to subsidizing the losses they were incurring in the small cities. Abolishing the price regulation, according to the industry brief, would reduce net earnings in the big cities, forcing the companies to close the small-town hotels.

The government brief might question whether the companies were really losing money on their small-town hotels. For example, shouldn't they have been able to earn a profit in the small towns as well by reducing the quality of service? The government brief might also make the point that the most likely outcome of abolishing the price regulation would be increased room rates in small towns, not a closing of the hotels altogether.

29-5. Agreements to restrict advertising will reduce the firms' costs, and could therefore benefit consumers by leading to lower product prices. On the other hand, without advertising, a firm that wanted to attract customers by reducing its price or increasing the quality of its products would find it more difficult to do so. Thus the intensity of competition may be reduced, leading to higher prices and/or lower product quality.

29-6. (a) One possible explanation was that Bell and Northern Telecom were effectively able to raise their combined profits by charging high prices for "optional" equipment, since Bell's requirement had created a monopoly for Northern Telecom in the market for such optional equipment.

(b) The ruling certainly increased competitiveness in the market for optional equipment, and gave consumers access to a wider range of such equipment, both in terms of price and quality.

(c) They could have tried to extend price regulation to cover various forms of optional equipment as well. On the other hand, although this might have been effective in holding prices down, it probably would have slowed down the rate of introduction of new types of equipment, in comparison to what happened as a consequence of the ruling.

Chapter 30

∎ ∎

Government Regulation to Protect Our Quality of Life

MAJOR PURPOSE

Many people think that environmental pollution is simply a bad thing that should be prevented. They believe that it has nothing to do with economics and that economic considerations such as cost are irrelevant. Pollution, they contend, should be cleaned up, regardless of cost. The principal objective in this chapter is to show that pollution is, in fact, an economic problem—one that involves many of the principles that have already been developed in this book. Moreover, if economic considerations are ignored, pollution will be much more costly to control. Society will waste valuable resources in the clean-up effort. Or to put the same point another way: Our limited available funds for cleaning up will give us far less improvement in the environment if we ignore costs.

The second objective of this chapter is to show that creating safe products and safe jobs is also an economic problem. Here, again, costs cannot be ignored.

LEARNING OBJECTIVES

After you have studied this chapter in the textbook and the study guide, you should be able to
- Explain why pollution is an externality
- Explain why perfect competition does not lead to efficiency when there is pollution or any other kind of external cost
- Show the efficiency loss from pollution in a diagram similar to Figure 30-2 in the textbook
- Explain why we cannot and should not attempt to eliminate pollution completely
- Demonstrate why the policy of imposing a physical limit on pollution is a far less efficient way of reducing it than imposing a tax on emissions
- Show why a third option—imposing physical limits on pollution, but allowing pollution rights to be bought and sold—is at least as efficient as a tax would be
- Critically evaluate the policy of subsidizing pollution-control equipment
- Explain how the responsibility for protecting the environment is divided between the federal and provincial governments in Canada
- Describe some of the problems with the methods currently used by Canadian governments to control pollution
- Explain some of the problems that arise when pollution spills over provincial or international boundaries
- Explain how recycling reduces the pollution problem and, as a favourable side effect, also reduces the problem of resource depletion that we will be studying in the next chapter
- Explain why ensuring that products and jobs are safe requires dealing with a lack of information rather than an externality
- Demonstrate why information problems justify government intervention

• Show why information problems are more serious for health than for safety
• Demonstrate why benefit-cost analysis is important in designing government regulations
• Explain why benefit-cost analysis involves many problems; for example, this approach often requires us to attach a value to a human life
• Demonstrate why government policy becomes inconsistent, with too few lives saved, if no attempt is made to put a rough-and-ready value on a human life

HIGHLIGHTS OF THE CHAPTER

Pollution as an External Cost

Pollution is an external cost, because it is not borne by those responsible for it. For example, when smoke from a factory soils someone's clothes, the factory owner doesn't have to pay the cleaning bill.

Why Does a Perfectly Competitive Market Fail to Deal with the Pollution Problem?

When there is an externality like pollution, the "invisible hand" of a perfectly competitive free market does not provide an efficient outcome. The reason is that there is a violation of one of the conditions in Chapter 26 that allows perfect competition to deliver an economically efficient outcome. The condition that is violated is that the marginal cost to producers (MC) must be the same as the marginal cost to society (MC_S). This condition does not hold when there is an external cost such as pollution, because MC_S is more than MC. The difference between the two is the marginal external cost MC_E, as illustrated in Figure 30-1 in the textbook.

Efficiency requires that the marginal benefit to society (shown by the demand curve) be equal to the marginal cost to society MC_S. In Figure 30-2 of the textbook, we see that this efficient outcome is at E_2. However, this is not the equilibrium in a perfectly competitive free market. The reason is that, as always in such a market, supply reflects the cost facing producers. But this is only their private cost MC. The external cost of their actions is a cost they don't have to face. Because supply reflects private cost MC only, the perfectly competitive equality of demand and supply is at equilibrium E_1 rather than the efficient E_2. Thus, perfect competition is inefficient; too much output of this polluting good is produced (Q_1 rather than the efficient output Q_2). The efficiency loss is measured by the red triangle in this figure. Be sure you can explain this triangle: For each of the units of "excess" output between Q_2 and Q_1, social cost MC_S exceeds benefit D. There is, therefore, a net

cost involved in producing each of these units—with the sum of all these costs being the red triangle.

What Principles Should Guide our Antipollution Policy?

The above analysis suggests a simple way that the government can make a perfectly competitive market efficient. Impose a tax on polluting producers equal to the external cost they are creating; that is, impose tax r in Figure 30.2 of the text. This tax now becomes one of the costs producers have to face. In other words, the "external cost is now internalized," because it has now become a cost that producers have to face. Since producers will have to take this external cost—along with all their other costs—into account in making their supply decisions, the supply curve shifts up from S_1 to S_2. Supply now reflects both internal and external costs, and the perfectly competitive equilibrium of demand and supply is at the efficient point E_2. Thus, with this simple imposition of a tax, the perfectly competitive market does yield an efficient outcome after all. Adam Smith's invisible hand does work, because, with this tax, the government is applying the appropriate pressure on the market, and then letting the market work.

Figure 30.2 in the text illustrates another important principle: Polluting output can be cut back "too much." Limiting it to Q_3 is even worse than a "hands-off" policy that would allow output to continue unrestricted at Q_1. (At Q_3, the efficiency loss FE_2G is even greater than the red efficiency loss at Q_1.)

Antipollution Policies: The Canadian Experience

Canadian governments have not used the methods of taxing polluters as a way of controlling pollution; instead, they have imposed limits on the allowable amounts of pollution that individual firms may emit. (The federal government has taken the lead in setting standards for the quality of air and water; however, the constitutional authority for setting and enforcing limits on allowable pollution rests with the provincial governments.) Another method has also been used: subsidizing the purchase of pollution-control equipment. On the whole, these programs have resulted in a substantial reduction in pollution, but most economists believe that they could have been designed to be more efficient. They make the following criticisms:

a. Because governments have not attempted to conduct systematic benefit-cost analyses of different types of pollution control, there has been little consistency in the limits set on allowable pollution: Some limits have probably been too restrictive, while others have not been restrictive enough.

b. Even if the total physical limit were to be set correctly (for example, at Q_3 in Figure 30.3 of the text) imposing restrictions on individual polluting firms is a much more costly way of reducing pollution (by, say, a half) than is the imposition of a pollution tax. Under a pollution tax of T, pollution would be cut back by those firms that have the lowest cost of pollution reduction—that is, firms to the right of Q_3 that can cut pollution at a cost shown, for example, by the short arrow. Thus, the total cost of reducing pollution would be minimized. On the other hand, when a physical limit on pollution is imposed on each firm, some of the reduction in pollution must be undertaken by firms to the left of Q_3 at the relatively high cost shown by, for example, the tall arrow. There is the same reduction in pollution, but it is achieved at an unnecessarily high cost.

In the United States, environmental agencies have recently begun to introduce a third method which, like a pollution tax, also lets the market work and therefore reduces pollution at minimum cost. This is a policy of imposing a physical limit on pollution but then allowing permits to pollute to be bought and sold at a market price. This "price of polluting" acts as a deterrent just like the tax T, ensuring that pollution will be cut back at minimum cost.

A fourth method that governments have used has been to subsidize pollution-control equipment. However, this has involved problems:

a. The government has often failed to ensure that the pollution-control equipment it has subsidized is used effectively.

b. Pollution-control equipment provides, at best, an "end-of-pipe" solution that is often more costly than other solutions such as using cleaner inputs. (For example, less polluting Western coal could be used in power plants.) Again, either a pollution tax or a system of tradeable permits would be a lower-cost policy because it would give firms not only the incentive to "cure" pollution, but also the incentive to find the least expensive cure.

Political Problems Plaguing Pollution Prevention

Even though Canadian and American governments have had remarkable success in slowing down and even reversing the deterioration of the environment during the 1970s, there are signs that further progress will be difficult. One reason for this is political. The lobbying efforts mounted by the firms opposing specific antipollution policies are likely to be more intensive than the lobbying by representatives for the beneficiaries. For a particular firm, preventing tighter antipollution rules may be a matter of life and death, while for those who benefit from antipollution policies, the effects of the rules applied to any single firm are of negligible importance. Furthermore, the pollution issue is sometimes complicated by the fact that pollution spills over boundaries. For example, some of the air pollution generated in Ontario spills over into Quebec; pollution of the Great Lakes by industrial firms on the American side of the lakes is of concern to Canadians as well as to American fishermen and swimmers; emissions of sulphur dioxide by U.S. power plants also affect Canadians. The problem here is this: How does one ensure that the government that has jurisdiction over the polluting firms takes into account the benefits accruing to residents in other jurisdictions when they decide how tightly to control their polluters?

Recycling

This can play an important role in reducing the amount of pollution because it disposes of polluting wastes (such as empty beer cans). Such a policy would also mean that we will need to extract fewer natural resources from our environment. If we produce new beer cans out of old ones, we won't need to use as much bauxite.

Government Intervention to Ensure Safe Jobs and Safe Products

1. How is this intervention to be justified? If firms under pressure let products or workplaces become dangerous, the health and safety of the firm's customers or labour force may be compromised. This seems like an externality, but it isn't. The damage is not to an innocent bystander (like those living on a polluted river). Instead, it is to the firm's customers or labour force who are parties to the transactions, and who can consequently take some action to curb the damage the firm is doing to them. For example, airline passengers can avoid an unsafe airline and workers can insist on a premium wage for dangerous jobs—provided they know the risks involved. The evidence is that workers do insist on some premium in risky jobs, but not enough to compensate adequately.

Thus, the major problem is the lack of information about exactly what risks to health and safety there really are. By the time the public finds out an airline is dangerous, lives have been lost. This justifies safety regulations by the Department of Transport. As another example, workers can't know the cancer risks from handling chemicals. This justifies government intervention to ensure that chemicals are labelled.

2. Risks to health are a greater problem than risks to safety. Workers can see risks to safety such as an unprotected buzz saw, and can insist that it be safely installed. There is a much greater information problem with health. A cancer risk from chemicals that may kill people 20 years later cannot be "seen." Therefore, government intervention to provide information and to prevent risk is even more strongly justified where there is a health risk than where there is a safety risk; however, both are important.

3. The airlines provide two exceptions to these general principles:

a. There is a huge information problem with safety in the air. Unlike the case of a buzzsaw, where information about risk becomes available when one person is injured, information about risk on an airline may become available only after hundreds are killed. Since the information cost the public faces in this case is so high, the government is justified in imposing safety standards.

b. Government regulation of airline safety is further justified by externalities. A crash may not only kill the parties to the transaction (the passengers and crew), it may also kill innocent bystanders on the ground who are not parties to the transaction. (They have nothing to do with flying.)

Evaluating a Government Regulation with Benefit-Cost Analysis

A regulation cannot be justified just because it has a desirable objective such as improving health and safety.

It must be effective in achieving that objective; that is, it must provide *substantial* benefits. And those benefits should exceed its costs. The purpose of benefit-cost analysis is to perform just such a test.

One might expect that whenever policy makers are considering a new regulation, they would perform such a benefit-cost analysis. Unfortunately, this is not always the case. In some recent legislation, it is expressly stated that regulations must be enforced regardless of their costs.

If we take a benefit-cost approach to analyse a proposed new regulation, it is first necessary to estimate costs, such as the operating costs of the agencies that administer the regulations, and the costs incurred by firms in complying with the regulations.

Even greater problems are encountered in estimating the benefits of a regulation. For example, one of the benefits may be the saving of lives—and no one wants to put a value on a human life. It is far easier to say that the value of a life is infinite, and leave it at that. But that's not how we value our lives. We all take some small risk with our lives whenever we take a trip in a plane—or, for that matter, an even bigger risk when we travel by car. We don't sit at home and avoid the risk, as we would if we truly believed that our lives had an infinite value. But while it's easy to argue that the value of a life is less than infinite, it's very difficult to be more specific. For attempts to do so, see Box 30-4 in the textbook.

Even if the complete information necessary for a full benefit-cost test is not available, it is still possible to make government policy more effective using fragmentary information. To use an example cited in the text, a regulation imposing an arsenic standard has been saving lives at an estimated cost of $70 million per life. Alternatively, lives could be saved at a cost of only about $100,000 each by building more railroad overpasses. Obviously, we should switch to this policy; if we did, we could save the same number of lives at much lower cost. Or, to put the same point more appropriately, we could use our limited funds to save far more lives.

IMPORTANT TERMS: MATCH THE COLUMNS

Match each term in the first column with its corresponding explanation in the second column.

_____ 1. Internal cost	**a.** The cost of reducing pollution by one more unit
_____ 2. External cost	**b.** The cost that is paid by the producer. Also called private cost.
_____ 3. Social cost	**c.** The cost of having one more unit of pollution
_____ 4. The marginal cost of reducing pollution (MCR)	**d.** The cost not paid by the producer (or consumer) of a good, but by someone else
_____ 5. Marginal cost of having pollution	

_____ 6. "End-of-pipe" treatment
_____ 7. Recycling
_____ 8. International externality
_____ 9. Benefit-cost analysis
_____ 10. Quality-of-life regulation
_____ 11. Benefit-cost test

e. The policy of removing pollutants just before they enter the environment
f. Legislation to protect health, safety, working conditions, and the environment
g. Estimating and comparing benefits and costs of a program
h. The requirement that the benefits of a program be at least as great as its costs
i. A cost imposed on one nation by the actions of another
j. The total cost to society, that is, the sum of internal and external costs
k. Using materials again rather than throwing them away. This can reduce pollution and preserve natural resources.

TRUE-FALSE

T F 1. Restricting industrial growth is one of the best measures for controlling pollution.
T F 2. Inefficiency occurs if producers do not take external pollution costs into account.
T F 3. Marginal external cost equals marginal social cost minus marginal private cost.
T F 4. The main effort of Environment Canada has been to collect the taxes that the government has imposed to discourage pollution.
T F 5. A pollution tax "internalizes an externality" because the producer is forced to face not only internal costs, but also the external costs imposed on society.
T F 6. Without government intervention, the marginal cost of having pollution would be zero.
T F 7. Setting an arbitrary physical limit on pollution will always be better than doing nothing at all.
T F 8. The problem with pollution is that, in the absence of government intervention, firms view it as an internal cost.
T F 9. A problem with the federal standards for maximum allowable rates of pollution emissions is that they are the same in provinces with relatively clean air as in provinces or cities where the air is already heavily polluted.
T F 10. Benefit-cost analysis is designed to ensure that the total benefits of a policy will equal its total costs.
T F 11. If both the U.S. and Canadian governments agree to take into account the benefits to the citizens of the other country as well as to their own citizens when setting water quality standards for the Great Lakes, the lakes are likely to be cleaner than they would be if each country considers only the benefits of its own citizens.

MULTIPLE CHOICE

1. An example of an externality being internalized occurs if:
   a. an export firm is required to raise the price of a good it is also selling in the home market
   b. an export firm is required to export less and sell more goods on the home market instead
   c. a producer is forced to face the external cost his product imposes on society
   d. a producer is forced to face the internal cost his product imposes on society
   e. a tax is imposed on the producer equal to the marginal social cost of the good

2. In a perfectly competitive market, the marginal benefit of a polluting good will equal its marginal social cost if:
   a. a tax is imposed on the good equal to its marginal external cost
   b. a tax is imposed on the good equal to its marginal internal cost
   c. a subsidy is provided equal to the marginal internal cost

    d. a subsidy is provided equal to the marginal external cost

    e. the government does not intervene with either a tax or subsidy

3. In a perfectly competitive market for a polluting good where the government is following a "hands-off policy":

    a. less than the efficient amount will be produced

    b. more than the efficient amount will be produced

    c. the efficient amount will be produced

    d. price will be equal to the efficient level

    e. price will be higher than the efficient level

4. In the face of external costs, efficiency can be achieved in a perfectly competitive market by setting a tax equal to:

    a. the marginal social cost of producing the good

    b. the marginal internal cost of producing the good

    c. the marginal external cost of producing the good

    d. the total social cost of producing the good

    e. the total internal cost of producing the good

5. Airplanes flying low over houses near airports cause "noise pollution." The most efficient policy to deal with this would be to:

    a. rely on the "invisible hand" to take care of the problem

    b. provide a subsidy to each airline depending on the total amount of noise it creates in the affected neighbourhoods

    c. impose a tax on each airline depending on the total amount of noise it creates in the affected neighbourhoods

    d. impose limits on the number of flights of each airline

    e. subsidize airlines that install noise-abatement devices

6. The marginal external cost of a polluting good is equal to:

    a. its marginal social cost plus its marginal internal cost

    b. its marginal social cost less its marginal internal cost

    c. its marginal internal cost less its marginal social cost

    d. its marginal internal cost or its marginal social cost, whichever is greater

    e. its marginal internal cost or its marginal social cost, whichever is less

7. As time passes, pollution becomes a more difficult problem to deal with because the marginal cost of reducing pollution (MCR):

    a. shifts to the left, while the marginal cost of pollution (MCP) is rising

    b. shifts to the right while MCP is rising

    c. shifts to the right while MCP is falling

    d. shifts to the left while MCP is falling

    e. remains stable while MCP is rising

8. An effluent fee is:

    a. any tax imposed on the wealthy

    b. a special tax on the wealthy who pollute

    c. a tax on each unit of pollution

    d. a subsidy provided to polluters to encourage them to use cleaner fuels

    e. a subsidy provided to polluters who install pollution-abatement equipment

9. Which of the following is *not* a good example of an international externality?

    a. congestion of Canadian highways by American tourists

    b. leakage of chemicals from a plant on the Canadian side of the Niagara River

    c. smoke from a U.S. power plant that causes acid rain in Canada

    d. cutting down trees in Canada to produce newsprint for U.S. newspapers

    e. radioactive fallout in Sweden from a nuclear accident in the Soviet Union

10. If a physical limit is set on the amount of pollutants each firm can emit:

    a. pollution will be cut back at minimum cost—that is, by the firms that can do so least expensively

    b. pollution will cut back at zero cost

    c. the result will surely be an improvement on leaving pollution uncontrolled

    d. the result will surely be inferior to leaving pollution uncontrolled

    e. it is not clear how the result will compare with leaving pollution uncontrolled

11. To determine the appropriate tax on pollution in a lake where there are many polluting industries, the government must have information on:

    a. the marginal cost of reducing pollution (MCR) and the marginal cost of having pollution (MCP)

    b. MCP but not MCR

    c. only the marginal benefit of reducing pollution (MBR)

    d. the marginal cost of pollution control equipment

    e. the marginal benefit of pollution control equipment

12. If one is to argue—along with Ronald Coase (see Box 30-2 in the text)—that property rights should be created to deal with water pollution, then the question of who actually owns these rights:

a. must be resolved by giving them to local governments

b. must be resolved by giving them to polluting firms

c. is more important from the point of view of equity, than of efficiency

d. is more important from the point of view of efficiency, than of equity

e. is important from neither an equity nor an efficiency point of view

13. If a physical limit is set on the amount of pollutants each firm can emit:

a. pollution will be cut back, but at a higher cost than necessary

b. pollution will be cut back, at the minimum possible cost

c. there will be no change in the amount of pollution

d. there will be an increase in the amount of pollution

e. nothing can be said about the pollution that will result

14. The least-cost way of reducing pollution in a lake is to:

a. encourage all firms to cut back their pollution by the same percentage

b. force all firms to cut back their pollution by the same percentage

c. let the firms with the highest profits cut back the most

d. force the firms with the lowest profits to go out of business

e. provide an incentive for firms with the lowest cost of reducing pollution to make relatively large cutbacks

15. If permits to pollute in a lake can be bought and sold, and sell for a price T, then pollution will be reduced:

a. by those firms that can do so at a cost of less than T

b. by those firms that can do so at a cost of more than T

c. in equal proportion by all firms

d. by firms that can externalize this internality

e. by all firms that are physically able to do so, regardless of the cost

16. Consider the following three policies to reduce pollution:

1. imposing physical limits on pollution
2. imposing physical limits on pollution and allowing trade in pollution permits
3. imposing a pollution tax

The methods that use the market mechanism are:

a. 1 and 2

b. 1 and 3

c. 2 and 3

d. 1, 2, and 3

e. 2 only

17. The government's policy of subsidizing the purchase of pollution control equipment can be criticized because it:

a. places too great an emphasis on "end-of-pipe" treatment

b. places too little emphasis on "end-of-pipe" treatment

c. has led to an overemphasis by the government on how efficiently this machinery will subsequently be operated

d. has been supported by inadequate short-term financing during its construction

e. none of the above

18. The recycling of wastes:

a. can reduce the rate of depletion of natural resources

b. can increase the rate of depletion of natural resources

c. is economically efficient, no matter how costly it may be

d. causes pollution

e. has no effect on pollution

19. Almost all studies estimate the value of a human life in the broad range:

a. $330,000 to $5 million

b. $3 million to $6 million

c. $4.5 million to $15 million

d. $100 million to $200 million

e. $1 billion to $3 billion

20. In controlling the release of new drugs:

a. there is a cost of delay for further testing, but no benefit of delay

b. there is a benefit from delay, but no cost

c. there is neither a benefit nor a cost from delay, because health is a non-economic issue

d. there is a cost and benefit of delay; the cost is that lives may be lost because a life-saving drug can't be used yet

e. there is a cost and benefit of delay, but neither can be specified

21. In their daily decisions, most people implicitly value their own life as worth:

a. an infinite amount

b. zero

c. about half their current year's income

d. some value between **a.** and **c.**

e. some value between **b.** and **c.**

22. Workers who take risky jobs:

a. protect themselves fully by insisting on a higher wage that will completely compensate for the risk

b. protect themselves partly by insisting on a higher wage that will partly compensate for the risk

c. don't protect themselves at all

d. settle for a lower wage

e. settle for the same wage but lower fringe benefits

EXERCISES

1a. Figure 30.1 represents the market for a good that causes pollution.

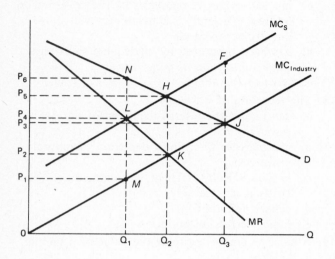

Figure 30.1

If the market is perfectly competitive, output will be _____, market price will be _____, marginal social cost will be _____, and the marginal external cost will be _____.

1b. If the commodity produces no external benefits, then the optimal output is _____. This output would be attained under perfect competition if the producers were faced with a tax of _____ per unit. This would result in a market price of _____. Without this tax, the efficiency loss will be area _____.

1c. Suppose that these firms were able to collude to form a monopoly. Then, the level of output (with no tax) would be _____, the market price would be _____, and the efficiency loss would be _____.

1d. Assume that the marginal external cost is constant—i.e., that the lines MC_S and $MC_{industry}$ are parallel, with $LM = HK = FJ$. Now suppose that the government imposes the same tax on the monopolist that it earlier charged to the perfect competitors. In this case, the monopolist will produce an output of _____, it will charge price _____, and the efficiency (gain, loss) will be area _____. Thus, a per unit tax on a polluting monopolist (will, will not) necessarily lead to greater efficiency.

2. If pollution is left uncontrolled in Figure 30.2, the amount of pollution will be _____. If the government imposes a tax T to reduce pollution, it will be cut back to _____. Those firms to the (right, left) of Q_1 will stop polluting while those firms to the (right, left) of Q_1 will continue to pollute.

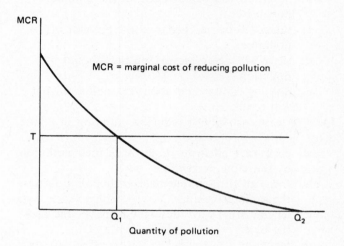

Figure 30.2

3a. (This problem requires Box 30-3 in the textbook.) If MCP_1 in Figure 30.3 is the marginal cost of having pollution and MCR is the marginal cost of reducing pollution, then, in the absence of any pollution tax, the quantity of pollution will be _____, MCR will be _____, and MCP will be _____. The economically efficient reduction in pollution is to quantity _____. This will result if firms are charged a tax of _____ per unit of pollution.

3b. Now suppose that the marginal cost of having pollution is MCP_2 instead of MCP_1. Then the economically efficient amount of pollution is _____. This will result if firms are charged a tax of _____ per unit of pollution. The efficient amount of pollution in this case is (more, less) because pollution is (more, less) damaging.

4. Now suppose that the marginal cost of having pollution is really MCP_1 but that the government makes a mistake and estimates it to be MCP_2. The government erroneously uses MCP_2 and sets the tax on pollution at _____. The resulting quantity of pollution is _____, which is (more, less) than the economically

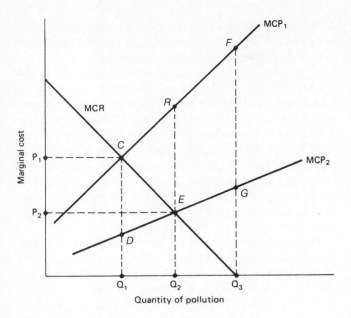

Figure 30.3

efficient amount. At this level of pollution, MCR is _____ and the true MCP is _____. There will be an efficiency (gain, loss) from the government's estimating error equal to area _____. Thus, we (may, may not) conclude that if the government underestimates the problem it will take inadequate action to counter it; that is, the government will set too low a pollution tax.

5a. The two lines in Figure 30.4 below show the marginal cost of reducing pollution MCR for two smoke-polluting firms (which are otherwise identical). Bars are added for detail. Reducing smoke pollution is less costly for firm (A, B). Suppose each firm is presently required

by law to limit its output of smoke to 10 units, as shown by the dark vertical line. Both firms together generate 20 units of pollution. Now suppose that a government official decides, after reading this book, to impose a pollution tax instead of limiting each firm's smoke. If he sets the tax at $650 for each unit of smoke emitted, then firm A will (cut back, expand) its emissions to _____ units of smoke, and B will (cut back, expand) its emissions to _____ units. Both firms together generate (more, less, the same) pollution as before. The firm with the higher MCR has (increased, decreased) its pollution and the one with the lower MCR has (increased, decreased) its pollution.

5b. Firm A's pollution-reduction costs have (increased, decreased) by _____, while firm B's pollution-reduction costs have (increased, decreased) by _____. Thus, the total pollution reduction cost of the two firms has (increased, decreased, stayed the same), while the total amount of pollution by the two firms has (increased, decreased, stayed the same). Therefore, the tax is (more, less) efficient in keeping down costs than the previous limits on pollution.

6a. Suppose that a company can produce a car that runs on gasoline, or one that runs on a newly invented fuel that sells for the same price, but that reduces the emission of pollutants by 50%. Unfortunately, the car using the new gasoline costs $200 more to construct. Suppose that, in all other respects, the two cars perform equally well, so that consumers do not care which fuel a car uses; if given the choice, they will buy the car with the lower purchase price. Therefore, with no regulations, the car producer will build the car using (gasoline, new fuel).

Suppose it is also possible to install an "end-of-pipe" pollution-control device on all its cars, which also reduces

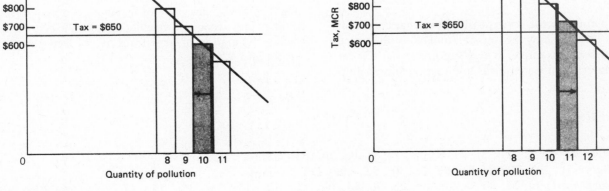

Figure 30.4

emissions by 50% but costs $500. Again, suppose that consumers do not care whether or not a car has this device. Then the auto producer will build the car using (gasoline, new fuel), and (with, without) the device. The cars (will, will not) pollute the atmosphere; but the car companies don't take this into account because this is an (external, internal) cost.

6b. Now suppose a government agency wants to cut back auto emissions by 50%. Therefore, it requires the company to install the pollution-control device. The company will now build cars using (gasoline, new fuel), and with the device. The cost to society of this end-of-pipe reduction in pollution is $_____ per car.

Now, suppose instead that the government merely requires the auto producer to cut back the emissions from its cars by 50%, leaving it up to the company to decide how to do this. Then, the cost to the company of complying with this requirement would be $_____ per car if it installed the device, or $_____ per car if it switched to the new fuel. Therefore, it would choose the (device, new fuel). In this case the cost to society of the reduction in pollution would be $_____ per car.

6c. In this example, the policy of telling the company how to reduce pollution is $_____ (more, less) costly per car than the policy of simply telling them to do it and leaving all the details to them. If, instead, the agency had told the company to do it by making cars that use the new fuel, the cost to society would have been (more than, less than, the same as) the cost of just telling them to do

it. What general rule does this example suggest about the relative cost of telling companies to comply compared with telling them exactly *how* to comply?

7. The Apex Company employs 2000 individuals working on high-steel construction. The firm has to pay its labour force a $1,000 per person wage premium each year in order to attract workers who are willing to risk their lives. The risks on this job raise the mortality rate by 2/1000; that is, the chance a worker will be killed during a year is 2/1000 higher than in other jobs. The question is: Should the government introduce a safety regulation that will reduce the risk by 1/1000, if this regulation costs $1.5 million (including both government administration costs and compliance costs by the firm)?

To answer this, we need to know the value of a human life. Because each worker is willing to take a 2/1000 chance of dying in return for an extra $1000 of pay, clearly, those workers value their lives at ($5 million, $500,000, $1,000, $500) which is the wage premium of $_____ divided by the _____ increase in risk.

Although this cannot be predicted precisely in advance, the expectation is that this regulation would save _____ lives, which is the _____ risk reduction from this regulation times the 2000 workers employed. Since each worker values his or her life at $_____, the benefit of this regulation is $_____. This is (greater than, less than, the same as) the $1.5 million cost of the regulation. Thus, this regulation (passes, fails) this benefit-cost test, and it would be (introduced, rejected).

ESSAY QUESTIONS

1. "One advantage of using taxes rather than physical limits to control pollution is that the former policy harnesses the forces of the marketplace to help find an efficient solution, whereas the latter policy does not." Do you agree or disagree? Explain your answer.

2. Explain why, in selecting the specific least-cost method of reducing pollution, private firms will do at least as good a job as government agencies, and often better.

3. Explain how the concept of an external cost (that is, a cost not borne by the decision maker) is illustrated by the following example. When Napoleon, the founder of the conscription system, was told that a planned mili-

tary operation would cost too many men, he replied: "That is nothing. The women produce more of them than I can use."

4. In recent years, a large Canadian distillery has paid for the tickets to enable people to travel free on the Toronto subway system on New Year's Eve. Explain how this self-imposed tax has helped to promote economic efficiency by internalizing an external cost.

5. Show why the value of a human life may have to be taken into account in calculating both the benefits and costs of regulation of new drugs by the Department of Health and Welfare.

ANSWERS

Important Terms: 1b, 2d, 3j, 4a, 5c, 6e, 7k, 8i, 9g, 10f, 11h
True-False: 1F, 2T, 3T, 4F, 5T, 6F, 7F, 8F, 9T, 10F, 11T
Multiple Choice: 1c, 2a, 3b, 4c, 5c, 6b, 7b, 8c, 9d, 10e, 11a, 12c, 13a, 14e, 15a, 16c, 17a, 18a, 19a, 20d, 21d, 22b

Exercises: **1a.** Q_3, P_3, Q_3F, *JF* **1b.** Q_2, *HK*, P_5, *HFJ* **1c.** Q_2, P_5, zero **1d.** Q_1, P_6, loss, *NLH*, will not **2.** Q_2, Q_1, right, left **3a.** Q_3, essentially zero, Q_3F, Q_1, P_1 **3b.** Q_2, P_2, more, less **4.** P_2, Q_2, more, Q_2E, Q_2R, loss, *CRE*, may **5a.** A, cut back, 9, expand, 11, the same, increased, decreased **5b.** increased, \$600, decreased, \$700, decreased, stayed the same, more **6a.** gasoline, gasoline, without, will, external **6b.** gasoline, \$500, \$500, \$200, new fuel, \$200 **6c.** \$300, more, the same, telling them exactly how to comply will cost more unless the government happens to pick the least-cost method—in which case it doesn't matter **7.** \$500,000, \$1,000, 2/1000, 2, 1/1000, \$500,000, \$1 million, less than, fails, rejected

ANSWERS TO SELECTED REVIEW QUESTIONS FROM THE TEXT

30-2. (a) This is a very misleading statement. Any policy to reduce (but not completely eliminate) pollution will leave some firms with some freedom (licence) to pollute. This is true whether the control measure is a tax or the imposition of a quantitative limit on pollution. A policy of removing any licence to pollute—that is, a policy of eliminating pollution—will not only be unsuccessful, but may also be worse than allowing all firms a "free licence" to pollute.

(b) This is a very accurate way of describing the policy of imposing a physical limit.

(c) This accurately illustrates the point that even a complete prohibition of any pollution whatsoever—costly though this would be—would not completely eliminate pollution. Some is the result of natural processes.

(d) In any particular case, there is a minimum-cost method of reducing pollution. If it is the end-of-pipe installation of pollution-control equipment, then subsidizing this equipment may be an effective way of reducing pollution. But if the minimum-cost method of reducing pollution is to attack the problem elsewhere—say, by purchasing higher cost, cleaner fuel—then an end-of-pipe subsidy will be relatively ineffective. It is far better to impose a tax that will force the firm to reduce pollution. In this case, the firm will respond by reducing it in the lowest-cost way.

30-3. It would be impossible for the thousands of buyers to get together and make a collective payment to the monopolist. Specifically, too many buyers would want to be free riders, enjoying the lower price charged by the monopolist without contributing to the payment made to the monopolist.

30-5. In one sense, the target rate of crime should obviously be zero. Through education and the solution of social abuses that lead to crime, we should be trying to

eliminate the desire of people to engage in crime. However, this is utopian: In the last analysis, there will always be some people left who want to commit crime. In such circumstances, the target should be to eliminate most—but not all—of this crime. The more we reduce crime, the more difficult and costly further reductions become. Even if half the population were engaged in police work, it is doubtful that crime could be eliminated altogether.

Another way of reducing crime is to make it more likely that someone who is arrested will be convicted. We could do so by setting up laws that make it easier to convict a suspect. But this too involves a cost. To see why, first note an essential problem: We don't know which suspects are guilty and which are innocent. (If we knew that, we wouldn't need to have trials.) The easier we make it to convict a suspect, the more likely it becomes that the guilty will (correctly) be convicted; but it also becomes more likely that an innocent individual will erroneously be convicted. And every time we jail an innocent individual, this is a cost of our policy of reducing crime by making convictions easier.

30-6. The tax should be lower in the desert because the cost of pollution is lower there. Most pollutants can still be "washed away" by natural processes, so the move by polluting firms from a crowded metropolitan area to the desert would reduce the overall cost of pollution facing the nation as a whole. In the limiting case in which all pollutants can be washed away in the desert, pollution still has zero cost, and the appropriate tax is still zero.

30-7. It may not be clear that the crash was caused by inadequate safety precautions, rather than terrorism or bad luck. Yes, it does illustrate this difficulty. Even after two crashes, it still may not be clear (although, as crashes increase, the odds become stronger in favour of the "inadequate safety" explanation).

Chapter 31

■ ■

Natural Resources: Are We Using Them at the Right Rate?

MAJOR PURPOSE

In the previous chapter, we saw that there was an external cost—in terms of damage to those living downstream—if chemicals are produced by a factory that dumps wastes into a river. The objective in this chapter is to use much of this same analysis to examine the external cost that is associated with resource extraction—namely, the cost to future generations because less of the resource will be available then. In this analysis, the question of who owns the resource is a critical one. If it is privately owned, then the owner will tend to take this future cost into account (since it's the owner's own resource that is being depleted) and decisions will therefore tend to be efficient. However, if the resource is common property (publicly owned), then those extracting the resource have no reason to take the future into account.

Because they tend to ignore the external cost to future generations, there is an inadequate conservation effort; an inefficiently large quantity of the resource is extracted.

In this chapter, we also return to the case study of oil, one of our most important natural resources. Earlier, in Chapter 28, we examined the attempt by OPEC to keep the world price of oil high; in this chapter, we examine the difficulties and inefficiencies introduced in the 1970s and early 1980s when the Canadian government kept the domestic price of oil low. Why did the government do this, and what was the effect of this policy on oil use? Finally, we examine alternative forms of energy, since these will determine how painful any shortage of oil may be to future generations.

LEARNING OBJECTIVES

After you have studied this chapter in the textbook and the study guide, you should be able to
- Describe the internal and external costs of extracting a common property resource, and explain why both of these are internal costs if the resource is privately owned
- Explain why a perfectly competitive market in a natural resource may be efficient if the resource is privately owned, but not if it is common property
- Describe the maximum sustainable yield (Box 31-1) and explain why harvests involve no future costs if the population of a species is greater than this; and why problems arise if the population is harvested down to a level below this
- Explain why simple projections of the use and availability of resources yield misleading predictions
- Give three reasons that population growth continues to be rapid in less developed countries despite the scarcity of resources
- Present the case in favour of economic growth, and the case against
- Describe how the domestic price of oil was controlled in the 1970s and early 1980s, and some of the practical problems that were encountered
- Explain the efficiency and transfer effects—domestic and international—of this policy, and how it affected the amounts of oil produced, consumed, and imported

• Present an argument for raising the domestic price of oil above the world price
• Explain the advantages and disadvantages of each of the three major alternative sources of energy—natural gas, coal, and nuclear power

HIGHLIGHTS OF THE CHAPTER

Since no one owns the fish in the sea, they are a common property resource, and provide a good illustration of one of the central problems addressed in this chapter: Common property resources are inadequately conserved in a free, perfectly competitive market. The reason is that fishing involves two costs—(1) the internal costs incurred by those who fish, such as the boats, nets, labour, and so on, and (2) the external cost that falls on future generations because there is less of this resource available to them. If the resource is common property, fishing firms don't pay any attention to this second cost. Like the polluting firm that ignores its external cost—such as the damage its pollutants do to those living downstream or downwind—the fishing firm that ignores the external costs it is imposing on future generations will produce more than the efficient amount. (Its output decision is influenced by its internal costs, but not by the external costs it creates.)

Policies to Reduce Inefficiency in Resource Extraction

There are three possible ways to reduce inefficiency:
1. Set a physical limit on the catch. The problem with this approach is that it does not use the market mechanism. A government official restricts the catch (perhaps by putting a limit on the size of nets or size of boats); and, as in the case of pollution discussed in the previous chapter, too severe a physical restriction may be worse than no restriction at all.

The two alternative ways to increase efficiency do use the market mechanism:
2. Impose a tax or fishing fee on fishermen according to the number of fish they catch—specifically, impose a tax on them equal to the external costs they generate, just like the tax on polluting firms analysed in the last chapter.
3. Create property rights; let the fish be privately owned. While this is not possible in the oceans or Great Lakes, it might be in inland lakes or ponds. (And it certainly is feasible for many other resources—such as timber—that are already privately owned to a substantial extent.) Once the schools of fish are privately owned, the owners will take into account both the harvesting costs and the cost of having a reduced catch in the future. (It is *their* future catch that will be reduced.) Thus, this future external cost is internalized once the resource is privately owned. Since the private owners will take all costs into account, the result is an efficient one. But it won't be equitable, unless the new owners are charged in some way for the asset (the fish) that they now own.

Special Problems of Nonrenewable Resources

Since schools of fish can eventually reproduce themselves, they are a renewable resource. On the other hand, there are other resources, such as coal, oil, or base metals that are not renewable. The key questions with such resources are: Will we run out, and if so, when? What can we do to prevent this? Simple projections of present trends point to an eventual doomsday, when rising population overtakes our limited resources. But such projections are oversimplified, because they do not allow for the adjustments that will take place as resources become scarce.

One of the most important kinds of adjustment is this: As a resource becomes more scarce, it becomes more expensive. This, in turn, leads to: (1) a substitution in production for the scarce resource by other factors that are more plentiful; (2) a substitution in consumption by goods that require less of the scarce resource; (3) induced innovation that economizes on these resources; and (4) a reduction in the rate of growth of population because raising children becomes costly as the price of resources rises.

Some have criticized this last point by noting that in the less developed countries, population growth has continued even though most parents can't afford to have children. However, the experience of these countries can be explained by three special factors: (1) poverty is so severe that people have children to provide them with support in their old age; (2) there are religious and social objections in these countries to birth control; and (3) their recent population growth is not just a reflection of high birth rates, but also of falling death rates, due to dramatic advances in medical services. However, falling death rates cannot continue to have the impact on population that they have had in the past.

In addition to the question of whether our future growth will be severely restricted by resource scarcity (as the doomsday models predict) or whether growth can continue because adjustment mechanisms work well, there is another overriding question: Do we really want substantial economic growth? The traditional argument in favour of growth is that it helps to relieve unemployment, reduce poverty, and raise our incomes and those of our children. However, a number of arguments have recently been put forward against continued growth. For example, it has been pointed out that growth contributes to pollution and depletes our natural resources. The main difficulty with such anti-growth arguments is that restricting growth is not the best way to attack these problems. Much more progress is possible if we design policies—such as taxes on polluters or on those firms extracting resources—that deal directly and specifically with each of these problems. In the case of resources, it is important to ensure that they are being priced high enough to provide adequate conservation.

What Is the Efficient Pricing of a Nonrenewable Resource?

The answer, illustrated in Figures 31-4 and 31-5, is that its price should keep rising as it becomes scarcer and scarcer; this will generate increasing pressure to conserve, for example, by using substitutes instead. It is important to understand why its price should not be the same in each year. This would be inefficient because $100 of a resource this year is worth more than $100 next year; used this year in investment it can grow to more than $100 next year. Therefore, it's efficient to use more this year and less next year—and a relatively low price this year and high price next year will generate that pattern.

It is also important to understand why, in a perfectly competitive market, the price of a resource will not (as well as should not) be the same in each year. If it were, the resource holders would sell it all off this year, and earn interest on the proceeds. (This is better than holding it until next year, selling it then for the same price, and earning no interest.) The price difference leaves them indifferent and therefore happy to sell it in either year.

Oil

Recently, this resource has been priced well above the requirements of conservation. Under the influence of OPEC—and, in particular, the Saudi Arabians—the world price of oil rose over ten times between 1973 and 1982. To provide some relief to oil users, the government instituted a policy of holding the domestic Canadian price down below the rapidly escalating world price. Full detail on the effects of this price ceiling—and the problems it raised—cannot be provided without a diagram, and you should be sure you have mastered Figure 31-6 in the text before proceeding. However, three of the broad effects

of this price control policy can be sketched out.

1. There were winners and losers. The winners were oil users—from Sunday drivers to the giant power-generating companies and their customers—who benefited because the price of oil was kept down. However, this lower price hurt oil producers in Western Canada, as well as the governments in the producing provinces whose royalty revenues were reduced.

2. There were two efficiency losses, shown by the two shaded triangles in Figure 31-6. One arose because the low price encouraged oil consumption, while the other arose because the low price discouraged domestic oil production.

3. To reduce the negative effects on production, the government added a twist to this policy and thus created a "blended price system." Under this system, the price of "new" currently produced oil was not kept down. It was allowed to rise to the world price. Thus, domestic production of oil would not, it was hoped, be discouraged after all. On the other hand, the price of "old" oil (that was already being produced, and would continue to be produced almost regardless of price) was still kept low. Finally, the price that oil buyers paid was a "blended" average of these various prices (including, in addition, the high world price of imported oil). Because Canadian oil users were paying the average of what these various kinds of oil cost, it was not necessary for the government to provide any subsidy of the kind typically required by a price-control policy. Unfortunately, however, it was an imperfect solution. Because it did not allow the domestic price paid by oil users to rise to the world price, Canadian consumption and, hence, imports of oil continued at a relatively high level. Furthermore, the system with different producer prices for new and old oil was difficult to administer because new and old oil cannot be physically distinguished. In the mid-1980s, the control system was gradually dismantled and, following the decline in world oil prices in 1986, the gap between the world price and the domestic Canadian price essentially disappeared.

Even though the world price of oil in the late 1980s and early 1990s has fallen well below its previous peak, energy policy remained an important issue. For one thing, there was the question of what steps could be taken to prevent another crisis if OPEC were once again to restrict oil exports. Furthermore, we have become more aware of the potential damage that carbon dioxide emissions (to which oil is a major contributor) may be doing to the world's climate. This raises the question: To what degree will North American energy users turn to other forms of energy such as natural gas and—perhaps most important in the long run—how soon will nuclear fusion (as opposed to the fission technology in use today) be developed to the point where it can, to a substantial degree, replace oil as a source of energy? As the 1990s began, that date was still a long way off.

IMPORTANT TERMS: MATCH THE COLUMNS

Match each term in the first column with the corresponding explanation in the second column.

_____ 1. Reservation price	a. A resource that is not privately owned
_____ 2. Sustainable yield curve	b. The curve relating the annual increase in a renewable resource (such as fish) to its population size. For any given population, this curve indicates the amount that can be extracted and still leave the population size constant.
_____ 3. Maximum sustainable yield	
_____ 4. Induced innovation	
_____ 5. Dynamic efficiency	
_____ 6. Renewable resource	c. The international cartel that raised the world price of oil by more than ten times between 1973 and 1982
_____ 7. OPEC	
_____ 8. Common property resource	
_____ 9. Blended price	d. The largest value on the sustainable yield curve. This is the largest amount of a renewable resource that can be extracted each year without reducing the population size.

e. The height of the supply curve for a privately owned resource. It includes (1) the cost of harvesting or extraction and (2) the amount necessary to compensate the owner for the reduction in the resource available in the future.

f. The average of the low price of old oil and the higher price of imported and new oil

g. A resource that reproduces itself naturally (such as fish) or that may reproduce itself with human assistance (such as timber)

h. The result when the price of a perfectly competitive nonrenewable resource rises each year by the amount of the interest rate

i. The development of new substitutes for increasingly expensive resources

TRUE-FALSE

T F   1. Under perfect competition, the rate of extraction of a privately owned resource is generally greater than the efficient rate.

T F   2. Those harvesting a common property resource take into account only the harvesting cost—not the cost to society of having less of this resource available in the future.

T F   3. For a common property resource, supply is determined by the marginal extraction cost only.

T F   4. A competitive equilibrium in the market for a privately owned natural resource is generally inefficient.

T F   5. If it were possible to tax those who fish for each fish caught, then, in theory, it would be possible to eliminate the efficiency loss that results because the oceans are not privately owned.

T F   6. An open border to fishermen from foreign countries would make the harvesting of fish more efficient, just as a border open to imports of foreign goods makes production within a country more efficient.

T F   7. When we run out of fresh water, all growth in population must cease.

T F   8. Allowing the domestic price of oil to rise to the world price makes us more dependent on foreign supplies.

T F   9. A policy of keeping the domestic price of a resource below the world price results in an inefficiently low level of domestic production.

T F   10. Raising the domestic price of oil above the world price will put upward pressure on the world price.

MULTIPLE CHOICE

1. In a perfectly competitive market, the last unit of a privately owned resource will be sold for:
    a. more than its reservation price
    b. less than its reservation price
    c. its reservation price
    d. more than its conservation price
    e. less than its conservation price

2. The height of the supply curve for a common property resource reflects:
    a. the extraction cost
    b. compensation for the reduced amount available in the future
    c. the extraction cost less compensation for the reduced amount available in the future
    d. the extraction cost plus compensation for the reduced amount available in the future
    e. the extraction cost or compensation for the reduced amount available in the future, whichever is larger

3. Which of the following is a common property resource?
    a. fish
    b. timber on privately owned land
    c. an oil company's reserves
    d. coal
    e. copper

4. In analysing resource use, economists use the term ''reservation price'' to mean:
    a. the lowest bid a seller will take in an auction
    b. the highest bid a buyer will pay in an auction
    c. the cost of harvesting or extracting a resource today
    d. the amount necessary to compensate for the reduced availability of the resource in the future
    e. c. and d.

5. The reservation price of a resource will decrease if:
    a. the expected future cost of extracting the resource rises
    b. the expected future price of the resource rises
    c. the expected future price of the resource remains constant
    d. auction prices have remained constant
    e. auction prices have been rising

6. The problem with doomsday models (that is, models that predict disaster because a growing population runs out of resources) is that typically:
    a. they are based on the assumption that current trends will continue long into the future
    b. they take inadequate account of the economic adjustments that will occur as resources become scarcer
    c. they take inadequate account of the social adjustments that will occur as resources become scarcer
    d. all of the above
    e. none of the above

7. Which of the following is an argument commonly used in favour of economic growth?
    a. unemployment is likely to be less severe in a rapidly growing economy
    b. faster economic growth helps to economize on scarce natural resources
    c. growth reduces pollution
    d. growth is necessary or our children will run out of natural resources
    e. growth reduces congestion

8. Which of the following is most important in explaining the increase in population in most less developed countries?
    a. the increase in the stock of natural resources relative to the labour force
    b. constant wages
    c. a change in the resource/capital ratio
    d. increasing wealth
    e. advances in medicine that have reduced the death rate

9. Between 1973 and 1982, the world price of oil (in U.S. dollars) rose from:
    a. less than $3 a barrel to $13 a barrel
    b. less than $3 to $23
    c. less than $3 to over $30
    d. $13 to $23
    e. $13 to over $30

10. The rapid increase in the price of oil in the 1970s:
    a. could be fully justified as a conservation measure
    b. could be partly justified as a conservation measure, but also reflected the exercise of monopoly power
    c. could not be justified, even in part, as a conservation measure
    d. represented a transfer from OPEC countries to oil-importing countries
    e. discouraged North American conservation efforts

11. Which of the following is a valid reason for raising the domestic Canadian price of oil above the world price?
    a. it would increase the revenues of oil exporters such as Venezuela and Mexico, with whom Canada has always had good diplomatic relations
    b. it would encourage consumers to substitute oil for natural gas

c. it would, indirectly, make us less vulnerable to an interruption of international oil supplies

d. **b.** and **c.**

e. none of these reasons is valid

12. Keeping the domestic price of oil below the world price:

a. encouraged production and consumption

b. discouraged production and consumption

c. discouraged consumption and encouraged production

d. encouraged consumption and discouraged production

e. encouraged consumption, but had no effect on production

13. Under the "blended oil price" policy of the 1970s and early 1980s, which was highest?

a. the price received by sellers of old oil

b. the price received by sellers of new oil

c. the price paid by buyers of new oil

d. none of the above because these prices were all the same

e. the policy was so confused that there was no way of telling

14. Which of the following contributed to the slowdown of the nuclear power industry in the 1970s and 1980s?

a. concern over how to dispose of radioactive wastes

b. concern over the possible proliferation of nuclear weapons

c. the fear of accidents, such as the one at Chernobyl in the Soviet Union

d. higher than expected plant costs

e. all of the above

15. Putting a common property resource under private ownership may raise which of the following problems?

a. the resource will be harvested too rapidly

b. if the new owners have monopoly power, they may use it to restrict the extraction of the resource more severely than conservation requires

c. if the new owners have monopoly power, they may use it to increase the quantity extracted of the resource

d. unless the new owners are charged adequately for this asset, it is unfair for society to provide them with such a windfall gain

e. **b.** and **d.**

16. The creation of private property rights over what was previously a common property resource:

a. is not legal for the government to do

b. would raise problems of fairness if the government were to sell these rights to a private owner for a price below their market value

c. would decrease the efficiency of the extraction of the resource

d. would have no effect on the extraction of the resource

e. would forever leave us with the same level of inefficiency in the extraction of the resource

17. An efficient pattern of resource use requires that:

a. the resource be priced at the same level each year

b. the price falls each year by the amount of the interest rate

c. the price rises each year by the amount of the interest rate

d. the cost of extracting the resource exceeds its price by the amount of the interest rate

e. the cost of extracting the resource is less than its price by the amount of the interest rate

18. If a perfectly competitive nonrenewable resource is being extracted efficiently, and more is extracted next year than this year, then:

a. the demand next year must have unit elasticity

b. the demand this year must have unit elasticity

c. the demand neither year must have unit elasticity

d. the demand must be greater this year than next

e. the demand must be greater next year than this

19. Conservation means:

a. to stop using any of the resource at all

b. to not use any of the resource until it is displaced by a substitute

c. to use it in an efficient pattern over time, starting today

d. to use it in an efficient pattern over time, starting as soon as its price starts to fall

e. to use it in an efficient pattern over time, starting as soon as its price stabilizes

20. Which of the following policies is the least efficient way of responding to a higher world price of oil?

a. limit the growth of GDP

b. conserve more

c. encourage more domestic production

d. intensify the search for alternative sources of energy

e. encourage energy-efficient technology

21. Allowing the domestic price of oil to increase to the world price results in:

a. increased oil imports

b. efficiency losses

c. no change in efficiency

d. increased domestic consumption of oil

e. reduced domestic consumption of oil

EXERCISES

1a. Figure 31.1 depicts a perfectly competitive market for a natural resource. The demand curve is D, the marginal cost of extraction is the height of the curve labelled S, and the marginal external (future) cost is the difference between the height of S and S′. The efficient quantity (assuming no external benefits) is _____, and this quantity will be demanded if the price is _____. If the resource is privately owned, the price will be _____, the quantity extracted will be _____, and the size of the efficiency loss will be _____.

1b. If the resource is not privately owned, the price will be _____, the quantity extracted will be _____, and the size of the efficiency loss will be _____. The efficiency loss could be eliminated by a (tax, subsidy) on extraction equal to _____ per unit.

2a. In Figure 31.2, a price ceiling of P_1 is imposed on the domestic oil market. Domestic production is _____, consumption is _____, and (exports, imports) are _____. Because importers have to buy

oil at the high world price P_2 and sell it domestically for only P_1, the government must compensate them by paying them a subsidy of _____ per barrel, times the _____ barrels they are importing, for a total government subsidy payment of area _____.

2b. When this price control is removed, price becomes _____, domestic production (increases, decreases) to _____, and domestic consumption (increases, decreases) to _____. (Imports, Exports) consequently (increase, decrease) to _____. Consumers (gain, lose) area _____ while producers (gain, lose) area _____ and the government (gains, loses) area _____ of (subsidy, tax) it no longer has to (pay, impose).

2c. When all these gains and losses are taken into account, the net (gain, loss) from decontrolling price is _____. This can be broken down into its two components: (1) The efficiency gain of area _____ because consumers are no longer buying oil they value at less than its true cost (the world price); and (2) the efficiency gain of area _____ because domestic firms are now producing oil for less than it previously cost to import. At the same time, there has been a transfer from consumers to _____ and _____.

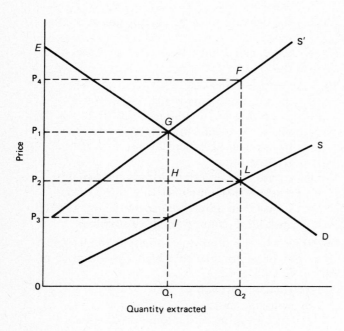

Figure 31.1

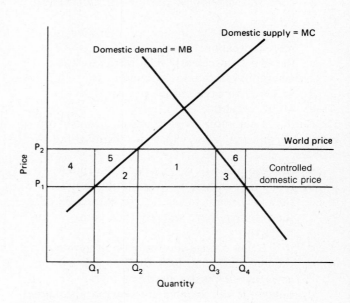

Figure 31.2

ESSAY QUESTIONS

1. Explain how the problem of excessive use of a common property resource is similar to the problem of environmental pollution. To deal with each of these problems, the government sometimes considers quantity restraints. Explain why you think these policies are effective or ineffective in dealing with each of these problems.

2. How does private ownership help to eliminate the inefficiency that exists when a resource is publicly owned (common property)? Would inefficiency be eliminated just as well if ownership were given to a single owner who then had a monopoly? What new problems might be created by allowing the resource to be monopolized?

3. "One of the shortcomings of the market mechanism is that private business interests are concerned, not with the future but, instead, with how much profit they can earn right now. We need the government to regulate the rate of extraction of natural resources to protect future generations from being deprived of their rightful share of resources." Do you agree or disagree? Why?

4. (This problem is based on Box 31-1 in the textbook.) "If the population of a species is now greater than the point of maximum sustainable yield, and if firms are now harvesting at a rate just large enough to maintain a constant size of population, then by increasing the rate of extraction they can harvest more now and more in the future." Explain this statement, using a diagram similar to Figure 31.2. If the cost of extraction is zero, what is the opportunity cost of raising the rate of extraction in this situation? Is this a case of being able to get something for nothing?

5. Suppose that scientists working on nuclear fusion make a major breakthrough, which means that the economic break-even point in fusion energy will be reached by the year 2000.

What would you expect the effects (if any) to be on the world price of oil (1) now and (2) in 2000?

What would you expect the effect (if any) to be on the Canadian price of natural gas (1) now and (2) in 2000?

6. The strict auto emission standard imposed by North American governments during the 1970s achieved its primary purpose of reducing pollution. But it had an unfavourable side effect because it increased our consumption of gasoline and thus damaged our attempts to conserve oil. Could the benefits of reduced pollution have been achieved without damaging the conservation effort if a policy of a higher oil price had been implemented instead? Explain.

7. Explain some of the external costs of producing and using oil. In your view, how do these costs compare with those arising from the production and use of natural gas? Coal? Nuclear fission?

ANSWERS

Important Terms: **1**e, **2**b, **3**d, **4**i, **5**h, **6**g, **7**c, **8**a, **9**f
True-False: **1**F, **2**T, **3**T, **4**F, **5**T, **6**F, **7**F, **8**F, **9**T, **10**F
Multiple Choice: **1**c, **2**a, **3**a, **4**e, **5**a, **6**d, **7**a, **8**e, **9**c, **10**b, **11**c, **12**d, **13**b, **14**e, **15**e, **16**b, **17**c, **18**e, **19**c, **20**a, **21**e
Exercises: **1a.** Q_1, P_1, P_1, Q_1, zero **1b.** P_2, Q_2, *GLF*, tax, P_1P_3 **2a.** Q_1, Q_4, imports, Q_1Q_4, P_1P_2, Q_1Q_4, 5 + 2 + 1 + 3 + 6 **2b.** P_2, increases, Q_2, decreases, Q_3, imports, decrease, Q_2Q_3, lose, 4 + 5 + 2 + 1 + 3, gain, 4 + 5, gains, 5 + 2 + 1 + 3 + 6, subsidy, pay **2c.** gain, 5 + 6, 6, 5, producers, the government

ANSWERS TO SELECTED REVIEW QUESTIONS FROM THE TEXT

31-1. Yes, it could be justified on conservation grounds (if, for example, such an agreement were to restrict the catch from, say, Q to Q^* in Figure 31.1). However, if the fish exist only in this area (so these owners monopolize its supply), there may be a natural temptation to restrict the catch even further as a means of exercising market power to raise price.

31-2. Myopic owners with a monopoly may harvest an inefficiently large amount if they don't adequately take into account the future costs of fishing today because they don't expect to live long. If they overestimate future costs of fishing today or if they exercise their market power to raise price, they may harvest an inefficiently small amount.

31-3. There is no further timber growth at point C. The proper timing of a timber harvest is every 30 years at point B. (This is where a straight line from the origin is tangent to the yield curve. This maximizes the slope of the line—that is, maximizes the average annual yield.)

31-5. The unit you are thinking of not using this year has a value, when extracted today, of P_1. (The height of the demand curve—i.e., the marginal productivity of this resource—is P_1.) Moving along PP' to the right, we see that this unit extracted today and put to productive use would have an increase in value to P_5 by year 5. This is more than its value if it is "held in the ground" and not extracted until year 5.

The demand curve in year 5—that is, the marginal productivity of the resource if extracted then—lies below P_5. Therefore, extract and use it now: Then its value will grow to P_5 in year 5. That's better than extracting it in year 5 when its value will be below P_5.

31-6. (a) The resource is recognized to be scarcer than previously estimated; the total available quantity Q is less. Thus, the price staircase shifts up—and with it the price in every year.

(b) The resource becomes scarcer relative to the demand for it. Same answer as in (a).

31-7. (a) We might have been impressed by it. But if we had known as much as we know now about how economies adjust, we would have been skeptical.

(b) Similarly, we are skeptical of a "doomsday conclusion" on oil today.

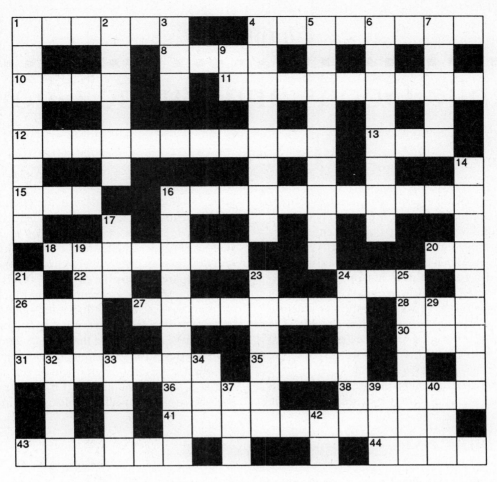

Across

1, 4. If a pasture or fishing area is owned in this manner, it may be overused.
8. partway open
10. Roman emperor who sometimes played music.
11. a common type of harmful externality
12. An emission fee is one way to protect our _____.
13. may be hard to get out of if you get into one
15. animal doctor (abbrev.)
16. The _____ yield is the amount of a renewable resource that can be harvested while still leaving the population constant.
18. One way to reduce pollution is to _____ waste.
20. exist
22. thing (Latin)
24. pig's home
26. famous Canadian hockey player
27. The efficient output occurs where the _____ social cost and social benefit are the same.
28. illegal organization in the United Kingdom (abbrev.)
30. When you pick it up, you pay.
31. what a doctor, lawyer, or teacher provides
35. is honked to give warning
36. leave out
38. rub out
41. what we will have to find if a natural resource runs out
43. be annoyed about
44. Blomqvist, Wonnacott, and Wonnacott, *Economics*

Down

1. High prices encourage people to _____ scarce raw materials.
2. If people suffer from this, they may use up scarce resources too quickly.
3. to constantly complain and criticize
4. The creation of _____ _____ is one way to discourage the overuse of a scarce resource.
5. what Petro-Canada hopes for when it drills in the Beaufort Sea
6. Overfishing today creates an _____ cost, which will be faced by future fishermen.
7. tasty fish
9. major chain of food stores (abbrev.)
14. Resources such as fish or timber, but not oil, are _____.
16. Private cost plus external cost equals _____ _____. (2 words)
17. in games of cards, may be high or low
19. Trial and _____ is often a hard way to learn.
21. At work you get your orders from this person.
24. Our _____ is sometimes called "spaceship earth."
25. substance used as an ingredient in fertilizer
29. sun god in ancient Egypt
32. one of the Great Lakes
33. see (Latin)
34. Australian bird
37. leading company in the computer business
39. We told you in 13 across not to get into one!
40. One is sometimes called fair.
42. opposite of out

Chapter 32

■■■■■■■■■■■■■■■■■■■■■■■■■■■■■■■■■■■■■■■

Public Goods and Public Choice

MAJOR PURPOSE

The last chapter dealt with external costs. In this chapter we use a parallel approach to analyse external benefits—that is, the benefits of a product that are enjoyed by others, above and beyond the internal benefits enjoyed by those who buy it. When external benefits exist, a free perfectly competitive market does not produce an efficient outcome. There is too little free-market production of such a good, just as there was too much production of a good with an external cost in the last chapter. The solution is to subsidize the good with the external benefits, just as the good with the external costs was taxed in the last chapter.

A further objective of this chapter is to extend this analysis of external benefits to describe the concept of a public good. A flood-control dam is an example of a public good, because no one can be excluded from enjoying its benefits, regardless of who pays for it. Typically, with such a broad distribution of benefits, no specific individuals play a significant enough role as purchasers to be prepared to buy the good. So, if it is to be provided at all, it must be the government that purchases it. In this chapter, we describe the difficulties a government faces in trying to decide whether or not such a purchase is justified; and we also describe the more general problems that arise whenever the government provides the public with any good or services. Even when the private market fails, and a good must be provided by the government (if it is to be supplied at all) problems remain.

LEARNING OBJECTIVES

After you have studied this chapter in the textbook and the study guide, you should be able to
* Demonstrate why a free, perfectly competitive market provides less than the efficient amount of a good with external benefits
* Measure, in a diagram like Figure 32-1 in the textbook, the efficiency loss resulting from the private provision of a good with external benefits
* Show why efficiency requires a good to be subsidized by an amount equal to the marginal external benefit it provides (assuming that there are not high costs of administering the subsidy)
* Define and fully explain the concept of a public good
* Construct the marginal social benefit curve (a) for a public good, and (b) for a private good, making clear the difference between the two
* Explain why the "free-rider" problem makes it difficult for the government to estimate the benefits of a public good simply by asking people how highly they value it
* Give the reasons for believing that when the government provides a good or service—whether or not this is in response to a failure by the free market—major problems remain, such as the problems of bureaucracy; efficiency is still not guaranteed
* Show why it may be necessary to view as a public good any wildlife species that is becoming extinct
* Explain the concept of "option demand" and demonstrate its significance in dealing with such a wildlife species

HIGHLIGHTS OF THE CHAPTER

Why is there too little production of a good with an external benefit?

The Inefficiency of a Private Market When There are External Benefits

A free, perfectly competitive market delivers less than the efficient output of a product with an external benefit because the marginal cost of the product (supply) is equated to its marginal *private* benefit (demand), rather than to its marginal *social* benefit. The reason is that, in deciding on their demand for the product, buyers take account of only the private benefit it will provide them, and ignore the external benefit it will provide to others. With the demand curve therefore reflecting only private benefit and any external benefit being ignored, it is no surprise that too little is produced, as Figure 32.1 demonstrates. The appropriate government policy is to subsidize this product by the amount of the external benefit it provides (assuming there are not substantial costs in administering the subsidy). Such a subsidy will increase the demand for the product and thus increase its output to the efficient amount.

Public Goods

In the case of products with an external benefit that we have been describing so far—such as gardening—you will receive an external benefit if your neighbour pays $100 for gardening services. But, of course, you will get an even larger benefit if you pay the gardener the $100 yourself in order to have the gardening done on your own lawn rather than on your neighbour's. Thus, the benefits you get depend on who buys the service. A *public good* can be viewed as the extreme case of a good with an external benefit, where the amount of benefit that an individual gets is just as great if someone else buys as it is if he or she were to buy it. In other words, the individual cannot be excluded in any way from enjoying it. For example, you get the same benefit from cleaner air, whether or not you help to pay for antipollution measures. That is not true of a private good. You can't enjoy a movie or a restaurant meal unless you pay for it. This is the reason that the benefits of a private good are horizontally summed in Figure 32-3 of the textbook, while the benefits of a public good are vertically summed in Figure 32.3.

The Free-rider Problem

If you will get the same benefit whether or not you help

pay for a good, why not be a "free rider" and not pay at all (or pay as small a share as you can get away with)? The incentive for people to ride free raises problems for an entrepreneur who believes (let's suppose, correctly) that the benefits people would get from a public good—such as a flood-control dam—exceed its costs and it, therefore, should be built. How can it be financed, when everyone the entrepreneur asks to contribute to it tries to minimize that contribution by understating the benefits the dam would provide? In short, each individual has an incentive to be a free rider, enjoying the benefits of the dam without contributing to it. Since all individuals have this incentive to understate the benefits of the dam, it appears not to be justified, and does not get built.

Suppose the government, rather than a private entrepreneur, tries to evaluate the dam by asking people how highly they would value it. If they think they will be taxed according to their answer, they will understate. On the other hand, if they think their taxes won't be affected by the project, they will tend to overstate their benefit—as a means of slightly increasing the chance that the project will be undertaken. In this case, they have nothing to lose, since the cost they incur is not affected by their overvaluation.

An Alternative Approach by the Government

In view of the difficulties in trying to get people to answer accurately, the authorities generally reject the approach of asking people for their evaluation of a project. Instead they often use a "benefit-cost" analysis based on a completely different kind of information. To use the example in the text, they may estimate the benefit of a dam by examining how frequently floods have occurred without it, and the average crop loss.

This approach may be superior, but it still involves major problems. For example, those who are running this analysis may have a vested interest in having the dam pass the benefit-cost test because they may hope to be employed in its construction. Or they may simply be trying to please their employer—a government that has promised this dam in the last election. They may therefore add benefits—perhaps at an inflated value—until these benefits exceed the costs, and the project is justified. Such an inflation of benefits may be easy, especially if one of the benefits of a flood-control project is to save lives. It is very difficult indeed to attach a dollar value to a human life. (Recall our discussion in Box 30-4 of the textbook.)

Other Problems with Government Expenditure Decisions

More generally, when decision-making shifts from the private marketplace to the government—as indeed it must in the case of a public good which the private market fails to deliver—then a new set of special problems arises:

1. Typically, private firms stop producing goods if they are no longer profitable—or, if they fail outright from the start—because these firms would lose money otherwise. On the other hand, government projects that are no longer justified are much more difficult to terminate for two reasons: (a) no politician wants to admit that a project may have been a mistake, for fear of losing the next election as a result; and (b) there is no natural check, like the bankruptcy of a private firm, to force termination of a government project.

2. Political votes are not as specific and frequent as the economic votes that people cast every day when they are deciding what to buy with their money. Thus private auto companies get a clear message of the models the public wants and does not want. Not so with public goods. It may be two or four years before the next election when the public can vote on how it likes or dislikes the dam and the other goods and services the government is providing. And even if people do approve of what the government is doing—and vote for it in the next election—it's hard to know whether the election victory is due to the dam the government has built, or to its foreign policy, or to some other completely different issue.

(Public opinion polls make this problem less severe, but don't remove it.)

3. Special interest groups can exert an inordinate influence on government decision making. Even if you have no particular interest in the government spending money on a proposed new road in northern Alberta, it probably doesn't pay you to invest a great deal of energy and resources in opposing it, since it may add only a trivial 10 cents to your tax bill. But those directly affected in the area have a strong incentive to support it and lobby for its construction. Thus, a few large benefits concentrated in one area may politically outweigh many small, widely dispersed costs, even if the sum of all these small costs exceeds the benefits economically.

4. Politicians are mainly interested in projects with benefits that are both obvious to the public and immediate. (If they don't have a payoff before the next election, it may be too late.) Thus, politicians often do not take a long-term point of view; there is a tendency for much government effort to be centred on short-term decision making.

5. The job of implementing—and sometimes initiating—government policies is performed by a bureaucracy. There is a constant tendency for bureaus and their budgets to expand, in part because of the incentives for bureau chiefs to expand their personnel. Accordingly, bureaus tend to grow beyond the efficient size. This tendency is not checked by the threat of economic loss or bankruptcy that faces a private firm that overexpands.

IMPORTANT TERMS: MATCH THE COLUMNS

Match each term in the first column with the corresponding explanation in the second column.

_____ **1.** External (spillover) benefit
_____ **2.** Public good
_____ **3.** Internal private benefits
_____ **4.** Benefit-cost analysis
_____ **5.** Option demand
_____ **6.** Free riders
_____ **7.** Logrolling
_____ **8.** Internalizing an externality

a. A product whose benefits are available to everyone, regardless of who pays for it
b. Forcing firms or individuals to face the external costs or benefits they are creating
c. The estimation of the dollar value of the costs and benefits that are likely to result from a particular government policy
d. Those who cannot be excluded from the benefits of a public good, even though they do not pay their share of its costs
e. The benefit derived from a product by those who do not buy it or produce it
f. The desire to have something available, whether or not we actually use it
g. The benefits from a good derived by the purchaser
h. An agreement by two voters that each will support the other's project

TRUE-FALSE

T   F   1. Internalizing externalities means that producers are forced to face any external costs of their actions; and buyers are allowed to enjoy any external benefits generated by their purchases.

T   F   2. One benefit of having the government provide public goods such as flood control dams is that these decisions are easily reversible.

T   F   3. The reason private firms can't be relied on to produce a public good is that they would externalize the internal benefits.

T   F   4. The marginal social benefit curve of a public good can be constructed by vertically summing the individual demand curves.

T   F   5. You cannot be excluded from enjoying the benefits of a public good even if someone else pays for it.

T   F   6. It is generally more difficult to cut out an expenditure program in the private sector than in the public sector.

T   F   7. The public can be more specific in expressing its preferences for goods by voting in elections than by making purchases in the marketplace.

T   F   8. It may make sense to vote for a party that has promised to make a certain government expenditure, even though you don't want this expenditure at all.

T   F   9. Politicians prefer policies with costs and benefits that are obscure.

T   F   10. Government policy should ensure that no damage whatsoever occurs to the environment.

MULTIPLE CHOICE

1. In producing two goods (one with an external benefit, the other with an external cost) a free, perfectly competitive market will generate:
   a. too much output of the good with the external benefit, and too little of the good with the external cost
   b. too little output of the good with the external benefit, and too much of the good with the external cost
   c. too little output of the good with the external benefit, and just the right amount of the good with the external cost
   d. too little of both
   e. too much of both

2. Which of the following comes closest to being a private good with no external benefits?
   a. national defence
   b. painting the outside of your house
   c. painting the inside of your house
   d. hiring a gardener
   e. the police force

3. If the government follows a "hands-off" policy, then the production of a perfectly competitive good with an external benefit will result in:
   a. marginal external benefit being greater than marginal social benefit
   b. marginal external benefit being equal to marginal social benefit

   c. marginal social cost being equal to marginal social benefit
   d. marginal social cost being greater than marginal social benefit
   e. marginal social cost being less than marginal social benefit

4. If a good has an external benefit, the government can ensure an efficient outcome by introducing a:
   a. tax equal to the external benefit
   b. tax greater than the external benefit
   c. subsidy less than the external benefit
   d. subsidy greater than the external benefit
   e. none of the above

5. If there are substantial administrative costs in subsidizing a good with an external benefit, the government should:
   a. tax it instead, to provide the same result
   b. subsidize the good regardless
   c. cancel the subsidy regardless
   d. cancel the subsidy if the efficiency gain it would produce is less than the administrative costs
   e. cancel the subsidy if the efficiency gain it would produce is greater than the administrative costs

6. The internal benefit of a good is the:
   a. benefit enjoyed by those who haven't purchased it

b. benefit enjoyed by the individual who has purchased it

c. benefit enjoyed by free riders

d. benefit enjoyed by the government, even though the public has purchased it

e. benefit enjoyed by the public, even though the government has purchased it

7. An example of internalizing an externality occurs when:

a. a firm building a ski lift buys a restaurant at the bottom of the hill

b. a firm buys from a domestic supplier a good that it used to buy from abroad

c. a city government subsidizes exterior home improvements

d. a. and c.

e. b. and c.

8. In defining the marginal benefit to society of a public good:

a. the demand curves by individuals are horizontally summed

b. the demand curves by individuals are vertically summed

c. the demand curves by individuals are horizontally summed and then vertically summed

d. we use the same technique that was used to derive the market demand curve for a private good from the individual demand curves

e. we take the demand curve of the individual who is most eager and able to buy the good

9. With a public good:

a. anyone can participate in the benefits except the actual purchaser

b. everyone can participate in the benefits including the actual purchaser

c. no one can participate in the benefits except the purchaser

d. only free riders participate in the benefits

e. free riders are prevented from participating in the benefits

10. Estimates that the government collects from individuals on how highly they value public projects tend to be unreliable because:

a. if people feel they will be taxed according to the value they state, they will tend to understate

b. if people feel they will be taxed according to the value they state, they will tend to overstate

c. if people feel they will not be taxed according to the value they state, they will tend to overstate

d. if people feel they will not be taxed according to the value they state, they will tend to understate

e. a. and c.

11. A free rider is someone:

a. who cannot be excluded from enjoying the benefits of a project even though this individual has paid nothing to cover its costs

b. who can be excluded from enjoying the benefits of a project

c. who is trying to encourage the government to continue its transportation subsidies

d. who has paid more than a fair share of the costs

e. who has paid his or her fair share of the costs

12. Benefit-cost analysis often involves the following problem:

a. questionable projects that have been promised in an election campaign may be justified by exaggerating benefits

b. questionable projects that have been promised in an election campaign may be justified by underestimating costs

c. it is very difficult to place a value on a human life

d. projects may be evaluated by those with a conflict of interest—for example, engineers who may eventually be employed in building the projects

e. all of the above

13. Typically, a government bureau that is a monopoly will produce:

a. too much output, while a private monopoly will produce too little

b. too little output, just like a private monopoly

c. too much output, just like a private monopoly

d. the right amount of output, while a private monopoly will produce too little

e. too little output, just like a private oligopoly

14. A species of wildlife in the wilderness:

a. cannot die out unless it is adversely affected by human action

b. will die out if it is left unprotected

c. may die out if it is left unprotected

d. will be prevented from dying out by free market forces

e. should not be protected by the government because of option demand

15. Suppose you voted for the NDP in 1988 because you were opposed to free trade with the United

States, even though you thought that the economic policies of the Progressive Conservatives were superior. Then this illustrates the problem that:

    a. public expenditure decisions are hard to reverse

    b. special interest groups have an inordinate influence on public decisions

    c. bureaucrats are not subject to the normal check of bankruptcy

    d. political votes are difficult to interpret because they are not as specific as market-place votes

    e. free riders are difficult to deal with

16. Many economists have argued that our farm subsidy programs are inefficient—that what farmers gain from higher food prices is less than what consumers lose. But these programs continue. According to the principles explained in this chapter, which seems the most likely explanation?

    a. food is a public good

    b. the farmers' special interest is politically stronger than the consumers' general interest

    c. the farmers' special interest is politically weaker than the consumers' general interest

    d. consumers do not adequately recognize the benefits of good food and must be forced to pay for them through taxes

    e. farmers have more votes than nonfarmers

17. Reversing a decision is more difficult for a government than a private firm because:

    a. this admission of error may damage the government in the next election

    b. business executives generally prefer to admit mistakes than to continue to lose money

    c. politicians don't directly suffer out of pocket when they continue uneconomic expenditures

    d. all of the above

    e. **b.** and **c.**

18. Logrolling:

    a. never damages the public interest

    b. always damages the public interest

    c. always promotes the public interest

    d. sometimes damages the public interest, and sometimes promotes it

    e. has an effect which is impossible to assess, no matter how much information is available on individual preferences

19. If the government asks individuals their valuation of a public good, they will:

    a. overstate if the government will tax them according to their stated valuation

    b. understate if the government will tax them according to their stated valuation

    c. understate if the government will finance the project without taxing them

    d. neither understate nor overstate if the government will finance the project without taxing them

    e. neither overstate nor understate if the government will tax them according to their stated valuation

20. Option demand is the demand for:

    a. a good, not because you want to use it now, but because you may want to use it in the future

    b. a good, not because you want to use it now, but because you are certain to want it in the future

    c. any public good that provides benefits now and in the future

    d. any private good that provides benefits now and in the future

    e. a good which is a private good now, but may be a public good in the future

21. In the case of a natural oligopoly, the appropriate role for the government is likely to be to:

    a. enforce competition legislation

    b. regulate price

    c. provide the good itself

    d. leave the market alone

    e. encourage price discrimination

EXERCISES

1a. Figure 32.1 on the next page shows the supply curve S and demand curve D for a perfectly competitive good that provides external benefits. Assume for now that there are no external costs of producing this good, and ignore MC_S.

In an unregulated market, the quantity that is produced is _____ and the market price is _____. If the marginal social benefit curve is MB_S, then the economically efficient quantity is _____ and the marginal external benefit is _____.

1b. The efficiency loss from relying upon the private market for the provision of this good is _____. The

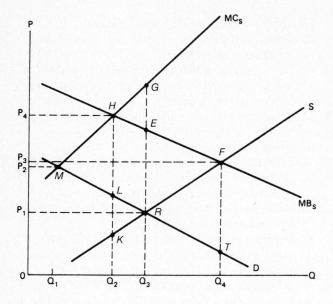

Figure 32.1

government could eliminate this efficiency loss by offering a per unit (subsidy, tax) of _____ to the producers of this good.

1c. Now suppose that the good involves external costs as well as external benefits. (An example would be a dam that provides flood control to farmers downstream but that floods out farmers upstream.) Let the curve labelled MC_S represent the marginal social cost of producing the good. Then the efficient amount of production of the good is _____. At that level of production, the marginal external cost would be _____ and the marginal external benefit would be _____. With no tax or subsidy, the private market would produce (more, less) than the economically efficient amount and the efficiency loss would be _____. This efficiency loss could be eliminated if the government were to (tax, subsidize) the production of the good by _____ per unit.

2. Figure 32.2 shows the marginal private benefit MB_A and MB_B that individuals A and B receive from a public good (a waste-treatment plant). In Figure 32.2 (c), show the marginal social benefit, assuming that A and B are the only members of society affected by the project.

3a. Suppose that there are 1000 farmers affected by a proposed dam. Each of them would receive a benefit of $1,000. The social benefit of the dam is $_____. If the dam costs $500,000, it (is, is not) worth building.

3b. Suppose you are one of the farmers. The government tells you that it intends to tax farmers according to how much each says the dam will be worth to him or her. If you tell the truth, it will cost you $_____. If you say $2,000, it will cost you $_____. If you say no benefit, it will cost you $_____. You will

have an incentive to (understate, overstate, reveal accurately) how much it is worth to you. Other farmers (will, will not) have the same incentive to provide this sort of answer, so the chances are that the dam (will, will not) be built—an (efficient, inefficient) outcome.

3c. As another example, suppose that the same 1000 farmers would get the same true benefits from the dam, but now suppose that the cost of building the dam is $1,500,000. In this case the dam (should, should not) be built. But suppose that now the government says that if it goes ahead with the dam it will tax the millions of taxpayers a few cents each to finance it. Your taxes will be scarcely affected. The only question the government has is: Should it go ahead or not? That depends on how highly farmers value it. If the government goes ahead, you will have a net gain (value to you of the dam minus your new taxes) of _____. You will maximize your chances of getting this gain if you (understate, overstate, reveal accurately) your benefit, and thus (increase, decrease) the chance that the dam will be built. Other farmers (will, will not) have the same incentive to give the same sort of answer, so the chances are that the dam (will, will not) be built—an (efficient, inefficient) outcome.

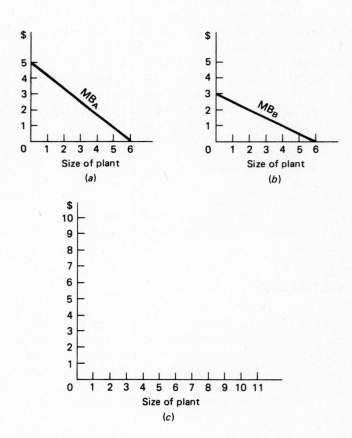

Figure 32.2

ESSAY QUESTIONS

1. Explain carefully whether or not each of the following might be considered to be a good with an external benefit:
   a. the Canadian Olympic Team
   b. your telephone
   c. driver safety lessons
   d. television programs

2. If the government asks people to reveal how much they would benefit from a public good, will they tell the truth? If the government asks them to reveal how much they are being damaged by a good with an external cost, will they tell the truth? Why or why not? How will their answers be affected if the government tells them that it is thinking of providing them with protection from this external cost, with this protection to be financed out of the government's general tax revenues?

3. Many industries pay lobbyists to influence regulatory agencies, House of Commons or Senate committees, and other government agencies and officials in Ottawa. Sometimes these lobbyists spend a lot of time promoting the idea that their industry is a source of external benefits. Why would the firms in an industry pay lobbyists to do this?

4. Criticize the following statement: "The government should not be providing money for vaccination programs. If people are unwilling to pay the full cost of vaccinations without subsidy, then vaccinations fail the market test and should not be provided at all."

5. Explain why you agree or disagree with the following statement: "You can rely on the government to provide you with the goods you want at a reasonable price just as much as you can rely upon private business firms. The reason is that the party in power wants you to be pleased with what it provides so that you will vote for it in the next election, just as a private business firm wants you to be pleased with what it provides so that you will buy the product again."

6. It has been argued that when the government spends more money, it provides a great deal of benefits to a small number of people and a very small cost to a large number of people (namely, taxpayers). Give an example. Why does a government judge that such a policy is in its interests? Will it necessarily be in the nation's economic interest?

ANSWERS

Important Terms: **1e, 2a, 3g, 4c, 5f, 6d, 7h, 8b**
True-False: **1T, 2F, 3F, 4T, 5T, 6F, 7F, 8T, 9F, 10F**
Multiple Choice: **1b, 2c, 3e, 4e, 5d, 6b, 7d, 8b, 9b, 10e, 11a, 12e, 13a, 14c, 15d, 16b, 17d, 18d, 19b, 20a, 21a**
Exercises: **1a.** Q_3, P_1, Q_4, *ER* (or *FT*) **1b.** *EFR*, subsidy, *TF* **1c.** Q_2, *KH, LH*, more, *HGE*, tax, *LK*
2. Figure 32.2(*c*) completed

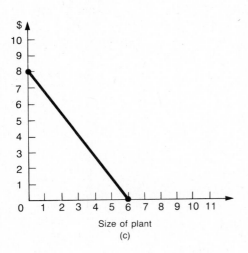

Size of plant
(c)

3a. $1 million, is **3b.** $1,000, $2,000, 0, understate, will, will not, inefficient **3c.** should not, almost $1,000, overstate, increase, will, will, inefficient

ANSWERS TO SELECTED REVIEW QUESTIONS FROM THE TEXT

32-2. Yes. According to the layman's definition, it is a public good because it is a service the government provides. According to the definition in the textbook, it is a public good because the benefit people get from national defence does not depend on who pays for it, and the defence protection you get is not diminished by the fact your neighbour is getting it as well.

Its benefits would be very difficult to estimate. First, it is not at all clear how much protection our total military budget actually provides. But, even if we knew this, how could we find out how high a value people place on this service? The government cannot simply ask people. If it were to try, then those who favour a big defence budget and feel that their answer will not substantially affect the taxes they have to pay, will tend to overstate the benefits they receive. On the other hand, those who do not favour military expenditure will also exaggerate—in this case, by inflating the negative value they place on it.

32-3. A private entrepreneur would not undertake this because he or she would face the same problem encountered in our dam-building example in the textbook. Even though the project may be justified, there is no way—in a world of potential free riders—that the private entrepreneur could raise the necessary funds from the public; people do not have an incentive to state honestly the benefits they would receive from the project.

32-4. Condition (26-1).

32-5. Agree: Since it's correct, this statement is self-explanatory.

32-7. In Table 32-2, change the two entries of $+3$ to $+4$.

Chapter 33

■ ■

What Are the Gains from International Trade?

MAJOR PURPOSE

Canadians in British Columbia gain from domestic trade with other Canadians in Alberta and Quebec. Similarly, Canadians gain from international trade with the Japanese and the Americans. The reasons are the same in either case. Our purpose in this chapter is to examine four broad sources of the gains from trade: (1) increased competition; (2) greater availability of products; (3) economies of scale; and (4) comparative advantage. This chapter also identifies the winners and losers from trade. While winners outnumber losers, and the nation as a whole benefits from trade, some Canadians are hurt. Their ability to organize themselves and apply political pressure is one of the main reasons that countries maintain restrictions on trade—restrictions that will be examined in the next chapter.

LEARNING OBJECTIVES

After you have studied this chapter in the textbook and the study guide, you should be able to
- Identify the four main sources of gains from international trade
- Explain why trade increases competition in the domestic Canadian market and reduces the market power of Canadian producers, thus generating an efficiency gain
- Explain why trade makes possible cost reductions because it provides opportunities to exploit economies of scale. Thus, income is increased and a wider variety of new products is available.
- Explain the difference between absolute advantage and comparative advantage
- Explain why countries export those commodities in which they have a comparative advantage, and how comparative advantage is determined by opportunity costs
- Explain the two respects in which international trade and technological change are similar, and the respects in which they are different
- Measure diagrammatically the gains from international trade using a production possibilities curve as in Figures 33-4 and 33-5 of the textbook or, alternatively, using the supply and demand diagrams shown in Figures 33-6 and 33-7
- Show the gains from trade in a supply/demand diagram by comparing the effect of trade on consumers with its effect on producers
- Identify the winners and losers from international trade

HIGHLIGHTS OF THE CHAPTER

The two broad questions addressed in this chapter are: Why are there gains from trade? Who are the winners and losers? First, consider why we gain from trade.

The Sources of Gain

1. *Increased competition.* There are two important changes that face domestic producers when trade is opened up. First, they face a much larger market; they can now sell to people anywhere in the world. Second, they now face many more competitors. Canadian General Electric (CGE) no longer competes just against Electrohome and other Canadian producers; instead, it now competes with an additional group of producers from Japan, the United States, and elsewhere. Because of increased competition, oligopolists such as CGE and Electrohome lose much of their market power—their ability to influence price. Thus, they move closer to perfect competition, with the increase in efficiency that this implies. Similarly, a Canadian monopolist may, as a result of trade, find itself an oligopolist, with several foreign competitors; this industry also moves closer to perfect competition.

2. *Greater availability of products.* Trade makes goods available that would otherwise not exist. Boeing might not have been able to develop the jumbo jet if it had been able to sell it only in the U.S. market, rather than in the entire world.

3. *Economies of scale.* Without international trade, each country must be self-sufficient; it must, therefore, produce a wide variety of products in the small quantity necessary just to satisfy its own needs. With international trade, each country can specialize, producing only a few items in large volume and trading to get the rest. Large volume often means reduced cost; that is, there are economies of scale. And reduced cost means that we can produce and therefore consume more. In other words, our real income rises. It also rises because other countries are specializing and reducing their costs. Thus, the products we trade for, as well as the goods we produce ourselves, fall in cost.

Not only are costs reduced; in addition, variety may be increased. For example, because of international trade, someone buying a car in the tiny European country of Liechtenstein can choose among Fords, Volkswagens, Datsuns, and many others that are produced elsewhere. Without international trade, consumers wouldn't have this choice. People in Liechtenstein would have to buy cars produced in Liechtenstein. But the market there is so small (the population is less than 30 000), that they would be lucky to have even one auto firm producing one model. There would be little or no variety.

4. *Comparative advantage.* To understand comparative advantage, you must first understand absolute advantage. Table 33-3 in the textbook can be used to clarify the difference between the two. In the right-hand column of this table, we see that Canada has an absolute advantage in food because a Canadian worker can produce 3 units of food, whereas a worker in Britain can produce only 1. In other words, it only takes a third as many workers to produce food in Canada as in Britain. The input requirement—that is, the labour requirement—to produce food in Canada is lower than in Britain. (This is the definition of absolute advantage: a country has an absolute advantage in a good if the input requirement in that country is lower than that in other countries.)

Canada also has an absolute advantage in clothing. (A Canadian worker outproduces a British worker in clothing by 6 to 4, as shown in the first column of Table 33-3.) Because Canada has an absolute advantage in producing both goods, absolute advantage cannot be the key to explaining which country will produce what. If it were the key, then Canada would produce both goods, and Britain neither—and that is inconsistent with the two-way trade we observe.

What then does determine the pattern of production and trade? The answer is: comparative advantage. But in which product does Canada have a comparative advantage? The answer is: food, because this is where Canada's absolute advantage is greater; a worker in Canada can outproduce a worker in Britain by 3 to 1 in food, but by only 6 to 4—that is, 3 to 2—in clothing. Because Canada has a comparative advantage in food, Britain has a comparative advantage in clothing; that's where Britain's absolute disadvantage is least.

Using a more formal definition, we say that Canada has a comparative advantage in food if it has a lower opportunity cost of producing food than does Britain. This is, indeed, the case. In the second row of Table 33-3, we see the high opportunity cost of food in Britain. Since a worker who is now producing 1 unit of food could instead be producing 4 units of clothing, the opportunity cost (the alternative forgone) of producing that 1 unit of food is 4 units of clothing. Compare this to the lower opportunity cost of food in Canada, derived from the top row in this table: Since a Canadian worker who is now producing 3 units of food could instead be producing 6 units of clothing, the opportunity cost in Canada of each unit of food is $6/3 = 2$ units of clothing. Because Canada has a lower opportunity cost of food than does Britain, Canada has a comparative advantage in food, and will specialize in this. Similar calculations for clothing will show that Britain has a comparative advantage here. With specialization in its products of comparative advantage, both Canada and Britain benefit, as is demonstrated in the calculations at the bottom of this table.

To sum up: Both absolute and comparative advantage refer to the cost of production. The difference is in how this cost is measured. For absolute advantage, cost is measured in terms of inputs required. For comparative advantage, cost is measured in terms of outputs forgone, that is, opportunity cost.

Here's an intuitive approach that may help you to understand better the gains from trade. Trade is the way a country can inexpensively acquire the goods in which it does not have a comparative advantage. Why produce these goods at home—where their opportunity cost is high—when they can be purchased from another country where their opportunity cost is low?

This gain from trade is further illustrated using the production possibilities curve shown in Figure 33-4 of the textbook. The gain comes when a country uses trade to move from point *B* to *D*. But you should be able to break down this move into its two components: (1) the move from *B* to *C*, as the country specializes in food, and (2) the move from *C* to *D*, as the country then trades food for clothing.

This production possibilities curve is also useful, as shown in Figure 33-5 in the textbook, when it is used to compare international trade and technological change. Both allow a country to consume a combination of goods lying beyond its current production possibilities curve. (Both may also be the source of unemployment that may have to be endured in the short run in order to realize income gains in the long run.)

Finally, the textbook also illustrates the gains from trade using familiar supply and demand diagrams. You should understand clearly why the nation gains from unrestricted exports, as shown in Figure 33-6, and unrestricted imports, as shown in Figure 33-7. We gain on the export side because we sell goods abroad for more than it costs us to produce them (or more than we lose when we switch these goods away from domestic consumption). At the same time, we gain on the import side because we can buy imports for less than it would cost us to produce them inefficiently at home; and imports also allow us to increase our consumption of bargain-priced goods from abroad. For both exports and imports there is a triangular efficiency gain shown in Figures 33-6 and 33-7. You should be able to confirm these gains in a diagram like Figure 33-8 that shows how trade affects consumers and producers. This technique then allows you to fill in the details on the second key question in this chapter.

Who Are the Winners and Losers?

Since opening our borders to an import lowers the domestic price of this good, consumers win and domestic producers lose. On the export side, there is also a conflict between these two groups—although the roles are reversed. Because opening foreign markets raises the price we can charge for our exports, producers win and consumers lose. Whenever trade policy is changed for a specific industry, a conflict between consumers and producers arises. This must be understood before turning to the contentious issues of trade policy discussed in the next chapter.

IMPORTANT TERMS: MATCH THE COLUMNS

Match each term in the first column with its corresponding explanation in the second column.

_____	1.	Economies of scale
_____	2.	Comparative advantage
_____	3.	Opportunity cost
_____	4.	Absolute advantage
_____	5.	International specialization
_____	6.	Terms of trade
_____	7.	Production gain on an export
_____	8.	Consumption gain on an import

a. Country A has this in good X if the opportunity cost of producing X is lower in country A than in any other country

b. Each country concentrating on one, or a small number of products, and acquiring the others through international trade

c. Country B has this in good Y if Y can be produced with fewer inputs in country B than in any other country

d. Falling average cost as output increases. This is one source of gain from international trade.

e. The quantity of good B that must be sacrificed in order to produce another unit of good A

f. The sale of a product abroad for more than it costs to produce at home

g. The price a country receives for its exports divided by the price it pays for its imports

h. The ability to purchase goods abroad more cheaply than they could be produced at home

TRUE-FALSE

T   F   **1.** Comparative advantage ensures that Canadian exports of any good will equal Canadian imports of that same good.

T   F   **2.** International trade tends to transform a natural oligopoly into a natural monopoly.

T   F   **3.** Although each member country in the European Community imposes tariffs in its trade with other member countries, it may trade freely with the rest of the world.

Table 33.1   Output per Worker

	Clothing	Food
in Canada	10	8
in Europe	2	4

T   F   **4.** In Table 33.1, Europe has a comparative advantage in food.

T   F   **5.** In Table 33.1, Europe has an absolute advantage in both goods.

T   F   **6.** If Canada has an absolute advantage in a good, then Canada will necessarily specialize in that good.

T   F   **7.** If Canada has a lower opportunity cost of producing good X than any other country, then Canada has a comparative advantage in X.

T   F   **8.** While improved technology allows a country to consume more by moving to a higher production possibility curve, international trade allows a country to consume more without moving its production off its existing production possibilities curve.

T   F   **9.** Large North American exports of grains following droughts overseas in the early 1970s benefitted North American farmers, hurt North American consumers, and resulted in an overall efficiency loss.

T   F   **10.** If a country imports oranges, then producers of oranges in that country probably gain from international trade in oranges.

MULTIPLE CHOICE

1. Manufactured goods are
   a. imported, but not exported by Canada
   b. exported, but not imported by Canada
   c. exported by Canada to Europe only
   d. imported and exported by Canada
   e. neither imported nor exported by Canada

2. Specialization and trade provide gains in
   a. domestic trade only
   b. foreign trade only
   c. domestic and foreign trade
   d. neither domestic nor foreign trade
   e. foreign trade, as long as countries do not have an absolute advantage

3. Which of the following is a possible result of international trade?
   a. a natural monopoly in the domestic market may be transformed into a natural oligopoly in the world market
   b. a perfectly competitive industry may be turned into a natural oligopoly
   c. a natural oligopoly may be turned into a natural monopoly

   d. a perfectly competitive industry may be turned into a natural monopoly
   e. large firms are able to exercise more market power because the size of the market is increased

4. International trade makes domestic firms more competitive in terms of
   a. price
   b. quality
   c. design
   d. the introduction of new products
   e. all of the above

5. International trade will lead a firm to introduce a new product if
   a. trade shifts demand to the right enough so that for the first time demand for the product overlaps its average costs
   b. trade shifts demand to the left enough so that for the first time demand for the product overlaps its average costs
   c. trade shifts demand to the left enough so that for the first time marginal cost of the product

intersects its average cost

  d. trade shifts demand to the right enough so that for the first time marginal cost of the product intersects its average cost

  e. trade shifts demand to the right enough so that for the first time marginal cost of the product intersects its average variable cost

6. Under international trade we export those goods for which we have a relatively low

  a. materials cost
  b. wage cost
  c. accounting cost
  d. opportunity cost
  e. overhead cost

7. The idea of comparative advantage was developed by

  a. Adam Smith
  b. Karl Marx
  c. David Ricardo
  d. Alfred Marshall
  e. John Maynard Keynes

8. If Canada has an absolute advantage in a good, then Canada

  a. may or may not export that good
  b. will necessarily export that good
  c. will necessarily avoid exporting that good
  d. will necessarily import that good
  e. will necessarily avoid importing that good

Table 33.2 Output per Worker

	Clothing	Food
in Canada	6	3
in Europe	4	1

9. In Table 33.2, international trade would induce Canada to import

  a. food
  b. clothing
  c. both
  d. neither
  e. one or the other; we can't say which

10. In Table 33.2, Canada has an absolute advantage in

  a. both goods, and a comparative advantage in food
  b. both goods, and a comparative advantage in clothing
  c. both goods, and a comparative advantage in neither
  d. neither good, but a comparative advantage in food
  e. neither good, but a comparative advantage in clothing

11. In Table 33.2, Europe has an absolute advantage in

  a. both goods, and a comparative advantage in food
  b. both goods, and a comparative advantage in clothing
  c. both goods, and a comparative advantage in neither
  d. neither good, but a comparative advantage in food
  e. neither good, but a comparative advantage in clothing

12. In Table 33.2, Europe's opportunity cost of producing food is

  a. 3 units of clothing
  b. 6/3 = 2 units of clothing
  c. 6/4 = 1 1/2 units of clothing
  d. 4 units of clothing
  e. 3 units of food

13. If the lower right-hand number in Table 33.2 is changed from 1 to 2, then Canada has an absolute advantage in

  a. both goods, and a comparative advantage in food
  b. both goods, and a comparative advantage in clothing
  c. both goods, and a comparative advantage in neither
  d. neither good, but a comparative advantage in food
  e. neither good, and a comparative advantage in neither

14. A nation's real income can be increased by

  a. international trade, but not by improved technology
  b. improved technology, but not by international trade
  c. neither technology nor international trade
  d. both technology and international trade
  e. international trade, provided there is protection for competing domestic industries

15. International trade allows a nation to increase its income by

  a. reaching a point beyond its production possibilities curve (PPC)
  b. reaching a point inside its PPC
  c. reaching along its PPC to a point to the northwest and staying there
  d. reaching along its PPC to a point to the southeast and staying there
  e. staying at the same point on its PPC

16. When Canada imports a good

  a. every Canadian citizen gains
  b. Canadian producers and Canadian consumers of that good benefit

c. Canadian producers and Canadian consumers of that good lose

d. Canadian consumers lose, but Canadian producers gain

e. there is an efficiency gain

17. The efficiency gain from the export of a good reflects a gain to

a. consumers, plus a gain to producers

b. consumers, minus a loss to producers

c. producers, minus a loss to consumers

d. consumers only

e. neither

18. A sudden move to free international trade is most likely to cause short-term unemployment in which of the following industries?

a. industries that don't export now, but could in the future

b. industries that export only

c. industries that export and sell domestically

d. import-competing industries

e. industries in which there are neither exports nor imports

19. Without trade in a world with two countries and two goods, real income will be

a. higher in the country that has an absolute advantage in both goods

b. lower in the country that has an absolute advantage in both goods

c. higher in the country that has an absolute advantage in neither good

d. higher in the country that has a comparative advantage in neither good

e. higher in the country that has a comparative advantage in both goods

20. In a world with two countries and two goods, opening trade will

a. benefit neither country

b. benefit only the country with an absolute advantage in both goods

c. benefit only the country with a comparative advantage in both goods

d. be a way for each country to benefit

e. benefit only the country with a comparative advantage in neither good

EXERCISES

1a. Suppose that Figures 33.1 and 33.2 represent the markets for shoes in England and Spain.

Without international trade, the price in England would be _____ and the quantity produced in England would be _____. The price in Spain would be _____ and the quantity produced in Spain would be _____. With trade, price will (rise, fall) in England and (rise, fall) in Spain.

1b. With international trade the single price at which the total demand—that is, the English demand plus Spanish demand—equals the total supply is _____. At that price English demand is _____ and English supply is _____; Spanish demand is _____ and Spanish supply is _____. In this situation, (Spain, England) will export _____ units of shoes. England has a comparative (advantage, disadvantage) in shoes, as reflected by the (lower, higher) price and cost of shoes in England before trade.

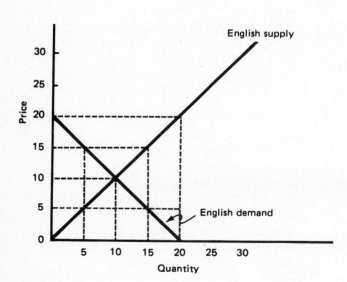

Figure 33.1

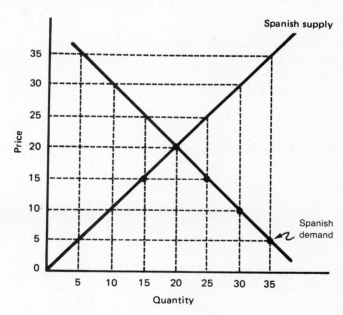

Figure 33.2

2a. This exercise is designed to help you understand comparative advantage. In Table 33.3, suppose that for country A, each acre of land will produce 100 bushels of wheat or 30 bushels of corn, whereas for country B, each acre of land will produce 40 bushels of wheat or 20 bushels of corn. Suppose that each country has 4000 acres. Fill in Table 33.3, giving the production possibilities for A and B.

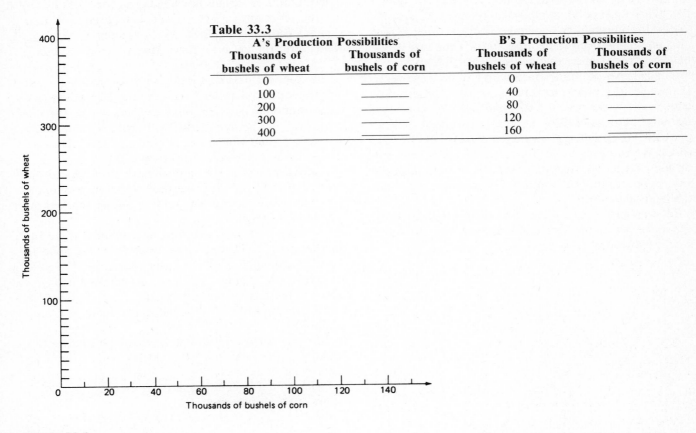

Table 33.3

A's Production Possibilities		B's Production Possibilities	
Thousands of bushels of wheat	Thousands of bushels of corn	Thousands of bushels of wheat	Thousands of bushels of corn
0	_____	0	_____
100	_____	40	_____
200	_____	80	_____
300	_____	120	_____
400	_____	160	_____

Figure 33.3

2b. Plot the PPCs for the two countries in Figure 33.3.

2c. Country _____ has an absolute advantage in producing corn; country _____ has an absolute advantage in producing wheat. Country _____ has a comparative advantage in producing corn; and country _____ has a comparative advantage in producing wheat. Suppose that, before trade, each country devotes half its land to each product. Then country B will produce and consume _____ thousand bushels of wheat and _____ thousand bushels of corn. Mark this on Figure 33.3. Also mark the production and consumption point for country A.

2d. Suppose that A and B were then to trade with each other at the price of 10 bushels of wheat for every 4 bushels of corn. (Note that this ratio of 10:4 is between A's pre-trade domestic exchange ratio of 100:30 = 10:3 cited at the beginning of this question, and B's ratio of 40:20 = 10:5. Therefore, it is a rate of exchange that will make trade beneficial for both countries.) Let's now see precisely why it is in B's interest to specialize in corn and purchase its wheat from A. If it does so, and devotes all its 4000 acres to corn, B will produce _____ thousand bushels of corn and _____ thousand bushels of wheat. B then keeps the original 40 thousand bushels of corn for its own consumption, and takes the additional 40 thousand it has produced and sells this for _____ thousand bushels of wheat. It is now able to consume the same 40 thousand bushels of corn as before, and 20 thousand (more, less) bushels of wheat. This 20 thousand bushels of wheat represents its (gain, loss) from specialization and trade. Graph B's specialization and trade with arrows in Figure 33.3, clearly indicating B's gains from trade.

Now plot similar arrows for A in Figure 33.3 to show how this exchange also benefits A. (Hint: A moves to the northwest along its PPC in order to produce the 100 thousand more bushels of wheat it needs to exchange with B. When it gives up this wheat to B, it acquires 40 thousand bushels of corn for it; this trade moves it back to the southeast. The question is: Does A go back to its original point or to a point superior to it and thus also acquire a gain from trade?)

Note how the trade arrows for the two countries have the same length and slope. They must; each trade arrow describes the exchange of 100 thousand bushels of wheat for 40 thousand bushels of corn. The only difference in the two arrows is the direction in which they are pointing. (They must point in opposite directions, because an export for one country is an import for the other.) Note also that gains from trade arise because the two PPCs have different slopes; therefore, it's possible to have a mutually beneficial trade arrow with a slope in between. If the two PPCs had the same slope, then opportunity costs would be the same in both countries. Consequently, neither country would have a _____ advantage, and mutually beneficial trade would (be possible, not be possible). We emphasize that we're concentrating here just on comparative advantage. Economies of scale also provide opportunities for mutually beneficial trade—but that's another story.

3a. In Figure 33.4, D is the Canadian domestic demand curve and MC is the Canadian marginal cost curve for a perfectly competitive good.

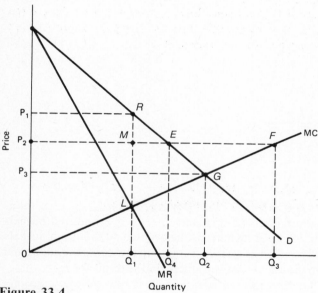

Figure 33.4

Suppose initially that there is no international trade. Then the amount _____ will be produced and the market price will be _____. Suppose now that international trade is introduced, and that it results in a price equal to P₂. Then consumption of the good in Canada will be _____, production of the good in Canada will be _____, and the difference between these amounts will be _____, which will be the amount of the good that Canada (exports, imports).

3b. As a result of allowing international trade in this good, producer surplus in Canada has gone (up, down) by the amount _____ and consumer surplus in Canada has gone (up, down) by the amount _____. Therefore, the net efficiency (gain, loss) to Canada is _____.

3c. Suppose next that there is no international trade in the good and that the market in Canada is an unregulated monopoly. Its marginal revenue will be the line _____. The monopolist will produce the amount _____ and will charge price _____. The efficiency (gain, loss) from monopoly will be _____.

Suppose now that international trade is introduced and that as a result the firm that used to have a monopoly in Canada is forced to behave as a perfect competitor, taking price as given.

Suppose as before that with international trade the market price is P_2. Then consumption of the good in Canada will equal _____, production of the good in Canada will equal _____, and the difference between these two amounts equals _____, which will be the amount of the good that Canada (exports, imports).

3d. As a result of allowing international trade in this good, the total revenue received by the producer in Canada has gone from _____ to _____, so the net gain in total revenue equals the rectangle _____, minus the rectangle _____.

3e. But the producer's cost has increased by the four-sided figure _____; thus the net gain to the producer equals the triangle _____, minus the rectangle _____. At the same time, consumer surplus (rises, falls) by _____; thus the net gain to the country (that is, the net gain to consumers plus the net gain to the producer) equals area _____. Shade in this area.

3f. In this case trade brings two efficiency gains: the standard gain from trade that results even in a world of perfect competition, shown by area _____, plus a gain because trade also ends monopoly inefficiency, as shown by area _____. Both gains make up the area _____, thus confirming our conclusion in part **e**.

3g. Does this illustrate a special case in which it is possible for international trade in a specific commodity to benefit both the consumers and the producers of that commodity?

ESSAY QUESTIONS

1. Who gains and who loses from a tariff that prohibits the import of a certain good? Do the gains outweigh the losses, or vice versa? Explain.

2. Looking ahead to the next chapter, can you think of any goods that we would not want to export, no matter how great the net economic benefits might be? Hint: Americans now trade military aircraft and equipment with Canada, and this trade provides economic benefits to both countries. Would you recommend that the Americans do the same with the Soviet Union?

3. "One of the gains from international trade is that it induces firms to reduce or eliminate technical inefficiency." Is this true? Why? Did we miss this point, or was it covered under one of our four broad sources of gains from trade?

4. Why do you think the leaders of the Canadian Auto Workers argue that the government should take steps to limit the number of Japanese autos imported into Canada? If you were one of these leaders, what would be your attitude towards a similar restriction on Canadian imports of steel? Why?

5. Why might trade between Ontario and Quebec benefit both provinces? In your answer, you may want to define the concept of an "export to another province" and an "import from another province."

6. A recent slogan has been "Trade, not aid. If we reduce Canadian restrictions on imports from the less developed countries, they will benefit, and so will we." Do you agree or disagree? Explain why.

7. Can you name any activities in your province that have developed as a result of inter-provincial specialization—that is, specialization between provinces? Any activities that have developed as a result of international specialization?

8. If the United States and Canada have an approximate balance in their trade, which country is more dependent on that trade? Why?

9. "There is no trade in cement between Australia and Germany. The reason is that transport costs on so bulky and heavy an item more than cancel out the gains from trade." Explain this statement. Do you agree with it? Does this mean that transport costs influence trade patterns? Explain how high transport costs in a good may explain "cross-hauling"—for example, the export of potatoes from Prince Edward Island to New York at the same time as potatoes are being imported into western Canada from the United States.

ANSWERS

Important Terms: **1**d, **2**a, **3**e, **4**c, **5**b, **6**g, **7**f, **8**h
True-False: **1**F, **2**F, **3**F, **4**T, **5**F, **6**F, **7**T, **8**T, **9**F, **10**F
Multiple Choice: **1**d, **2**c, **3**a, **4**e, **5**a, **6**d, **7**c, **8**a, **9**b, **10**a, **11**e, **12**d, **13**c, **14**d, **15**a, **16**e, **17**c, **18**d, **19**a, **20**d
Exercises: **1a.** $10, 10, $20, 20, rise, fall **1b.** $15, 5, 15, 25, 15, England, 10, advantage, lower
2a and **2b.** Figure 33.3 completed (see next page)

Table 33.3 completed

A		B	
Wheat	Corn	Wheat	Corn
0	120	0	80
100	90	40	60
200	60	80	40
300	30	120	20
400	0	160	0

2c. A, A, B, A, 80, 40 **2d.** 80, zero, 100, more, gain, comparative, not be possible **3a.** Q_2, P_3, Q_4, Q_3, Q_4Q_3, exports **3b.** up, P_2FGP_3, down, P_2EGP_3, gain, EGF **3c.** MR, Q_1, P_1, loss, RGL, Q_4, Q_3, Q_4Q_3, exports **3d.** P_1RQ_10, P_2FQ_30, MFQ_3Q_1, P_1RMP_2 **3e.** LQ_1Q_3F, MLF, P_1RMP_2, rises, P_1REP_2, $RLFE$ **3f.** EGF, RLG, $RLFE$ **3g.** yes

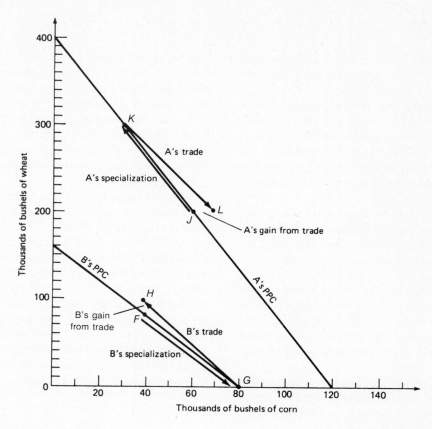

Figure 3.3 completed

ANSWERS TO SELECTED REVIEW QUESTIONS FROM THE TEXT

33-1. (a) It is an advantage for consumers, since foreign competition often lowers price (or keeps it from rising as fast) and, therefore, results in greater consumer surplus. The existence of foreign products on the market also provides the consumer with greater variety.

(b) It is a disadvantage for producers, since lower price reduces producer surplus.

(c) By increasing efficiency, it benefits the nation as a whole. (The disadvantage for producers is more than offset by the advantage for consumers, as shown in Figure 33-8.)

33-2. Yes, both may benefit—even in the special case where cost curves in both countries are exactly the same. Economies of scale mean that the AC curve for each product is falling. As Britain specializes in good X, the average cost of producing it is reduced. As Canada specializes in good Y, the average cost of producing it also falls. With specialization and the reduced cost of producing each good, resources are released that can be used in other productive ways. Therefore, each country may benefit—even though neither may have a comparative advantage. (In other words, both countries may benefit, even though there is no difference in their cost curves. Of course, if cost conditions do differ—if comparative advantage does exist—then this is a further source of benefit.)

33-3. This can be shown using a PPC in Figure 33-5(*a*); or using supply and demand curves in Figures 33-6 and 33-7 (or 33-8). Note in any of these cases that trade is being reduced, rather than increased, so the analyses are reversed.

33-6. (a) Britain specializes by moving up the PPC from G to H, increasing its production of clothing and decreasing its production of food.

(b) From the production point H, Britain exports clothing, in an amount given by the vertical distance between H and J) and imports food (the horizontal distance from H to J).

(c) Since there are only two countries in this example, Britains's exports of clothing must be equal to Canada's imports of clothing, and Britain's imports of food equal to Canada's exports of food. Thus, arrow *CD* in Figure 33-5(*a*) has the same length and slope as the arrow in Figure 33-9, though its direction is the opposite.

33-7. This statement is wrong. Economists do not say that trade and technological change are similar because both increase our ability to produce. Instead, economists say that they are similar because both increase our ability to consume (i.e., increase our real income). Technological change does this by shifting our production possibility curve outward (increasing our ability to produce). Trade does this by allowing us to move to a point beyond our PPC.

33-9. (b) This policy induces production of "too much" output (that is, more than the perfectly competitive amount); thus, there is the efficiency loss shown in Figure 26-3(*a*).

Chapter 34

■ ■

International Trade: Policy Debates

MAJOR PURPOSE

Even though the gains from trade have been evident since the days of Adam Smith, and even though tariffs have been on a downward trend over the last 50 years, many trade barriers still remain. We are still a long way from free trade. The primary objective of this chapter is to answer the question "How is it possible that these barriers still exist? Can they, or can they not, be justified?" We will also address a number of other important and closely related questions: What are the historical develop-

ments that have moved Canada and other nations toward freer trade? As we have been moving two steps forward, what are the new barriers to trade that have been moving us one step back? Another issue of particular significance to Canada is, of course, the 1989 free trade agreement with the United States. What are the likely advantages and disadvantages to Canada as the provisions of this agreement are implemented and further provisions are negotiated in the 1990s?

LEARNING OBJECTIVES

After you have studied this chapter in the textbook and the study guide, you should be able to
- Explain the military, political, and cultural reasons that trade barriers still exist
- State three fallacious economic arguments for protection, explaining why they are fallacious
- State eight economic arguments for protection that contain some element of truth, and the difficulties with each of these arguments
- Describe the historical development of international trade policy in Canada and elsewhere in the world, including the multilateral efforts at trade liberalization over the last 50 years, with special reference to the creation of the GATT and the Kennedy, Tokyo, and Uruguay Rounds
- Evaluate the European Community (EC) with special reference to the problems it raises for North American exporters
- Give several examples of non-tariff barriers, explaining why each distorts trade
- Explain the concept of tariff escalation and its significance to Canada
- Describe the main provisions in the 1989 Canada/United States free trade agreement (FTA), and explain their likely effects on the Canadian economy in the years to come

HIGHLIGHTS OF THE CHAPTER

The trade barriers that remain throughout the world—and new ones that have been introduced—have been defended by their supporters as "in the national interest." Do the arguments they use make sense?

Arguments for Protection

Several of the arguments for protection have little to do with economics.

The main non-economic reason for protection is political. The loss that results from allowing a good to be freely imported is felt very heavily by the few people who specialize in producing that good; in many cases, their jobs are threatened by the competition of imports. These people will often vote for a politician who promises to work for restrictions on such imports. In the debate over the Canada/United States free trade agreement during the 1988 election, the fear that the agreement would lead to major job losses was a major theme in the Liberal and NDP campaigns opposing it. As we saw in the last chapter, the damage to those who become losers under free trade is likely to be more than offset by the benefits to the winners—all the people who are able to enjoy a wider variety of less expensive goods, or who get jobs in the expanding export industries. But these expected gains by the winners are either hypothetical, or widely dispersed over the public as a whole, with the benefit received by each individual being relatively small. Thus, winners usually vote for other issues on which they feel more deeply, and the politician who promises to work for restrictions on imports is often elected. Thus, trade restrictions that make no economic sense are still introduced for political reasons.

In some countries, especially the United States, tariffs and other trade restrictions have also been justified by considerations of national security. The argument here is that some industries produce goods that are vitally important to a country's national defence. If there were no trade restrictions protecting domestic producers from import competition, some of these industries might not survive. But this would leave the country in a vulnerable position in times of war. However, in small countries that belong to military alliances (such as NATO), this national security argument loses much of its validity if the country's military needs can be supplied from other countries within the alliance.

A third non-economic argument for protection is especially relevant to a small country like Canada which is geographically close to, and has extensive economic relations with, a large neighbour: that restrictions on trade may be needed in order to protect and foster the small

country's unique cultural identity. Because of scale economies in such industries as book and magazine publishing, TV programming, or film making, it is difficult for domestic producers to compete with American publishers, film makers, and so on. But if Canadians read primarily foreign books and magazines and watch foreign-made movies and TV programs, will it be possible to preserve our separate and distinct identity?

Because many Canadians feared that the answer was no, they pushed hard for special provisions in the FTA to protect our cultural industries and, in the end, the Americans agreed to put in a number of safeguards for cultural industries.

Now let's turn to the economic arguments that have been used to try to justify protection. Some are fallacious, but some contain an element of truth.

1. "Buy Canadian because it keeps our money at home. When we buy goods from Italy we lose our money to the Italians." This argument is fallacious. When we buy Italian goods, our money eventually comes back when the Italians buy our goods. The Italians want our goods, not our money.

2. "We can't compete with cheap foreign labour." This argument is also fallacious. Labour in many foreign countries is less expensive because it is less productive. Our higher productivity means that, on average, we *can* compete with cheap foreign labour. We do particularly well in goods in which we have a comparative advantage (where our productivity advantage more than offsets our higher wage rate). We can't compete where we don't have a comparative advantage (where our productivity advantage does not offset our higher wage rate).

3. "Tariffs should be tailored to equalize costs at home and abroad." This, too, is a fallacious argument. According to the theory of comparative advantage, we gain from international trade because there are differences in costs between countries. Tailoring tariffs to eliminate these differences would eliminate trade, and all the gains it provides.

4. "If we buy steel from Hamilton rather than Japan, employment will rise in Hamilton rather than Japan." There is a grain of truth in this argument. Restricting imports of steel from Japan may stimulate employment in Hamilton at least in the short run. However, there are two problems. First, Japan may retaliate with her own restrictions against our exports, and this will reduce employment in Canada. Thus, we don't get employment gains after all. In short, we are following a "beggar-my-neighbour" policy that doesn't provide employment benefits, but results in shrinking trade and a loss of the gains from trade. Second, blocking out Japanese competition makes it more difficult to control costs and prices in Canadian industries. If Canadian workers don't feel that they have to compete with the Japanese, they will be less restrained in their wage demands. We saw in Chapter 33 that one of the gains from trade is that it makes our economy more competitive. We lose this gain whenever we protect our industries.

5. "Restricting trade will diversify a nation's economy." This may be true for some countries. Trade may lead a country to specialize in producing just a few goods. If world prices drop for these few goods, the country will suffer from having "put all its eggs in one basket." But even though Canada does have very large exports of a few primary products such as wheat, timber, and natural gas, it also exports a whole range of other primary and manufactured products as well. Thus, a lack of diversification in international trade is not a serious enough problem in Canada to justify increased tariff protection. Moreover, heavy specialization may sometimes put a country in a particularly favourable position if the world price of its main export good rises; a prime example is the group of OPEC countries which produces almost nothing but oil.

6. "We need to protect our infant industries." This argument is sometimes valid. Without the protection of trade restrictions, some industries may never reach the size where they can realize the economies of scale necessary to compete in world markets. However, there are three difficulties with this argument. (a) Infant industries never seem to grow up. They typically continue to demand protection, and no government wants to lose votes by cutting the apron strings. (b) Even if an industry were to "grow up," it still might not be able to compete effectively. (c) If the infant industry really does have a promising future, then why aren't private lenders willing to lend it enough money to survive until maturity?

7. "Restricting imports may reduce the price we have to pay for them." This may make sense if Canada buys so much of a good that a cutback in this demand (as a result of a Canadian import restriction) would reduce the world price. However, the Canadian demand for most goods represents only a very small fraction of the world demand for those goods. Hence, Canada's ability to influence the world prices for the goods it imports is very limited.

8. "Restricting imports may reduce our vulnerability to a cutoff in foreign supplies." Cutbacks in oil supplies from OPEC countries in the 1970s made clear the force of this argument. But oil is special; for most other commodities, the risk of having our supply cut off is minimal. If one country stops selling to us, we can turn to other sources of supply.

9. "Use protection to engineer (that is, create) a comparative advantage." Just as past accumulation of capital by some nations have given them a comparative advantage in products that require a lot of capital, the accumulation of human capital in protected high-tech industries today could give us a comparative advantage in those industries in the future. There is some truth in this, but:

a. It is similar to the infant industry argument, and subject to the same criticisms.

b. Like other arguments it assumes that our trading partners won't retaliate.

c. Protecting one high-tech industry like computer chips increases the cost of other high-tech industries that use chips.

10. "Protect industries with positive externalities." High-tech industries are again a good example. (There were huge external benefits to the general public when AT&T developed the transistor.) It's true that positive externalities justify a subsidy, but protection may be the worst kind—again, since it invites retaliation.

There are only a few strong arguments for free trade. However, the many arguments against it are often seriously flawed and universally assume partners won't retaliate if we protect. So, don't just count the number of arguments. The case for free trade is still a strong one.

Non-tariff Barriers

There are several kinds:

1. Quotas are quantitative limits on imports. These include the voluntary export restraints that Canada and the United States pressured the Japanese into imposing on their exports to North America. The United States subsequently removed this pressure and the Japanese were free to drop the VERs on shipments to the United States. However, they did not. Why should they? The United States and Canada had shown them how to profitably cartelize their export sales to North America. Because of this, the Japanese auto companies were making more profit in North America than in Japan.

An alternative form of quota is a limit that a country imposes on its own total imports of a particular good.

2. Health or quality standards. An example is the European ban on hormone-fed beef from North America. How much is this a policy to protect health and how much is it a policy to block out import competition? It is hard to say.

3. Bureaucratic red tape can be used to discourage imports. An example was the French requirement that all imported VCRs be cleared through the tiny, inland customs house at Poitiers—the same town that Frederic Bastiat used to satirize protection 150 years ago. (See Box 34-1.)

History of Canadian Trade Policy

Perhaps the most important period in Canadian trade policy was the 1880s, when the Conservative government under Sir John A. Macdonald introduced very high tariffs as part of its National Policy—aimed at stimulating Canada's manufacturing industry and promoting interprovincial trade. Since that time, Canada's tariffs have generally been falling (except during the early 1930s when Canada and many other countries raised tariffs as a way of stimulating domestic aggregate demand and reducing unemployment). Since the Second World War, the trend toward lower Canadian tariffs can be partly explained by Canada's participation in the programs of multilateral tariff reductions negotiated by most of the world's industrialized countries under the General Agreement on Tariffs and Trade (GATT). Especially important international tariff reductions came as a result of the "Kennedy Round" of tariff negotiations in the late 1970s. The "Tokyo Round" of negotiations dealt not only with tariffs, but also with "non-tariff" barriers (NTBs), such as import quotas, special customs procedures which make import trade more costly, and the discrimination in government purchasing against imported goods. A new round of multilateral negotiations—the Uruguay Round—began in 1986.

From the viewpoint of Canada and the United States, the process of multilateral tariff reductions has been especially important since the formation of the European Economic Community (EEC) in the late 1950s. Since the countries that are members of the EEC have abolished tariffs on trade with each other, Canadian and U.S. exporters (who still face a tariff on their sales to an EEC importer) are at a disadvantage relative to suppliers in any EEC country. (For Canada, this problem became especially important in 1973 when the United Kingdom, one of Canada's important trading partners, joined the EEC.) However, this disadvantage has become less severe since the EEC has participated in all multilateral agreements to reduce tariffs on *all* imports.

The 1988 Canada/United States Free Trade Agreement (FTA)

Proponents of free trade have long argued that it would be in Canada's interest to enter into bilateral negotiations with the United States, with the aim of ultimately abolishing all tariffs and other restrictions on Canada-U.S. trade. Advocates of such an agreement have argued that the resulting gains from industrial specialization and from an increased ability for Canadian firms to exploit econ-

omies of scale could lead to a large increase in Canada's GDP. Some studies conducted in the mid-1980s suggested that this increase would be as much as 8 to 9% of GDP. (However, other analysts predicted gains as small as 1 to 2%.) Furthermore, free trade advocates argued that an important objective of a free trade arrangement would be to protect Canada against the effects of future protectionist moves by the United States, in the form of increased tariffs or NTBs.

Following the recommendations of the MacDonald Commission in 1985, Canada formally requested that the United States enter into negotiations about an agreement. The United States accepted, and during 1986-88, a draft agreement was negotiated. Following an election completely dominated by this issue, the victorious Progressive Conservatives brought in legislation ratifying the agreement, which came into effect on January 1, 1989.

The main provisions of the agreement stipulate that all tariffs and many other obstacles to Canada-United States trade will be eliminated over a ten-year period ending in 1998. In addition, there is provision for joint Canada-United States scrutiny of application of existing trade laws by either country to restrict imports from the other, and for continued negotiations over the issue when either country will be *allowed* to impose such restrictions.

Because the agreement is so recent, it is still too early to assess what its main effects will be. Critics argue that an elimination of our tariffs on imports from the United States will make it impossible for most of our manufacturing firms to stand up against the increased competition from U.S. firms. Hence, Canada's manufacturing sector will shrink substantially, with considerable job losses, and we will be pushed further in the direction of producing mostly primary products (being "hewers of wood and drawers of water"). Further, free trade will greatly increase our political dependence on the United States, in the critic's view. However, other observers are more optimistic and suggest that even though some manufacturing industries will contract as a result of increased international competition, others will remain competitive by specializing in the production of a narrower range of products for both the U.S. and Canadian markets; still others will expand as they increase their export sales when U.S. tariffs are eliminated. Moreover, while increased trade with the United States in one sense makes us more vulnerable to political pressure from that country (since Canadian producers become more dependent on the U.S. market), in another sense the agreement may *reduce* our vulnerability: Under the FTA the United States has agreed to refrain from imposing certain types of restrictions on imports from Canada.

A problem that continues to be important for Canadian international trade is the problem of tariff escalation. Because importing countries often have higher tariffs on processed goods than on raw materials, there is a tendency for the processing of many Canadian raw materials to be done in the importing country rather than in Canada. In order to promote more processing in Canada, Canadian trade negotiators have been trying to get our trading partners to reduce the escalation in their tariff schedules.

IMPORTANT TERMS: MATCH THE COLUMNS

Match each term in the first column with its corresponding explanation in the second column.

_____ **1.** Tariff
_____ **2.** NTB
_____ **3.** Quota
_____ **4.** Trade restriction
_____ **5.** Protection
_____ **6.** "Beggar-my-neighbour" policy
_____ **7.** Infant industry
_____ **8.** Terms of trade
_____ **9.** Canada/United States FTA
_____ **10.** Multilateral
_____ **11.** Bilateral
_____ **12.** The General Agreement on Tariffs and Trade (GATT)
_____ **13.** EEC
_____ **14.** Kennedy Round
_____ **15.** Tokyo Round

a. The common market in Europe formed in the late 1950s by Germany, France, Italy, the Netherlands, Belgium, and Luxembourg, and later joined by other countries such as Britain

b. The policy of imposing barriers to trade in order to shield domestic industries from foreign competition

c. Between only two countries

d. A tax imposed on imported goods as they enter a country

e. The multilateral GATT negotiation in the 1970s that cut tariffs by about a third

f. An industry that has not yet reached the size at which it can capture sufficient expertise and/or economies of scale to compete in world markets

g. A non-tariff barrier, that is, any government measure—other than a tariff—that restricts trade

h. A treaty signed in 1947 that provides for multilateral negotiations to reduce trade restrictions

i. The use of trade restrictions to reduce imports, increase domestic production and, therefore, reduce unemployment

j. A limit on the number of units of a good that can be imported into a country

k. Between many countries

l. The multilateral negotiation by GATT countries in the 1960s that reduced tariffs by about a third

m. The price we receive for our exports, compared to the price we pay for our imports

n. Any tariff or non-tariff barrier that impedes international trade

o. Bilateral agreement that came into effect on January 1, 1989

TRUE-FALSE

T F **1.** Tariffs are often imposed because producers have more political influence than consumers.

T F **2.** When international trade is opened up in a good, Canada as a whole gains only if we end up exporting that good.

T F **3.** Diversifying an economy may reduce the gains from trade.

T F **4.** If Canada were to increase restrictions on imported steel, this would tend to increase employment in Hamilton in the short run.

T F **5.** After an infant industry has been supported by the government for a year or two, political pressure to remove the protection becomes almost irresistible.

T F   6. Canadian processing of raw materials before they are exported to foreign countries is discouraged because many of the countries with which we trade have lower tariffs on unprocessed raw materials than on processed goods.

T F   7. Because wages in Canada are higher than in Mexico, it follows that costs of production are also higher—and this justifies protecting our goods from cheap Mexican products.

T F   8. One of the strongest arguments for trade restrictions is that they keep us from losing our dollars to foreigners.

T F   9. If the government were to do nothing about our unemployment problems, this would constitute a "beggar-my-neighbour" policy.

T F   10. By restricting its imports, a large country may be able to improve its terms of trade, but for a small country such a strategy is unlikely to work.

MULTIPLE CHOICE

1. The national security argument for protecting essential defence industries:
   a. has been opposed by economists since the days of Adam Smith
   b. is not heard as often in Canada as it is in the United States
   c. is justified as a method of creating employment, but can't be justified in any other way
   d. all of the above
   e. none of the above

2. If we take into account the interests of both producers and consumers, then restrictions on the imports of Japanese cars into Canada are:
   a. in the interest of the nation as a whole, and in the interest of the province of Ontario
   b. in the interest of the nation as a whole, but not in the interest of the province of Ontario
   c. not in the interest of the nation as a whole, nor in the interest of the province of Ontario
   d. not in the interest of the nation as a whole, but it may well be in the interest of the province of Ontario
   e. not in the interest of Ontario, and has little or no effect on the nation as a whole

3. The strongest political pressure for a change in trade policy usually comes from:
   a. producers lobbying for import restrictions
   b. producers lobbying for export restrictions
   c. consumers lobbying for import restrictions
   d. consumers lobbying for export restrictions
   e. consumers lobbying for a reduction in trade restrictions

4. In dealing with a serious problem of unemployment, a country that trades heavily should normally look first to:
   a. increasing tariffs
   b. increasing quotas
   c. increasing other non-tariff barriers
   d. restricting its exports

   e. domestic monetary and fiscal policy

5. Which of the following arguments for protection makes economic sense?
   a. we should tailor tariffs so as to equalize costs at home and abroad
   b. when we import, the country loses money that wouldn't be lost if we produced domestically instead
   c. we can't compete with cheap foreign labour
   d. for a large country such as the United States, restricting oil imports may significantly reduce the world price of oil
   e. all of the above

6. Problems that arise when a country protects an infant industry include:
   a. the industry's cost may never fall below those in foreign countries, because foreigners may enjoy some natural advantage
   b. it may be very difficult to know when infant protection has become an old age pension
   c. the new industry may hire a large number of employees whose voting power may make it difficult to remove protection later—even when it is no longer justified
   d. all of the above
   e. none of the above

7. A beggar-my-neighbour policy involves:
   a. encouraging the purchase of essential materials from abroad
   b. export controls to prevent the sale of our natural resources to foreign countries
   c. import restrictions designed to capture employment from foreign countries
   d. subsidies to encourage imports of foreign natural resources
   e. subsidies to encourage imports of foreign luxury goods

8. The infant industry argument for protection makes sense if the infant is:

a. able to compete against foreign firms now, but not in the future
b. not able to compete against foreign firms now, but will be able to in the future
c. won't be able to compete now or in the future
d. will be able to compete now and in the future
e. won't be able to compete now; the future is irrelevant

9. "If I buy a radio from India, I get the radio and India gets the dollars. But if I buy a Canadian-built radio, I get the radio and the dollars stay here." This argument is:
a. misleading because the Indians seldom keep the dollars they earn from us in trade; they eventually spend them on our goods
b. misleading because the dollars I spend buying a Canadian-built radio also leave this country
c. correct; this is why we should stop trading
d. correct; we should trade only for political reasons
e. true for radios, but not for most goods we import

10. The argument that an industry with positive externalities should be protected is most similar to the argument that:
a. a polluting industry should be taxed
b. a polluting industry should be subsidized
c. a polluting industry should be left alone
d. vaccinations should be subsidized
e. vaccinations should be taxed

11. If an industry has large positive externalities:
a. it must be protected
b. it should be protected
c. it should be subsidized, with protection being the best method
d. it should be subsidized, but not by protection because this invites retaliation
e. it should be subsidized, but not by protection because this guarantees against retaliation

12. Non-tariff barriers are:
a. designed solely to restrict trade
b. designed solely to improve health standards
c. designed solely for other non-trade reasons
d. sometimes designed to restrict trade, and sometimes designed to improve health standards; but in either case, they restrict trade
e. justified so long as they provide a benefit, regardless of their cost

13. The National Policy introduced by Sir John A. Macdonald:
a. was a policy intended to nationalize the Canadian oil and gas industry
b. proposed the establishment of a free trade arrangement with the United States as a means of raising Canada's national income
c. was an early version of the CBC program "The National"
d. introduced high tariffs on imported goods as a means of promoting trade between Canada's provinces
e. provided a large subsidy for VIA Rail passenger service

14. Canadian tariffs today are:
a. higher than in the 1930s
b. slightly lower
c. much lower
d. about the same
e. higher in most goods, but lower in some

15. Under the Canada/United States free trade agreement:
a. all tariffs and non-tariff barriers will be eliminated by 1992
b. all tariffs will be eliminated by 1998
c. all tariffs will be eliminated by 1995, but existing non-tariff barriers will remain
d. Canada is obliged to eliminate several of its existing social programs
e. none of the above

16. With free trade between Canada and the United States, it is likely that Canada will:
a. give up the production of industrial goods in order to concentrate on agricultural goods
b. give up the production of agricultural goods in order to concentrate on industrial goods
c. give up one industry (say, electrical machinery) in order to specialize in another, (say, chemicals)
d. give up the production of some items of electrical machinery in order to specialize in other items of electrical machinery; and do the same in chemicals
e. in both electrical equipment and chemicals, produce an even wider range of items than at present

17. According to estimates by Harris and Cox, a Canada/United States free trade agreement will lead to an increase in Canadian GDP of:
a. 0.5 to 1%
b. 4 to 5%
c. 8 to 9%
d. 14 to 15%
e. a small decrease in Canadian GDP

18. The concept of "tariff escalation" refers to:
a. the policy of charging higher tariffs on more expensive goods
b. the tendency for countries to raise their tariffs in order to reduce unemployment during the Great Depression
c. the policy of countries importing raw

materials to charge higher tariffs on raw
materials in order to drive down the price of
such imports

   d. the policy of some countries to charge lower
tariffs on imports of unprocessed raw
materials than on imports of other goods

   e. the policy of charging higher tariffs on goods
imported from low-wage countries

19. The formation of the European Economic Community:

   a. was one of the reasons for the severe scarcity
of agricultural goods in the early 1980s

   b. has made it easier for Canadian firms to
compete against the French in the German
market

   c. has made it more difficult for Canadian firms
to compete against the French in the German
market

   d. has made it more difficult for Canadian firms
to compete against the Japanese in the German market

   e. has had no effect on Canadian firms competing in the German market

20. In the Kennedy Round, participating countries
cut their tariffs by about a third. In the Tokyo
Round that followed:

   a. almost no further progress was made

   b. no further progress was made

   c. participating countries cut their remaining
tariffs by about 10%

   d. participating countries cut their remaining
tariffs by roughly another one-third

   e. participating countries cut their remaining
tariffs by roughly 90%

21. The Tokyo Round resulted in an average tariff
reduction of about:

   a. 5%

   b. 15%

   c. 25%

   d. 35%

   e. 45%

EXERCISES

This exercise covers the same ground as the appendix to
the chapter. You will probably be able to do the exercise
and find it helpful, even if you are not being asked to
study the appendix. However, if you get stuck, you can
refer to the appendix for help. In any case, first try to
do the exercise on your own.

   1a. Figure 34.1 shows the domestic Canadian supply
and demand for a good that is traded internationally.
Without international trade the price would be
_____ and the quantity produced would be
_____. If this good is available on the world mar-

ket at a price P_2, then the price in Canada, under free
trade, will be _____. Domestic production will be
_____, domestic consumption will be _____,
and the country will (import, export) the amount
_____. As a result of this international trade, the
(gain, loss) to consumers is area _____, while
producers are (better, worse) off by area _____. If
we consider both producers and consumers, the effect of
international trade on the nation, on balance, is an efficiency (gain, loss) of area _____.

   1b. Suppose that the government imposes a tariff on
this good, shown by arrow t. Suppose that this has no
effect on the world price of the good. Because of the tariff, the domestic price will (rise, fall) to _____.
(Importers who are willing to bring this good in for a price
P_2, will need this higher price to compensate them for
the tariff t that they now have to pay the government.)
The quantity of imports will be _____. As a result
of the tariff, consumers (gain, lose) area _____,
while producers are (better, worse) off by area
_____. Moreover, the government is now collect-
ing a tariff t on imports of _____, for a total revenue of area _____. Therefore, there is a net (gain,
loss) to the nation from this tariff of areas _____.

   1c. Now suppose that, instead of this tariff t, the
government imposes an import quota that restricts
imports to the quantity FG. With imports of FG, P_2 (is,
is not) an equilibrium price, because the demand for this
good at price P_2 is (more than, less than) the domestic
plus imported supply. Thus, price will be (above, below)

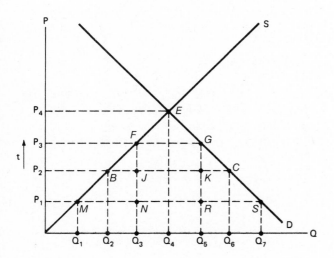

Figure 34.1

P_2. P_3 (is, is not) an equilibrium price because, with imports FG, the demand for this good at P_3 is (more than, less than, equal to) the domestic plus imported supply. Thus, this quota of FG is the quota equivalent of tariff _____, because both raise the domestic Canadian price by _____, and reduce imports to _____.

1d. Because of the quota, the price in the domestic market will rise to _____, consumers will (gain, lose) area _____, and producers will (gain, lose) area _____. Suppose that the quota rights are held by foreigners exporting to Canada. They can then make a profit by acquiring this good outside Canada for _____ per unit and selling it in Canada for _____. The revenue the government gets from the imposition of this quota is _____. Therefore, the net effect on the nation of this quota is its effect on producers and consumers, which is a (gain, loss) of area _____.

1e. When the Canadian government imposes an import quota, and gives away these quota rights to foreigners, then a quota will result in a (larger, smaller) amount of (gain, loss) to the nation than will an equivalent tariff. The additional (gain, loss) from the quota occurs because duty revenue is collected by the Canadian government if there is a (tariff, quota), but is not collected if there is this type of (tariff, quota). Instead, this revenue goes as profit to (Canadian producers, foreign holders of quota rights).

ESSAY QUESTIONS

1. When a country is in a severe recession, the political pressure to reduce imports becomes stronger. Why? Critically evaluate such a proposal.

2. It is sometimes argued that trade restrictions protect our high standard of living from being eroded by competition from low-income countries. Evaluate this. Do trade restrictions erode our standard of living or increase it for the nation as a whole? For the industry that's being protected?

3. Even though the complete elimination of tariffs in all countries would be likely to promote economic efficiency both in Canada and throughout the world, Canadian policy makers of course have no control over tariffs in foreign countries, and we cannot expect to be able to persuade all other countries to remove their tariffs on imports from Canada. On the other hand, it would be possible for Canada to eliminate unilaterally all tariffs on imports into Canada even if other countries do not reduce their tariffs on imports from us. Discuss arguments for and against such a unilateral tariff elimination.

4. Explain carefully how a tariff tends to reduce the benefits of international specialization.

5. Consider a tariff high enough, not just to reduce, but to completely prevent imports. How would it affect consumers? producers? the nation as a whole? Would the government collect any duty revenue from such a tariff? From a tariff that only reduces imports?

6. The text argued that a country may improve its terms of trade by restricting imports. In 1973 the oil-producing countries of OPEC managed to improve their terms of trade by restricting their exports. Explain carefully what are the similarities and differences between the "terms of trade" argument for restricting imports and the "terms of trade" argument for restricting exports.

ANSWERS

Important Terms: 1d, 2g, 3j, 4n, 5b, 6i, 7f, 8m, 9o, 10k, 11c, 12h, 13a, 14l, 15e

True-False: 1T, 2F, 3T, 4T, 5F, 6T, 7F, 8F, 9F, 10T

Multiple Choice: 1b, 2d, 3a, 4e, 5d, 6d, 7c, 8b, 9a, 10d, 11d, 12d, 13d, 14c, 15b, 16d, 17c, 18d, 19c, 20d, 21d

Exercises: **1a.** P_4, Q_4, P_2, Q_2, Q_6, import, BC, gain, P_4ECP_2, worse, P_4EBP_2, gain, EBC **1b.** rise, P_3, FG, lose, P_3GCP_2, better, P_3FBP_2, FG, $FGKJ$, loss, FJB and GKC **1c.** is not, more than, above, is, equal to, t, t, FG **1d.** P_3, lose, P_3GCP_2, gain, P_3FBP_2, P_2, P_3, zero, loss, $FGCB$ **1e.** larger, loss, loss, tariff, quota, foreign holders of quota rights

ANSWERS TO SELECTED REVIEW QUESTIONS FROM THE TEXT

34-2. This statement can't be true, since it is possible to raise a tariff so high that it eliminates all imports—and therefore any duty paid on them. Thus, as tariffs are increased from an initial zero level, duty revenue rises at first; but eventually it must fall.

34-4. (a) Since trade is now being cut off, rather than opened up, just reverse the analysis in Figure 33-8. Price rises rather than falls. (That is, all gains in Figure 33-8 become losses, and vice versa.)

(b) Eliminating exports has exactly the opposite effect as allowing exports in the first place.

(c) If exports are eliminated, it does not make any difference how this occurs. Export restrictions may be imposed for political reasons.

34-5. In one respect, tariff and transport costs are the same: They both deter trade. But, in another respect, they are different. If Canadian exporters were to incur higher costs because they went back to using clipper ships, this would be a waste—money down the drain. But if they incur a higher cost because they pay a foreign tariff, this is not all waste. Instead, some is a transfer from exporters to the foreign countries that are now collecting duty revenue.

34-7. As long as Japanese wages were considerably lower than American and Canadian wages, Japan had a comparative advantage in the production of textiles (which require a relatively large amount of labour per unit of output). As Japanese wages have risen, Japan has been losing its comparative advantage in such products. However, in countries such as South Korea and Taiwan, wages remain relatively low. Thus the comparative advantage in textiles is shifting away from Japan, toward these low-wage countries.

34-8. The statement is wrong. Because fish is a common-property resource, allowing unrestricted entry into the fishing industry will result in overfishing, as explained in Chapter 31.

However, it is less clear that it is efficient to protect the fish stock by restricting catches of foreign fishermen by more than those of Canadian ones. In a system of "stinted landing rights" such as described in Box 31-2, it could be argued that foreign fishermen should be allowed to bid for these rights on the same terms as Canadian fishermen.

Part Nine

Microeconomics: How Income Is Distributed

Chapter 35

■ ■

Wages in a Perfectly Competitive Economy

MAJOR PURPOSE

In this chapter, the objective is to use the familiar tools of supply and demand developed in earlier chapters to analyse how wages are determined in perfectly competitive labour markets. The labour market for a specific industry will be perfectly competitive if:

(a) there are so many buyers and sellers of labour service that none can affect the wage rate;

(b) labour is standardized, with all workers being equally productive; and

(c) workers are mobile and can move in and out of this industry.

Given these assumptions, the text shows (1) how the labour demand by an industry reflects the productivity of labour in that industry, and (2) how labour supply reflects the wages and productivity of labour in other industries. The conclusion that follows is that perfect competition yields an efficient outcome in a labour market, just as it did in a product market.

A number of real world complications in labour markets are recognized. For example, in this chapter we study what happens when the government intervenes to set a minimum wage. Furthermore, we examine what happens when assumption (c)—that labour is mobile—does not hold. Specifically, what happens when discrimination prevents women from entering jobs traditionally held by men? In the next chapter, assumption (a) above is relaxed in order to show the effects when workers form a union to raise wages—or employers form an association to lower wages. In Chapter 37, assumption (b) is relaxed in order to analyse what happens when workers are not equally productive.

LEARNING OBJECTIVES

After you have studied this chapter in the textbook and the study guide, you should be able to

- Explain why, under perfect competition, the curve showing a firm's demand for labour is the same as the curve showing the marginal revenue product of labour
- State two reasons the labour demand curve might shift to the right
- Illustrate how the labour demand curve can be used to show the total income of labour in an industry and the total income of other factors of production
- Explain why the height of the labour supply curve for an industry reflects the opportunity cost of labour—that is, labour's wage and productivity in other industries
- Explain why, in the absence of externalities, perfect competition in the labour market typically results in an efficient wage and employment level
- Measure diagrammatically the efficiency loss that results when a labour market is not perfectly competitive
- Explain why one cannot necessarily jump from the conclusion that a perfectly competitive labour market is efficient to the much stronger conclusion that a free, unregulated labour market is "best"

- Explain the effects of a minimum wage in an otherwise perfectly competitive labour market, and its effects in a labour market that is not competitive
- Discuss the effects of discrimination in a labour market
- Describe and evaluate the concept of work of equal value (comparable worth)

HIGHLIGHTS OF THE CHAPTER

As a first approximation, a wage can be viewed just like the price of any other good or service that is traded in the market. In this case, the service is labour, the demanders are employers, and the suppliers are workers.

The Demand for Labour

In defining its demand for labour, a firm begins with its marginal physical product (MPP). This schedule, shown in column 3 of Table 35-1 in the textbook, shows how the firm's output increases—in physical units—as it hires more labour. By multiplying this increase in physical output by the price at which the firm can sell that output, it is possible to calculate the additional revenue the firm receives as it hires more labour. This is called its marginal revenue product (MRP), and is shown in column 5 of Table 35-1. MRP will also be the value of the marginal product (VMP) provided the firm is selling its output in a perfectly competitive market.

The profit-maximizing firm will demand labour up to the point where the MRP is just equal to the wage rate W. The reason is that, if MRP were greater than W, the firm could increase its profits by hiring more workers; and if MRP were less than W, the firm could increase its profits by hiring fewer workers. Thus, the MRP curve shows how much the firm will hire at each possible wage. In other words, the MRP curve is the firm's labour demand curve.

A firm's demand for labour schedule slopes down because of diminishing returns. (Recall this concept from Figure 24-2.) As a firm hires more and more labour (with other factors fixed), it eventually finds that the marginal physical product of labour—and therefore MRP—decreases. In other words, its demand for labour slopes downward.

There are several reasons why a firm's demand curve for labour might shift: (1) If the price of the firm's output falls, MRP and, therefore, the demand for labour will shift down; (2) If the marginal physical product of labour shifts up, MRP and the labour demand curve will also shift up. Such an upward shift might occur, for example, if the firm increases the amount of capital it employs; this would make labour physically more productive by providing it with more machinery to work with. Another example might be a technological improvement that allows a firm to get more physical output from its workers. (Often, increased capital equipment and technological change go together, but it is possible for one to occur without the other.)

The market demand curve for labour is merely the horizontal sum of the demand curves of all the individual hiring firms. This is similar to the summation of the individual demand curves for a good described in Figure 22-1 in the textbook.

Before turning to the supply curve for labour, we pause briefly to consider a further important interpretation of labour demand.

How the Labour Demand Curve Shows the Distribution of Income

The total income of an industry is the sum of the contributions of all workers employed in that industry. That is, in Figure 35-4 in the textbook, it is the sum of all the individual contributions—such as arrows *a* and *b* on the left—of all *N* workers in this industry. In total, this is area 1 and 2 under the labour demand curve. Of this area representing total industry income, rectangular area 2 is labour income, since it is the quantity of employment (the base of this rectangle) times the wage (the height of this rectangle). The rest—that is, area 1—goes to other factors of production, in the form of rent, interest, and profit.

The Supply of Labour

The height of the labour supply curve indicates how much must be paid to attract one more worker into the industry—that is, the worker's transfer price. This is (roughly) the wage and productivity of this worker in another industry. In other words, the height of the labour supply curve is just the opportunity cost of an additional worker.

Is a Perfectly Competitive Labour Market Efficient?

Efficiency requires that labour be hired in an industry up to the point where its marginal benefit is just equal to its marginal costs. (If there are no externalities—as assumed here—then there is no difference between social and private benefits, and no difference between social and private costs.) The marginal benefit of labour is its productivity in this industry, as given by the labour demand curve. The marginal cost of labour is its opportunity cost—that is, its wage and productivity elsewhere; this is given by its supply curve. Since supply and demand for labour are equated in a perfectly competitive labour market, the marginal cost of labour is equal to the marginal benefit of labour, and this market is, therefore, efficient.

When a labour market has been shifted away from a perfectly competitive equilibrium, there is an efficiency loss that can be measured by the triangle between the demand curve, the supply curve, and the vertical line at the actual quantity of employment. Examples are provided in panels (b) and (c) of Figure 35-6 in the textbook. If such triangular efficiency losses are not clear, you may wish to review the similar analysis that was used in Figure 26-3 to show efficiency losses in product markets. It is essential that you understand these fully, because they will be used frequently.

Although a perfectly competitive labour market is efficient, it does not necessarily follow that a free unregulated labour market is "best," for the following four reasons: (1) In an unregulated market, employers may discriminate against minorities, and thus violate the mobility assumption of perfect competition; labour is not free to move into any industry; (2) In an unregulated market, employers may have market power, thus violating another assumption of perfect competition; (3) There may be externalities; (4) Even if none of these problems arise—and an unregulated labour market is efficient—it may not be best because of the way it distributes income.

The Effect of a Minimum Wage

There are four effects when a minimum wage (above the existing equilibrium wage) is introduced into a perfectly competitive labour market. (1) Employment is reduced. (2) Reduced employment leads to an efficiency loss, similar to the red triangle in panel (c) of Figure 35-6. (The efficiency loss is even more than this if the minimum wage is imposed across all labour markets.) (3) Although the wage received by workers who are still employed in this industry rises, the wage of those who no longer have a job here falls (or disappears altogether). Therefore, on balance, the overall effect on total labour income is uncertain. (4) The amount of income going to other factors of production will definitely decrease, because the higher wage that must be paid to labour will put a squeeze on these other incomes.

While these four effects can be predicted from our theory, there is another effect that experience has taught us: The unemployment created by minimum wage legislation falls most heavily on teenagers.

The important qualifications to this minimum wage analysis include: (1) Even if the minimum wage raises total labour income, workers may not feel that they benefit overall from the change. Even though jobs pay better, they are harder to find; and employers paying a higher wage may no longer feel that they can afford the cost of on-the-job training that is so beneficial to workers. (2) The more industries covered by minimum wage legislation, the greater the unemployment it will create. The reason is that it becomes harder for an unemployed person to find a job elsewhere, because there are fewer and fewer other jobs available.

The Effects of Discrimination in the Labour Market

Figure 35-8 in the text shows the economic effects when employers discriminate by hiring women only for jobs with a low marginal product; the offensive moral and social dimensions are also recognized, even though they cannot be dealt with in this analysis.

When women are forced into jobs where they produce less, there is an efficiency loss roughly equal to the reduction in their output. Moreover, because they work in jobs where they are less productive, women receive a lower wage. Thus the entire efficiency loss in essentially borne by women. It is true that male workers benefit from a higher wage, due to the artificial scarcity of labour created in their part of the market because women are no longer able to work there. However, other factors of production lose because their interest, rent, and profit income is squeezed by the higher wage for men. Since most other factors of production are owned by families with a male wage earner, it is not clear that such families benefit overall, or lose: They gain because of the higher wage for the male earner, but lose because of the reduced income of their other factors of production; if there is a working woman in the family, the reduction in her wage constitutes part of the loss. The one clear message is that there is an efficiency loss, and this loss will be borne primarily by single women and families without a male wage earner.

Work of Equal Value

With equal pay for men and women in the *same* job now a widely accepted principle, the focus has shifted to the question, What should be done when men and women are in *different* but equally demanding jobs, and women are paid less? Should nurses be paid less than truck drivers? Proponents of the principle of "equal pay for work of equal value" say no. If these jobs are judged comparable, in terms of the education, responsibility, skills, etc., that they require, then pay should be equalized. Moreover, certain federal and provincial labour laws now reflect this principle. However, critics are concerned because this policy requires that specific jobs be compared; and these comparisons will be based on subjective and arbitrary judgements by bureaucrats or judges who will be second-guessing labour markets. They will be imposing a detailed and complex system of wage controls that will leave many labour markets in a chronic condition of excess demand or supply.

IMPORTANT TERMS: MATCH THE COLUMNS

Match each term in the first column with its corresponding explanation in the second column.

_____ 1. Marginal physical product (MPP) of labour

_____ 2. Marginal revenue product (MRP) of labour

_____ 3. Opportunity cost of labour

_____ 4. Value of the marginal product (VMP) of labour

_____ 5. Transfer price of labour

a. The additional revenue that a firm can earn by hiring one more worker

b. The wage necessary to induce a worker to change jobs

c. The additional number of units of output that a firm can produce by hiring one more worker

d. The wage or productivity of labour in another industry

e. Marginal physical product of labour times the price of the employer's product

TRUE-FALSE

T   F   1. The marginal revenue product curve shows the cost to the firm of hiring additional workers.

T   F   2. A profit-maximizing firm that is operating in perfectly competitive labour and product markets will hire labour to the point where the value of the marginal product equals the wage rate.

T   F   3. The demand for labour schedule shifts to the right whenever the marginal revenue product of labour schedule shifts to the right.

T   F   4. If the marginal revenue product of labour is less than the wage, a perfectly competitive firm can increase its profits by hiring more labour.

T   F   5. One effect of an increase in the minimum wage is a decrease in the income going to factors of production other than labour.

T   F   6. Even if there is an external cost of employing labour, a perfectly competitive labour market will still be efficient.

T   F   7. The marginal revenue product of labour is the amount the firm's revenue increases when it hires one more worker.

T   F   8. The value of the marginal product of labour is the same as the marginal revenue product of labour, if the hiring firm is a monopolist in its product market.

T   F   9. The demand for labour by an industry is the horizontal sum of the demand by the individual firms in that industry.

T   F   10. If the wage rate rises elsewhere in the economy, the wage and employment in a perfectly competitive industry will tend to rise.

T   F   11. There is a greater efficiency loss if the minimum wage is applied to only one industry rather than to all industries.

MULTIPLE CHOICE

1. The marginal physical product of labour:
   a. is based on the assumption that the firm uses a given capital stock as the employment of labour increases
   b. is based on the assumption that the use of capital increases by the same proportion as labour employment
   c. shows the additional revenue a firm can earn because it hires one more worker
   d. is set equal to the wage rate by an employer in equilibrium
   e. is the same as the value of the marginal product

2. A firm's demand curve for labour is the curve showing its:
   a. total physical product of labour
   b. average revenue product of labour
   c. marginal physical product of labour
   d. average physical product of labour
   e. marginal revenue product of labour

3. The demand for labour by a firm producing bolts shifts up in response to:
   a. a rise in the price of bolts
   b. a fall in labour productivity in the bolt-making industry
   c. a downward shift in the demand for bolts
   d. a decrease in the stock of machinery in the industry
   e. a decrease in the stock of other investment equipment in the industry

4. A leftward shift in the labour supply schedule may be the result of:
   a. a rightward shift in the marginal revenue product of labour schedule
   b. a leftward shift in the marginal revenue product of labour schedule
   c. higher available wages in other industries
   d. a fall in labour productivity
   e. a falling opportunity cost of labour

5. Perfect competition in a labour market requires the assumption that workers are:
   a. so numerous that each individual can affect the wage rate
   b. so numerous that no individual can affect the wage rate
   c. so few that no individual can affect the wage rate
   d. so few that any individual can affect the wage rate
   e. any of the above, since no assumption is required on this

6. If there is a perfectly competitive market for farm labour, and there is a fall in the price of grain and other farm outputs, then there will be:
   a. a shift to the left in the labour supply curve
   b. a shift to the right in the labour supply curve
   c. a shift to the left in the labour demand curve
   d. a shift to the right in the labour demand curve
   e. a. and c.

7. The value of the marginal product of labour is equal to the marginal revenue product of labour:
   a. always
   b. never
   c. only if the hiring firm is a monopolist in its product market
   d. only if the hiring firm is a perfect competitor in its product market
   e. only if the hiring firm is an oligopolist in its product market

8. The opportunity cost of labour in an industry:
   a. is approximately measured by the height of the labour demand schedule
   b. is approximately measured by the height of the labour supply schedule
   c. decreases as employment in the industry increases
   d. is completely vertical because labour can switch between industries
   e. is the income that capital can earn elsewhere

9. Which of the following will cause a rightward shift in the labour demand by an industry?
   a. an increase in labour productivity in this industry
   b. a decrease in labour productivity in this industry
   c. an increase in the minimum wage
   d. an increase in the transfer price of labour
   e. a decrease in the transfer price of labour

10. Labour demand by a firm will shift to the left if there is:
    a. a decrease in the minimum wage
    b. an increase in the marginal revenue product of labour
    c. a decrease in the marginal revenue product of labour
    d. an increase in wages in other industries
    e. a decrease in wages in other industries

11. The total area under an industry's demand for labour schedule to the left of the existing quantity of employment equals:
    a. the income received by other factors in the industry
    b. the total income of labour in the industry

c. the total income of labour and all other factors in the industry
d. total profits in the industry
e. the marginal revenue received by the industry

12. If the labour supply curve is vertical, then a technological improvement that increases the marginal physical product of labour will cause:
   a. an increase in the wage and no change in employment
   b. an increase in both the wage and employment
   c. an increase in employment and no change in the wage
   d. a decrease in the wage and no change in employment
   e. a decrease in the wage and an increase in employment

13. In a perfectly competitive labour market for an industry, an increase in wages elsewhere in the economy will result in:
   a. a shift to the right in the labour supply curve
   b. an increase in wages and employment in this industry
   c. a decrease in wages and employment in this industry
   d. a decrease in wages, and an increase in employment in this industry
   e. an increase in wages, and a decrease in employment in this industry

14. Which of the following does not affect an individual worker's transfer price?
   a. the wage in the industry from which the worker is moving
   b. the wage in the industry to which the worker is moving
   c. financial moving costs
   d. psychological moving costs
   e. differences in the attractiveness of working conditions in the new and old industries

15. In a perfectly competitive labour market for an industry, there will be an efficiency loss unless labour is hired up to the point where:
   a. the marginal productivity of labour in this industry exceeds its marginal productivity elsewhere
   b. the marginal productivity of labour in this industry is less than its marginal productivity elsewhere
   c. the marginal productivity of labour in this industry is equal to its marginal productivity elsewhere
   d. the marginal opportunity cost of labour exceeds its marginal productivity in this industry
   e. the marginal opportunity cost of labour is less than its marginal productivity in this industry

16. If less than the perfectly competitive number of workers is hired in an industry:
   a. the marginal productivity of labour in this industry will exceed its marginal productivity elsewhere
   b. the marginal productivity of labour in this industry will be less than its marginal productivity elsewhere
   c. the marginal productivity of labour in this industry will be equal to its marginal productivity elsewhere
   d. the marginal opportunity cost of labour will exceed its marginal productivity in this industry
   e. the marginal opportunity cost of labour will be the same as its marginal productivity in this industry

17. In a perfectly competitive labour market:
   a. employers hire labour up to the point where they maximize their profit
   b. employers hire labour up to the point where their marginal benefit is equal to their marginal cost
   c. employees supply labour services up to the point where their marginal benefit is equal to their marginal cost
   d. there is an efficient level of employment
   e. all of the above

18. In Canada, the minimum wage:
   a. is set by the federal government for the whole country
   b. is higher for teenagers than for older workers in most jurisdictions
   c. covers every industry in those provinces where minimum wage legislation exists
   d. is generally higher for women than for men in federal jobs
   e. none of the above

19. A minimum wage can increase efficiency if:
   a. there is a major problem with teenage unemployment
   b. all wages in the economy are already above the minimum wage
   c. all wages in the economy are below the minimum wage
   d. all wages in the economy are the same as the minimum wage
   e. the labour market is not perfectly competitive

20. The efficiency loss from sex discrimination in a perfectly competitive labour market:
   a. is borne to a large extent by single women, whose income is reduced
   b. occurs because women are employed in more productive activities, while men are in less productive ones

c. occurs because income is transferred from male workers to other factors of production

d. occurs because income is transferred from female workers to non-labour factors of production

e. occurs because the other factors of production are owned by outsiders

For those who have studied the appendix to this chapter:

21. An economy-wide labour supply curve will "bend backwards" if:

a. an increase in the wage rate induces labour to work more

b. workers decide to use their increase in wages to "buy more leisure"

c. workers decide to use all their increase in wages to buy more goods

d. the substitution effect of a higher wage dominates the income effect

e. there is no cost of living allowance in wage contracts

EXERCISES

1a. Fill in the missing data in Table 35.1 for a hypothetical firm with a given stock of capital which sells its output in a competitive market at a constant price.

If the wage rate is $55 per worker per day, then the firm will want to hire _____ workers if the price of its output is $10, and _____ workers when this price is $15.

Table 35.1

Number of workers	Total physical output	Marginal physical product of labour	Marginal revenue product (MRP) when price of output is $10 per unit	Marginal revenue product (MRP) when price of output is $15 per unit
0	0			
1	12			
2	19			
3	24			
4	28			
5	30			

1b. Fill in the missing data in Table 35.2 for another hypothetical firm, assuming that the wage it faces is $40 per worker per day and the price of its output is $5.

Table 35.2

Number of workers	Total physical output	Marginal physical product	Marginal revenue product
0	0	—	—
1		10	
2		9	
3		8	
4		7	
5		6	

The firm will be willing to hire no more than _____ workers. With this amount of employment, the firm's total revenue will be _____, its total wage payment will be $_____, and the income of other factors will be $_____.

2. Plot the labour demand schedule of this firm in Figure 35.1. Draw a horizontal line at the wage rate of $40 per worker per day. Label as 1 the area representing labour income. Label as 2 the area representing the income going to other factors.

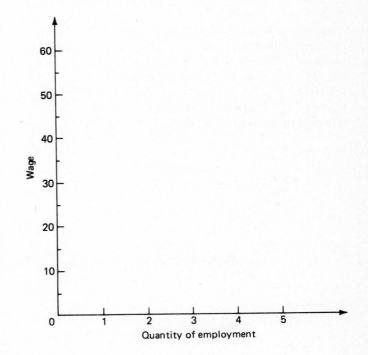

Figure 35.1

3. Figure 35.2 depicts a perfectly competitive labour market with no externalities. The equilibrium wage rate is _____ and the equilibrium quantity of employment is _____. Suppose a minimum wage of U is imposed. Then employment will be _____. Next, suppose the minimum wage is H. Then employment will be _____ and the difference between demand and supply will be _____. Fill in Table 35.3.

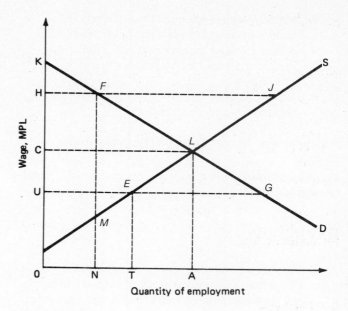

Figure 35.2

Table 35.3

	Efficiency loss is area:	Total labour income is area:	Income of other factors is area:
No minimum wage			
Minimum wage at U			
Minimum wage at H			

(This requires study of the text, especially Box 35-1.) A perfectly competitive labour market is shown in Figure 35.3.

4a. The marginal productivity of labour (VMP) in this industry is shown by the _____ curve, while the marginal productivity of labour elsewhere is shown by the _____ curve. The equilibrium is at _____, with wage _____ and employment of _____ workers. At this equilibrium, employers have (maximized, minimized) their profit by hiring labour up to the point where its marginal benefit—that is, the marginal productivity of labour in this industry as shown by the _____ curve—is equal to the marginal cost the employers face, as shown by _____. At the same time, employees have (minimized, maximized) their own net benefit by offering their labour up to the point where their marginal benefit—as shown by _____—is equal to their marginal cost, shown by _____. This marginal cost to employees is called a (substitute, opportunity) cost, because it represents their potential earnings in their (least, most) attractive alternative job.

4b. If employment is at N_2, there is an efficiency (gain, loss) of area _____ because the N_2N_1 extra workers employed would have (higher, lower) marginal productivity elsewhere—as shown by the _____ curve—than in this industry where their marginal productivity is shown by the _____ curve. On the other hand, if employment in this industry is at N_3, then there is an efficiency (gain, loss) because N_3N_1 workers should be employed in this industry, but are not. These workers would have marginal productivity here shown by the _____ curve compared to their (lower, higher) marginal productivity elsewhere, as shown by the height of the _____ curve. Only at an employment level of _____ can one or the other of these types of efficiency losses be avoided.

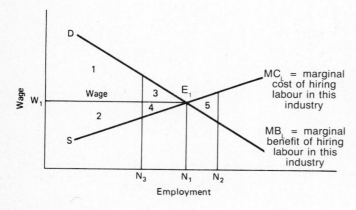

Figure 35.3

ESSAY QUESTIONS

1. "The labour demand schedule slopes down for the same reason that the demand curve for a consumer good slopes down." Explain to what extent this is or is not true.

2. List and explain some influences that could shift the labour supply curve for an industry. In each case, indicate in which direction the shift would occur.

3. Over the past 50 years, the number of domestic servants in North America has fallen dramatically. Do you think this is because of the price and availability of labour-saving household appliances? Or is it due to rising wages in other occupations? Or do both factors play a role? Explain how each affects the supply and demand for domestic help.

4. Discuss the influences that affect the elasticity of demand for labour, by first reviewing the influences affecting the elasticity of demand for a consumer good discussed in Chapter 21 in the text.

5. How would the supply of labour in a particular market be affected by a decrease in the cost of moving from one city to another?

6. Would you expect labour market discrimination to be more of a problem in a perfectly competitive industry or in a monopolistic industry?

ANSWERS

Important Terms: 1c, 2a, 3d, 4e, 5b
True-False: 1F, 2T, 3T, 4F, 5T, 6F, 7T, 8F, 9T, 10F, 11F
Multiple Choice: 1a, 2e, 3a, 4c, 5b, 6c, 7d, 8b, 9a, 10c, 11c, 12a, 13e, 14b, 15c, 16a, 17e, 18e, 19e, 20a, 21b
Exercises:

1a.
Table 35.1 completed

W	O	MPP	MRP if $P = \$10$	MRP if $P = \$15$
0	0	—	—	—
1	12	12	120	180
2	19	7	70	105
3	24	5	50	75
4	28	4	40	60
5	30	2	20	30

2, 4

1b.
Table 35.2 completed

Number of workers	Total physical output	MRP
0	0	—
1	10	$50
2	19	45
3	27	40
4	34	35
5	40	30

3, $135, $120, $15

2. Figure 35.1 completed

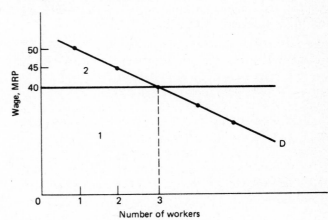

3. C, A, A, N, *FJ*

Table 35.3 completed

Zero	0CLA	KLC
Zero	0CLA	KLC
FLM	0HFN	KFH

4a. D, S, E_1, W_1, N_1, maximized, D, W_1E_1, maximized, W_1E_1, S, opportunity, most **4b.** loss, 5, higher, S, D, loss, D, lower, S, N_1

ANSWERS TO SELECTED REVIEW QUESTIONS FROM THE TEXT

35-1. (a) Total revenue is $420 (21 units at $20). The total wage bill is $240 (4 workers at $60). The difference of $180 is the return to other factors of production.

(b) Total revenue is the total area of the first four bars in Figure 35-1; payments to labour is the area of these same bars below the horizontal line at $60, while the return to other factors is the area above that line.

35-3.

35-2. If the product price falls to $10, the height of each bar in Figure 35-1 would be cut in half, as would the height of the firm's labour demand curve. At a wage of $60, the firm could hire 3 workers who would produce 18 units at $10, which would be just enough to pay the firm's wage bill.

Table 35-1　Marginal Revenue Product vs. Value of Marginal Product

Workers	Output	MPP	Price	Total Revenue	MRP	VMP
0	0		—	0		
1	5	5	$24	$120	$120	$120
2	12	7	$23	$276	$156	$161
3	18	6	$22	$396	$120	$132
4	21	3	$21	$411	$45	$63
5	23	2	$20	$460	$19	$40

35-4. Loosely speaking, with a lower labour productivity in Newfoundland, the labour demand curves of firms there would be lower than in other provinces with higher productivity. With a given minimum wage rate, this could be expected to lead to a lower rate of employment—that is, a higher rate of unemployment—in Newfoundland. Comparative unemployment statistics do in fact show higher unemployment rates in Newfoundland than elsewhere in Canada.

35-5. A minimum wage will be more likely to raise total income if labour demand elasticity is low. If elasticity is more than one, then a higher wage will lower labour income. And beware: Even if labour income is increased, it may be a questionable objective if it leaves many workers unemployed.

Across

1, 3. Proponents say this raises the incomes of the poor; critics say it causes unemployment.

6. gas commonly used as a refrigerant

7. He explained the idea of comparative advantage.

10. historical period

11. a barrier to international trade

12. one of the arguments for the protection of domestic industry from foreign competition

15. Bastiat suggested that these people might object to the unfair competition from the sun.

19. new (German, fem.)

20. a flying mammal

22. wept

23. the key to rising living standards

26. tool for propelling a boat

27, 28. Where this is low, a country has a comparative advantage.

30. form an association of workers

31. large mammal

32. a third type of efficiency (in addition to allocative and technological efficiency)

33. He is associated with idea that, in aggregate, supply creates its own demand.

Down

1, 23. In a perfectly competitive economy, the wage is equal to the value of this.

2. picture

3. In an efficient economy, this is avoided.

4. the goal of getting the most out of our productive efforts

5. one of the major arguments for tariffs (2 words)

8. ungentlemanly chap

9. Do this to oil to produce gasoline.

13. African river

14. He suggested that tariffs were equivalent to a "negative railway."

16. indefinite article preceding vowel

17. sweet, melodious

18. externalities

20. prefix meaning "two"

21. A good lawyer can often help clients to _____ taxes.

24. industry with only two sellers

25. attempt (verb)

29. organization for negotiating over tariffs and other trade barriers (abbrev.)

Chapter 36

■■■■■■■■■■■■■■■■■■■■■■■■■■■■■■■■■■■

Wages in Imperfectly Competitive Labour Markets

MAJOR PURPOSE

The key objective in this chapter is to analyse what happens when labour markets are not perfectly competitive. Typically, the result is inefficiency, and this is compared with the efficient outcome when labour markets are perfectly competitive, as described in the last chapter.

Elements of imperfect competition may appear on either side of the labour market. On the one side, workers may form a union which, as a monopoly (a single seller of labour services), is able to raise the wage rate. On the other side, there may be a monopsony firm (a single buyer of labour services) that is able to lower the wage rate. In either case, an inefficiently low amount of labour is hired. The interesting case of bilateral monopoly arises when there is a monopoly (a union) on the workers' side of the market, and a monopsony on the employer's side. Illustrations are provided to show how difficult and complicated wage bargaining can be in this case. In particular, special problems arise in any bargaining between a monopoly union of public service workers and their monopsony employer—the government.

LEARNING OBJECTIVES

After you have studied this chapter in the textbook and the study guide, you should be able to

• Describe how union membership has changed in various periods of Canadian labour history
• Describe the changing relationship between Canadian and American union movements
• Explain the differences between Canadian and U.S. labour legislation in the question of compulsory union membership
• Show in a diagram the inefficiency that results when a union succeeds in raising wages in an otherwise perfectly competitive labour market
• Describe, on the other hand, the special ways that a union may improve efficiency
• Show, in particular, how efficiency may be increased if a union is formed in a labour market that has previously been monopsonized
• Analyse bilateral monopoly, where market power is held by a monopoly (a single seller) on one side of the market and by a monopsony (a single buyer) on the other
• Explain why a strike may occur even though there is a large collective loss from it
• Show why there may be large internal and external costs if labour negotiations break down and a strike occurs
• Identify three ways of trying to avert an imminent strike
• Explain the possible imbalance of bargaining power when a public service union negotiates with a government
• State four reasons workers get different wages

HIGHLIGHTS OF THE CHAPTER

The major topics covered in this chapter include: (1) the history of the labour union movement in Canada and its relationship with the labour movement in the United States; (2) the effects of introducing a union into an otherwise perfectly competitive labour market; (3) the effects of a monopsony (a single buyer) in an otherwise perfectly competitive labour market; (4) a description of bilateral monopoly, where a monopoly union bargains with a monopsony employer; (5) the reasons public service employees form a union, but the special problems that then arise; and (6) the reasons wages aren't the same for all workers.

History

As Figure 36-1 in the text shows, there have been four distinct periods in the modern history of the Canadian labour movement.

1. During the 1920s and 1930s, union membership in Canada did not grow by very much. The most important labour organization, the Trades and Labour Congress of Canada (TLC), was essentially a federation of *craft* unions—like its U.S. counterpart, the American Federation of Labor (AFL). As a result, it did not appeal to unskilled workers in mass-production industries who did not belong to a particular "craft." Furthermore, there was strong employer resistance to the growth of unions, and the labour legislation during that period made it hard for unions to overcome this resistance.

2. During the 1940s and early 1950s, union membership grew very rapidly in Canada. In part, the reason for this was the rapid rise in *industrial* unions, which brought the unskilled workers in mass-production industries into the union movement. Canada's industrial unions were organized in the Canadian Congress of Labour (CCL), the counterpart of the American Congress of Industrial Organizations (CIO). Furthermore, Canada's labour legislation changed during this period, with the right of workers to unionize becoming explicitly recognized; the 1945 *Rand formula* set a precedent by making it legal for a labour contract to compel all workers to contribute financially to the union.

3. In the decade between the early 1950s and early 1960s, union membership in Canada grew only slowly, in part reflecting the relatively slow growth of employment in industries in which unions have traditionally been important and in part reflecting continued strife between craft unions and industrial unions. However, this strife has gradually diminished, and most unions of either type are now affiliated with the Canadian Labour Congress (CLC), which was created in 1956 through a merger of the TLC and CCL. (In the United States, a similar merger created the AFL-CIO.)

4. Since the early 1960s, union membership has remained relatively stable in the aggregate, but its *composition* has been changing. Union membership in the private sector and in the traditional international unions has continued to grow slowly. Most of the growth in union membership in the 1960s and 1970s has occurred instead in *national unions* which are not affiliated with U.S. labour organizations. In particular, there has been rapid growth in union membership in the public service and, of course, public sector unions are national unions.

(In the United States, union membership as a proportion of the labour force has *declined* during the last few decades. Part of the reason for this has been public hostility to unions in the United States, as well as the passage of legislation such as the Taft-Hartly Act, which outlaws compulsory checkoff of union dues and gives the individual states the right to pass laws prohibiting union shops or closed shops. Closed shops and union shops are legal in Canada.)

The Effects of Unions

A union gives workers a voice in presenting grievances to their employer. It also negotiates with management to establish seniority rules and improve working conditions. These benefit not only the workers but also the employer who is able to offer more attractive jobs and therefore reduce quit rates.

But the main objectives of a union are to protect the jobs and raise the wages of its members. According to recent estimates, unionized workers get anywhere from 10% to 30% higher wages than comparable non-unionized workers. If a union is established that raises the wage in a previously competitive labour market, there are three main effects: (a) there is a reduction in employment and in the income of workers who consequently lose their jobs; (b) there is an increase in the wages and incomes of workers who still have jobs, but this increase comes at the expense of other factors of production; and (c) there is a triangular efficiency loss that can be measured by the usual geometric technique. Study Figure 36-2 in the textbook until you can demonstrate these three effects on your own.

Finally, a union tries to protect its members' jobs in several ways. For example:

1. It may try to negotiate a shorter work week. If there is unemployment, fewer hours per worker means more workers can get jobs.

2. It can press the government to restrict imports. In

Chapter 34 we saw that this may indeed increase domestic employment in the short run. However, any employment gains are likely to be wiped out if our trading partners buy less exports from us in retaliation; and, even if they don't, such protection will have damaging effects on the economy.

The analysis in Figure 36-2 of the efficiency loss that results from a union is overly harsh, because in some ways not shown in this diagram, unions improve efficiency. First, by giving workers a voice, unions provide them with an alternative to quitting or being fired when a problem arises. Thus, they save unnecessary costs of labour turnover. Second, by improving working conditions they can reduce the tension between workers and employers, and thus create a more productive atmosphere. Third, a union's bargaining power may simply offset the bargaining power of monopsonist employers; in this case, a union may increase efficiency. (Remember that our earlier discussion of the efficiency losses from a union applies only if the labour market is perfectly competitive otherwise.)

Monopsony

As a single employer of labour, a monopsony tries to exploit its market power by reducing wages. If it succeeds—in an otherwise perfectly competitive labour market—the three main effects will be to (a) transfer income from labour to other factors of production; (b) reduce employment; and (c) create an efficiency loss. Study Figure 36-3 in the textbook until you can demonstrate these three effects on your own.

Bilateral Monopoly

In this case of "two-sided" monopoly, market power is held both by a union on the one side, and by a monopsonistic employer on the other. This case is the most difficult to analyse.

To illustrate, suppose a union is formed in a labour market where a monopsonist employer has been keeping the wage rate below the perfectly competitive level. In this case, the formation of the union may raise the wage back toward the perfectly competitive level. If this is the outcome, the union will be simply undoing some of the effects of the monopsony. Specifically, the union will (a) transfer income back from other factors of production to labour, (b) increase employment, and (c) reduce the efficiency loss from monopsony. Before reading further make sure you can illustrate these effects with a diagram similar to Figure 36-5 in the textbook.

However, the outcome is not this simple to predict, because there is no guarantee that a newly formed union

will only raise wages toward the perfectly competitive level; it may raise wages beyond this. If this happens we can no longer be sure that the union will increase efficiency. This is the basic problem in analysing bilateral monopoly: We don't know where the wage will be set. All we know for sure is that the wage will be somewhere between the high wage the union seeks, and the lower wage the monopsonistic employer seeks. At what point the wage will be determined within this range depends on the bargaining power of each side. This, in turn, depends partly on the ability of each to outlast the other in the event of a strike. Thus, the bargaining power of the union depends upon the size of the union's strike fund. The bargaining power of the employer depends upon the size of its inventories of finished goods that it can continue to sell during a strike.

Strikes

In a sense, everyone is damaged by a strike. The employer loses profits and the labour force loses wages. Nevertheless, strikes do occur, because (a) each side may see a strike as a way of getting a more favourable wage rate than the other side's final offer on the eve of the strike; (b) each side may want to increase its future credibility and bargaining power by clearly demonstrating that it is prepared to allow a strike to take place; or (c) either side may make a bargaining mistake that prevents an agreement from being reached before a strike deadline. In comparison to other countries, Canada has a record of relatively frequent and long-lasting strikes. Nevertheless, in an average year the typical Canadian worker spends less than one day on strike.

One reason strikes pose an important issue for public policy is *spillovers*—that is, costs of strikes to people not involved in the bargaining. For example, a transit strike prevents people from getting to their jobs.

There are several possible ways of averting a strike when the two sides are unable to reach agreement on their own. (a) The government (federal or provincial, depending on who has the jurisdiction over labour relations in the industry involved) may appoint an outsider to act as a mediator or conciliate between the parties. (b) Both sides may agree to voluntary arbitration, in which a third party decides upon a settlement that both sides agree in advance to accept. (c) If they don't agree to voluntary arbitration, the government may force them to accept compulsory arbitration.

Unions of Public Service Employees

Unions in the public sector raise problems because they

have such a strong bargaining position, for the following reasons.

1. There are large spillover costs to the voting public when public servants such as transit workers or the police go on strike. Thus, voters may exert great pressure on the government to settle the dispute.

2. Public servants know that, in the last analysis, it is typically easier for a government than for a private company to raise the funds necessary to pay a higher wage. The government can tax or borrow in a way that is not available to private employers.

3. A union has much greater bargaining power over a financially weak government than it would have over a financially weak private employer. The reason is that a strike won't force a government out of business, but it might drive a private employer bankrupt, in which case there are no jobs to negotiate about.

4. Because public service employees now constitute a large bloc of voters, politicians are reluctant to fight hard against their wage demands.

Because public servants have such a strong bargaining position, it is often suggested that they should not be allowed to strike, or even form a union. But this would raise a problem. If these workers cannot form a union, how can they defend themselves against a monopsonistic employer (the government)? If not with a union, what else?

Wage Differences

Wage differences can exist for at least five different reasons: First, there may be *dynamic* wage differentials. When new job opportunities open up in an industry, wages must rise temporarily to attract workers from other industries. Eventually, the influx of new workers will bring the wages back down. Second, *compensating* wage differentials give workers more pay for especially hazardous or unpleasant jobs. Third, monopoly or monopsony power may be greater in some labour markets than in others. Fourth, barriers to entry can keep wages artificially high in some jobs. Fifth, those with special talents and skills earn a higher wage because they are more productive, as we shall see in the next chapter.

IMPORTANT TERMS: MATCH THE COLUMNS

Match each term in the first column with its corresponding explanation in the second column.

_____ **1.** Seniority rules
_____ **2.** Industrial union
_____ **3.** Craft union
_____ **4.** Collective bargaining
_____ **5.** Trades and Labour Congress of Canada
_____ **6.** Rand formula
_____ **7.** Canadian Congress of Labour
_____ **8.** Closed shop
_____ **9.** Union shop
_____ **10.** Open shop
_____ **11.** Right-to-work law
_____ **12.** Jurisdictional dispute
_____ **13.** Checkoff
_____ **14.** National union
_____ **15.** Monopsony
_____ **16.** Strike fund
_____ **17.** Canadian Labour Congress (CLC)
_____ **18.** Mediation
_____ **19.** Arbitration
_____ **20.** Dynamic wage differentials
_____ **21.** Compensating wage differentials

a. A collection of industrial unions, like the American CIO

b. A union whose members all belong to the same craft or profession, although they may work in different industries. Examples are the plumbers' union and the carpenters' union.

c. The specification of a third party to suggest a compromise settlement in a labour dispute. The third party cannot make binding recommendations.

d. Differences that may arise if labour views some jobs as less attractive than others. (Employers have to pay a higher wage to fill the unattractive jobs.)

e. Preference in hiring and firing to those who have been longest on the job

f. A union whose members all work in the same industry, or group of industries, although they may belong to different crafts or professions. Examples are the Canadian Auto Workers and the United Mine Workers.

g. A union not affiliated with a similar foreign union

h. A statute making closed shops or union shops illegal

i. A firm in which anyone hired by an employer must join the union within some specified period
j. Differences in wages that arise because of changing demand or supply conditions in the labour market. These differences tend to disappear over time as labour moves out of relatively low wage jobs and into those that pay a relatively high wage.
k. A collection of craft unions, like the American AFL
l. Negotiations between a union and an employer over wages, fringe benefits, hiring policies, job security, and working conditions
m. Formed through a merger of the TLC and the CCL
n. A firm in which an employer can hire only workers who are already union members
o. A sum of money owned by a union for the purpose of supporting its members while on strike
p. A single buyer
q. The practice of having employers collect union dues by deducting them from workers' paycheques
r. Court decision legalizing a system of dues checkoffs
s. A conflict between unions over whose members will do specific jobs
t. A firm in which employees do not have to be in a union
u. The specification of a third party to suggest a compromise settlement in a labour dispute. The decision of the third party is binding on both labour and management.

TRUE-FALSE

T F 1. Bilateral monopoly in the labour market means that employers are exercising monopsony power and labour is exercising monopoly power.

T F 2. An industrial union draws its members from any industry, provided they have a common skill (such as plumbing).

T F 3. The Canadian Auto Workers (CAW) is a craft union.

T F 4. Like Samuel Gompers' American Federation of Labour, the Trades and Labour Congress of Canada was an attempt to organize labour for a political class struggle, rather than for the pursuit of improved wages and working conditions.

T F 5. If wages are reduced below what they would be in perfect competition, there will be a loss in efficiency.

T F 6. A monopolist in the labour market will seek to raise wages, while a monopsonist will seek to lower them.

T F 7. Other things equal, a company producing perishable goods is more vulnerable to strike threats than one producing durable goods.

T F 8. The spillover cost of a strike must be less than the internal cost to the industry in which the strike occurs.

T F 9. Public service unions have recently been growing less rapidly than other unions.

T F 10. Compensating wage differentials would not exist if workers viewed all jobs as equally attractive.

MULTIPLE CHOICE

1. When a union negotiates seniority rules, workers with seniority are typically:
   a. the first to be laid off and the first to be rehired
   b. the first to be laid off and the last to be rehired
   c. the last to be laid off and the last to be rehired
   d. the last to be laid off and the first to be rehired
   e. left unaffected in terms of being laid off or rehired

2. Craft unions draw their membership from:
   a. workers in companies that build pleasure boats
   b. workers in companies that build any boats
   c. all workers in a specific industry regardless of their skills
   d. all workers in a specific industry provided they have the same skill
   e. all workers from any industry provided they have the same skill

3. Unions, in Canada and elsewhere:
   a. negotiate higher wages
   b. negotiate improved working conditions
   c. have occasionally been getting voting seats on boards of directors
   d. act as a social forum for their members
   e. all of the above

4. According to labour market studies, unionized workers in Canada are estimated to earn wages that are higher than comparable non-unionized workers by:
   a. 6 to 12%
   b. 10 to 30%
   c. 35 to 40%
   d. 55 to 73%
   e. less than 4%

5. The Rand formula:
   a. specifies that all workers must contribute to the union, whether or not they are union members
   b. specifies that a strike cannot be held unless there has been a vote by all employees
   c. specifies that illegal strikes during the time the agreement is in force will be penalized
   d. was originally contained in a 1945 court decision
   e. all of the above

6. Labour contracts in Canada specifying a closed shop:
   a. were prohibited by a federal law passed in 1967
   b. are illegal for workers belonging to industrial unions
   c. are generally legal in Canada
   d. are the only kinds of labour contracts that are legal in Canada
   e. are required under the Rand formula

7. Which of the following provides the greatest barrier to entry into a work force?
   a. an open shop
   b. a closed shop
   c. a union shop
   d. the Rand formula
   e. right-to-work legislation

8. In a union shop, a firm:
   a. can hire only workers who are already union members
   b. can hire only workers who have already worked in a union shop
   c. can hire only workers who have already worked in an open shop
   d. can hire non-union workers provided they join the union within a brief specified period
   e. can hire any workers, who then have the option of joining or not joining the union

9. Which of the following is the clearest example of featherbedding?
   a. seniority rules
   b. sexual harassment on the job
   c. firefighters employed on diesel trains
   d. shorter work weeks
   e. the firing of technologically displaced workers

10. As a fraction of the non-agricultural labour force, union membership in the second half of the 1980s was about:
    a. 1/3 in Canada and 1/5 in the United States
    b. 1/4 in both Canada and the United States
    c. 1/3 in Canada and less than 1/10 in the United States
    d. 1/2 in Canada and just over 1/3 in the United States
    e. about 40% in Canada and about 25% in the United States

11. If a union formed in a perfectly competitive labour market successfully raises wages, then:
    a. income is transferred from other factors of production to all workers
    b. income is transferred from other factors of production to workers who still have a job in this industry
    c. there is an efficiency gain from increased employment
    d. there is an efficiency loss from increased employment
    e. there is an efficiency gain from reduced employment

12. Unions improve efficiency by:
    a. raising wages above what they would be under perfect competition
    b. reducing labour turnover by giving workers the chance to present their grievances rather than quit or be fired
    c. increasing labour turnover by negotiating higher wages
    d. increasing employment above its perfectly competitive level
    e. b. and d.

13. If a firm can hire only workers who are already union members, it is described as a:
    a. constrained shop
    b. closed shop
    c. union shop
    d. open shop
    e. restricted shop

14. Which of the following is most likely to occur if a union is introduced into a previously competitive labour market with no externalities?
    a. Total income to labour will decrease
    b. The income of some individual workers will increase
    c. Employment in that market will increase
    d. Incomes of non-labour factors of production will increase
    e. An efficiency gain will result

15. The introduction of labour-saving machinery:
    a. may create temporary unemployment, and result in worse jobs for labour in the long run
    b. may create temporary unemployment, but results in higher wages for labour in the long run
    c. may temporarily raise employment, but results in worse jobs for labour in the long run
    d. may create temporary unemployment, and results in lower wages in the long run
    e. has no effect on employment in either the short or the long run

16. Unions may have beneficial effects on efficiency:
    a. by removing labour's collective voice and thus reducing distractions in the workplace
    b. by reducing communication between labour and management, and thus reducing distractions facing managers
    c. by increasing quit-rates
    d. by reducing quit-rates
    e. by increasing management's market power to raise wages

17. Employment will be increased in an otherwise perfectly competitive labour market by:
    a. the introduction of a union whose main effect is to raise wages
    b. collusion by employers to act together like a monopsonist
    c. an increase in the minimum wage
    d. the introduction of a closed shop
    e. none of the above

18. A union's negotiating power will be increased most by:
    a. a large union strike fund
    b. a small union strike fund
    c. a right-to-work law
    d. large inventory holdings by the employer
    e. reduced tariff protection on the employer's output

19. In a labour market with a strong union, the creation of a monopsony bargaining association by employers tends to:
    a. raise wages even further
    b. lower wages
    c. transfer income from other factors of production to labour
    d. a. and c.
    e. none of the above

20. Baseball salaries before and after the players' escape from the reserve clause illustrate:
    a. how much unions can raise salaries
    b. how much unions can lower salaries
    c. how much monopsonists can raise salaries
    d. how much monopsonists can lower salaries
    e. the countervailing power of a union

EXERCISES

1a. In Figure 36.1, MC_L is supply and MB_L is demand in a perfectly competitive labour market with no externalities. The equilibrium wage is _____ and the equilibrium quantity of employment is _____. In perfect competition the income of labour is area _____ and the income of other factors is area _____.

1b. Suppose now that a union is formed, which increases the wage to W_2. Then the quantity of employment will be _____, the income going to labour still in this industry will be _____, the income going to other factors will be _____, and the efficiency (gain, loss) will be _____.

1c. Now suppose that there is an external benefit from

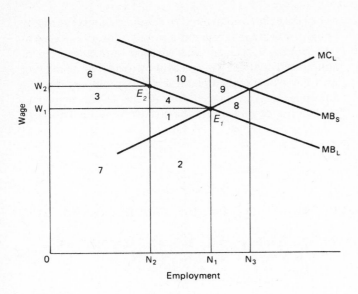

Figure 36.1

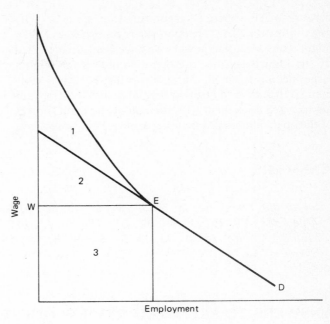

Figure 36.2

hiring labour in this activity. (To use the example cited in Chapter 35: Suppose the workers being hired are musicians. They provide not only a direct benefit to their employer—the symphony orchestra—whenever they play in a concert, but also an external benefit because of their other contributions to the cultural life of the community.) Because of this external benefit, the marginal social benefit of labour is MB_s rather than just the employers' benefit MB_L. Then the efficient quantity of employment will be _____. In perfect competition the wage will be _____, the quantity of employment will be _____, and the efficiency (gain, loss) will be _____.

1d. With this externality, if a union is formed to raise wages to W_2, then the quantity of employment will equal _____ and the efficiency (gain, loss) will equal _____.

2. In Figure 36.2, D represents the demand for labour while area 1 represents the external cost of a strike.

If a strike occurs, the cost to labour—in terms of lost wages—is area _____, while the loss of income by other factors in this industry is area _____. This means that the total internal cost to all factors in this industry is _____. In addition, there is an (external, internal) cost of area _____. Therefore, the total cost to society of a strike in this industry is _____. The problem with a strike is that the labour and management participants in the negotiation take into account only (external/internal) costs. No account may be taken of the additional cost to other groups shown as _____.

ESSAY QUESTIONS

1. Discuss several differences between American and Canadian labour laws that give the union movement a stronger legal position in Canada than in the United States.

2. Do you think that unions help or hinder the attempt to achieve (a) stable prices and (b) an equitable distribution of income?

3. If there is no union on one side of the market to raise wages, and no collusion or association by employers on the other side of the market to lower wages, compare the bargaining position of the individual worker and the individual employer.

4. Describe the conditions under which an increase in the minimum wage may increase the amount of employment.

5. Describe the spillovers if each of the following went on strike:
   a. Municipal garbage workers
   b. Air traffic controllers
   c. City police
   d. Steel workers

6. In the summer of 1980, the orchestra members of New York's Metropolitan Opera went on strike. Their union leaders thought they had a lot of bargaining power because of the opera's recent financial success. Why might this strengthen the union's bargaining power? Why might that bargaining power also have been strengthened by the knowledge that the opera would be receiving a large income from the nationally televised live performances that were to begin in the fall of 1980? After failing to reach agreement with the union, the management of the opera announced that the whole season would have to be cancelled, and offered to refund the tickets already bought. Eventually, one more round of negotiations was undertaken, agreement was reached, and management announced that the season could proceed after all, but with fewer operas than planned. Do you suppose that the announcement of cancellation of the season helped to speed up a resolution of the strike? Why or why not?

ANSWERS

Important Terms: 1e, 2f, 3b, 4l, 5k, 6r, 7a, 8n, 9i, 10t, 11h, 12s, 13q, 14g, 15p, 16o, 17m, 18c, 19u, 20j, 21d
True-False: 1T, 2F, 3F, 4F, 5T, 6T, 7T, 8F, 9F, 10T
Multiple Choice: 1d, 2e, 3e, 4b, 5e, 6c, 7b. 8d, 9c, 10a, 11b, 12b, 13b, 14b, 15b, 16d, 17e, 18a, 19b, 20d
Exercises: **1a.** W_1, N_1, 7 + 1 + 2, 6 + 3 + 4 **1b.** N_2, 3 + 7, 6, loss, 1 + 4 **1c.** N_3, W_1, N_1, loss, 9 **1d.** N_2, loss, 1 + 4 + 9 + 10 **2.** 3, 2, 2 + 3, external, 1, 1 + 2 + 3, internal, 1

ANSWERS TO SELECTED REVIEW QUESTIONS FROM THE TEXT

36-1. Yes, one would expect that deregulation would make them more competitive in setting their fares and in negotiating their wage and salary contracts. (Facing stiffer competition, the companies no longer had the previous high levels of profit to share with employees.) Wages did, in fact, rise more slowly, or not at all. In some cases, wages and salaries fell. In 1985, Canadian unions were strong opponents of deregulation.

36-3. The first condition. Employers do not hire labour until its marginal benefit (VMP) is equal to the wage rate. [They stop hiring at a point such as N_2 in Figure 36-3, where VMP is G, but the wage is only W_2.]

36-5. Increases. Workers with bulldozers. Another example: Airline pilots can effectively strike, because (like bulldozer operators) they operate expensive capital equipment. It is very costly to the airlines to leave this idle; thus the airlines are under great pressure to meet pilots' demands.

36-6. (a) The union of subway workers. If the subways are not running tomorrow morning, irate voters will be putting great pressure on municipal politicians to "do something" (i.e., resolve the strike). If there is a strike of the workers who manufacture trains, the delivery of the trains may be delayed—but the subways can still operate, using old equipment.

(b) The union of firefighters. If they strike, a city may burn down. If teachers strike, students' education is tem-porarily disrupted. But, to some degree, they can pick up missed material later.

(c) Probably the union of public school teachers. The public at large is often more concerned that all children get an elementary education than that a few get a higher education.

36-7. If both groups get the same percentage wage increase, then it is indeed true that any initial wage difference will persist. Since most people would trade some of their income for greater job security, equity suggests that, *ceteris paribus,* those who get more of one (security) should get less of the other (income).

36-9. (a) It may be a way of helping an unprofitable firm avoid bankruptcy (which would lead to a loss of jobs for all workers).

(b) Efficiency improves: With the marginal worker being paid the competitive wage, the firm will expand its hiring to the competitive, efficient level. (The return to other factors of production will be lower than in the competitive equilibrium, because of the higher wages paid to some workers.)

(c) In one way, it may improve job security: It may help the firm stay in business. In another way, however, job security may be reduced: It is now in the firm's interest to put pressure on the more highly paid workers to leave, since they can be replaced by new workers who are paid a lower wage.

Chapter 37

■ ■

Other Incomes

MAJOR PURPOSE

In the previous two chapters, we analysed labour income. The objective of this chapter is to analyse other forms of income—specifically, interest, profits, and rent. For example, in discussing interest rates, we see how they are determined by supply and demand in the market for loanable funds. This simple analysis is then extended to show the efficiency and equity effects when the government intervenes to impose a ceiling on interest rates.

Our initial emphasis in this chapter is on the income earned by physical capital, such as buildings and machinery. We analyse the role of the rate of interest in determining the amount and allocation of capital services in the economy, and how the presence of foreign capital affects the capital market and the return to capital in Canada. The focus later shifts to another important kind of capital—human capital in the form of education and training. One form of human capital is a university or college education, and returns to such investments are examined. Finally, this chapter analyses rent—the return to a factor of production above its opportunity cost (that is, above the income it could earn in an alternative activity). Rent is earned not only by land, but also by any other highly productive factor. Examples include the rent earned by highly skilled baseball players or business executives.

LEARNING OBJECTIVES

After you have studied this chapter in the textbook and the study guide, you should be able to
- Explain how the public receives an interest income for providing business with debt capital, and how the public receives a profit income for providing business with equity capital
- Explain how the demand for loanable funds is related to the marginal efficiency of investment schedule
- Show in a diagram how an interest rate ceiling imposed on a perfectly competitive market for loanable funds will affect efficiency and redistribute income
- Explain why it is a fallacy to suppose that interest rate ceilings necessarily help poor people
- State the basic reason that a substantial proportion of the capital used in Canada has been provided by foreign investors
- Describe the transfer effects that take place when foreign capital comes into Canada
- Explain why there is an efficiency gain when foreign investors are allowed to invest their funds in Canada
- Compare an investment in human capital and an investment in physical capital
- Describe the conditions under which investment in human capital could be less than the efficient amount, and the conditions under which it could be more than the efficient amount
- Explain why it is difficult to measure the rate of return on human capital

- Define rent and explain why it can be earned not only by land, but by any factor of production
- Give three examples of rent, in addition to rent on land
- Describe how rent is capitalized in the value of land

If you have studied the appendix to this chapter, you should be able to
- List several reasons that multinational corporations (MNCs) exist
- List several criticisms of the role of foreign capital in Canada

HIGHLIGHTS OF THE CHAPTER

About one-quarter of domestic factor income in Canada goes to factors of production other than labour. This chapter is about the income earned by other factors, that is, the income earned by capital and the income earned by land.

First, consider the income earned by physical capital such as plant and machinery. This income goes as:

a. interest to those who have made loans to business to buy plant and equipment—that is, to those who have provided debt capital to business;

b. profit to those who have provided funds to business to buy plant and equipment by buying shares (stock) in that business—that is, to those who have provided equity capital to business.

The Rate of Interest and Normal Profit

The interest rate may be viewed as a price—the price that equates the demand and supply of loanable funds. The demand for loanable funds reflects the *marginal efficiency of investment*—that is, the productivity of investment. Whenever you see a demand curve for loanable funds you should visualize it as enclosing the vertical bars in Figure 37-1 in the textbook, with each of these bars representing the marginal efficiency of investment.

The supply of loanable funds measures the willingness of savers to part with present income—that is, their willingness to defer present consumption until the future when the loan is repaid. The higher the rate of interest, the greater their reward and the more they are willing to save. Whenever you see a supply curve for loanable funds you should visualize it as enclosing a whole set of vertical bars (like the one shown in Figure 37-2). Each reflects the value of funds in their alternative use—present consumption.

In practice, there is not one rate of interest, but many, because of differences in risk. The greater the risk that a borrower will be unable to repay a loan, the higher the rate of interest that this particular borrower will have to pay. Interest rates are also influenced by a number of other factors, such as the expectation of inflation and the length of term of the loan. In addition, the expectation of a change in future interest rates will affect today's interest rates.

An important policy question studied in this section is: What happens if the government imposes an interest-rate ceiling? If the market for loanable funds is perfectly competitive, there are likely to be four main effects of such a policy: (1) The public saves less because the interest reward for savings has been reduced. Consequently, fewer loans are made and there is less investment. (2) Because investment is reduced, there is an efficiency loss, shown by the familiar triangle in Figure 37-3. (3) There is likely to be an additional efficiency loss, because investment funds must be rationed, and the borrowers who do succeed in acquiring the limited funds may not be those with the most profitable investment projects. (4) Income is transferred from lenders to those borrowers who are still able to acquire loans. (They now pay a lower interest rate.)

However, it is a fallacy to suppose that interest-rate ceilings necessarily help the poor. The people who benefit are the borrowers who get the limited funds at a bargain price. But these borrowers may be quite rich, while those who don't get funds may be poor.

Normal profits are earned by owners of equity capital. Normal profit is defined as the return that could be earned in an alternative investment—in this case, the interest the owner could have earned lending these funds out instead.

Foreign-owned Capital in Canada

A large amount of the capital being used in Canada has been provided by foreign savers (today mostly from the United States, but earlier from the United Kingdom). The main reason Canada relies on a large amount of foreign saving is *not* that Canadians are less willing to save than people in other countries; instead, it is because Canada has a very large number of profitable investment opportunities in resource-based industries (like the mining industry) and elsewhere. Foreign capital in Canada includes both equity capital (mostly as a result of foreign direct investment) and debt capital (resulting from portfolio investment).

The presence of foreign capital in Canada has led to a much lower return on capital than would prevail if there were no foreign capital here. As a result, *Canadian* savers earn a lower rate of return on their capital than they otherwise would (and supply less saving than they otherwise would). However, the additional capital provided by foreign savers raises the value of Canadian GDP and leads to higher incomes to other Canadian factors of production (primarily labour). As Figure 37-7 in the textbook shows, the gain to these other factors of production is larger than the loss to Canadian savers; hence, there is an efficiency gain (shown by areas 2 + 3 in the figure) from allowing foreign capital to come into Canada.

The efficiency gain shown in Figure 37-7 is computed on the assumption that the total return to foreign-owned capital (area 4 + 5 in the figure) is paid to the foreigners. In reality, however, part of the return represents a benefit to Canadians: that part which is paid to the government as taxes. (Foreign-owned firms pay corporate income tax at the same rate as Canadian-owned firms, and interest and dividends paid to foreigners are subject to Canadian "withholding tax.") Thus, the efficiency gain shown in Figure 37-7 may be an underestimate.

The possibility of efficiency gains provides an argument for letting foreign capital in with no restrictions. However, there are several arguments that can be used to justify *some* restrictions on the inflow of foreign capital. One argument noted in the text is that by limiting the amount of capital that we allow to come in, we may be able to attract it into Canada at a lower cost. (Other arguments against allowing unrestricted foreign investment in Canada—such as the possible erosion of Canada's political sovereignty or cultural identity if we get too much of it—are discussed in the appendix to Chapter 37.)

Factor Prices and the Allocation of Scarce Resources

In a free market, the wage rate screens labour into its most productive use. (Employers with less productive jobs don't hire labour because they can't afford to pay the market wage.) Similarly, a free market screens investment funds provided by savers into the most productive investments, i.e., those with the highest MEI. (Businesses that want to invest in less productive projects can't do so, because they can't afford to pay the market interest rate.) In either case, the market price is a rationing device which ensures that the most productive activities will be undertaken.

Human Capital

There are two main forms of investment in human capital: (1) formal education and (2) apprenticeship, or on-the-job training.

There are two reasons investment in human capital may be less than the efficient amount:

1. Employers are sometimes reluctant to provide on-the-job training because trainees may quit and take their skills elsewhere.

2. There are often external benefits from education. For example, when a highly educated scientist discovers a cure for a disease, it benefits the entire population. Because such external benefits are not taken into account by those making the decision to invest in education, investment in human capital may fall short of the efficient level. This underinvestment in human capital provides a justification for government subsidies to education.

In practice, estimating the returns to a university education is very difficult for a number of reasons. For example, people with high incomes tend to have a lot of both education and talent. It's hard to sort out how much of their higher income is due to each.

Further complications arise if we wish to calculate the social return to education. For example, it is difficult to measure the external benefits of education. (How do you measure the benefits to society when a highly educated scientist discovers a new strain of wheat?)

Rent

Perhaps the most important thing to understand about rent is that it can be earned not only by land, but also by other factors of production. It is defined as the earnings of any factor above its opportunity cost. The textbook gives five examples of economic rent:

a. The return to agricultural land because of differences in quality.

b. The return to urban land because of differences in location.

c. The return to mineral deposits because of differences in quality.

d. Above-normal profits earned in an industry with barriers to entry.

e. The income (above opportunity cost) of an individual with a valuable talent or skill. (See Figures 37-9 and 37-11.)

It is important to understand how rents are capitalized in the value of land. Suppose you own two plots of farmland, and one (A) earns more income—and therefore more rent—than the other (B). A will clearly be worth more; you can sell it for a higher price. But how high will its price go? The answer: it will rise until the rent it earns is about the same percentage return that you can earn elsewhere. For example, if you can rent it out for $200 a hectare and the interest rate you can earn by lending out your money instead is 10%, then you will be willing to sell it (and someone else will be willing to buy it) if its price rises to $2,000. Thus, rents on land (or on other things such as the right to produce agricultural commodities whose prices are regulated by marketing boards) determine the values of land, production quotas, and so on.

IMPORTANT TERMS: MATCH THE COLUMNS

Match each term in the first column with its corresponding explanation in the second column.

_____ 1. Debt capital
_____ 2. Equity capital
_____ 3. Human capital
_____ 4. Physical capital
_____ 5. Marginal efficiency of investment
_____ 6. Time preference
_____ 7. Roundabout production
_____ 8. Foreign direct investment
_____ 9. Foreign portfolio investment
_____ 10. Withholding tax
_____ 11. Economic rent
_____ 12. Monopoly rent

a. Includes foreign purchases of Canadian bonds
b. The process of deferring the production of consumer goods, in favour of producing capital goods that can be used in the future to produce even more consumer goods
c. The above-normal profits accruing to any individual or business because of the possession of monopoly power
d. Funds that are lent to businesses
e. The schedule that ranks investments in terms of their percentage return
f. Funds that go into acquiring a share in the ownership of a business
g. A desire to consume now rather than in the future. This determines the supply curve for loanable funds
h. The return to any factor of production in excess of its opportunity cost
i. The plant, machinery, and other forms of equipment that can be used for producing goods and services
j. Affects dividends and interest paid to foreign residents
k. Results in more capital in foreign-controlled firms in Canada
l. Skills, training, and education of individuals that can be used for producing goods and services

TRUE-FALSE

T F 1. Interest income is earned by those who provide equity capital.
T F 2. The return to capital (foreign-owned and Canadian-owned) is a larger share of Canadian domestic income than the income of all Canadian workers.
T F 3. An interest rate ceiling benefits all those who wish to borrow.
T F 4. A substantial increase in the price of a factor of production will typically induce a firm to change the combination of factors it is using.
T F 5. If a ceiling is imposed on the price of any good or service, then any necessary rationing of this good or service is likely to lead to an efficiency loss.
T F 6. Factor prices act as a screening device to help allocate factors of production.
T F 7. Human capital is like physical capital in so far as it represents an expenditure today that is expected to pay off in the future.
T F 8. The costs of a university education include more than living, tuition, and book costs.

T F   9. The private rate of return to a university education is not necessarily the same as the social rate of return.

T F   10. Very little of the income of hockey star Mario Lemieux is rent.

T F   11. An inflow of foreign capital into Canada is likely to harm both Canadian labour and Canadian capital owners.

MULTIPLE CHOICE

1. What is the annual rate of return on a machine that costs $10,000 and generates enough sales over its 1-year lifetime to cover labour, materials, and other costs, plus $12,000?
   a. 120%
   b. 20%
   c. 12%
   d. 10%
   e. 2%

2. The demand curve for loans reflects
   a. the marginal revenue product of labour
   b. the marginal efficiency of investment
   c. either **a.** or **b.** depending on whether the good being produced is labour or capital intensive
   d. the time preference of savers
   e. none of the above

3. Savers in our society receive an interest return because of their decision to
   a. buy domestic rather than imported goods
   b. speed up import purchases
   c. delay consumption
   d. speed up consumption
   e. deposit money in a bank savings account rather than to buy government bonds

4. An interest rate ceiling helps all
   a. the rich who want to lend
   b. the poor who want to lend
   c. the poor who want to borrow
   d. borrowers
   e. those borrowers who can still obtain funds

5. Which of the following is the most likely result of an interest rate ceiling in a perfectly competitive market for loanable funds?
   a. a transfer of income from poor borrowers to some lenders
   b. a transfer of income from all borrowers to some lenders
   c. a transfer of income from rich to poor
   d. a transfer of income from lenders to some borrowers
   e. a reduction in the amount of credit rationing

6. An interest rate ceiling
   a. redistributes income, but has no effect on efficiency
   b. leads to an efficiency gain that is likely to be underestimated by the usual triangular measurement
   c. leads to an efficiency gain that is likely to be overestimated by the usual triangular measurement
   d. leads to an efficiency loss that is likely to be overestimated by the usual triangular measurement
   e. leads to an efficiency loss that is likely to be underestimated by the usual triangular measurement

7. A company in a shaky financial position pays
   a. a higher interest rate on its borrowing than it would if it were financially sound
   b. a lower interest rate on its borrowing than it would if it were financially sound
   c. the same interest rate on its borrowing as it would if it were financially sound
   d. a higher or lower rate, depending upon the rate of inflation
   e. a lower rate because of the expectation of inflation

8. Since the interest rate is greater than zero, we know that
   a. present goods are worth more than future goods. The reason is that a given amount of present goods can be transformed into more future goods.
   b. present goods are worth less than future goods. The reason is that a given amount of present goods can be transformed into more future goods.
   c. present goods and future goods have an equal value if interest rates are rising
   d. present goods and future goods always have an equal value
   e. nothing can be said about the relative value of present and future goods

9. A rightward shift in the marginal efficiency of investment is likely to
   a. decrease the rate of interest and decrease the amount of funds loaned
   b. decrease the rate of interest and increase the amount of funds loaned
   c. increase the rate of interest and increase the amount of funds loaned

    d. increase the rate of interest and decrease the amount of funds loaned

    e. increase the rate of interest and leave unchanged the amount of funds loaned

10. An increase by the public in its valuation of current (compared to future) consumption will

    a. decrease the rate of interest and decrease the amount of funds loaned

    b. decrease the rate of interest and increase the amount of funds loaned

    c. increase the rate of interest and increase the amount of funds loaned

    d. increase the rate of interest and decrease the amount of funds loaned

    e. increase the rate of interest and leave unchanged the amount of funds loaned

11. An increase in wages will induce a firm to

    a. hire more labour

    b. lower its prices

    c. use more labour-saving techniques

    d. use fewer labour-saving techniques

    e. produce more output

12. Minimum wage laws

    a. discourage on-the-job training of apprentices

    b. encourage on-the-job training of apprentices

    c. increase allocative efficiency

    d. transfer income from workers who still have jobs to other factors of production

    e. transfer income from workers who lose their jobs to other factors of production

13. If during the last 50 years the Canadian government had been following a policy of not allowing any foreign capital into Canada, then

    a. Canadian wage rates would most likely have been higher than they currently are

    b. Canadian GDP would most likely be higher than it currently is

    c. the rate of return to capital in Canada would most likely have been higher than it currently is

    d. the amount of Canadian-owned capital used in Canada would most likely have been lower than it currently is

    e. none of the above

14. The amount of net direct foreign investment (that is, direct foreign investment in Canada less direct Canadian investment in foreign countries)

    a. was lower (as a proportion of GDP) in 1950 than during subsequent decades

    b. was negative during much of the 1970s and 1980s

    c. increases when a foreigner purchases bonds issued by Quebec Hydro

    d. has been larger than foreign portfolio investment since 1970

    e. increases whenever a foreigner buys shares in any Canadian corporation

15. A high-school education can be viewed as

    a. a bad investment, because it yields a lower return than a university education

    b. a bad investment, even though it yields a higher return than a university education

    c. a bad investment, because it yields a lower return than physical capital

    d. a good investment, even though it yields the same return as a university education

    e. a good investment, because it yields a higher return than physical capital

16. To estimate the social return to investment in higher education, the private rate of return should be

    a. adjusted downward to take account of government subsidies to higher education

    b. adjusted upward to take account of government subsidies to higher education

    c. adjusted downward to take account of the external benefits of education

    d. **a.** and **c.**

    e. left unadjusted in any of these ways

17. In explaining why the private and social returns to a post-secondary education differ, we must take into account

    a. the external benefits of a post-secondary education, but not its subsidization by the government

    b. its subsidization, but not its external benefits

    c. both its subsidization and its external benefits

    d. both, but only if they are roughly equal

    e. neither

18. Land may earn rent because it is

    a. productive in growing crops

    b. attractively located for business development

    c. the site of mineral resources

    d. the site of oil deposits

    e. any of the above

19. If the quantity of wheat that can be produced on a hectare of land doubles, while the quantity and cost of inputs remain constant, then the rent per hectare

    a. increases by 50%

    b. almost doubles

    c. doubles

    d. more than doubles

    e. none of the above

20. The income of the typical physician includes

    a. rent on innate talents

    b. a return to human capital accumulated in medical school

    c. a return to human capital accumulated as an intern

    d. none of the above

    e. all of the above, except **d.**

EXERCISES

1a. Figure 37.1 shows a perfectly competitive market for loanable funds. The equilibrium rate of interest in this market is _____ and the equilibrium quantity of loans is _____. In a competitive equilibrium the interest income received by lenders would equal _____.

1b. If the government imposes an interest rate ceiling at M, then the quantity of loans will be _____, the MEI will be _____, the excess demand for loans will be _____, the interest income received by lenders will be _____, and the size of the efficiency loss will probably be (more, less) than the area _____.

1c. If the interest ceiling is set at *J*, then the size of the efficiency loss will be _____.

2a. Figure 37.2 shows a perfectly competitive market for a factor of production, where D is the demand curve and S_1 is the supply curve. In a competitive equilibrium, the factor price would be _____ and the quantity of employment of the factor would be _____. The income received by the owners of this factor would equal _____ and the income received by the owners of all other factors would equal _____.

2b. Now suppose that a tax is imposed on the owners of this factor, equal in amount to *LE* per unit of the factor that they are supplying. This would shift the supply curve up vertically by the amount *LE*, so that the after-tax supply curve is the one labelled S'_1. With the tax, the after-tax equilibrium price paid by firms for the factor will equal _____, the equilibrium price received by the owners of the factor will equal _____, the after-tax income accruing to owners of the factor will be _____, the amount of the tax collected will be _____, the income received by other factors will be _____, and the size of the efficiency loss will be _____.

2c. Now suppose that there is no tax; instead, suppose that supply shifts from S_1 to S_2. S_2 is (more, less) elastic than S_1. With supply curve S_2 the equilibrium factor price will be (no different, more, less) than with S_1, and the equilibrium quantity of employment of the factor will be (no different, more, less) than with S_1.

2d. With S_2 the same tax *LE* will shift the supply curve up to S'_2. With the tax, the equilibrium price paid by the firms for the factor will be _____, the after-tax equilibrium price received by owners of the factor will equal _____, the quantity of employment of the factor will equal _____, the after-tax income accruing to owners of the factor will equal _____, the amount of the tax collected will equal _____, the income received by other factors will equal _____, and the size of the efficiency loss will equal _____.

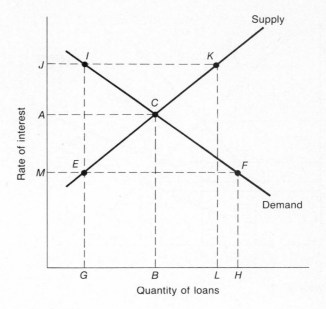

Figure 37.1

2e. To sum up: If we consider the effects of a tax in the face of these two pre-tax supply curves S_1 and S_2, the one generating the greater tax revenue is (S_1, S_2); the one that produces the smaller efficiency loss from the tax is (S_1, S_2); the one generating the smaller reduction in employment is (S_1, S_2); the one generating the least reduction in the factor's after-tax income is (S_1, S_2), and the one reducing other incomes the least is (S_1, S_2).

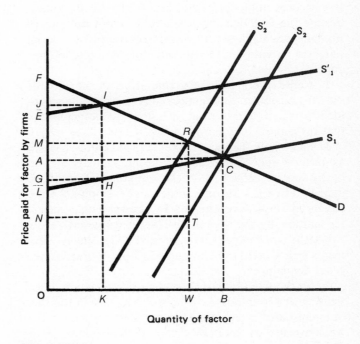

Figure 37.2

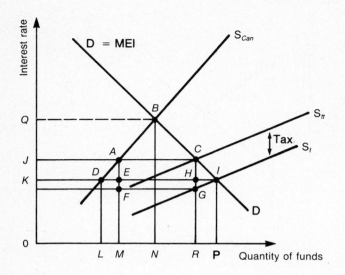

Figure 37.3

3a. In Figure 37.3, the curve D = MEI represents the demand for capital funds in Canada, S_{Can} is the supply of funds from Canadian savers, and S_t is the total supply curve of funds, including foreign funds. The curve S_{tt} is the total supply curve of funds if a tax, given by the vertical distance T = (CG) = (AF) is imposed on the earnings of foreign capital.

If no foreign capital is allowed into Canada, the amount of funds used in the economy will be _____ and the return to capital will be _____.

3b. If foreign capital *is* allowed to come in and there is no tax, the total amount of funds used in the Canadian economy will be _____, of which _____ will be supplied by foreign savers. The total return on the foreign capital will be equal to the rectangle _____, and the efficiency gain will be the triangle _____.

3c. If a tax T is imposed on the earnings of foreign capital, the total supply curve shifts up to S_{tt}. The amount of foreign capital used in Canada will shrink to _____. The total return going to foreign capital owners (after payment of the tax) will be the rectangle _____. Canadian taxpayers will benefit by the tax paid by the foreign capital owners; the revenue from this tax is the rectangle _____. This tax revenue, plus the triangle *ABC*, is now the total net benefit to Canadians of having this amount of foreign capital invested in Canada.

(The imposition of the tax will increase the gain to Canada from having foreign capital here if the tax paid by the foreigners is greater than the reduction in the net gain to Canadian factors of production as the tax is imposed; that is, if the tax revenue rectangle is greater than the area *DICA*.)

ESSAY QUESTIONS

1. The discoverers of insulin, Banting and Best, did not become millionaires as a result of their discovery, despite the fact that it has probably saved millions of human lives. Explain what this means if we wish to compare the private and social rates of return to human capital.

2. Name several influences that affect the position of the MEI schedule, explaining in each case how the schedule is affected, and in what direction, by an increase in that influence.

3. Show how the income of a surgeon can be viewed as partly a wage, partly a return to human capital, and partly a rent. Which of these components would be increased by the surgeon's success in developing a more advanced surgical technique? By the surgeon's special recognition by the Royal College of Surgeons? How would the rent component be affected if licensing requirements were relaxed to permit more people to practise surgery? Explain.

4. As the interest rate rises, the price of bonds falls. Bearing this in mind, show how an increase in the rate of interest affects potential lenders differently from those who have already lent money by purchasing bonds. Show also how it affects potential borrowers differently from

those who have already borrowed money by selling bonds.

5. Suppose that a factor had a totally inelastic supply. What would its opportunity cost be to society? Would it be accurate to classify all its income as rent?

6. Why is it difficult to measure the social rate of return on investment in human capital?

7. Suppose Canada imposes a high tariff on the imports of a good such as washing machines. Thus, whenever a washing machine is imported, Canadian taxpayers benefit from the tariff collected by the government.

Suppose now that a foreign firm comes into Canada and establishes facilities to produce a large number of washing machines in Canada; as a result, there is a sharp reduction in the number of washing machines imported into Canada, and the government loses the tariff revenue that would have been collected on the imported machines.

If we want to measure the net benefit to Canada of this foreign investment, how should we treat the loss of tariff revenue? Is it generally in Canada's interest to have foreign firms invest in production facilities in Canadian industries that are protected by tariffs? Is the possibility of foreign investment relevant when we try to measure the efficiency loss from imposing a tariff?

ANSWERS

Important Terms: 1d, 2f, 3l, 4i, 5e, 6g, 7b, 8k, 9a, 10j, 11h, 12c
True-False: 1F, 2F, 3F, 4T, 5T, 6T, 7T, 8T, 9T, 10F, 11F
Multiple Choice: 1b, 2b, 3c, 4e, 5d, 6e, 7a, 8a, 9c, 10d, 11c, 12a, 13c, 14b, 15e, 16a, 17c, 18e, 19d, 20e
Exercises: **1a.** *A, B, 0ACB* **1b.** *G, J* (or *GI*), *EF* (or *GH*), *0MEG*, more, *ICE* **1c.** zero because the ceiling is ineffective **2a.** *A, B, 0ACB, AFC* **2b.** *J, G, 0GHK, JIHG, FIJ, ICH* **2c.** less, no different, no different **2d.** *M, N, W, 0NTW, NMRT, MFR, RCT* **2e.** S_2, S_2, S_2, S_2, S_2 **3a.** *0N, 0Q* **3b.** *0P, LP, LDIP, DBI* **3c.** *MR, MFGR, FACG*

ANSWERS TO SELECTED REVIEW QUESTIONS FROM THE TEXT

37-1. Our wages and salaries are high because our labour, with its large content of human capital (education, training, etc.) is highly productive. Its productivity is increased even further because of the large quantities of physical capital with which it is combined, and the advanced state of technology in our nations.

We also earn a large amount of income on capital, because of our large capital stock. Rents on land and natural resources are high because of the high quality of land and resources available here though not as high as in the Persian Gulf countries where rents on oil deposits are very large.

37-4. Suppose interest rates are expected to fall next year because of a decrease in the demand for loans by business. In this case, lenders will increase their purchases of long-term bonds, to lock in the interest rate before it falls. Thus, the price of long-term bonds rises, that is, the interest rate today on long-term bonds falls.

37-5. Examples of adjustments that took place in response to higher prices of oil (and energy in general) include building more energy-efficient (but more expensive) houses—that is, a substitution of capital for energy in the production of housing services—and substitution of capital and labour for energy as airlines flew their planes at slower speeds to save fuel (at lower speeds, each plane and crew will produce fewer passenger miles; thus, reducing speed means an increase in the inputs of labour and capital in the production of air travel).

Products which required high energy inputs, such as plastics and fertilizer, became more expensive. In response, buyers tried to substitute other materials for plastics, and farmers reduced their inputs of fertilizer per acre (that is, substituted land for fertilizer in the production of food).

37-7. A firm may pay high salaries to such individuals in order to acquire their human capital (experience in marketing, management, design, etc.). It may also wish to acquire their knowledge of the products and processes the competing firm is now using and developing, and of what that firm plans for the future.

37-9. To an economist, rent is the return of a factor of production in excess of its opportunity cost. In ordinary language, rent is periodic payments for the temporary use of various assets (such as apartments, rental cars, or farmland) owned by someone other than the user.

To an economist, the earnings of individuals such as professional athletes or movie and TV actors have a large rent component, but the public does not generally consider those earnings as rent. Payment for the use of an apartment is considered by the public as being rent, though to an economist it mostly reflects the opportunity cost of the capital invested in apartment buildings. Payment for the use of farmland would be considered rent by both economists and the general public.

37-10. For Gordon Lightfoot, it is likely that rent is very significant, with his income in music now far exceeding the amount he could earn in an alternative occupation. In cases (b) and (c), rent is not significant. These people could earn roughly their present wage in some alternative endeavour.

37-11. Correct, except for the last sentence. An increase in the price of oil does increase rent on existing oil fields.

37-12. Define the productivity of land as the value of the corn it can produce, minus the cost of shipping it to market. Then, the ring of farms surrounding Toronto has higher productivity (just like the higher productivity of land A in Figure 37-14). The ring of farms beyond the innermost ring has lower productivity, because of the greater transport cost involved in shipping corn to market. And so on.

37-15. According to these figures, his opportunity cost is $500,000—his expected income in basketball, his best alternative occupation. Of his $2 million total income, this leaves a balance of $1,500,000, which is the rent he earns in baseball.

Chapter 38

■ ■

Income Inequality

MAJOR PURPOSE

In the three preceding chapters, we have described how incomes are determined in our society. For example, some people have a higher income because of some innate talent or a large investment in human capital. Others may earn rent from land they own. Our first objective in this chapter is to summarize these economic reasons for differences in incomes, and complete that list with the additional reasons—such as just plain luck—that have not been dealt with in earlier chapters because they don't yield to economic analysis.

Our second objective is to examine the Canadian income distribution that results from all these influences. How much income inequality is there? This question is answered with a *Lorenz curve* which gives an immediate picture of how much of the nation's income is earned by low-income Canadians, and how much by high-income Canadians. The conclusion is that a great deal of inequality exists.

The third broad question we then address is: How effective are the government's programs of taxation and expenditure that have been designed, at least in part, to reduce inequality? The answer is that government expenditures, especially transfer payments, have had considerable effect, but taxes have had surprisingly little effect in equalizing incomes.

This then provides the background for tackling one of the most difficult issues in economics—the normative question: "How unequal should incomes be?" While economists cannot answer that question in a definitive way, they can throw a great deal of light on this issue. Specifically, we show that it is difficult to argue that either (a) income equality or (b) the free-market distribution of income is fair.

LEARNING OBJECTIVES

After you have studied this chapter in the textbook and the study guide, you should be able to
- Explain the reasons some people have more income than others
- Explain how the Lorenz curve is constructed and why it provides a good picture of the nation's income distribution
- Explain why the Lorenz curve may exaggerate the degree of inequality
- Identify the government policies that have been designed, at least in part, to make incomes more equal, and specify which of these has been most successful in achieving this objective
- Explain why the direct effects of policies designed to increase equality are at least partially offset by their negative indirect effects on incentives
- Demonstrate why it cannot be claimed that a free market leads to a fair distribution of income
- Demonstrate why complete equality of income is not necessarily fair; that is, show why equality is not the same as equity (fairness)
- Explain why it is reasonable to aim for some compromise between the extremes of a free market and complete equality
- Show why a conflict often exists between equity and efficiency
- Specify at least one policy where these two are not in conflict

HIGHLIGHTS OF THE CHAPTER

Four broad questions are addressed in this chapter: (1) Why is there income inequality? (2) How much income inequality exists in Canada? (3) How much of this inequality has been eliminated by government expenditures and taxes? (4) How much inequality should there be? That is, what is an equitable distribution of income?

Why Is There Inequality?

There are at least eight reasons some people may have more income than others: (1) their greater investment in human capital, (2) some innate ability on which they earn rent, (3) greater financial wealth, either because they have inherited it or saved it, (4) greater market power due to membership in a union or possession of some other form of monopoly power, (5) a willingness to work harder or longer hours, (6) discrimination in their favour in the labour market, (7) good connections and other benefits of family background, and (8) just plain luck—being at the right place at the right time. To illustrate how costly it can be if you are in the right place at the wrong time, consider the classic complaint of the failing stock-market speculator: "I got all the decisions exactly right; it was just the timing I got wrong."

While we don't have enough information to state precisely how much income inequality is due to each of these factors, there is some evidence that human capital may be the most important: In an early U.S. study it was found that as much as 60% of income differences were due to differences in human capital.

How Much Inequality Is There in Canada?

This question is answered by the Lorenz curve shown in Figure 38-1 of the text. This curve shows the percentage of the nation's income received by the poorest 20% of the population; by the poorest 40%; and so on. If everyone had exactly the same income each year, then the Lorenz curve would be the 45° "complete-equality" line shown in that diagram. In this case, the poorest 20% would get 20% of the nation's income; the poorest 40% would get 40% of the nation's income; and so on. This is not true for the Canadian Lorenz curve shown in this diagram. Its large bow indicates a substantial degree of inequality.

Actually, this overstates the case. Even if there were perfect equality, with all families receiving exactly the same *lifetime* pattern of income, there would still be some bow in the Lorenz curve, since it measures income *in a single year*. The reason is that some families would be at the height of their earning power. They would be observed with far more income in that year than younger families who would be just beginning their careers at a low income.

How Much Do Government Expenditures and Taxes Reduce Inequality?

The Lorenz curve in Figure 38-2 in the text shows that government taxes and transfers reduce inequality by some 20 to 25%. That is, the area between the complete equality line and the Lorenz curve is reduced by between one-fifth and one-quarter. This reduction has been accomplished by three broad government programs:

1. *Taxation.* Taxes generally reduce inequality, because most taxes fall more heavily on the rich than on the poor.

2. *Cash transfer programs*, which include not only programs such as social assistance to needy families, but also Unemployment Insurance, Old Age Security, and family allowances.

3. *Transfers in kind*, such as education, housing, and health care services that are provided by the government.

Taken together, government transfers in cash and in kind are considerably more important than taxation in reducing inequality.

While these programs have the *direct* effect of reducing inequality, they also have an offsetting *indirect* effect. They *increase* inequality because they reduce the incentive for the poor to find and hold jobs. Furthermore, they reduce the incentive for families at all income levels to stay married. (When a family breaks up, its income is split between two smaller families, lowering the income per family. In particular, a break-up is very likely to create a single-parent family—usually headed by a woman—with low income. Government support to one-parent families obviously helps them—but it also reduces the financial incentive to stay together.)

What is a "Fair" or "Equitable" Distribution of Income?

This question cannot be answered with complete certainty, because it is a normative question of "what ought to be," rather than a positive question of "what is." Nevertheless, most people would agree on two points:

1. The outcome of the free market has no special claim to being fair. One reason is that there is no way of justifying huge profits to those who can exercise market power and raise price because they operate in markets that are not perfectly competitive. But there are problems that go deeper than this. Even if markets were perfectly competitive, it would be difficult to argue that their outcome would necessarily be fair. The example in the text is of the individual who makes no effort or contribution to the nation's output, yet who receives a very high income because he owns inherited agricultural land. The only claim for perfect competition—and it's an important one—is that, in the absence of externalities, it provides an outcome that is efficient. But no claim can be made that this outcome is necessarily fair.

2. At the other extreme, complete equality of income would not be fair either, because some people work harder and longer than others, and some people have more dangerous jobs than others. Most would agree that it is fair for such people to have a higher income. After reading this section, it is essential that you be able to explain why equality and equity are not the same. Equality means "being equal" while equity means "being fair."

With these two extremes—the free market's distribution of income and a completely equal distribution of income—being judged unacceptable, what is a reasonable compromise? Here are two of the guidelines suggested in the text:

1. Set *equality of opportunity* as our objective rather than equality of reward. View life as a race that should be fair, with all participants starting out together although, of course, not finishing that way. No cheating should be allowed: High incomes acquired by dishonest means should not be tolerated. There should be no handicaps; for example, no one should be denied the opportunity of an education because of discrimination. But this doesn't mean that everyone should be awarded a university degree—that should depend on what people are willing and able to do with their equal opportunity.

2. We should modify the rewards of the race. Some must finish last, but they should not be left in an impoverished state.

The Conflict Between Equity and Efficiency

Perhaps the most important concept in this chapter is this: In striving for equity, it must never be forgotten that there is typically (though not always) a conflict between equity and efficiency. To take the extreme case: If everyone were guaranteed an equal income, who would want to fight fires or work the long hours of the computer engineer? Equalizing the nation's income pie would reduce the size of that pie.

The Rawlsian Solution

The ideas of Professor John Rawls discussed in Box 38-1 of the text are of considerable interest because for some time many people thought he had the solution to the problem of what the nation's income distribution should be. Rawls suggests that we imagine everyone to be in an "original position," in which no one knows what his or her particular income will be. Then ask what kind of income distribution reasonable people would choose from behind this "veil of ignorance." They would be choosing a distribution of income—that is, an "income ladder"—without knowing on which of the rungs they themselves would be located.

Rawls argues that in these circumstances, everyone would agree to his "difference principle": There should be complete equality in the distribution of income, unless there is an unequal distribution that leaves everyone better off. But he arrives at this conclusion by supposing that all the people who make this decision would figure that with their luck, no matter what "income ladder" they may choose, they would end up on the lowest rung; so, they would choose an income distribution in which the lowest rung is as high as possible. In other words, they would chose the income distribution with the largest minimum income. This is the *maximin* criterion.

In this box, we give examples to show that Rawls' theory only applies to people who won't take a risk under any circumstances. Therefore, it just doesn't apply to average Canadians—let alone those who visit Las Vegas in search of risk. Thus, Rawls did not answer the question of what our income distribution should be. To this question, there may never be a clear answer.

IMPORTANT TERMS: MATCH THE COLUMNS

Match the term in the first column with its corresponding explanation in the second column.

_____   **1.** Lorenz curve
_____   **2.** Complete equality line
_____   **3.** Transfers in kind
_____   **4.** Original position
_____   **5.** Difference principle
_____   **6.** Maximin criterion
_____   **7.** Cash transfers

a. This appears in the Lorenz curve diagram with a 45° slope. The Lorenz curve would coincide with this only if all families received exactly the same income in the year of observation.

b. The theory that income should be equally distributed unless there is some other distribution that makes everyone better off

c. Government payments to individuals and families, such as Unemployment Insurance or social assistance benefits and family allowance cheques

d. This shows the percentage of national income that is received by the lowest-income 20% of families, by the lowest-income 40% of families, and so on

e. It is in this location that Rawls would ask everyone to choose the best income distribution, without knowing what his or her position on that income scale will be

f. Goods or services such as education or medical care provided by the government at no direct charge to the recipient

g. Making the choice that maximizes the minimum value

TRUE-FALSE

T   F   **1.** Transfers-in-kind are those transfers that do not affect the distribution of real income.

T   F   **2.** Government expenditures are more effective than taxes in reducing inequality.

T   F   **3.** If government tax and transfer programs were to redistribute a large amount of a nation's income, part of a country's Lorenz curve might end up above the 45° line.

T   F   **4.** Between 1951 and 1981, the income after taxes and transfers of the poorest 20% of Canada's population grew at least as fast as that of the rest of the population.

T   F   **5.** If income is defined broadly to include both money and leisure, then fairness requires that those who take a lot of their income in one form (leisure) should get less in the other form (money).

T   F   **6.** The only reason that complete equality is rejected as a target is that this division of the nation's income pie would shrink its overall size.

T   F   **7.** Equity is a normative, rather than a positive issue.

T   F   **8.** Scientific evidence indicates that complete equality is the only fair way of distributing the nation's income.

T   F   **9.** The provable virtues of a free, perfectly competitive market have to do with its equity—not its efficiency.

T   F   **10.** Equity requires that everyone be paid the same income.

T   F   **11.** It is possible to have an absolutely fair competition, but a bad system of rewards.

MULTIPLE CHOICE

1. In the mid-1980s, what proportion of the nation's net wealth (that is, taking into account a family's debts as well as its assets) was held by the least wealthy 25% of the population?
   a. 15%
   b. 12%
   c. 5%
   d. 3%
   e. essentially none at all; their average net wealth was about zero

2. In the mid-1980s, how much of the nation's wealth was held by the richest 5% of the population?
   a. 8%
   b. 18%
   c. 28%
   d. 38%
   e. 58%

3. Early research on inequality in the United States tended to indicate that, in determining differences in income
   a. the least important influence is wealth
   b. the least important influence is family background
   c. the most important influence is human capital
   d. the least important influence is luck
   e. the least important influence is human capital

4. The Lorenz curve measures how close the nation's actual income distribution is to
   a. a fair distribution
   b. an equal distribution
   c. the distribution in the previous year
   d. the distribution that would exist if all markets were perfectly competitive
   e. the distribution that would exist if no markets were perfectly competitive

5. The greater the degree of income inequality
   a. the smaller the bow in the Lorenz curve (i.e., the closer the Lorenz curve is to the 45° line)
   b. the larger the bow in the Lorenz curve
   c. the steeper the initial slope of the Lorenz curve
   d. the higher the point the Lorenz curve eventually reaches
   e. none of the above

6. In the late 1980s, what percentage of the total Canadian income (before taxes and transfers) was earned by the lowest-income 40% of Canadian families?
   a. less than 2%
   b. about 4%
   c. about 8%

   d. about 14%
   e. about 31%

7. Because all government taxes taken together are
   a. highly progressive, they are more effective than government expenditures in making incomes more equal
   b. highly progressive, they are less effective than government expenditures in making incomes more equal
   c. not highly progressive, they are less effective than government expenditures in making incomes more equal
   d. not highly progressive, they are more effective than government expenditures in making incomes more equal
   e. regressive, they are more effective than government expenditures in making incomes more equal

8. Putting an end to racial discrimination is likely to
   a. increase the bow in the Lorenz curve
   b. decrease the bow in the Lorenz curve
   c. change the Lorenz curve so that its bow is above rather than below the 45° line
   d. make the Lorenz curve start from a different initial point
   e. make the Lorenz curve end at a different point

9. If some individuals acquire more and more human capital, while others do not, then this is likely to
   a. increase the bow in the Lorenz curve
   b. decrease the bow in the Lorenz curve
   c. change the Lorenz curve so that its bow is above, rather than below, the 45° line
   d. make the Lorenz curve start from a different initial point
   e. make the Lorenz curve end at a different point

10. If we were to pursue only the goal of equity, we would find that our policies would
   a. always reduce efficiency
   b. often reduce efficiency
   c. always increase efficiency
   d. expand the size of the total income pie
   e. leave the size of the total income pie unchanged

11. It is difficult to argue that the free market would do a completely equitable job of distributing income because
   a. the free market is often not perfectly competitive; some people raise their income through the exercise of market power

b. even if the free market were perfectly competitive, it would still often provide luxuries for the wealthy, without providing adequate necessities for the poor
c. the free market is efficient
d. **a.** and **b.**
e. none of the above

12. The most difficult concept for economists to pin down is
a. efficiency gain
b. efficiency loss
c. equity
d. equality
e. inequality

13. A policy of trying to equalize incomes completely has been criticized because it would
a. be inefficient
b. be unfair, because it would give people who work hard the same reward as those who do not
c. require a change in our present system of inheritance
d. shrink the total income pie
e. all of the above

14. The major virtue of a perfectly competitive free market is its
a. efficiency when there are no externalities
b. efficiency when externalities do exist
c. equity
d. tendency to ensure equality of income
e. tendency to ensure equality of wealth

15. A criticism of Rawls' theory is that it:
a. is based on an unrealistic assumption about how people view risk
b. concentrates only on the individual (or group) that is lowest on the income scale
c. doesn't take into account those who are near to, but are not at, the bottom of the income scale
d. is based on the maximin principle
e. all of the above

16. John Rawls argues that income should be divided equally
a. in all circumstances
b. in no circumstances
c. unless an unequal distribution benefits the majority
d. unless an unequal distribution benefits at least a large minority

e. unless an unequal distribution benefits everyone

17. According to Rawls' maximin criterion, which of the following income distributions is best?
a. everyone gets $3,000 per year
b. everyone gets $5,000 per year except for one person who gets $3,100
c. half the people get $10,000 per year and the other half get $1,000
d. everyone gets $20,000 per year except for one person who gets $2,900
e. everyone gets $40,000 per year except for one person who gets $3,000

18. Which of the following is not an example of a transfer in kind?
a. subsidized housing
b. provincial health insurance
c. government job-training programs
d. Old Age Security
e. free primary education

19. In the mid-1980s, taxes and transfer payments eliminated approximately what percentage of income inequality?
a. 20 to 25%
b. 30 to 35%
c. 40 to 45%
d. about half
e. about 75%

20. The share of total income, before taxes and transfers, going to the richest 20% of Canadian families in 1987 was
a. 20 to 25%
b. 30 to 35%
c. 40 to 45%
d. about half
e. about 75%

21. According to 1987 data, the share of total income (before taxes and transfers) going to the richest 20% of Canadian families was about how many times larger than the share going to the poorest 20% of families (that is, average family income among the richest 20% was about how many times larger than the average income among the poorest 20%)?
a. about 3 times
b. about 5 times
c. about 8 times
d. a little less than 10 times
e. about 15 times

EXERCISES

1. Table 38.1 below gives the income distribution of a hypothetical economy, as in panel (*a*) of Table 38-1 in the textbook. In Table 38.2 below, fill in the cumulative income distribution in the last row.

Plot this as a Lorenz curve in Figure 38.1 below, and label it L_1.

Suppose that the government then taxes away half the income of every family in the top 20% of the income distribution and gives it in equal amounts to every family in the lowest 60% of the distribution. Fill in the resulting income distribution in Table 38.3 and the resulting cumulative income distribution in Table 38.4.

Plot the Lorenz curve for income after taxes and transfers in Figure 38.1 and label it L_2. Note how important taxes and expenditures can be in reducing inequality, at least in theory.

2. Consider the five following ways of distributing income among five families in an economy:

a. Four families receive $1,000 per year each, and the fifth family receives $600 per year.

b. Four families receive $501 per year each, and the fifth receives $3,000 per year.

c. Each family receives $500 per year.

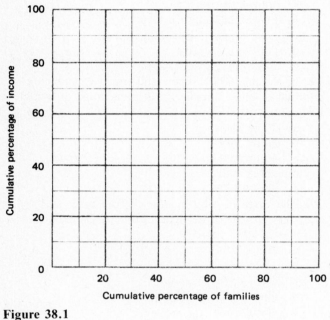

Figure 38.1

Figure 38.2

Table 38.1

	Lowest 20%	Second 20%	Third 20%	Fourth 20%	Highest 20%
Percent of income	4	6	10	20	60

Table 38.2

	Lowest 20%	Lowest 40%	Lowest 60%	Lowest 80%	Total
Percent of income					

Table 38.3

	Lowest 20%	Second 20%	Third 20%	Fourth 20%	Highest 20%
Percent of income					

Table 38.4

	Lowest 20%	Lowest 40%	Lowest 60%	Lowest 80%	Total
Percent of income					

d. Four families receive $1,100 per year each, and the fifth family receives $5,600.

e. Four families receive $5,000 per year each, and the fifth receives nothing.

Fill in Table 38.5, giving the total national income according to each distribution.

Table 38.5

Distribution	Total national income
A	
B	
C	
D	
E	

Fill in Table 38.6 for each of the distributions, showing the cumulative percentages.

Draw and label the Lorenz curve for each of these distributions in Figure 38.2.

Table 38.6 (percent of income)

Distribution	Lowest 20%	Lowest 40%	Lowest 60%	Lowest 80%	Total
A					
B					
C					
D					
E					

Indicate in Table 38.7 below the way that these distributions would be ranked according to Rawls' maximin criterion.

Table 38.7

Rank	Distribution
Best	
Second best	
Third best	
Fourth best	
Fifth best	

According to Rawls' ranking, does the best distribution have the largest total income? Does it have the least inequality as measured by the Lorenz curve?

The reason that egalitarians—that is, those who believe in equal incomes—were disillusioned by Rawls is illustrated in Figure 38.2, where we see that Rawls (does, does not) recommend the "complete-equality" distribution _____. Instead, he recommends distribution _____, which is one of the (most, least) equal of the distributions.

ESSAY QUESTIONS

1. "With a problem as perplexing as determining the best income distribution for the nation, the best approach is a simple one that strikes right to the heart of the matter: Make all incomes equal. This is philosophically and morally the fair and just solution." Do you agree? Explain your position.

2. In your view, is it possible for an unequal income distribution to be equitable? Use examples to support your position.

3. Is it fair for Steffi Graf to earn such a high income from doing something—playing tennis—that many others in the world enjoy?

4. In what way do you think the shape of the Lorenz curve would be affected by:

(a) an end to racial discrimination

(b) some individuals acquiring more and more human capital, while others do not

(c) unemployment insurance

(d) a highly progressive tax

(e) a special new tax on wage income

(f) a special new tax on incomes over $100,000

5. Along with four of your friends, estimate the income of each of your next-door neighbours. Plot a Lorenz curve for this sample of 10 incomes.

6. Marxists believe in the principle, "to each according to his needs, from each according to his abilities." Do you agree or disagree? Why or why not? Do you think that this principle would lead to a straight-line Lorenz curve? Why or why not? Do you think that a government that tried to put this principle into effect would run into problems?

ANSWERS

Important Terms: **1**d, **2**a, **3**f, **4**e, **5**b, **6**g, **7**c
True-False: **1**F, **2**T, **3**F, **4**T, **5**T, **6**F, **7**T, **8**F, **9**F, **10**F, **11**T
Multiple Choice: **1**e, **2**d, **3**c, **4**b, **5**b, **6**d, **7**c, **8**b, **9**a, **10**b, **11**d, **12**c, **13**e, **14**a, **15**e, **16**e, **17**b, **18**d, **19**a, **20**c, **21**e
Exercises: **1.** Table 38.2: 4, 10, 20, 40, 100

Figure 38.1 completed

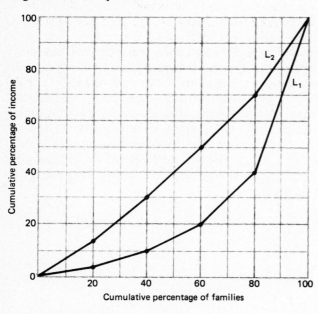

Figure 38.2 completed

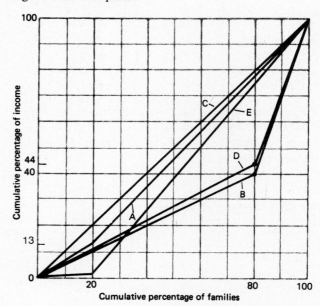

Table 38.3: 14, 16, 20, 20, 30
Table 38.4: 14, 30, 50, 70, 100

2.

Table 38.5 completed

Distribution	Total national income
A	$ 4,600
B	$ 5,004
C	$ 2,500
D	$10,000
E	$20,000

Table 38.6 completed

Distribution	Lowest 20%	Lowest 40%	Lowest 60%	Lowest 80%	Total
A	13	35	57	78	100
B	10	20	30	40	100
C	20	40	60	80	100
D	11	22	33	44	100
E	0	25	50	75	100

Table 38.7 completed

Rank	Distribution
Best	D
Second best	A
Third best	B
Fourth best	C
Fifth best	E

No, no, does not, C., D., least

ANSWERS TO SELECTED REVIEW QUESTIONS FROM THE TEXT

38-2. Our guess is (b): He seems to have been lucky in knowing just the right sports stars at just the right time. In addition, we might speculate one some other reasons for his success: He saw the opportunity for sports stars to exploit their market power. (It now appears that when he was establishing his company, these stars were earning far less than the value of their marginal product, measured in potential box office receipts.) Moreover, he seized the initiative in becoming their agent to exploit this market power while they were busy playing tennis or golf.

38-3. The one thing that is financially more rewarding than being the world's best is to have people think you are the world's best. Then they will pay a very large rent for your services (or for that matter, for your appearance at some function or on some board).

38-5. This statement is basically true, and represents another view of the difficulties in Rawl's approach.

38-6. Clark's argument is one of the classic defences of the free-market distribution of income. Although a perfectly competitive market (without externalities) would reward factors according to what they create (their marginal product), free markets for factors are seldom perfectly competitive. Even when they are, little claim can be made that they generate an equitable distribution of income. Again, see the example cited in problem 38-2.

Chapter 39

■ ■

Government Policies to Reduce Inequality:
Can We Solve the Poverty Problem?

MAJOR PURPOSE

The objective of this chapter is to evaluate what we are now doing—and what we might possibly do in the future—to alleviate the grinding effects of poverty on the poorest individuals in our population. Specifically, we will address three sets of questions: (1) How is the poverty line defined, and who are the poor below it? (2) What policies do the federal and provincial governments now have in place to reduce poverty, and how successful have they been? (3) What income maintenance programs have been proposed to replace the present income support systems, and how likely is it that they would be successful?

LEARNING OBJECTIVES

After you have studied this chapter in the textbook and the study guide, you should be able to
- Describe how the poverty line is defined
- Explain why, over long periods of time, our definition of the poverty line tends to drift up to a higher level of real income
- State the factors that increase the likelihood of a family being poor
- Describe the government policies that attack the causes of poverty, and the policies that reduce its symptoms
- Explain the difference between universal social programs and "targeted" programs specifically designed to help the poor, and give examples of each
- Describe some problems that exist in our present welfare system
- Explain the concept of the implicit tax in a welfare program and why this is important in evaluating such programs
- Critically evaluate the guaranteed minimum income proposal
- Argue the case that income maintenance programs are the cure for poverty
- Argue the opposite case that such programs are the cause of poverty
- Describe how a negative income tax program would work
- Explain the theoretical advantages of a negative income tax program
- Explain why three objectives come into conflict when the government is trying to design a negative income tax: (1) to raise the minimum income to an acceptable level; (2) to increase the incentive to work, and (3) to keep the costs of the program from escalating
- Describe some results of experimental studies on the negative income tax
- Explain the pros and cons of a wage subsidy

HIGHLIGHTS OF THE CHAPTER

Here are the broad questions that are addressed in this chapter.

How Is the Poverty Line Defined?

The most common definition of poverty is based on poverty lines (called "low-income cutoff" lines) estimated by Statistics Canada for different groups of families or individuals. It is defined by finding the income level at which the average family or individual would have to devote as much as 58.5% of income to the basic necessities of life—namely, food, clothing, and shelter. (Studies have shown that as family income increases, families spend a smaller and smaller proportion of income on these necessities.) Any family or individual below this low-income cutoff line is defined as being poor. The estimated poverty line is different for urban and rural families and for large and small families; in 1988, the poverty line for an urban family of four was $23,500 per year. The poverty line is adjusted every year to take inflation into account. It also drifts higher in real terms over long periods of time because our idea of what is barely acceptable tends to increase.

Who Are the Poor?

Table 39-1 in the text shows that the incidence of poverty in 1986 was substantially higher in the Atlantic provinces and Quebec and lower than average in Ontario and the prairie provinces. Table 39-2 shows how various characteristics of families and individuals affect the likelihood of poverty. Families (or individuals) are more likely to be poor if (1) the head of the household is female; (2) the head of the household has little education; (3) the family or individual has been unable to find full-time work; (4) the family has three or more children. You should be able to explain how each of these factors is related to poverty.

What Are the Government Policies that Reduce Poverty?

Several government programs attack the *causes* (as opposed to the symptoms) of poverty: (1) subsidizing investment in human capital, such as free primary and secondary schooling and subsidized job training under the Adult Occupational Training Act; (2) laws and programs that are intended to reduce the extent of poverty that arises from disability and illness, including laws regulating safety in the workplace and universal health insurance; (3) other policies, such as provision of subsidized day care, to make it easier for women in low-income families to earn an income outside of the home.

The programs that help alleviate the symptoms of poverty include several universal social insurance programs of government transfer payments in cash or in kind: Old Age Security, the CPP/QPP, the Family Allowance program, Unemployment Insurance, provincial health insurance programs. These programs have become very expensive and are going to become even more costly as the proportion of old people (who receive a large proportion of these payments) in Canada's population increases during the next several decades.

Other government transfer programs are *targeted*; that is, they are designed to help poor people only. These include the federal Guaranteed Income Supplement (GIS), which goes to poor people whose only source of income is Old Age Security, the federal Child Tax Credit, and provincial social assistance (or "welfare") programs.

How Successful Have Government Anti-poverty Policies Been?

The incidence of poverty in Canada has declined rapidly during the twentieth century. As Figure 39-1 in the textbook illustrates, during the last 25 years, the estimated proportion of families living in poverty has declined from about 1 in 3 families to about 1 in 9. Some people argue that most of the credit for this is due to our welfare programs. They also argue that these programs have given us the additional, "non-economic" benefit of knowing that we live in a decent society that provides for the poor.

However, critics point to a number of problems with our current welfare programs. One problem arises because the system imposes an "implicit tax" on any income the poor may earn. When a poor family earns another $1,000 of income, it may consequently have to give up, say, $800 of welfare benefits it receives from the government. (Sometimes it's more than this, sometimes less.) This $800 is called an 80% "implicit tax" because, from the point of view of the poor, it's as though they had $800 of their additional $1,000 of income "taxed away." If they only get $200 net benefit when they go out and earn $1,000, why bother? It is critical that you understand this concept of an implicit tax, and why a high rate of this tax weakens the incentive of the poor to work. For some families in our present welfare system, this implicit tax has been very high indeed—in some instances approaching, or even exceeding, 100%. In such cases, the poor who earn another $1,000 will lose $1,000 of welfare payments from the government. Their income doesn't increase at all; they have no monetary incentive to get a job.

What Are the Proposals to Replace the Present Welfare System?

1. A guaranteed minimum income (GMI). Under this program, shown in Figure 39-2 of the textbook, the government would guarantee a family a minimum income of, say, $10,000. Any shortfall in the family's earnings would be covered by a payment from the government. The problem with this policy is that it has a built-in 100% implicit tax that leaves no incentive for the poor to go to work. If they do, and earn another $1,000, their welfare payments from the government are reduced by this same amount. It doesn't matter whether they earn $5,000 or $6,000. Their income is fixed by the government at a $10,000 level. So they don't benefit at all when they earn that $1,000 more. Ensure that you fully understand this scheme in Figure 39-2 of the textbook before you proceed to the more complicated proposal for a negative income tax in Figure 39-4 of the text.

2. A negative income tax (NIT). This proposal also provides the poor with a guaranteed minimum income; but, in addition, it provides them with an incentive to go out and earn income on their own. The implicit tax in this program can be set at, say, 50% (rather than the 100% implicit tax in the GMI proposal above). Thus, a family that earns another $1,000 of income has its payments from the government reduced by only $500. It, therefore, gets a net benefit of $500, which provides it with an incentive to work. Note that the "income-after-subsidy" line CA that was completely flat in the GMI proposal in Figure 39-2—and, therefore, provided no incentive to work—has now been replaced by the upward-sloping line CQ in Figure 39-4. Since some of the benefit from increased income can now be kept—it is no longer all lost—there is an incentive to go to work.

If, as its proponents recommend, the negative income tax were to replace the entire inconsistent set of present welfare policies, it would provide another benefit. It would be more equitable because all the poor would be treated alike; all would face the same minimum income, and the same implicit tax. However, this policy would not be problem-free. Like any other anti-poverty program it could not simultaneously achieve the three desirable but conflicting goals of (1) providing an acceptable minimum income for everyone, (2) preserving the incentive for people to work, and (3) keeping costs down. As an example of how these goals may conflict, suppose the government decides to achieve the first goal by raising the minimum income level from $10,000 to $12,000. This will shift the "income after" line CQH in Figure 39-4 up by $2,000 throughout its whole length, thus increasing the gray "subsidy gap" that the government must fill. Thus, this measure may conflict with objective (3) of keeping costs down.

Unfortunately, results of NIT experiments in the United States suggest that, in practice, the negative income tax doesn't work as well as many economists had hoped. In fact, compared with even the existing welfare system, it had disappointing results because it was not successful in inducing people to work more.

A Wage Subsidy

Disappointment in the NIT experimental results has led some to suggest this alternative: a wage subsidy that would provide financial assistance to the poor by increasing their wages. Because it would increase the reward for work (the wage rate) it is hoped that this scheme might provide a stronger work incentive. Its main drawback is that it would remove any guaranteed minimum income, and thus would provide no assistance to those individuals who, because of age or disability, cannot work to support themselves. Accordingly, some method would have to be devised to "tag" such people, so that they could qualify for special government support. While such a system would be necessary, it would be far from foolproof. One problem is that some of the able-bodied who do not want to work may try to have themselves fraudulently tagged as disabled.

Concluding Remarks

In the analysis of the GMI and NIT proposals, the focus has been on the cost of a welfare system, in terms of the reduced incentive to work by the recipients of welfare. But there is another cost as well—the cost of raising the taxes from the general public to finance the welfare expenditure. There is evidence that there is about a 25-35% loss when taxes are raised, because those who are taxed are left with less incentive to work. Make sure—in Figure 39-3 of the text—that you can clearly distinguish between these two costs—that is, the disincentive to work imposed on the public that has to pay for welfare payments, and the disincentive to work of the poor who receive the welfare payments.

IMPORTANT TERMS: MATCH THE COLUMNS

Match each term in the first column with its corresponding explanation in the second column.

_____ 1. Poverty
_____ 2. Poverty line
_____ 3. Adult Occupational Training Act
_____ 4. Human rights legislation
_____ 5. Workers' Compensation
_____ 6. Old Age Security
_____ 7. Canada Pension Plan/Quebec Pension Plan
_____ 8. Family Allowances
_____ 9. Wage subsidy
_____ 10. Guaranteed Income Supplement
_____ 11. Targeted transfer program
_____ 12. Implicit tax
_____ 13. Guaranteed minimum income
_____ 14. Negative income tax
_____ 15. Tagging
_____ 16. Child tax credit
_____ 17. Unemployment Insurance

a. The identification of those who, because of age or disability, are unable to earn an income and, therefore, deserve special support from the government

b. Provincial programs that pay pensions to people who have been disabled through work-related injuries

c. A proposed government program which would ensure people a minimum income but give them no incentive to work

d. Any government transfer program in which benefits go primarily to those with low incomes

e. Provincial laws prohibiting various kinds of discrimination in the labour market and elsewhere

f. That income at which a typical family would pay as much as 58.5% of its income for food, clothing, and shelter

g. Targeted tax relief for low-income families with children

h. Pays the same support to all Canadians over the age of 65

i. A program that guarantees everyone a minimum income and provides a work incentive by allowing people to retain part of any income they earn

j. Government payments to all families with children

k. Government program that pays part of the cost of retraining people who have lost their old jobs

l. Government pension plan providing retirement benefits that depend on previous employer-employee contributions

m. Government cash transfers to those who have lost their jobs

n. Supplements OAS for low-income retirees

o. When increased earnings lead to loss of government benefits

p. Inadequate income to buy the necessities of life

q. When the government provides funds for increasing the wages of low-income earners

TRUE-FALSE

T F 1. By 1987, only one Canadian family in 20 was below the poverty line.
T F 2. Average real family income in the 1920s was well below the poverty-line income in 1987.
T F 3. The poor are located in the lower left-hand corner of the Lorenz curve.
T F 4. The poverty-line income estimated by Statistics Canada is lower for a family in an urban area than for a comparable family in a rural area.
T F 5. The poverty line is not adjusted over time to take account of inflation, because inflation is not the problem.

T F   **6.** Unemployment insurance benefits are an example of an in-kind transfer.

T F   **7.** Families in which the head of the household is a woman are more likely to be poor than are other families.

T F   **8.** Transfer programs such as social assistance relieve the symptoms of poverty rather than attacking its causes.

T F   **9.** Under a guaranteed minimum income, all Canadians would receive the same income after taxes and subsidies.

T F **10.** The implicit tax in a welfare system is the sum of the benefits lost divided by the additional earned income.

T F **11.** All Canadian provinces have about the same proportion of families living in poverty.

MULTIPLE CHOICE

1. In 1988, Statistics Canada estimated that the poverty-line income for a rural family of four was:
- **a.** more than $17,000 per year
- **b.** higher than the poverty line for an urban family of four
- **c.** the same as the poverty line estimated for 1982
- **d.** about the same as for a single individual in a city
- **e.** less than $12,000

2. By recent standards, the proportion of the population living in poverty in the early 1960s was about:
- **a.** 1 in 10
- **b.** 1 in 5
- **c.** 1 in 3
- **d.** 50%
- **e.** 2 out of 3

3. It becomes impossible to lift all Canadians out of poverty, if we define poverty as:
- **a.** the bottom half of the income distribution
- **b.** any income less than $10,000
- **c.** the bottom tenth of the income distribution
- **d.** a. or c.
- **e.** b. or c.

4. Select the correct word to put in the blank spot: It is _____ better to attack the causes of poverty than its symptoms.
- **a.** always
- **b.** usually
- **c.** seldom
- **d.** almost never
- **e.** never

5. In the 1920s, a family with a real income close to today's poverty line would have been considered well off. This reflects the fact that:
- **a.** productivity has decreased
- **b.** our standards of what constitutes a poverty line income have risen
- **c.** government welfare programs have been reduced

- **d.** population has expanded
- **e.** food was cheaper in 1920 than it is today

6. The percentage of all families with annual incomes below Statistics Canada's low-income cutoff:
- **a.** was estimated to be about 1/3 of all families in the early 1960s
- **b.** decreased more during the period 1960-80 than during 1980-86
- **c.** was estimated to be less than 15% in 1986
- **d.** was higher in the Maritime provinces than in the rest of Canada in 1986
- **e.** all of the above

7. Which of the following government transfer programs is *not* specifically targeted at people with low incomes?
- **a.** Unemployment Insurance
- **b.** social assistance programs
- **c.** child tax credit
- **d.** Guaranteed Income Supplement
- **e.** low-income housing

8. Which of the following kinds of government programs relieve only the symptoms of poverty?
- **a.** those that subsidize investment in human capital
- **b.** social assistance payments under the cash deficit method
- **c.** universal health insurance
- **d.** policies to reduce unemployment and disability
- **e.** subsidized day care

9. Which of the following government programs does *not* create an implicit tax on the recipients?
- **a.** social assistance payments
- **b.** child tax credit
- **c.** Guaranteed Income Supplement
- **d.** subsidized housing
- **e.** Old Age Security payments

10. Which of the following combinations accounted for the largest share of total federal and provincial government expenditures in 1982/83?

a. hospital and medical insurance, Unemployment Insurance, and Old Age Security
b. social welfare assistance, Unemployment Insurance, and Old Age Security
c. hospital and medical insurance, family allowances, and the child tax credit
d. Old Age Security, social welfare assistance, and family allowances
e. Unemployment Insurance, Guaranteed Income Supplement, and Workers' Compensation

11. A guaranteed minimum income:
a. would increase efficiency by increasing the incentive to work
b. would be very costly, especially because it would reduce the incentive to work
c. would cost less than we would expect, because it would increase the incentive to work
d. would have no effect on the incentive to work
e. would have no effect on efficiency

12. A guaranteed minimum income has an implicit tax on very low income families of:
a. 0%
b. 25%
c. 50%
d. 75%
e. 100%

13. The income-maintenance program that would provide the poor with the largest incentive to work is one in which the "income-after-subsidy" line:
a. has zero slope
b. has a slope close to zero
c. has a slope of 30°
d. has a slope of almost 45°
e. has a negative slope

14. The estimated "leak in the welfare" bucket in which income is transferred to the poor has been estimated at about:
a. zero when taxes are collected, and 50% when the welfare expenditures are made
b. 30% when taxes are collected, and 60% when the welfare expenditures are made
c. 30% when taxes are collected, and 20 to 25% when the welfare expenditures are made
d. 50% when taxes are collected, and 20 to 25% when the welfare expenditures are made
e. 50% when taxes are collected, and zero when the welfare expenditures are made

15. The maximum implicit tax on any family facing the present set of federal and provincial welfare policies may be:
a. about 50%

b. about 80%
c. just under 100%
d. 100%
e. more than 100%

16. A family will have the strongest financial incentive to stop working if the implicit tax it faces is:
a. zero
b. so close to zero that the difference is not significant
c. 50%
d. almost 100%
e. more than 100%

17. If a family living in government-subsidized housing is required to pay 25% of its income in rent, then for this reason alone it is facing an implicit tax of:
a. zero
b. 25%
c. 75%
d. 100%
e. 125%

18. A welfare program that pays you $5,000 if you earn nothing, and $4,500 if you earn $2,000, has an implicit tax of:
a. zero
b. 25%
c. 40%
d. 50%
e. 105%

19. Which of the following should offer the greatest work incentive to the very poor?
a. no taxes or subsidies
b. the present welfare system
c. a wage subsidy
d. a guaranteed minimum income
e. a. and d. equally

20. With a negative income tax, an increase in the implicit tax rate will:
a. increase the slope of the "income-after-tax" line
b. decrease the slope of that line
c. leave the slope of that line unchanged
d. raise the point where the income-after-tax line intersects the vertical axis
e. lower that point

21. Suppose a negative income tax is set up with the minimum income set at $8,000, and the implicit tax rate set at 50%. In this case, a subsidy would be paid by the government:
a. to no one
b. only to those earning less than $4,000
c. only to those earning less than $8,000
d. only to those earning less than $12,000
e. only to those earning less than $16,000

EXERCISE

Consider the following four tax-subsidy programs:

A. Every family earning less than $5,000 receives enough subsidy to give it an income of $5,000 after taxes and subsidies. On every dollar earned over $5,000, a family must pay a 20% tax.

B. Every family receives a subsidy of $5,000, but then pays a 50% tax on every dollar earned.

C. Every family receives a subsidy of $3,000, but then pays a tax of 30% on every dollar earned.

D. Every family receives a subsidy of $3,000 but then pays a tax of 50% on every dollar earned.

In Figure 39.1, plot the line for each program showing how a family's income after taxes and subsidies is related to its income before taxes and subsidies. For each program, indicate in Table 39.1 the marginal tax rates on income earned above $5,000.

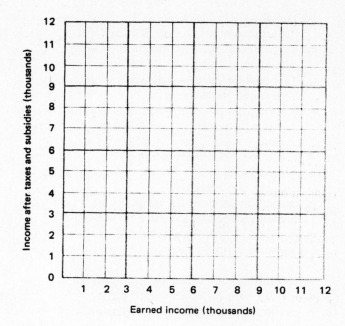

Figure 39.1

Table 39.1

Program	Marginal tax rate on income earned above $5,000
A	
B	
C	
D	

Suppose that the distribution of earned incomes (before taxes and subsidies) in the economy is given by Table 39.2.

Table 39.2

Annual income before taxes and transfers (thousands of dollars)	0	3	5	6	10	15	20	50
Number of families earning this income	1	2	4	4	3	2	1	1

In Table 39.3 fill in the net tax (i.e., tax minus subsidy) paid to each family under each of the programs.

Table 39.3

Income (in thousands)		0	3	5	6	10	15	20	50
Net tax of each	A								
family under	B								
program:	C								
	D								

In Table 39.4 show the total net taxes collected—that is, total taxes collected minus total subsidy paid. Assume that, regardless of the tax-subsidy program that is imposed, there is no change in the amount of work and, therefore, no change in the earned income of each family. In other words, the income distribution in Table 39.2 doesn't change, regardless of the tax-subsidy program.

Table 39.4

Program	Total net taxes
A	
B	
C	
D	

ESSAY QUESTIONS

1. "Universal social insurance and welfare programs may be desirable, but they are totally unproductive. They don't add anything to the nation's capacity to produce." Do you agree with this statement, or not? Explain your answer. (Use provincial medicare as one of your examples.)

2. Use a numerical example to show that if poverty is defined as the income of the bottom 10% of the population, it becomes a meaningless and useless measure of hardship.

3. If you observe that the children of the poor are poor, and that the children of the rich are rich, does this prove the ability of the rich to secure a high income for their children (by providing them, for example, with special educational opportunities)? Or does it reflect different genetic capabilities? Or both? Discuss.

4. If the main ill effect of social assistance programs is to encourage fathers to leave home so their families can qualify for welfare, what do you think of maintaining the program but disqualifying any family whose father has abandoned them?

5. If the government gave equivalent cash transfers instead of subsidized housing, education, or other types of assistance in kind, would the recipients be better off? Why? Would their children be better off? Why does the government provide assistance in kind?

6. In the United States, the poverty line is simply defined as three times the cost of feeding a family a diet that meets certain minimal nutritional standards at the lowest possible cost. Do you think this is a better way of defining the poverty line than the method used by Statistics Canada? Why or why not?

ANSWERS

Important Terms: 1p, 2f, 3k, 4e, 5b, 6h, 7l, 8j, 9q, 10n, 11d, 12o, 13c, 14i, 15a, 16g, 17m
True-False: 1F, 2T, 3T, 4F, 5F, 6F, 7T, 8T, 9F, 10T, 11F
Multiple Choice: 1a, 2c, 3d, 4b, 5b, 6e, 7a, 8b, 9e, 10a, 11b, 12e, 13d, 14c, 15e, 16e, 17b, 18b, 19c, 20b, 21e
Exercise:

Figure 39.1 completed

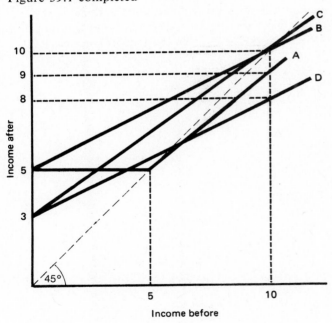

Table 39.1   completed

A	20%
B	50%
C	30%
D	50%

Table 39.4 completed

A	10,800
B	0
C	0
D	36,000

Table 39.3 completed

−5,000	−2,000	0	200	1,000	2,000	3,000	9,000
−5,000	−3,500	−2,500	−2,000	0	2,500	5,000	20,000
−3,000	−2,100	−1,500	−1,200	0	1,500	3,000	12,000
−3,000	−1,500	−500	0	2,000	4,500	7,000	22,000

ANSWERS TO SELECTED REVIEW QUESTIONS FROM THE TEXT

39-1. A family facing an implicit tax of 90% (or 105%) will lose 90 cents (or $1.05) in benefits from the government for every additional $1 of income it earns. If it faces an implicit tax of 90%, it will have very little incentive to work, since it will only be able to keep 10 cents on the dollar. If its implicit tax is 105%, this family would be better off not earning additional income; it can have a higher income by working less.

39-2. If the breadwinner in familiy *h* goes fishing, the efficiency loss is $8,000 (red bar *QF*), the income earned before this policy was introduced. If the breadwinner in family *j* goes fishing, the efficiency loss is $11,000—again, it's the income earned before this policy was introduced. If *j* goes fishing one of his five working days a week, the efficiency loss is $11,000/5 = $2,200. The efficiency loss from subsidizing family *g* is zero, since the work this family does is unaffected. (It does no work either before or after the subsidy.)

If the minimum income level is raised from $10,000 to $12,000, the efficiency loss would almost certainly increase, since the incentive for families like *j* to work would disappear. (The breadwinner of *j* would no longer lose $1,000 by quitting work.)

39-4. (a) The new figure will be similar to Figure 39-4, but the line *CH* will be flatter, intersecting the 45° line at about $14,300 (rather than at $20,000).

(b) The incentive to work has been reduced: a family now gets to keep only $300 out of each $1,000 it earns (rather than $500 per $1,000 in Figure 39-4).

(c) The implicit tax has risen. It is now 70%, rather than 50% in Figure 39-4.

(d) Yes, they are: the higher the implicit tax, the lower the incentive to work.

(e) If each family continues to work the same amount as before, the total government subsidy is less than before, since each family's subsidy has been reduced.

However, because the incentive to work has been decreased, some families are now likely to work less, and thus move to the left in the diagram. Such a move increases the subsidy they will receive. On balance, therefore, it is not clear whether the total subsidy the government pays out will increase or decrease.

(f) Because some families are now likely to reduce the work they do (that is, move to the left in the diagram), the transfer bucket has become leakier.

(g) In this case, the line *CH* shifts down by $2,000, in a parallel fashion, starting at $8,000 on the vertical axis and intersecting the 45° line at an income of about $16,000. In comparison with Figure 39-4, the incentive to work may not be affected much, because the implicit tax remains the same (at 50%). However, a family that does not work at all will now have an income of only $8,000, not $10,000. This may induce some families to work more, simply to eke out a bare living.

The total amount of subsidy the government pays is likely to be reduced in this case. This is both because each family is subsidized up to a lower level, and because some families that previously contributed nothing or very little to their own support are now likely to feel that they have to work more, given the reduced support level.

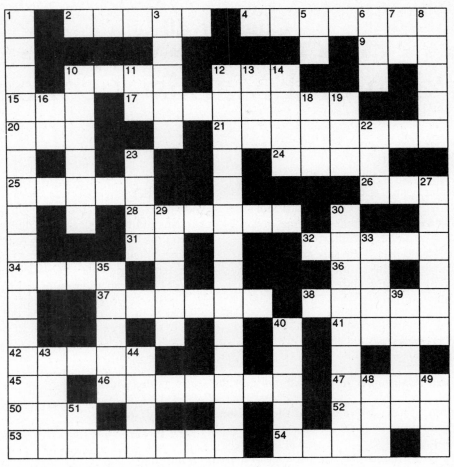

Across

1, 4. Education and training are examples of this.
9. consumed
10. Birds do this with their wings.
12. During a recession, there is at least a _____ in real output.
15. illegal organization in the United Kingdom
17. popular name for provincial health insurance in Canada
20. organization fighting for the rights of blacks in South Africa (abbrev.)
21. Canada's federal and provincial programs of income support and social insurance are designed to provide more economic _____.
24. falls when you weep
25. really like
26. tried to fight inflation in the 1970s (abbrev.)
28. not the same as equality; fairness
31. second person singular pronoun (French)
32. name used for troops from Australia and New Zealand during World War I (abbrev.)
34. charged particles
36. last two initials of Canadian institution where stocks are traded
37, 38. a diagrammatic device for illustrating inequality
41. enables plant to draw water and nourishment from the soil
42. change
45. negative
46. When you retire, you will probably get one from the government and another from your employer.
47. negative (Russian)
50. ocean fish
52. give up
53, 54. a way to discourage pollution

Down

1. based on the cash deficit method in most provinces (2 words)
3. northern deciduous tree
5. Italian river
6. a source of revenue for the government
8, 27. This illustrates the idea that something is lost when money is transferred from rich to poor.
10. Labour is a _____ of production.
11. before noon (abbrev.)
12. one of the causes of poverty—for single women and minorities, for example
13. frozen water
14. agreement
16. health care professional (abbrev.)
18. street (French)
19. long time period
22. outlawed political organization in the United Kingdom
23. Sugar can be produced from one variety of this.
29. Imperial volume measure
30. contract whereby one party agrees to indemnify the other against loss for a fee
33. nil
35. Get plenty of this before your economics final, but not during the lectures.
39. cast a ballot
40. ski resort in the Rockies
43. machine for weaving
44. colloquial word for communists
48. positive response
49. substitute for coffee
51. nickname for future queen of England

Chapter 40

■ ■

Marxism and Marxist Economies

MAJOR PURPOSE

Historically, the most influential criticism of the capitalistic, free enterprise system was that set out by Karl Marx. He charged that this system distributes income in an unfair way because it provides income to owners of capital—that is, to "capitalists." In this chapter, we examine Marx's criticism and his proposed alternative: a revolution followed by a socialist state in which capital would be owned by the state on behalf of all the people.

We then describe the two most important Marxist experiments—those in the Soviet Union and China. What problems did the Soviets and Chinese encounter? Why is it that the Marxist philosophy that promises so much, delivers so little when put into practice? What will be the major challenges that they—or any other Marxist states—will face in attempting to reform their economies and move toward freer markets?

LEARNING OBJECTIVES

After you have studied this chapter in the textbook and the study guide, you should be able to
- Describe the labour theory of value, and the subsistence theory of wages
- Explain Marx's concepts of surplus value and the exploitation of the working class
- Define and clearly distinguish between socialism and communism
- State two predictions of Marx that have not been verified by history
- Criticize both the theory and practice of socialism
- Explain how capital is raised for investment purposes in a socialist state
- Describe the problems associated with central planning
- Explain why there is typically less innovation in a socialist state than in a free enterprise economy
- Explain the problems the Soviets face in setting production targets in their 5-year plans
- Describe the "second economy" in the Soviet Union
- Describe the problems facing the consumer in an economy that is not closely oriented to the marketplace
- Compare the Soviets' disguised unemployment with our overt unemployment
- Compare the Soviets' suppressed inflation with our inflation
- Explain to what degree the Soviets have succeeded in equalizing incomes, and the problems they have encountered because of the increasing importance of human capital
- Explain why growth has been disappointing in the Soviet Union
- Describe eleven challenging questions that will have to be faced by the Soviet Union or any other communist country that tries to reform its economic system

HIGHLIGHTS OF THE CHAPTER

This chapter can be broken down into four broad topics: (1) Marx's criticism of a free enterprise system; (2) the socialist-communist alternative that he proposed; (3) the application of Marxism, especially in the Soviet Union; and (4) the economic problems the Soviet Union and other Marxist states will face as they attempt to reform their economies by moving toward freer markets.

Marxism

Karl Marx based his philosophy on (1) the labour theory of value and (2) the subsistence theory of wages. He claimed that there is a *class struggle* in which workers (the "proletariat") are exploited by the capitalists (the "bourgeoisie" who own the capital equipment and other means of production). Instead of enjoying all the fruits of their labour, workers receive just enough to subsist, with the rest going in the form of "surplus value" to the capitalists. According to Marx, the only way of resolving this class struggle is a revolution in which workers forcibly seize the ownership of physical capital from their exploiters. They then set up a socialist state in which there is a dictatorship of the proletariat and capital is owned by the state. In turn, this is followed by a communist system in which the state has withered away, and capital and other forms of property are owned by the community as a whole.

One criticism of Marxist theory is that its predictions have not been borne out by history. (1) The dictatorship of the proletariat, instead of withering away, has remained powerful in Marxist states. (2) Under capitalism, workers have enjoyed rising real income instead of the increasing misery predicted by Marx.

Another criticism of Marxist theory is that if capitalists are eliminated, some other way must be found to generate physical capital for investment. The Marxist solution is to generate capital by taxation—in particular, heavy taxes on consumer goods—rather than by personal saving. However, this raises three problems: (1) taxes (forced saving) may be more burdensome than voluntary saving; (2) when governments invest the funds they have raised, they typically lack the inventiveness of private capitalists; and (3) some substitute must be found for the profit motive as a means of allocating capital among different industries.

The concept of profit raises an important issue in the debate between capitalism and Marxism. Supporters of Marxism and capitalism alike generally agree that monopoly profits should not go unchecked. Supporters of capitalism argue that this can be done in a capitalist system by government regulation. Marxists argue that regulation is ineffective because big business interests are so powerful that they end up controlling their own regulators. A capitalist response to this criticism is that big business does indeed have power; and so does the government. But this is better than having all of the power in the hands of the government—as happens in a communist state.

The Soviet System

Two important features of the Soviet system are: (1) most physical capital is owned by the state rather than by private individuals and (2) the decisions on how much of each good to produce and how much to invest in each industry are not made by market forces, but are instead made by a central government planning agency (Gosplan) in its 5-year plans. These plans set yearly production targets, or quotas, for each industry and—in even more detail—for each plant. There are three major problems with central planning of this sort:

1. It is difficult for the government to determine a set of consistent output quotas. For example, the right output for the steel industry depends on the output of those industries that use steel, such as machinery and autos. But at the same time, the right output for the machinery industry depends on the output of those industries that use machinery, such as steel. How do you solve for the output of either steel or machinery, when each depends on the other? The answer is that it is not easy. Although there are mathematical techniques for solving such problems, it is seldom possible for a planning agency to get the quotas just right. Consequently, bottlenecks—such as a shortage of steel—are common in the Soviet Union.

2. Consumers' wants tend to be ignored in the Soviet system. When steel is in short supply, it goes to produce bridges or machinery, not refrigerators for consumers. Thus, consumer goods are in chronic short supply, and this leads to the long line-ups that are a feature of Soviet life. Another reason the Soviet consumer is short-changed is that each production manager tends to concentrate on satisfying a quota rather than on producing the types of goods that consumers want. (For more on the plight of the Soviet consumer, see Box 40-1 in the textbook.)

3. It is not clear that the Soviet degree of central planning could be made to work without a repressive Soviet-style political dictatorship. Marxists reply that our freedom is enjoyed only by the rich and powerful. And they point to one apparent advantage of central planning: It produces very little measured unemployment. However, critics point out that if someone is working to produce unwanted goods this really constitutes "disguised" unemployment.

The 5-year plans of the Soviet Union have emphasized rapid growth. For example, between 1950 and 1970, the average rate of growth of Soviet GDP was almost 5%, which far exceeded the 3% growth rate in the United States. However, the reason for this was not that the Soviet Union has a better system for generating growth. Instead, it was due to the fact that investment in the Soviet Union has run about 30% of GDP, compared to 15% in the United States. When one compares the Soviet Union with a country like Japan that also invests this high a percentage of its GDP, Soviet growth does not compare favourably. Moreover, despite the heavy diversion of its GDP into investment, Soviet growth has recently become particularly disappointing; it has fallen close to zero.

There have been four reasons for this poor performance.

1. Inefficiency exists because firms aren't under competitive pressure. They are not subject to our hard budget restraint—that is, bankruptcy if they continue to lose money. Instead they face a soft budget restraint; the government will bail them out.

2. Poor development and adaptation of new technology. Because their objective is to meet a quota, Soviet managers don't experiment. If you don't experiment in our system, you go out of business.

3. Isolation from the world economy. Little competition from imports means there is no pressure in the Soviet Union to match quality standards of the international marketplace.

4. Morale problems have led to alcoholism and absenteeism. The difficulty here seems to be lack of incentives, partly because a higher income can only be used to purchase inferior goods.

Problems in Moving any Marxist Economy toward Freer Markets

The Soviet Union or any other Marxist country will have to address a number of very difficult issues in moving from a government-controlled system to freer markets:

1. Will firms face a hard budget restraint? That is, will the inefficient be allowed to go bankrupt? If they are not, waste and inefficiency will persist.

2. Will prices be set free? They must be or allocative inefficiency and disguised unemployment will continue; shoes that won't fit will continue to be made.

3. Will the economy be opened to foreign competition? This is needed to get the gains from trade and to pressure Soviet firms into improving quality.

4. How much private ownership will be allowed? If there isn't a major shift toward private ownership, incentives to produce more and better goods will remain weak.

5. Will foreign ownership be allowed? Foreign investment can bring large benefits because foreign firms:

(a) bring in new technology

(b) bid up wages

(c) pay taxes

But foreign ownership would severely compromise Marxism. The philosophical problems of allowing the Soviets to own Soviet industry would be magnified if Soviet industry can be owned by firms in capitalist countries.

6. Will agriculture or industry by reformed first?

(a) The Chinese chose agriculture and this reform was, by and large, successful.

(b) The Soviets started with industry, and found it much more difficult.

7. Should reform be phased in by sector or be across-the-board? There's a problem with phased-in reform: It may be like a phased-in change of traffic from the right lane to the left—cars this year, trucks the next. For example, if even the most efficient firm in the economy still has its price frozen but its input prices are allowed to rise, it will go bankrupt.

8. Can the institutions required for a free market be developed, such as civil courts to settle disputes? (These have never been adequately developed because of the assumption that conflicts don't exist in a Marxist state.)

9. Can government regulations be developed? For example:

(a) pro-competitive regulations to prevent monopoly abuse by private firms;

(b) controls to prevent pollution by private firms.

10. Can aggregate demand be constrained? Recent financing of the large Soviet fiscal deficit by printing money has increased inflationary pressure. Because prices are controlled, this has meant more severe scarcity and longer queues. If this "suppressed inflation" is not dealt with, prices will rise rapidly once they are set free. If inflationary pressure cannot be contained, this may destroy the whole reform process.

11. As democracy develops, will it be possible to set prices free? In our democratic society, the public will often not allow a single price—rent—to be decontrolled because it would rise. How can all prices be allowed to rise in the Soviet Union if the public is allowed to vote? But isn't political reform even more important than economic reform?

IMPORTANT TERMS: MATCH THE COLUMNS

Match each term in the first column with its corresponding explanation in the second column.

_____	1. Capitalism
_____	2. Socialism
_____	3. Communism
_____	4. Labour theory of value
_____	5. Subsistence wage theory
_____	6. Surplus value
_____	7. Hard budget restraint
_____	8. 5-year plan
_____	9. Proletariat
_____	10. Bourgeoisie
_____	11. Dictatorship of the proletariat
_____	12. Disguised unemployment
_____	13. Soft budget restraint

a. The Marxist term for the working class

b. The situation that exists if people are employed, but in useless tasks

c. In Marxist theory, this is the ideal system in which all means of production and other forms of property are owned by the community as a whole and the central government has "withered away"

d. An economic system in which most physical capital is privately owned

e. A plan that sets up production and investment targets for each industry

f. The theory that, in a capitalist economy, workers' wages can never rise, except temporarily, above a socially defined minimum level

g. The transitory stage, according to Marx, that follows the workers' revolution, before the government withers away and the ideal state of communism is achieved

h. An economic system in which physical capital and other means of production, such as land, are owned by the state

i. The Marxist term for the capitalist class

j. The difference, according to Marx, between the total value of output (all of which "belongs" to labour) and the wages actually received by labour

k. The theory that the value of any good is determined solely by the amount of labour that goes into producing it, including the labour embodied in the capital used to produce it

l. The ability of a firm that has continuously suffered losses to stay in business

m. The requirement that a firm that has continuously suffered losses should go bankrupt

TRUE-FALSE

T F 1. According to Marx, labour in a capitalist system receives a socially defined subsistence income barely sufficient to meet the workers' basic needs.

T F 2. The government of the Soviet Union does not regard itself as having achieved communism.

T F 3. According to Marxist theory, a communist society is one in which the state has withered away.

T F 4. A major reason why it has been difficult to control the abuse of personal power in the Soviet Union is that there have not been free elections in which the public can remove the party in power and replace it with another.

T F 5. Marx believed that the labour time spent on producing machinery and the income earned by capitalists on that machinery were both surplus value.

T F 6. According to Marx, economic history was a story of the proletariat exploiting the bourgeoisie in a class struggle.

T F   7. According to Marx, the amount of labour going into the production of a good includes the labour spent on (or congealed in) the machinery used to produce the good.

T F   8. Marx's analysis is positive, rather than normative.

T F   9. Marx spent a great deal of time discussing how, in his communist society, conflicts would be resolved by groups with conflicting interests.

T F   10. The Soviet planning system leads to more efficient production.

T F   11. Many workers in the Soviet Union (as well as in North America and Western Europe) have become capitalists, in the sense that they have accumulated substantial quantities of human capital.

MULTIPLE CHOICE

1. Marx's analysis was based on:
   a. the labour theory of value
   b. the theory that wages tended toward a socially defined subsistence level
   c. the marginal productivity theory of wages
   d. **a.** and **b.**
   e. **a.** and **c.**

2. Marx's recommended system for production and income distribution was:
   a. from each according to his need; to each according to his ability
   b. from each according to his ability; to each according to his need
   c. from each according to his ability; to each according to his wants
   d. from each, and to each, according to his ability
   e. from each, and to each, according to his need

3. Marx believed that once a communist society was established:
   a. power would corrupt, and absolute power would corrupt absolutely
   b. power would corrupt, but absolute power would provide freedom
   c. the power of the state would increase, but the power of any individual would decrease
   d. the power of the state and all individuals would increase
   e. the state would wither away

4. Marx charged that capitalism was unfair because of its:
   a. income payments to capitalists; he recommended having ownership of capital by the state
   b. income payments to capitalists; he recommended taxing capitalists' income more heavily
   c. inadequate income payments to capitalists; he recommended the transfer of some labour income to capitalists

   d. high income payments to highly skilled workers; he recommended paying unskilled workers more
   e. high income payments to highly skilled workers; he recommended paying highly skilled workers less

5. Marx argued that:
   a. surplus value goes to labour under a capitalist system
   b. surplus value goes to capitalists under a capitalist system
   c. surplus value goes to capitalists under a communist system
   d. deficit value goes to capitalists under a communist system
   e. deficit value goes to capitalists under a capitalist system

6. In Marxist countries, communism refers to:
   a. a period of violent class struggle
   b. a transitional period leading to socialism
   c. a period in which the means of production (capital equipment, etc.) are owned by the state
   d. a period in which the means of production are owned by the community as a whole
   e. a period in which there is a dictatorship

7. Historically, the Soviet system has:
   a. provided enormous political power to its leaders, but inadequate means of controlling them
   b. provided its leaders with enormous political power, but inadequate economic power to do the job
   c. provided its leaders with enormous political power, but inadequate income
   d. provided its leaders with enormous political power, but inadequate financial power to do the job
   e. not provided employment opportunities

8. In the Soviet Union, profits:

a. exist and play a more important role in allocating resources than in North America

b. exist and play as important a role in allocating resources as in North America

c. exist but they don't play as important a role in allocating resources as in North America

d. don't exist

e. exist and are paid out to managers of Soviet plants

9. Human capital is owned by:

   a. the state in a capitalist system

   b. the state in a communist system

   c. the employing firm in a communist system

   d. the employing firm in a capitalist system

   e. neither state nor employing firm in either system

10. The Soviet Union has:

   a. more overt unemployment than North America, but less disguised unemployment

   b. less overt unemployment than North America, but more disguised unemployment

   c. more overt and disguised unemployment

   d. less overt and disguised unemployment

   e. the same overt and disguised unemployment

11. According to Marx:

   a. under socialism there is democracy; under communism there is dictatorship

   b. under socialism there is dictatorship; under communism there is no state

   c. under both there is dictatorship

   d. under both there is democracy

   e. under both there is no state

12. The saving necessary to finance the expansion of automobile factories:

   a. is provided voluntarily in our system. (Those whose incomes are low are not required to save at all.)

   b. is provided voluntarily in the Soviet Union

   c. is "forced saving" in the Soviet Union. (It is paid in taxes to the government by all the public, whether or not they wish to save.)

   d. a. and b.

   e. a. and c.

13. The Soviet system of political dictatorship:

   a. is not consistent with Marx's views

   b. is consistent with Marx's views that the overthrow of capitalism would be followed by a dictatorship

   c. makes it more difficult for central planners to impose their authority

   d. makes it more difficult to divert resources from consumer goods to heavy industry

   e. none of the above

14. In the Soviet system:

   a. the state owns most productive assets

   b. prices are determined largely by a central planning agency

   c. consumers choose from a relatively narrow selection of goods

   d. preference in production is given to heavy industry over consumer goods

   e. all of the above

15. Bottlenecks arise in the Soviet Union because:

   a. of the problems of setting up a completely consistent system of production quotas

   b. workers receive all the income

   c. there is no disguised unemployment

   d. investment is a smaller percentage of GDP than in the United States and Canada

   e. the overt unemployment rate is higher than in North America

16. Between 1980 and 1985, the Chinese government moved:

   a. from the Cultural Revolution to the Great Leap Forward

   b. toward more orthodox Marxism

   c. away from more orthodox Marxism to the Great Leap Forward

   d. away from more orthodox Marxism toward Stalinism

   e. toward a greater degree of free enterprise

17. In the Soviet Union there is:

   a. private ownership but long queues to buy consumer goods

   b. private ownership but no queues to buy consumer goods

   c. state ownership and no queues to buy consumer goods

   d. state ownership but long queues to buy consumer goods

   e. state ownership and uncontrolled prices

18. In the Soviet Union, compared to an economy such as Canada's:

   a. production is more responsive to consumer preferences, and there is less overt unemployment

   b. production is more responsive to consumer preferences, and there is more overt unemployment

   c. production is less responsive to consumer preferences, and there is more overt unemployment

   d. production is less responsive to consumer preferences, and there is less overt unemployment

e. production is less responsive to consumer preferences, and there is the same amount of overt unemployment

19. Soviet planners direct production away from consumption by:
   a. giving investment priority, and imposing no tax on consumer goods
   b. giving investment priority, and imposing a tax on consumer goods that accounts for about 10% of their price
   c. giving investment priority, and imposing a tax on consumer goods that accounts for about a third of their price
   d. giving investment priority, and imposing a tax on consumer goods that accounts for over half of their price
   e. imposing no priorities and an insignificant tax on consumer goods

20. A firm that doesn't face bankruptcy if it continues to make losses is subject to a:
   a. steel budget restraint
   b. soft budget restraint
   c. inflexible budget restraint
   d. hard budget restraint
   e. fixed budget restraint

21. The Chinese iron rice bowl system guaranteed:
   a. all families protection against an increase in the price of food
   b. all families protection against an increase in all prices
   c. all farmers protection against imports of rice
   d. all farmers protection against imports of all food
   e. all workers protection against unemployment

EXERCISES

1. Marx contended that in a free enterprise system (workers, capitalists) exploit (workers, capitalists) by acquiring the surplus value—that is, the difference between _____. Marx's solution was a (violent, non-violent) revolution in which the (proletariat, bourgeoisie) would seize the property of the (proletariat, bourgeoisie). A (communist, socialist) system would then follow in which there would be a (democratic government, dictatorship) of the (bourgeoisie, proletariat) and property would be owned by the (community as a whole, state). Eventually, this would pave the way for a (communist, socialist) system in which the state would (wither away, further consolidate its political power) and all property would be owned by the (community as a whole, state).

2. In the Soviet Union, investment is largely financed by (forced, voluntary) saving in the form of (taxation, subsidization) of (consumer, producer) goods. The big surprise is that the (high, low) investment in the Soviet Union has recently generated such a (high, low) rate of growth. The central planning agency often miscalculates in setting investment and output targets, and these errors lead to (excess supply, bottlenecks). In such circumstances, it is (producers, consumers) who do without. This group is also at a disadvantage because decisions on the models, styles, sizes, etc., of what should be produced are not determined by the (marketplace, hired managers) but instead by (the marketplace, hired managers).

In the Soviet Union, the problem of inequality (has, has not) been solved, in large part because workers have been investing in (physical, human) capital which (can, cannot) be owned by the state.

ESSAY QUESTIONS

1. "A communist society inevitably follows a dictatorship of the proletariat." Explain the degree to which you agree or disagree.

2. What are the problems facing Soviet planners that do not arise in our system?

3. It was often argued in the 1960s that Soviet growth exceeded that of the United States because the Soviets were playing "catch-up ball." Growth is easier in a less advanced economy because it's easier to copy technology than to develop it. Explain why you agree or disagree with this view.

4. "The growth of the labour union movement has severely damaged the credibility of Marxist theory in two respects: First, it has played a role in invalidating one of Marx's predictions. Second, events in Poland in the early 1980s made it clear that a Marxist government does not necessarily represent the interests of the working class." Explain why you agree or disagree.

5. Describe what is, in your view, the ideal organization of society. Try to ensure that the system you suggest would work in practice as well as in theory.

6. The Soviets do not appear to suffer as seriously

from inflation as we do. In what sense do you think that the Soviets have replaced measured inflation with a less obvious kind? (Hint: Is the value of your money really constant if prices remain the same but bottlenecks make goods harder to find?)

7. Can the labour theory of value explain why land has value? Why oil deposits have value? (You may wish to review the discussion in Chapter 37 of how land and resource values are determined.)

8. What do you think the practical problems are in defining a "subsistence wage"? (Hint: Do you think the problems of defining a poverty line in Chapter 39 apply here as well?)

9. Suppose you are a non-communist politician in an African state. For the last 20 years the communist members of your parliament have been recommending a switch to a Soviet-type system because it offers a more rapid growth rate. What is your view?

ANSWERS

Important Terms: 1d, 2h, 3c, 4k, 5f, 6j, 7m, 8e, 9a, 10i, 11g, 12b, 13l
True-False: 1T, 2T, 3T, 4T, 5F, 6F, 7T, 8F, 9F, 10F, 11T
Multiple Choice: 1d, 2b, 3e, 4a, 5b, 6d, 7a, 8c, 9e, 10b, 11b, 12e, 13b, 14e, 15a, 16e, 17d, 18d, 19c, 20b, 21e
Exercises: **1.** capitalists, workers, what labour produces and what it is paid, violent, proletariat, bourgeoisie, socialist, dictatorship, proletariat, state, communist, wither away, community as a whole **2.** forced, taxation, consumer, high, low, bottlenecks, consumers, marketplace, hired managers, has not, human, cannot

ANSWERS TO SELECTED REVIEW QUESTIONS FROM THE TEXT

40-1. (a) Marx's concept of surplus value refers to that part of the value of the nation's total output that is not paid to labour. Surplus value includes interest and profit paid to those who supply the funds for capital investment. It does not include the labour "congealed" in the value of the machinery.

(b) Ensuring that all owners are workers doesn't solve the problem. There will still be workers who aren't owners and, to a Marxist, they can be exploited. Ensuring that all workers are owners doesn't solve the problem either, unless they become "equal owners" with the same share as all the others. (If they are only "token owners" with a small share of ownership, then they can be "partly exploited.") But it's impossible to insist that a worker buy equal ownership in a firm before he can be hired. Workers can't afford to. Thus, the firm could not hire labour.

40-2. Overt unemployment (with people unable to find work) is worse in our system. Disguised unemployment (with people in jobs, but doing little or nothing that is really productive) is worse in the Soviet Union. See the section in the text on macroeconomic balance.

40-3. Concerned over their short-run interest (avoiding the loss of jobs to machines), workers may overlook their long-run interest—which is to be working with large amounts of capital, hence enjoying high productivity and a high wage. (Not all workers are hostile to an accumulation of capital. Indeed, North American unionists who have recently complained that multinationals are exporting capital and technology when they invest abroad, recognize the desirability of working with large amounts of capital in North America.)

40-4. The steel/machinery loop in the text provides a good example. Suppose the steel target is increased and, because steel production requires machinery, the machinery target is also increased. If the planners now fail to recognize that increased machinery output will require more steel, the steel target won't be set high enough and there will be a bottleneck in steel.

Another example might be: Cement is required to build factories, and factories are required to make cement.

Answers to Crossword Puzzles

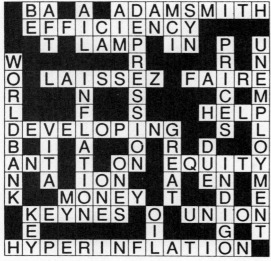

CHAPTER 1

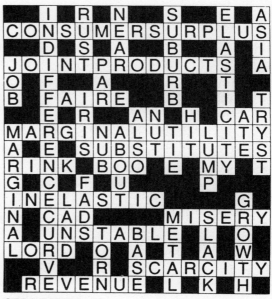

CHAPTER 22

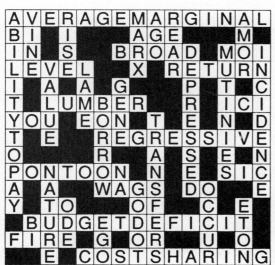

CHAPTER 5

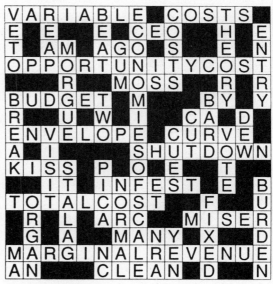

CHAPTER 25

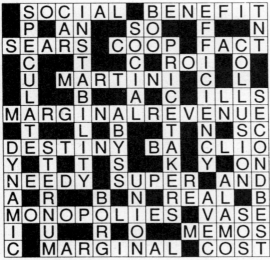

CHAPTER 27

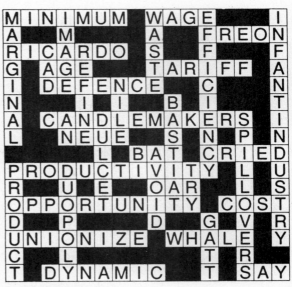

CHAPTER 35

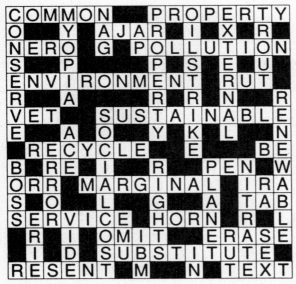

CHAPTER 31

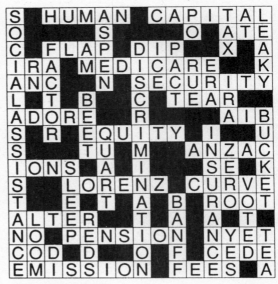

CHAPTER 39

─ ─ ─ ─ ─ ─ ─ ─ ─ ─ ─ ─ ─ ─ ─ _CUT HERE_ ─ ─ ─ ─ ─ ─ ─ ─ ─ ─ ─ ─ ─ ─ ─

STUDENT REPLY CARD

In order to improve future editions, we are seeking your comments on **STUDY GUIDE to accompany AN INTRODUCTION TO MICROECONOMICS, Third Canadian Edition, by Blomqvist, Wonnacott, and Wonnacott.**

After you have read this text, please answer the following questions and return this form via Business Reply Mail. *Thanks in advance for your feedback!*

1. Name of your college or university: ───────────────────────────

───

2. Major program of study: ──────────────────────────────

───

3. Are there any sections of this test which were not assigned as course reading? ──────

   If so, please specify those chapters or portions. ─────────────────────

   ───

   ───

   ───

─ ─ ─ ─ ─ ─ ─ ─ ─ ─ ─ ─ ─ ─ ─ _FOLD HERE_ ─ ─ ─ ─ ─ ─ ─ ─ ─ ─ ─ ─ ─

4. What did you like *best* about this book? ─────────────────────

   ───

   ───

5. What did you like *least*? ──────────────────────────────

   ───

   ───

6. How can we improve future editions? ──────────────────────

   ───

   ───

   ───

If you would like to say more, we'd love to hear from you. Please write to us at the address shown on the reverse of this card.

CUT HERE

------------------------------ *CUT HERE* ------------------------------ ┐
                                                                         │
                                                                         │
                                                                         C
                                                                         U
                                                                         T

                                                                         H
                                                                         E
                                                                         R
                                                                         E
                                                                         │
------------------------------ *FOLD HERE* ------------------------------ ┤

**BUSINESS
REPLY MAIL**

No Postage Stamp
Necessary if Mailed
in Canada

Postage will be paid by

7115

Attn: Sponsoring Editor Business and Economics

The College Division
McGraw-Hill Ryerson Limited
330 Progress Avenue
Scarborough, Ontario
M1P 9Z9

TAPE SHUT